Learn Blender Simulations the Right Way

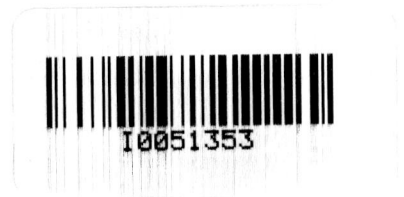

Transform your artistic vision into stunning, realistic simulations with Blender 4.0

Stephen Pearson

Learn Blender Simulations the Right Way
Second Edition

Portfolio Director: Rohit Rajkumar
Relationship Lead: Neha Pande
Content Engineer: Anuradha Joglekar
Program Manager: Sandip Tadge
Growth Lead: Namita Velgekar
Technical Editor: Tejas Mhasvekar
Copy Editor: Safis Editing
Proofreader: Anuradha Joglekar
Indexer: Tejal Soni
Production Designer: Ponraj Dhandapani
Marketing Owner: Nivedita Pande

First edition: November 2022

Second edition: April 2025

Production reference: 1070425

Published by Packt Publishing Ltd.
Grosvenor House
11 St Paul's Square
Birmingham
B3 1RB, UK

ISBN 978-1-83620-005-5

www.packtpub.com

To my parents, who helped me start on this journey of learning 3D. And to my wife, Jamie, for her encouragement and inspiration as we both write and create together.

– Stephen Pearson

Contributors

About the author

Stephen Pearson is a 3D artist, graphic and product designer, video producer, and the founder of BlenderMadeEasy. He has worked in the 3D industry for over 11 years and has produced several best-selling courses on architectural visualization, **Visual Effects** (**VFX**) simulations, and animation. He started using Blender in 2014 as a fun hobby, but now he uses it to teach other 3D artists around the world. In his spare time, he enjoys exploring local breweries, going for a ride on his motorcycle, and playing with his two dogs.

I would like to first thank my family, friends, and loving wife for all the encouraging words and support throughout the process of writing this book. I would also like to thank all the Blender developers for making such an amazing program free and open source for anyone to try. And, of course, thank you to all the people who have watched my tutorials and supported me throughout the years.

About the reviewers

Mariselvam M is a VFX artist who works on visual effects, animation, and movie projects that demand technical precision and artistic creativity. Their passion for the field was sparked by a love for cartoons and movies, which continues to inspire their work today. Known for their expertise in Blender and Houdini, Mari is passionate about crafting visually compelling narratives In addition to their professional endeavors, Mari enjoys traveling with friends, drawing creative inspiration from new experiences.

I extend my heartfelt thanks to my parents and friends for their unwavering support.

Thirunavukkarasu M is an AR/VR Developer and 3D Artist with a strong focus on creating immersive experiences using Unity, Blender, and Meta Quest devices. Currently, he is working at the Logistics Sector Skill Council, developing cutting-edge AR/VR solutions to enhance training and visualization for the logistics and supply chain industry.

In his current role, he designs and implements interactive simulations and 3D assets that improve learning outcomes and operational efficiency. His expertise spans Unity development, 3D modeling, and mixed reality (MR) applications, with a proven track record of delivering projects like **Caddy VR** for industrial visualization and **Fighter Jet Training Modules** for defense preparedness. His work is driven by a commitment to innovation and a desire to push the boundaries of what's possible in extended reality (XR).

Table of Contents

Part 1: Using Mantaflow for Fire, Smoke, and Fluids

1

2

Part 2: Simulating Physics with Soft Bodies and Cloth

6

7

8

Part 3: Diving into Rigid Bodies

Part 4: Understanding Dynamic Paint in Blender

12

13

14

15

Creating a Burning-Up Effect   363

Preface

Over the last couple of years, Blender has surged in popularity due to the 2.8 release, which completely changed the user interface. Not only are thousands of people downloading Blender every day but many big studios, such as EA Games, Infinity Ward, and Ubisoft, have also taken notice and started using it as well. Now, with the introduction of 4.2, Blender has become even more common across various studios. This open source, cross-platform software has everything a 3D creation suite should have. Modeling, rigging, animation, rendering, compositing, motion tracking, game creation, and – what this book is all about, simulating physics – are just a taste of what can be done using Blender!

Physics simulations in 3D have become standard in movies, games, and animation. Most explosions, crashes, destruction, fire, and fluid effects are all done on the computer. In this book, we will be covering the five main simulation types in Blender, which are fluid simulation (including fire, smoke, and liquid), soft bodies, cloth, rigid bodies, and dynamic paint. We will be going through each one in detail, and there will be hands-on projects for each simulation type. By the end, you should have a good grasp of every simulation in Blender and how to use them together seamlessly. It's time for you to feel confident in creating your own **Visual Effects** (VFX) projects and animations!

Who this book is for

This book is for VFX artists, 3D artists, game designers, and any Blender user who wants to learn about creating physics simulations. Readers are expected to have basic knowledge of the Blender interface and how to use it.

What this book covers

Chapter 1, *An Introduction to Mantaflow*, begins our journey of learning Blender simulations by taking a look at Mantaflow. You will get an understanding of the basics and what it takes to create a fire, smoke, or fluid simulation.

Chapter 2, *Understanding Domains, Flows, and Effectors*, gets technical. It's hard to know exactly what each setting and value does, so in this chapter, we will cover each one in an easy-to-understand way. By the end, you will have a good grasp of what every setting does in a mantaflow simulation.

Chapter 3, *Creating a Realistic Campfire Simulation*, puts your technical knowledge to the test by creating a realistic campfire simulation. Step by step, we will go through the entire process, and by the end, you will have created a nice, satisfying campfire scene.

Chapter 4, Creating a Waterfall Using Mantaflow, looks at the liquid side of mantaflow by creating a realistic waterfall scene. In this chapter, we will walk through the process of creating a waterfall, adding foam particles, and rendering the animation.

Chapter 5, Creating a Realistic Explosion, explores explosions, which are very fun and exciting but can be a bit tricky to create in Blender. That's why, in this chapter, we will go through how to create a realistic explosion from start to finish, using particle systems, smoke simulations, and complex materials!

Chapter 6, Getting Started with Soft Bodies, examines soft body simulation, which allows you to deform your object in a soft and organic way. In this chapter, we will cover everything there is to know about the soft body simulation and all its settings and values.

Chapter 7, Creating a Soft Body Obstacle Course, covers creating an obstacle course for a soft body sphere to go through. We will cover collisions, cloth, soft bodies, goals, glass materials, and more. Then, we will render the animation in Eevee.

Chapter 8, An Introduction to Cloth Simulations, delves into cloth simulation in Blender and how to use it effectively and efficiently. We will discuss each setting and value with screenshots and images so that it's easy to understand.

Chapter 9, Creating a Realistic Flag, looks at creating an animation using cloth simulation, and what better way than to create a flag? In this chapter, we walk you through the process of creating a realistic flag, from adding the flagpole to attaching the rope to creating a fabric material.

Chapter 10, An Introduction to Rigid Bodies, explores rigid bodies, which allow you to simulate physics while not deforming your object. In this chapter, we will discover how to use this simulation and how to work with constraints, as well as all the settings and values that come with it.

Chapter 11, Creating a Rigid Body Physics Course, covers rigid body simulation in a practical way by creating a physics-based obstacle course in Blender. We will learn how to create a domino effect, create an elevator using constraints, simulate thousands of cubes all at once, and much more in this chapter.

Chapter 12, An Introduction to Dynamic Paint, delves into dynamic paint in Blender. Dynamic paint is a way to simulate the behavior of brushes and canvases. This can be used to create colormaps, displacement, weight, and waves.

Chapter 13, Creating a Paintbrush Effect, looks at using dynamic paint in Blender to create a paintbrush effect! We will start by animating a brush following a curve, then look at creating a hair particle system, simulating dynamic paint, and creating the materials.

Chapter 14, Creating a Raindrop Effect, shows you how to create a raindrop effect using particles and dynamic paint. We will first create a nice lake scene, adding in rain particles, simulating ripples, and creating water materials!

Chapter 15, Creating a Burning-Up Effect, shows how to combine multiple simulations together to create a unique animation! We will start by using dynamic paint and a mask modifier. From there, we'll simulate cloth flowing in the wind, and finally use the fire simulation to create the burning-up effect!

To get the most out of this book

You will need at least Blender 4.2 installed on your computer. It is, however, recommended to have the most up-to-date version of Blender, as some of the later chapters were written in 4.4.

Software/hardware covered in the book	Operating system requirements
Blender 3D	Windows, macOS, or Linux

Basic knowledge of Blender and its interface is recommended, as this will help you to follow along with the projects.

If you are using the digital version of this book, we advise you to type the code yourself or access the code from the book's GitHub repository (a link is available in the next section). Doing so will help you avoid any potential errors related to the copying and pasting of code.

Download the example code files

You can download the example code files for this book from GitHub at `https://github.com/PacktPublishing/Learn-Blender-4-Simulations-the-Right-Way`. If there's an update to the code, it will be updated in the GitHub repository.

We also have other code bundles from our rich catalog of books and videos available at `https://github.com/PacktPublishing/`. Check them out!

Download the color images

We also provide a PDF file that has color images of the screenshots/diagrams used in this book. You can download it here: `https://packt.link/gbp/9781836200055`.

Conventions used

There are a number of text conventions used throughout this book.

`Code in text`: Indicates code words in text, database table names, folder names, filenames, file extensions, pathnames, dummy URLs, user input, and Twitter handles. Here is an example: "Let's begin by opening the `Burning Effect Setup.blend` file."

A block of code is set as follows:

```
html, body, #map {
  height: 100%;
  margin: 0;
  padding: 0
}
```

When we wish to draw your attention to a particular part of a code block, the relevant lines or items are set in bold:

```
[default]
exten => s,1,Dial(Zap/1|30)
exten => s,2,Voicemail(u100)
exten => s,102,Voicemail(b100)
exten => i,1,Voicemail(s0)
```

Any command-line input or output is written as follows:

```
$ mkdir css
$ cd css
```

Bold: Indicates a new term, an important word, or words that you see onscreen. For instance, words in menus or dialog boxes appear in **bold**. Here is an example: "On **Frame 1**, press *K* and add a **Location** keyframe to the brush."

> **Tips or important notes**
> Appear like this.

Get in touch

Feedback from our readers is always welcome.

General feedback: If you have questions about any aspect of this book, email us at customercare@ packtpub.com and mention the book title in the subject of your message.

Errata: Although we have taken every care to ensure the accuracy of our content, mistakes do happen. If you have found a mistake in this book, we would be grateful if you would report this to us. Please visit www.packtpub.com/support/errata and fill in the form.

Piracy: If you come across any illegal copies of our works in any form on the internet, we would be grateful if you would provide us with the location address or website name. Please contact us at copyright@packt.com with a link to the material.

If you are interested in becoming an author: If there is a topic that you have expertise in and you are interested in either writing or contributing to a book, please visit authors.packtpub.com.

Subscribe to Game Dev Assembly Newsletter!

We are excited to introduce **Game Dev Assembly**, our brand-new newsletter dedicated to everything game development. Whether you're a programmer, designer, artist, animator, or studio lead, you'll get exclusive insights, industry trends, and expert tips to help you build better games and grow your skills. Sign up today and become part of a growing community of creators, innovators, and game changers. `https://packt.link/gamedev-newsletter`

Scan the QR code to join instantly!

Join our community on Discord

Join our community's Discord space for discussions with the author and other readers:
`https://packt.link/learn-blender-simulations-discord-invite`

Free Benefits with Your Book

This book comes with free benefits to support your learning. Activate them now for instant access (see the "*How to Unlock*" section for instructions).

Here's a quick overview of what you can instantly unlock with your purchase:

PDF and ePub Copies

Next-Gen Web-Based Reader

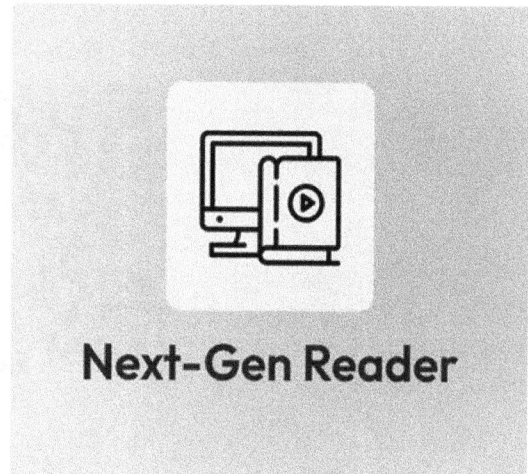

Access a DRM-free PDF copy of this book to read anywhere, on any device.

Use a DRM-free ePub version with your favorite e-reader.

Multi-device progress sync: Pick up where you left off, on any device.

Highlighting and notetaking: Capture ideas and turn reading into lasting knowledge.

Bookmarking: Save and revisit key sections whenever you need them.

Dark mode: Reduce eye strain by switching to dark or sepia themes

How to Unlock

UNLOCK NOW

Scan the QR code (or go to packtpub.com/unlock). Search for this book by name, confirm the edition, and then follow the steps on the page.

Note: Keep your invoice handy. Purchases made directly from Packt don't require an invoice.

Share Your Thoughts

Once you've read *Learn Blender Simulations the Right Way, Second Edition* we'd love to hear your thoughts! Scan the QR code below to go straight to the Amazon review page for this book and share your feedback.

`https://packt.link/r/1-836-20005-6`

Your review is important to us and the tech community and will help us make sure we're delivering excellent quality content.

Part 1:
Using Mantaflow for Fire, Smoke, and Fluids

To start our journey of learning about Blender simulations, we will be taking a look at the fluid and smoke simulation system known as **Mantaflow**. Step by step, we will learn the basics and what it takes to create fire, smoke, and liquid simulations. From campfires to explosions to waterfalls, we will learn all there is to know about Mantaflow and how to use it in Blender.

This part has the following chapters:

- *Chapter 1, An Introduction to Mantaflow*
- *Chapter 2, Understanding Domains, Flows, and Effectors*
- *Chapter 3, Creating a Realistic Campfire Simulation*
- *Chapter 4, Creating a Waterfall Using Mantaflow*
- *Chapter 5, Creating a Realistic Explosion*

1

An Introduction to Mantaflow

Over the past five years, **Blender** has surged in popularity by an extraordinary margin. With the introduction of version 2.8 in July 2019 came a whole lot of new users wanting to learn what this free open source program is all about. More users are coming in every day, and in 2022, Blender was downloaded over 17 million times, plus another 1.6 million times from other sources such as Microsoft Store, Steam, and Snap!

This software includes the entire 3D workflow of creating 3D models, texturing, animation, rigging, compositing, motion tracking, game design, video editing, and, of course, the topic of this book, simulating physics! We will be covering all the simulations that Blender has to offer, starting with the liquid and smoke simulations.

Creating a liquid or smoke simulation in Blender is complicated and sometimes quite frustrating when you are just starting. From personal experience, trying to figure out how all the settings work in Blender by trial and error is hard and can take a lot of time.

If you feel overwhelmed by the hundreds of settings and values in Blender's fluid simulator, there is no need to worry! The goal of this chapter is to ease you into working with **Mantaflow** and to help you get a basic understanding of what creating a simulation looks like.

If you didn't know, Mantaflow is Blender's default liquid and smoke simulator. In this chapter, we will discuss how it was developed, what you can create using it, and what you need to get started to create a simulation. Finally, we will create a fire simulation together. Step by step, we will go through all the settings and render out an animation so that you can upload and share it!

In this chapter, we'll be covering the following topics:

- What is Mantaflow?
- Gas and liquid simulations
- What you need to create a simulation
- Creating your first simulation

> **Free Benefits with Your Book**
>
> Your purchase includes a free PDF copy of this book along with other exclusive benefits. Check the *Free Benefits with Your Book* section in the Preface to unlock them instantly and maximize your learning experience.

Technical requirements

This chapter requires that you have Blender version 4.2 or above installed. To download Blender, visit www.blender.org.

You can find the assets for this chapter in this book's GitHub repository: https://github.com/PacktPublishing/Learn-Blender-4-Simulations-the-Right-Way/tree/main/Chapter%201.

What is Mantaflow?

Mantaflow is the framework in Blender for simulating gas and liquid. Mantaflow was introduced in Blender 2.82 and has seen many updates since then. It was first developed back in 2009 at the ETH Computer Graphics Laboratory. Now, it's being maintained and developed by the Thuerey group at the **Technical University of Munich** (**TUM**).

In Blender version 2.81 and below, the smoke and fluid simulations were two completely different things, and they weren't very compatible with each other. When 2.82 came out, the Blender developers removed these two simulations and introduced Mantaflow. This was a much better system because it combined both the fluid and smoke simulations into one.

To enable Mantaflow on an object, you need to head over to the **Physics** properties area (it will look like a circle with a dot in the middle) and select **Fluid**:

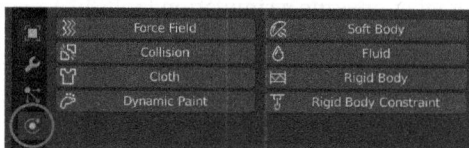

Figure 1.1 – Blender's Physics properties area

Don't get confused when you only see **Fluid** in Blender's **Physics** panel. **Fluid** is just the name used for the overall simulation. Once you select it, you'll be able to choose between **Gas** or **Liquid**.

Now that we've covered what Mantaflow is, let's take a look at the simulations you can create with it in Blender!

Gas and liquid simulations

You've seen me throw around the terms *gas*, *liquid*, and *fluid*, but what are the differences? As mentioned previously, **Fluid** is used to describe the entire simulation. Inside the simulation, there are two options to choose from:

- **Gas**: Used to create things such as smoke, fire, or airborne solids
- **Liquid**: Used to simulate things such as water or honey

Let's talk about each one separately so that you can understand the differences between them and how each one works.

Gas simulations

Gas simulations allow you to create smoke and fire in Blender. But what can you do with it? Well, you can combine fire and smoke to create a massive explosion. Other examples might include a flame thrower, campfire, steam, mist, or fog.

Figure 1.2 – Flame thrower example

There so are many things that you can create, and the possibilities are almost endless. The following figure shows what we will learn to create in *Chapter 5*:

Figure 1.3 – Explosion example

Smoke and fire simulations are made up of what we call **voxels**. You can think of a voxel as a 3D pixel of the simulation. The smaller the pixel, the better the simulation will look. You can change the size of these voxels by increasing the **resolution** of a simulation. Higher values will make the simulation more detailed but will cause the simulation to run slower and take longer to bake:

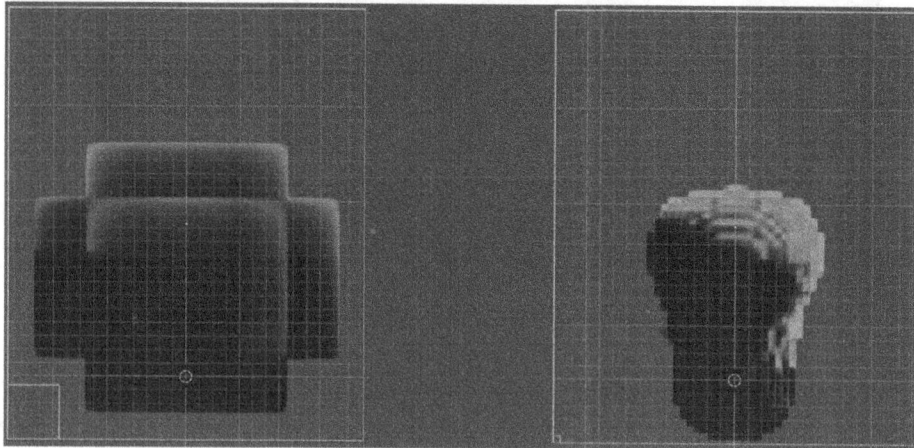

Figure 1.4 – Example of a voxel

In the preceding screenshot, the left simulation has a resolution of 8. This is quite small, so that is why the voxel is very large. The simulation on the right has a resolution of 64 and, as you can see, the voxel size is much smaller. You can also tell the size of the voxel by looking at the bottom-left corner of the **domain** object:

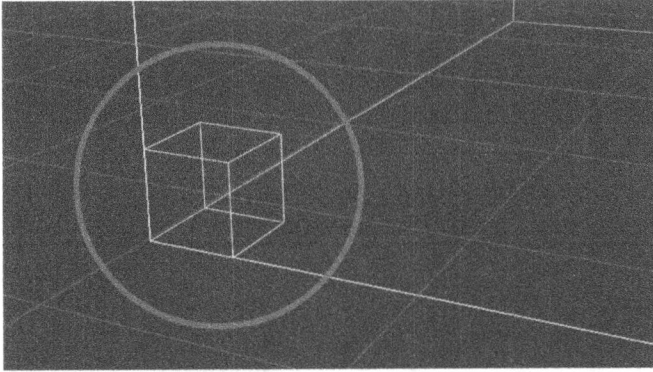

Figure 1.5 – Domain voxel size

The domain is the container for the entire simulation. We will cover them in detail in the *What you need to create a simulation* section.

These voxels represent all the attributes of the simulations such as heat, density, temperature, and velocity, just to name a few.

What is an attribute?

An attribute is simply a term used to describe data that is being stored. You can take this data and use it to influence materials, modifiers, and more.

The smoke that gets created in the domain can be from either a **mesh** or a **particle system**. These objects that emit smoke are called **flows**. Flows are used to add or remove smoke from the domain. Using a particle system as the emitter, you can easily create an explosion, which we will learn about in *Chapter 5*.

The movement of the smoke or fluid is controlled by the flow of air. This airflow can then be controlled by the following properties:

- **Density and Heat**: These values are within the domain object's settings. These values control how fast the smoke will rise.

- **Effectors**: These are mesh objects that will collide with the smoke, restricting its movement.

- **Flow**: These objects affect how fast or slow the movement of the fluid will be.

- **Force fields**: These also offer a way to affect the movement of the smoke. Depending on which force field you add, you can give your simulation a much more dynamic and interesting look! For example, the **Wind** force field will give a constant force in the direction you point it in. This can be very useful for adding just a little bit of movement to the smoke and making it look a lot more interesting!

Now that we have covered gas simulations, let's talk about liquid simulations.

Liquid simulations

Liquid simulations are very powerful, and there are many things you can do with them. Do you want to have a glass explode when it hits the ground, causing fluid to fly everywhere? What about creating a waterfall, waves, lava, or honey? All of this is possible with the liquid simulation:

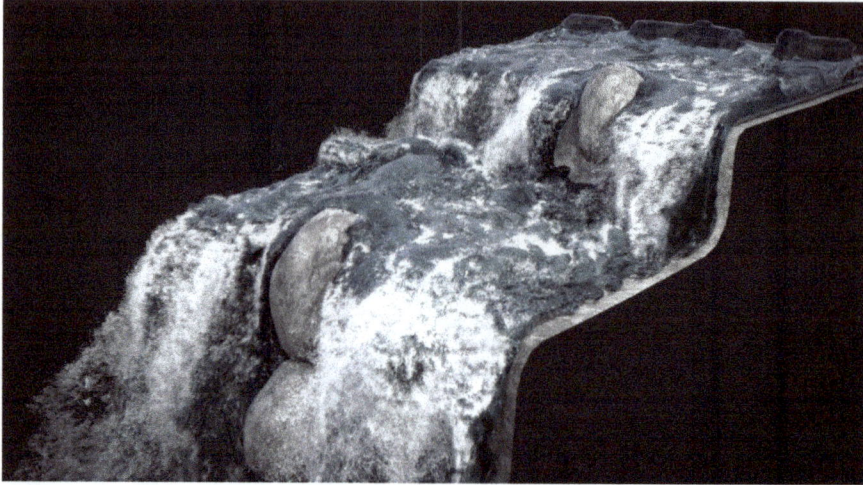

Figure 1.6 – Waterfall example

These simulations are used to simulate the real physics and behavior of fluids. Unlike the gas simulation, if you increase the resolution of the fluid, it will add geometry to the scene:

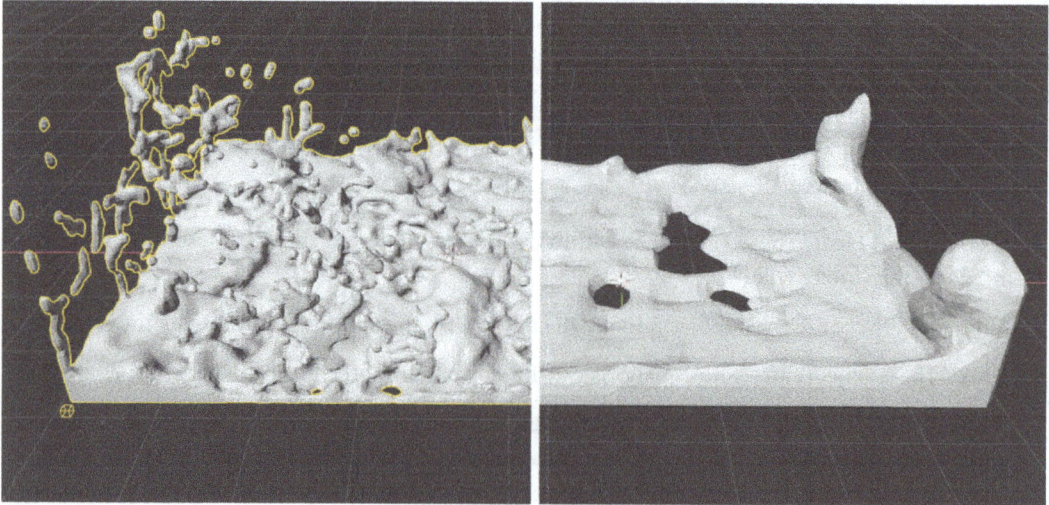

Figure 1.7 – Fluid resolution example

In the preceding screenshot, the left-hand side has a resolution of 96; on the right, it's set at 32. The left-hand side looks highly detailed with a lot of geometry, creating lots of splashes. However, the right-hand side has low detail, giving the look of low poly. Sometimes, a lower resolution might be what you are going for; it all depends on what you are trying to create.

The fluid can only be emitted into the domain using a mesh object such as a cube, sphere, or plane. Particle systems will not work for fluid simulations.

> **Increasing the resolution of fluid will drastically change the vertex count**
>
> The vertex count went from around 8,000 up to 200,000, just by increasing the resolution by 64 to 96. This will add to the total memory of the scene, making Blender run a bit slower. You can view the total memory of the scene by right-clicking on the **Status Bar** area at the bottom of the screen and selecting **System Memory**.

Both gas and liquid simulations are powerful, and they allow you to create so many different things very easily. Now that we've covered the differences between them, let's get into what you need to create simulations!

What you need to create a simulation

In short, there are two things you will always need for a Mantaflow simulation, as follows:

- A domain object
- A flow object

We will look at each in more detail, along with effectors, which are not mandatory but are still useful.

Domain objects

A domain object is the container for the entire simulation. No gas or liquid will be allowed outside this domain. When the simulation gets close to the edge, it will either collide or disappear, depending on what setting you have set.

> **The bigger the domain, the more resolution you will need**
>
> This will cause the simulation to bake longer. A general rule is to have the domain just big enough to fit the simulation.

The domain object is always going to be the shape of a cube. Even if the domain isn't a cube, the simulation will treat it as one and will simulate outside the original mesh:

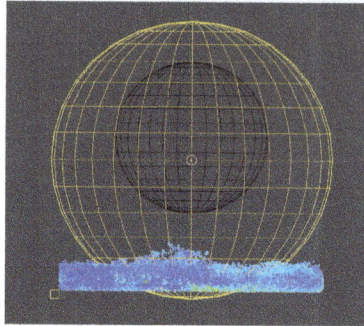

Figure 1.8 – Domain example

The sphere in this example is the domain and, as you can see, the fluid is going outside the mesh. It is probably best to only use a cube as the domain for any simulation. As I stated earlier, you can also see the resolution of the simulation by viewing the size of the little box in the bottom-left corner.

To assign a domain to a mesh object, have it selected, go to the **Physics** panel, and select **Fluid | Type | Domain**.

Flow objects

Flow objects are used in simulations to either add or remove fluid from the domain. It's important to note that the flow object needs to be inside the domain to simulate properly; having it outside will do nothing.

Unlike the domain, with a flow object, you can have any shape you want but it needs to be a mesh object 🔽. This means that curves ✏️, meatballs 🟡, empties 📐, or other objects like that will not work:

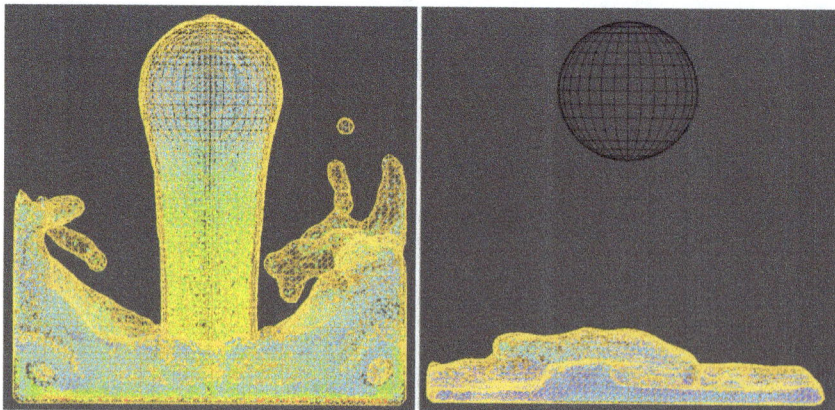

Figure 1.9 – Flow examples

We will cover flow objects in detail in *Chapter 2*, but I wanted to provide this example so that you can understand how they work. In the flow's properties, you can change its **Behavior**. There are three options you can choose from. This will affect how the smoke/fluid is emitted into the domain:

- **Inflow**: This will constantly add fluid to the simulation (left-hand side of *Figure 1.9*).
- **Geometry**: The fluid added is based on the exact amount of geometry of the mesh itself (right-hand side of *Figure 1.9*).
- **Outflow**: This will delete the fluid.

To assign a flow object, go to **Physics | Fluid | Type | Flow**.

Effectors

Effector objects can be used to collide with the liquid or smoke, restricting the movement of the simulation and creating interesting results in the process. Another way to use effectors is to set them as **guide effectors**. Guides basically allow you to change the velocity and movement of the simulation. They do get a little complicated so we will save that for *Chapter 2*. Effectors aren't necessary to create a simulation, but they can add another level of detail and interest to your scene.

To assign an effector object, make sure you have a mesh object selected, and go to **Physics Properties | Fluid | Type | Effector.**

To summarize, there are two types of simulations that you can create with Mantaflow: a gas or liquid simulation. When you decide which one you want, the next step is to add all the objects you need, those being a domain and a flow object. Do you want multiple flow objects? Do you want to add any collision objects to give more interest to the simulation? There are an endless number of simulations that you can create, and it's up to you to decide what you want to do.

In the last part of this chapter, we will be creating a fire simulation together. Step by step, we will learn exactly what it takes to create fire using Blender and Mantaflow. So, strap in, open Blender, and let's get started!

Creating your first simulation

Now that we understand what creating a Mantaflow simulation in Blender looks like, let's create one together. In this section, we will go through the entire process of creating a fire simulation in Blender; this process will include doing the following:

- Adding the objects
- Creating the simulation
- Creating a material for the fire

- Setting up the camera
- Rendering the animation

This may sound like a lot but don't get overwhelmed. I will be going through every step, and together, we will create something awesome! This section is aimed at beginners, but it also assumes you have basic knowledge of Blender's interface and how to use it.

With that out of the way, let's get started!

Adding the objects

Let's start by adding the objects we will need in the scene. Remember, we need a domain object and a flow object for every simulation. With the default scene open in Blender, we already have a cube that we can use for the domain object. Currently, it's a bit small, so let's scale it up:

1. To scale an object in Blender, make sure it's selected and press S. You can now move your mouse to scale the cube, or you can type a number in. Let's scale the cube by 2 and then press *Enter*. I also think it can be a bit taller, so let's scale it along the *Z* axis. To do this, press S, then *Z*, and then type 1.5 as the value.

2. Once you are happy with the scale of your object, you can add the flow. You can use whatever object you like, but for my simulation, I'm going to add a UV sphere. Press *Shift + A*, then select **Mesh | UV Sphere**. Scale it down to around 0.5 and place it near the bottom of the domain.

    If you did all that correctly, it should look something like this:

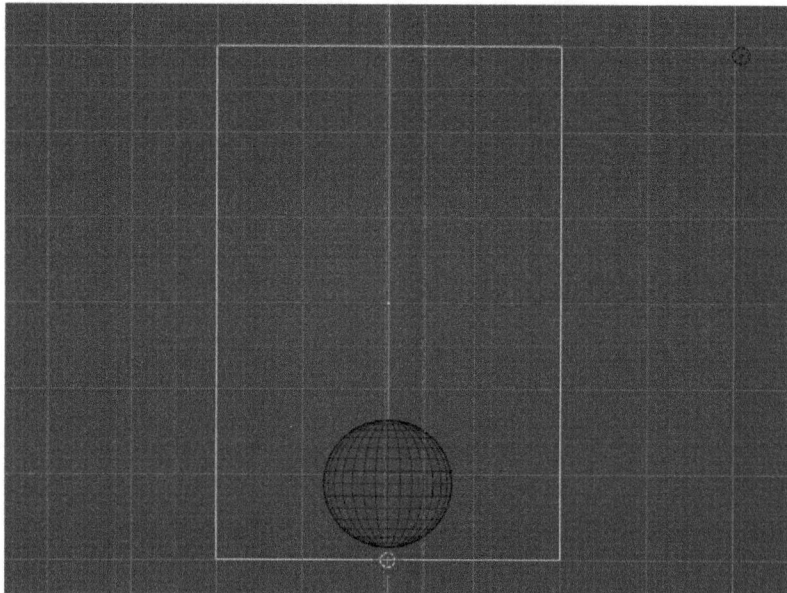

Figure 1.10 – Domain and flow

3.   The final step is to apply the scale to our objects. If you select the domain object and look in the **Properties** tab by pressing *N*, you will see the following scale numbers:

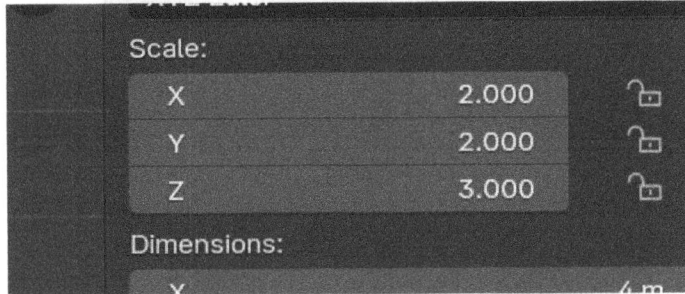

Figure 1.11 – Domain scale values

Before we changed the size of the domain object, these values were 1 each for **X**, **Y**, and **Z**. But since we scaled the domain by 2 and **Z** by 1.5 in *step 1*, it changed those values to what you see in *Figure 1.11*. Generally, you always want these values to be set at 1. This will make sure modifiers, textures, UV maps, and physics calculations are accurate.

4.   To change these values to 1 and to keep the current size of our objects, we need to apply the scale. We can do this by pressing *Ctrl + A* and *Cmd + A* and selecting **Scale** with both the domain and flow selected. Now, those **Scale** values should be back at 1 and everything will work properly!

Now that we have our objects in place, it's time to start working with the domain and flow!

Creating the simulation

Everything is in place, so the next step is to assign the cube as a domain object and change the settings. After that, we will create the flow and edit some of the values.

Setting up the domain object

Let's start by setting up our domain object:

1.   Select your domain and head over to the **Physics Properties** panel on the right-hand side (it should look like a circle with another circle inside it):

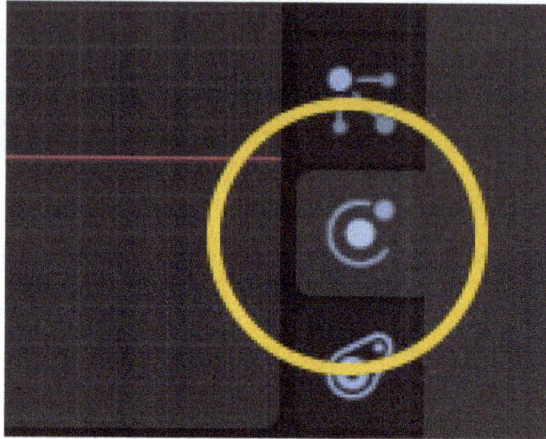

Figure 1.12 – The Physics properties panel

2.   Once you're there, click on **Fluid**, and for **Type**, select **Domain**. (Yes, there are quite a lot of settings; let's take it one step at a time.)

3.   The first thing we should do is change the cache type. Scroll down until you see the **Cache** panel. We don't need to bake in 250 frames, so let's set the **End** frame property of the simulation to 150. As for **Type**, let's select **Modular**, and check the box that says **Is Resumable**. This will allow us to stop the bake halfway through if we need to.

The **Cache** panel should look like this:

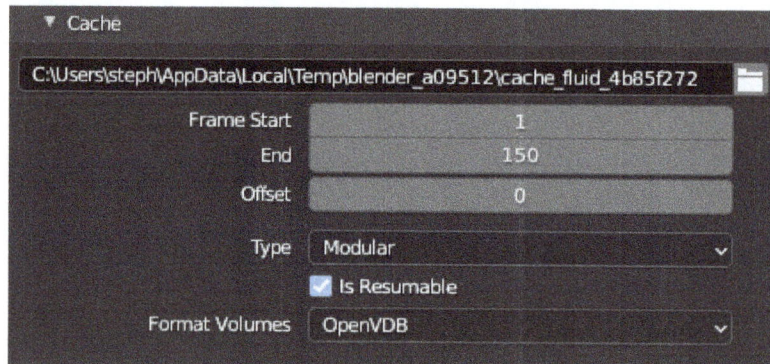

Figure 1.13 – Cache

4.   Now, let's set up the other domain settings. Starting at the very top, set **Resolution Divisions** to 128. This will give us a nice, high-quality fire:

Figure 1.14 – Resolution Divisions

5. **CFL Number** basically changes the number of simulation steps per frame. Higher values decrease the number of steps resulting in faster computation time. And, of course, lower values increase the steps, making it more accurate but slower. We don't need a value of 2 for this simulation so let's go with a value of 4 and this will help speed up bake times.

6. Check the **Adaptive Domain** box. This will change the size of the domain based on where the fire is, which, in turn, will decrease the bake time:

Figure 1.15 – Adaptive Domain

We can leave all the default settings as-is.

7. In the **Gas** panel, open the **Fire** section. **Reaction Speed** controls the height of the flames. Higher values mean lower flames, while lower values mean taller flames. Let's set it a bit lower to 0.5:

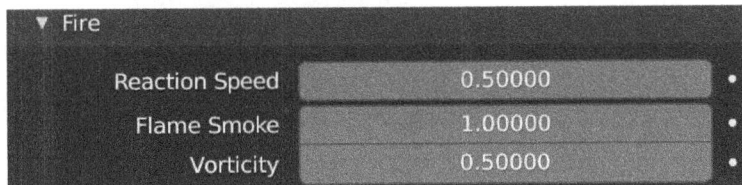

Figure 1.16 – Fire settings

8. (Optional) If you want more swirls in your fire, you can turn up the **Vorticity** amount in the flames to 0.6 or 0.7. Don't set it too high or your fire will go crazy!

The domain settings are now done; the next step is the flow object!

Setting up the flow object

Follow these steps to set up your flow object:

1. Select your sphere and, in the **Physics Properties** panel, select **Fluid**. As you've probably guessed, set **Type** to **Flow**.

2. As for **Flow Type**, change it from **Smoke** to **Fire**.

3. Setting **Flow Behavior** to **Geometry** will make the fire disappear very quickly when we play the animation. However, we want it to constantly add fire, so let's change it to **Inflow**.

4. We can bring up **Fuel** to 1.2. This will make the fire a bit taller and move more quickly.

5. In the **Flow Source** section, **Surface Emission** is currently set at 1.5. This means that the fire will emit slightly away from the mesh surface. I would rather have it closer to the mesh, so let's set this value to 1.

6. With all that done, we are ready to bake our simulation! Select your domain, and click the big **Bake Data** button at the top to start baking the simulation. Keep in mind that this might take a little bit of time, depending on how fast your computer is.

Now, all we have to do is sit back and wait for it to finish baking. Once it's done, we can create the fire material!

Creating the material

Creating a basic fire material is pretty simple to do:

With the domain object selected, let's jump over to the **Material** properties panel (it will look like a red circle):

Figure 1.17 – Material properties

1. The base **Principled Shader** is what we call a **surface shader**. This controls the colors, textures, and light bounces on the surface of a mesh. Since the fire is not a mesh, this won't work, so let's remove it. Click on **Surface Principled BSDF** (it will have a green dot next to it) and select **Remove**.

2. What we need instead is a **volume shader**. These kinds of shaders are for the interior of a mesh or fire and smoke. So, let's add one. Open the **Volume** panel and select **Principled Volume**:

Figure 1.18 – Volume shader

3. The first color option is for the smoke. Let's set it to a slightly darker gray.

4. You can also set the **Density** property higher if you want more dense smoke. Let's go with a value of 8.

5. There are many ways to create fire. The most basic way is to turn up the **Blackbody** intensity. You will notice that if you drag the **Blackbody** value up, you can only go to 1; however, if you type a number in manually, then you can go higher. The higher you set this, the brighter the fire will appear. Let's go with a value of 4!

And that's it! You've created your fire material. Now, let's set up our camera so that we can see the fire! If you aren't happy with the look, you can always come back later and change it.

Our fire is looking good so far! Now, we need a way to see it!

Setting up the camera

Let's set up the camera and position it where we want:

1. Press *0* on your numpad to go into **Camera View** or go up to **View | Cameras | Active Camera**.

2. To move the camera around easily, go into the **Properties** panel (*N*) section and, in the **View** tab, check the **Camera to View** checkbox. Now, you can move the camera around just like how you would move around the 3D space:

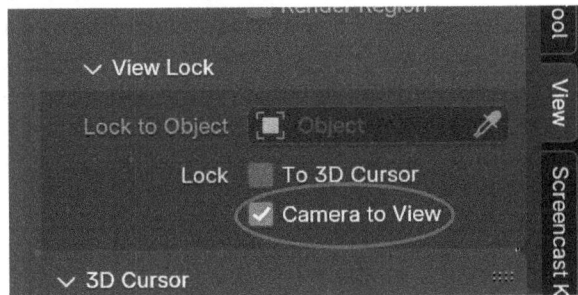

Figure 1.19 – Camera

3. Move the camera to where you can see the entire simulation. Then, make sure to uncheck **Camera to View**; otherwise, you may accidentally move the camera when you don't mean to.

4. As for the lighting for the scene, let's jump over to the **World** settings and set **Color** to black:

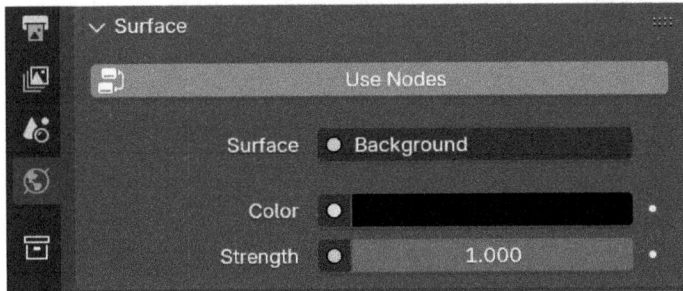

Figure 1.20 – World lighting

Now that our camera, lighting, and material are all done, it's time to set up the render settings!

Rendering the animation

Now would be a good time to match the simulation to the end frame. Since we baked 150 frames, let's set the **End** frame property in the Timeline to 150 as well:

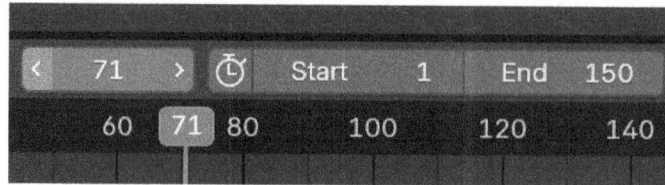

Figure 1.21 – Timeline example

Next, let's choose which rendering engine to use. There are two default render engines to choose from in Blender: **EEVEE** and **Cycles**. Both have their strengths and weaknesses. For example, EEVEE will render much faster than Cycles, but the fire won't look as good. If you have a slower computer, I recommend using EEVEE because rendering smoke/fire in Cycles is pretty GPU/CPU-intensive. To choose a rendering engine, head over to the **Render** properties section and click **Render Engine**:

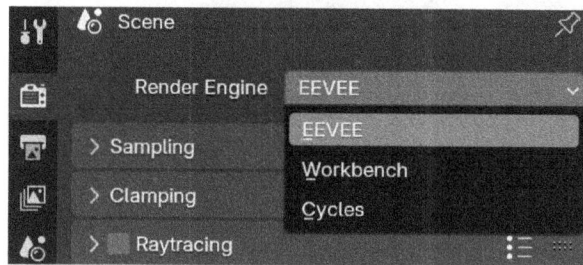

Figure 1.22 – Render Engine

For my animation, I used EEVEE, but if you want to use Cycles, I will provide instructions for both!

Cycles

With the **Cycles** engine selected, let's change some of the settings so that Blender will render faster and get a better result:

1. Open the **Sampling** panel and, in the **Render** tab, set the **Max Samples** number to 20.

2. Open the **Color Management** tab, set **View Transform** to **Filmic**, and set **Look** to **High Contrast**. This will give the fire much more of a pop and make it not look as dull.

Now that you've completed the steps for rendering in Cycles, feel free to skip the EEVEE instructions and head on over to the *Setting the output* section!

EEVEE

In the coming chapters, we will be learning a lot more about rendering volumes in EEVEE! For now, let's go over some basic settings to help the fire look much better. Switch over to the **EEVEE** render engine and let's get started:

1. In the **Sampling** panel, set **Render Samples** to `16`. Between 16 and 128 samples, there is not much difference, so lowering it will help speed up render time.

2. In the **Volumes** tab, set **Resolution** to `1.1`. This will make the fire have more detail and look better.

3. Open the **Color Management** tab, set **View Transform** to **Filmic**, and set **Look** to **High Contrast**.

If you would like to add some glow to the fire, you can jump over to the **Compositing** workspace at the top. Check **Use Nodes**, then press *Shift + A* and go to **Filter | Glare**. Place the node between the **Render Layers** and **Composite** nodes. Feel free to customize these values to find what you like or you can copy the following ones:

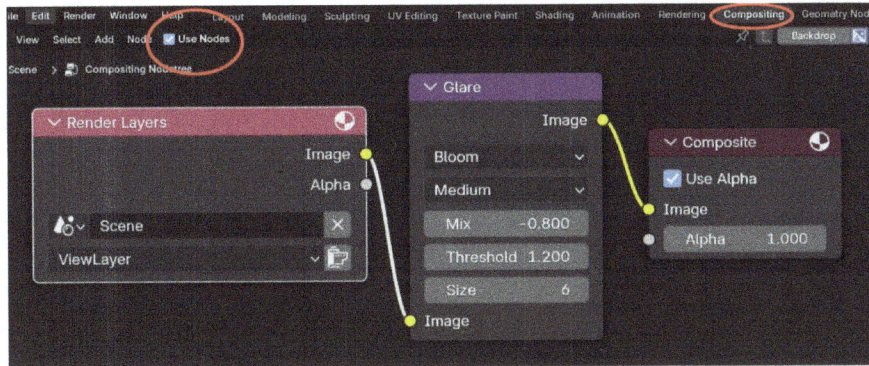

Figure 1.23 – Adding Bloom

The final step in this tutorial is to set up an output for our animation.

Setting the output

Whenever you render an animation in Blender, you need to set an output folder. To do this, head over to the **Output** properties section and set a directory for where you want your animation to render by clicking on the little **Open Folder** icon on the right. After that, set up the file format of your choosing. I'm going to set mine to **FFmpeg Video** and **Container** to **MPEG-4**. It should look something like this once you are done:

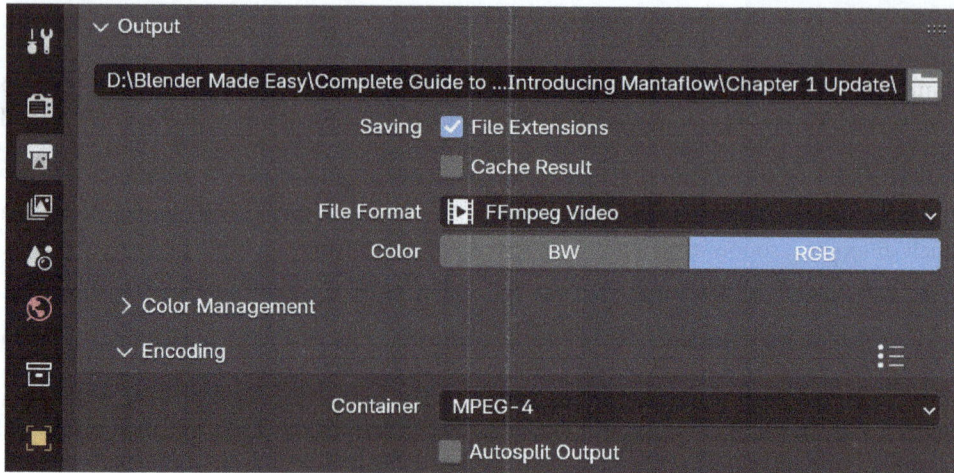

Figure 1.24 – Output

Now, you are ready to render! Go to **Render | Render Animation** or press *Ctrl + F12* or *Cmd + F12*. Once the render has finished, it will be in the output directory you set!

To view my result and download this `.blend` file, you can visit `https://github.com/ PacktPublishing/Learn-Blender-4-Simulations-the-Right-Way`.

The following is a frame of my simulation:

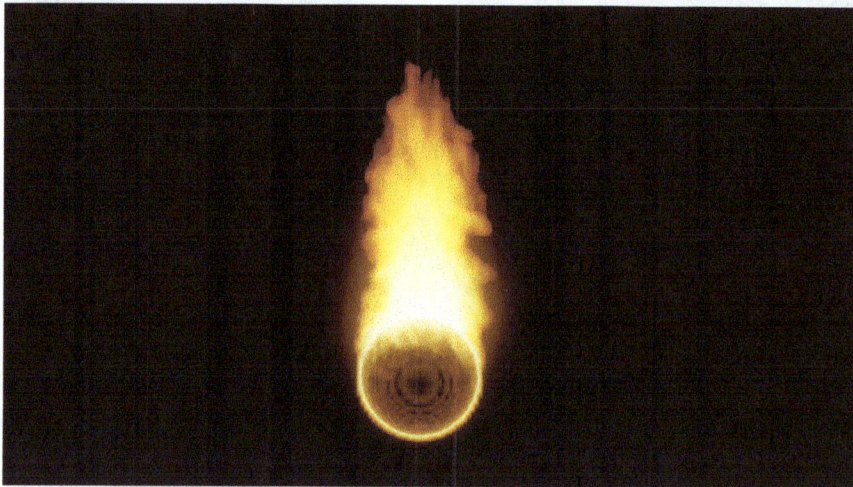

Figure 1.25 – Final result

And there you have it! You've completed the first tutorial of this book. Hopefully, you made it through with ease and learned something new along the way!

Summary

If you have never touched Mantaflow simulations in Blender until today, congratulations on making it through this chapter and creating your first fire simulation!

We covered quite a few topics in this chapter, so let's recap! First, we learned what Mantaflow is and how it was introduced to Blender. We looked at what creating a simulation is about and the two types to choose from – *gas* and *liquid*. We also covered all the objects you can add to your simulations – that is, *domains*, *flows*, and *effectors*.

After that, we worked together and created an awesome fire simulation. Using Mantaflow can be a bit challenging at times but, hopefully, this chapter gave you a clear understanding and a boost of confidence to go and create simulations!

I encourage you to open Blender and try to create a simulation and have fun with it! You can do something interesting such as setting a custom text object on fire and having the color of the flames be purple! Or you could do something a bit more serious such as using force fields to create a tornado effect! The things you can create with Mantaflow are almost endless!

The next chapter is all about the domains, flows, and effectors. We will look at each in detail and talk about their settings so that you understand exactly what values to change to get your desired simulation!

2

Understanding Domains, Flows, and Effectors

Now that we have covered the basics of Mantaflow, it's time to get a little more advanced! In this chapter, we will be diving deep into Blender and learning all about domains, flows, and effectors – all the objects that make up a simulation.

There are hundreds of settings and values to tweak to your liking, and it can be frustrating not knowing what they are or how to use them in a practical way. The goal of this chapter is to give you a technical understanding of the liquid and fire simulation in Blender. That way, you will know exactly what all the settings and values do, without having to guess. You will always be able to come back and reference this chapter if you forget something. We will be going through each setting, and there will be a brief description of what it does in the simulation, with screenshots for easy learning!

While we briefly touched upon domain, flow, and effector objects in the previous chapter, in this chapter, we will go into much more detail and learn all the ins and outs, starting with the domain object.

In this chapter, we'll be covering the following topics:

- Domains
- Flow objects
- Effectors

We have a lot of things to cover in this chapter, so let's jump right into it!

Technical requirements

This chapter requires that you have Blender version 4.2 or above installed.

To download Blender, visit www.blender.org.

Domains

We learned a little bit about domains in *Chapter 1*, in the *What you need to create a simulation* section, but let's have a quick refresher!

A domain object is a container for the entire simulation, in which no fluid or smoke can leave the boundaries. The shape of this container is always going to be a cube. Even if you use an object that is not a cube, Blender will use the bounding box of the object as the domain size.

Another thing to keep in mind is the size of the domain. The bigger it is, the higher the resolution you will need to make the simulation look good. This results in longer bake times, bigger file sizes, and more computation power.

To add a domain first, add a new cube object, then head to the **Physics** panel and select **Fluid | Type | Domain**.

There are two types of domains: *gas* and *liquid*. Gas is used for fire and smoke simulations, whereas liquid is used for fluid simulations. Inside the domain, many settings and values exist that can be tweaked to affect the look of the simulation. Most of these panels and settings are the same for both the gas and liquid domains:

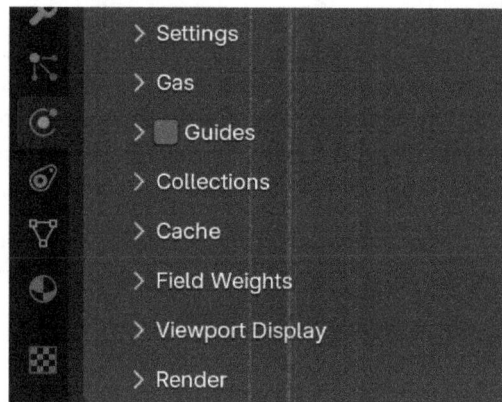

Figure 2.1 – Gas domain settings

Let's go through each of the different panels and talk about them separately. To fully understand them, I highly recommend opening Blender and following along as we discuss each setting.

Settings

When you assign a mesh to be a domain object, here are the settings you will see:

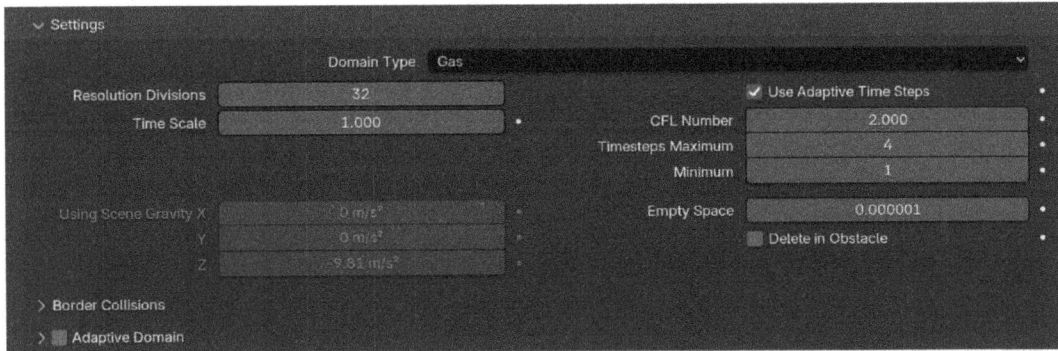

Figure 2.2 – Domain settings

Let's go through each one; I will describe exactly what it does:

- **Domain Type**: This allows you to choose between **Gas** and **Liquid**.

- **Resolution Divisions**: This controls how good the simulation will look. We mentioned this setting in *Chapter 1*, but let's review it again. Higher values will result in smaller voxels, making the simulation look better but run slower. The bigger the domain, the higher you need to set this value. If you double the size of your domain, you will also need to double the size of the resolution to get the same look.

- **Time Scale**: This controls the speed of the simulation. Higher values will result in faster simulations and lower values will give the look of slow motion. If you set this setting to 0, the simulation won't stop completely; there will be a tiny amount of motion.

- **CFL Number**: This stands for Courant–Friedrichs–Lewy; it is a little bit technical. When baking a simulation, there is a certain number of *time steps per frame*. Time steps are how many times the solver will calculate the simulation per frame. The more velocity an object has, the more time steps it will need to be physically accurate. Higher values will result in fewer time steps and faster bake times, which will give less accurate simulations. Lower numbers will give the simulation more time steps, thus increasing the bake time but giving better results. Leaving it at the default value of 2 will work for most simulations.

- **Use Adaptive Time Steps**: This checkbox will have Blender automatically decide when to give more steps per frame. It's usually a good idea to have this checked; that way, when there are fast-moving fluids, Blender will add more time steps, and when there are slow-moving fluids, you won't need as many time steps. This will help decrease the bake time.

- **Timesteps Maximum** and **Minimum**: These values control how many steps there will be per frame of the simulation. Usually, if you have collisions that aren't working properly or smoke/fluid that is moving too fast, you will want to turn these numbers up.

- **Using Scene Gravity**: This, just like in real life, gives the scene some physics and allows the fluid to fall. You can control the values here so that instead of falling, the fluid might fall to the side or even upside down if you set **Z** to a positive value.

You will notice that this is currently grayed out in *Figure 2.2*. This is because the scene is using Blender's default gravity. You can turn this off by heading to the **Scene** panel and unchecking **Gravity**:

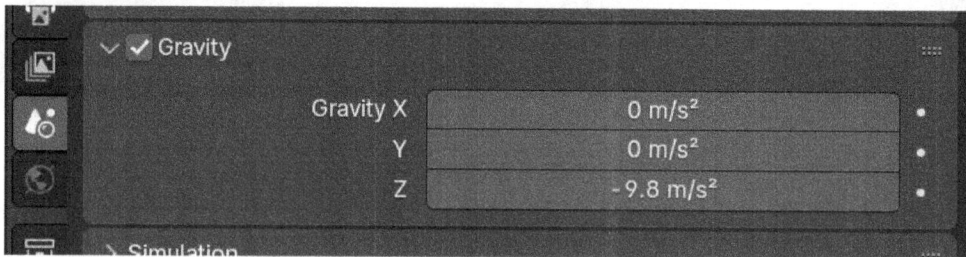

Figure 2.3 – Gravity

Now, you can change the gravity in the domain settings. This can be useful if you want multiple domains with different gravity settings. Keep in mind that if you uncheck **Gravity** in the **Scene** panel, other physics, such as particle systems and rigid bodies, won't have gravity.

- **Empty Space**: This is for gas domains only. It is used to get rid of smoke as it gets very thin. This will help with render times and baking times:

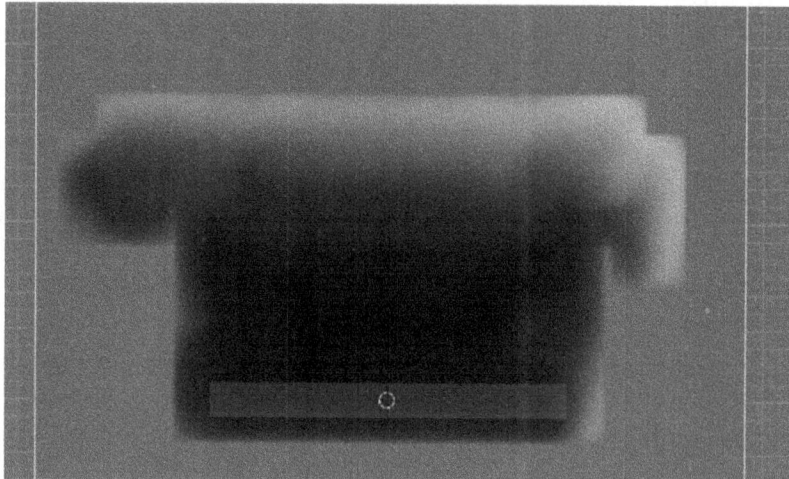

Figure 2.4 – Empty Space example

You will notice that with **Empty Space** set to 0 . 7, the top and sides of the simulation have been clipped off. Make sure that this is set very low; otherwise, you might delete some smoke that you don't mean to.

- **Delete in Obstacle**: This will delete any fluid/smoke inside an obstacle if this is checked.

- **Border Collisions**: This is a way to have the smoke/fluid collide with the edges of the domain. The options in this tab that can be checked and unchecked are **Front**, **Back**, **Right**, **Left**, **Top**, and **Bottom**. If left unchecked, the smoke will pass out of the domain without colliding and disappear.

- **Adaptive Domain**: This is used for gas domains only. This option is great and should almost always be checked. It allows the size of the domain to change dynamically to fit the simulation:

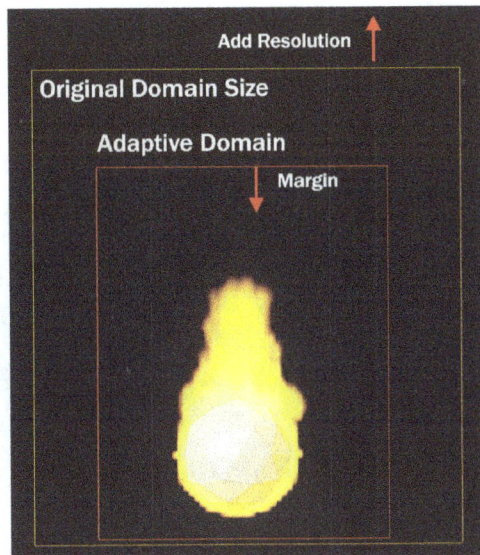

Figure 2.5 – Adaptive Domain example

There are three settings that you can change here:

- **Add Resolution**: This will expand the domain past its original size if the smoke reaches the edge.

- **Margin**: This is the amount of space between the domain and the smoke. Lower values will bring the edge of the domain closer, while higher values will push it away.

- **Threshold**: This is another way to clip the smoke. If the density of the smoke is smaller than the threshold, **Adaptive Domain** will cut it off, deleting that smoke from the simulation.

Adaptive Domain is very useful and is a huge time-saver when baking a simulation! In some rare cases, this option can cause problems with smoke clipping or importing OpenVDBs, but most of the time, you will want to have this turned on.

That is all the settings for the first panel of the domain. Now, before we jump into the smoke and liquid options, I want to mention the **Cache** panel!

Cache

The **Cache** panel is the directory that's used to set where all the smoke/fluid data will be stored when baked in. The default directory is a temporary folder. This means that the simulation data will be deleted after you close your project. In some cases, this might be useful because simulations can take up a lot of hard drive space. In other cases, it might be annoying having to rebake the simulation every time you reopen the project.

To save your data so that it doesn't get deleted, you need to click on the little folder icon and select a different folder. Usually, it's a good option to put the cache in the same folder as your project blend file:

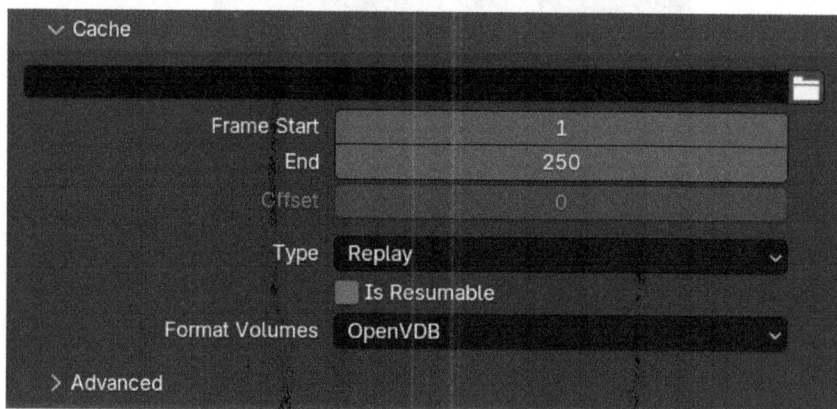

Figure 2.6 – The Cache panel

Below the directory, we have **Frame Start** and **End**, which control when the simulation will start and when it will end, respectively. The **Offset** parameter allows you to delay the start of the simulation. For example, setting **Offset** to 50 will allow the simulation to start at frame 50 instead of 1. This can also be changed after the simulation has finished baking.

In the **Type** dropdown menu, there are three ways to bake the simulation:

- **Replay**: This bakes the simulation in real time as you are playing it in the viewport. This can be useful when testing out settings at a low resolution.

- **Modular**: This splits up the domain into different modules that need to be baked separately. If you select this type, the noise, guide, mesh, and particle panels will all need to be baked individually. This is also useful when you want to change something in one of these panels without rebaking the entire simulation.

- **Final**: This, unlike **Modular**, will bake everything all at once.

With the **Modular** or **Final** type selected, the **Bake** button will appear. Once you click **Bake**, the simulation will start the baking process and you will be able to see the progress by looking at the percentage at the bottom of the screen:

Figure 2.7 – Bake progress

When the simulation has finished baking, the settings will be grayed out and you won't be able to change anything. However, you can click **Free Data**, which will delete the bake, allowing you to change the settings.

The **Is Resumable** checkbox allows you to cancel the bake halfway through and resume it later. I almost always keep this option on just in case I need to stop the bake. One thing to keep in mind is that enabling this will cause more simulation data to be written, thus increasing the bake size.

Finally, the two **Format Volumes** options that store all the data are **Uni Cache** and **OpenVDB**:

- **Uni Cache**: This is Blender's way of storing the simulation data. Each object in the simulation will have its own Uni Cache file (.uni).
- **OpenVDB**: This will store all the objects in the simulation in one OpenVDB file per frame, instead of having every object have its own .uni file. This is more efficient, and most of the time, I will be using this format.

Now that we understand what baking a simulation in Blender looks like, let's discuss all the settings for the gas and liquid domains!

Gas domains

When creating a gas domain, there are a lot of options that differ from liquid domains, such as the density of the smoke, when the smoke will dissolve, and the height of the flames. In the upcoming chapters, we will learn how to use gas domains to create realistic flames and explosions.

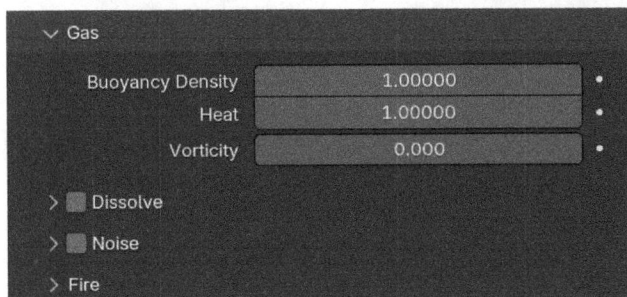

Figure 2.8 – Gas settings

The **Gas** panel is located underneath the **Settings** panel. All these options will affect the look and behavior of the smoke when simulating! Let's go through them together:

- **Buoyancy Density**: This controls whether the smoke will rise or sink. Higher values will make the smoke rise faster and negative values will make the smoke sink.

- **Heat**: This controls the temperature of the smoke. This also affects whether the smoke will rise or sink. One thing that needs to be mentioned is that this setting is based on the **Initial Temperature** property in the **Flow Object** settings, which we will discuss more in the *Flow objects* section.

  If the flow's initial temperature is set to a negative value and the heat is set to a positive value, the smoke will sink. If both values are positive or negative, the smoke will rise. The reason it's set up this way is so that you can have multiple flow objects that will rise or sink.

- **Vorticity**: This controls the swirls and randomness of the smoke! You want to be careful with this setting because if you go too high, the smoke will fill up the entire domain. I would recommend staying below a value of 0.5.

  In the following figure, the vorticity values go from 0 to 0.1 to 0.4, from left to right. As you can see, with just a small amount of vorticity, it will still add a lot of swirls and randomness to your simulation:

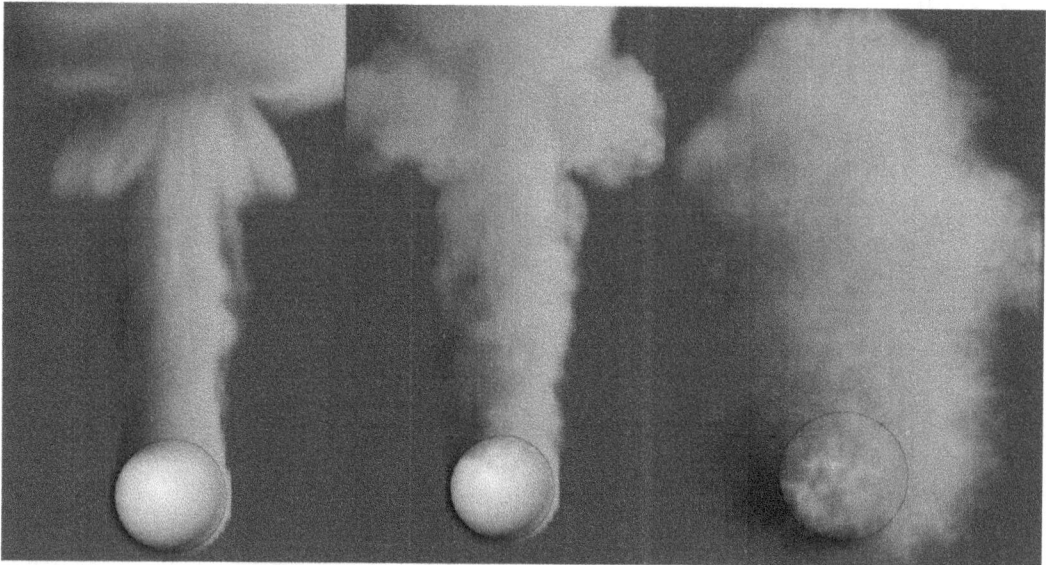

Figure 2.9 – Vorticity

- **Dissolve**: When this option is checked, the smoke will dissolve over time. How fast it dissolves is based on the **Time** value. For example, if **Time** is set to 10, the smoke will be emitted and will start to dissolve 10 frames later. The **Slow** checkbox allows the smoke to dissolve a little more smoothly and slowly:

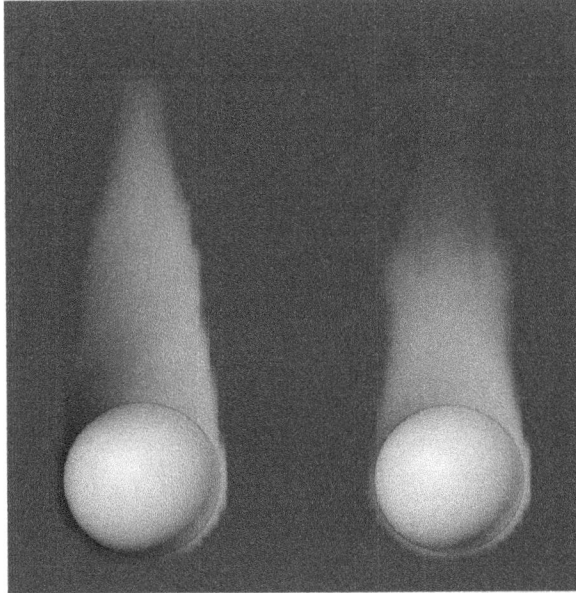

Figure 2.10 – Dissolve example

In *Figure 2.10*, the simulation on the left has a time of 20 with **Slow** set to **OFF**. The simulation on the right has a time of 5 but **Slow** is set to **ON**. As you can see, the right one is much smoother.

- **Noise**: One thing we need to mention is that if you increase the resolution division in the **Settings** panel, this will change the shape and look of the smoke. **Noise**, on the other hand, is great for adding fine detail to the smoke without changing the overall shape. So, if you like the look of your simulation but want to add more detail, **Noise** is the way to go!

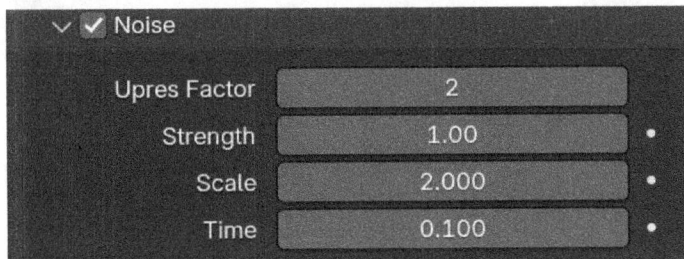

Figure 2.11 – Noise settings

Let's discuss each of the settings:

- **Upres Factor**: This takes your resolution divisions and multiplies the detail by the number you set. The higher you go with this value, the more levels of detail will be added:

Figure 2.12 – Noise upres example

In the previous figure, the example on the left has no noise, the middle has an **Upres** value of 2, and the right has an **Upres** value of 4.

- **Strength**: This controls how strong the noise will appear in the smoke:

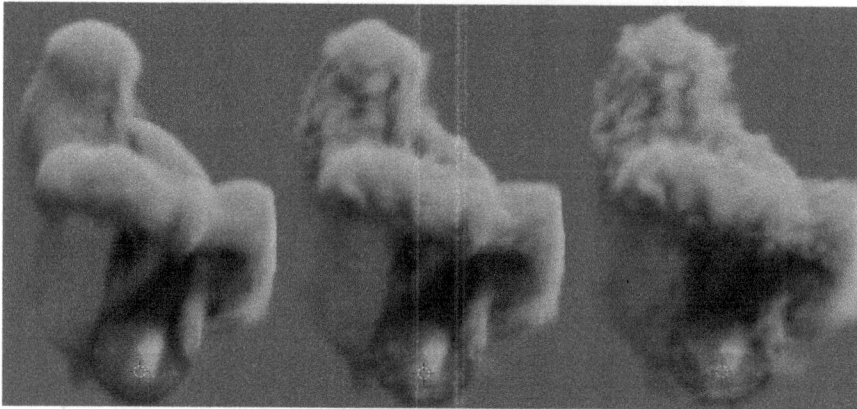

Figure 2.13 – Strength example

In the preceding figure, the **Strength** values from left to right are 0.2, 1, and 2. Lower values will make the noise appear more subtle and higher values will appear stronger and noisier!

- **Scale**: This is the setting that controls the size of the noise. Higher values will result in larger swirls, while lower values will give you smaller swirls:

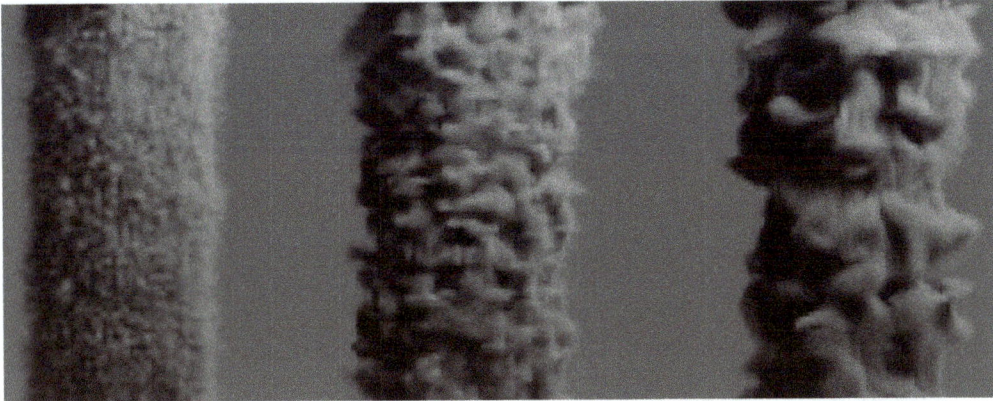

Figure 2.14 – Scale example

- **Time** is a setting that allows you to get a different pattern of noise in the smoke. Changing this value will move the noise pattern around and give slightly different results.

Using different **Resolution Divisions** and **Upres Factor** values will give you a lot of variating results. For example, let's view the following figure. A simulation with a division of 64 and an upres of 4 (left) will look drastically different from a simulation with a division of 256 and no noise (right):

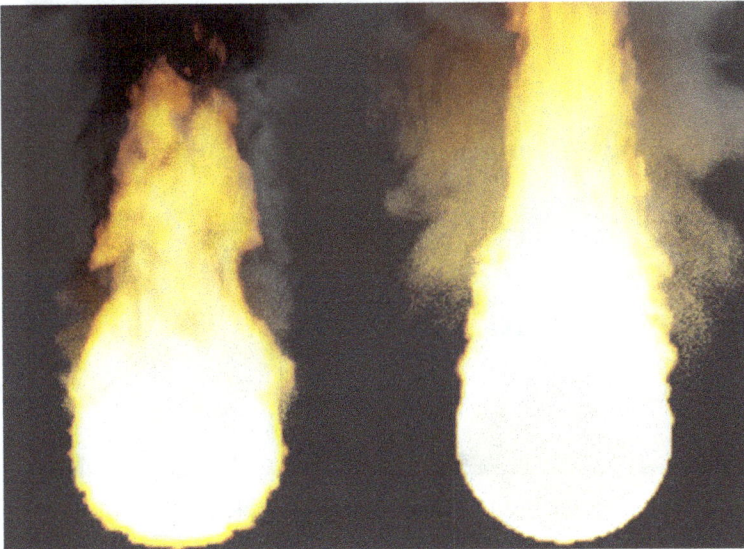

Figure 2.15 – Noise and resolution

In general, **Noise** is a great way to add small details to your simulation. Normally, a simulation with low division and high upres will make the smoke/fire look small, based on a real-world scale.

- **Fire**: This has six settings that we can change to alter the look of the fire. Let's go through each one:

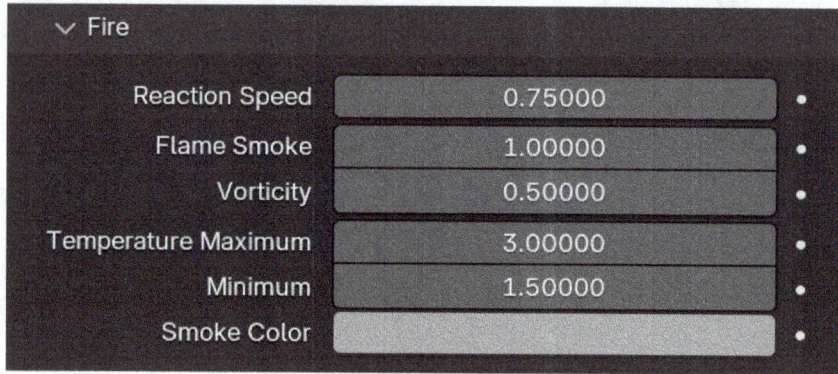

Figure 2.16 – Fire settings

- **Reaction Speed**: This controls how fast the fuel will burn. Lower values will result in taller flames, while higher values will make the fuel burn quickly, resulting in smaller flames.

- **Flame Smoke**: This controls how much smoke will appear for the fire. In the following figure, the values are 0.25, 1, and 4:

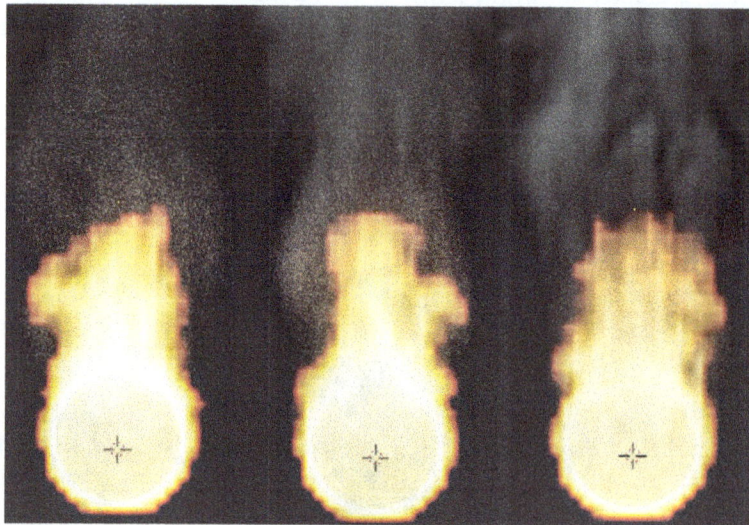

Figure 2.17 – Flame Smoke example

- **Vorticity**: This adds randomness and swirls to the flames! Be careful not to go too high with this value; otherwise, the fire will fill up the entire domain, making it look very strange. The values shown in the following figure are `0.1`, `0.7`, and `1.5`:

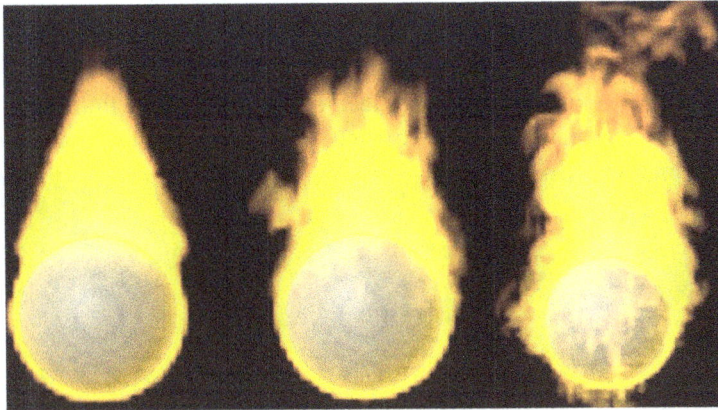

Figure 2.18 – Flame vorticity

- **Temperature Maximum** and **Minimum**: These control how fast the flames will rise. Higher values will result in faster simulations, while lower values will make the flames rise very slowly.

- **Smoke Color**: This changes the color of the smoke that's emitted.

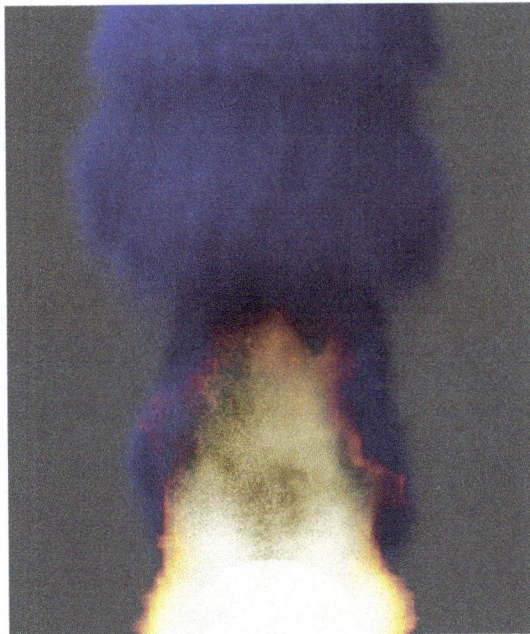

Figure 2.19 – Smoke color

And there it is! We have covered all the settings for the gas domain! In the next chapter, we will learn even more about fire and how to create a realistic campfire! For now, let's switch over to the liquid domain and talk about all the settings for fluid simulations.

Liquid domains

The liquid domain type has many settings that affect the look and way a fluid acts; these include thickness, particle density, splash, foam, bubble particles, and meshes, just to name a few.

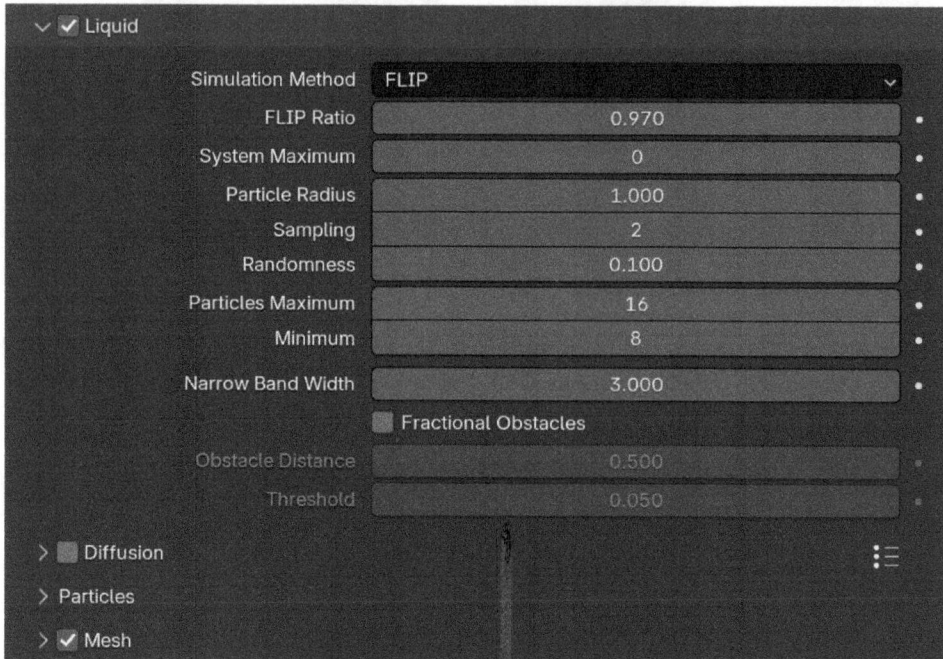

Figure 2.20 – Liquid settings

If **Liquid** is checked, Blender will create a particle system that will help visualize the flow of the simulation. There are many more settings and values to cover in the liquid domain, so let's jump right into it:

- **Simulation Methods**: There are two methods to choose from – **FLIP** and **APIC**. To see these, view the following figure:

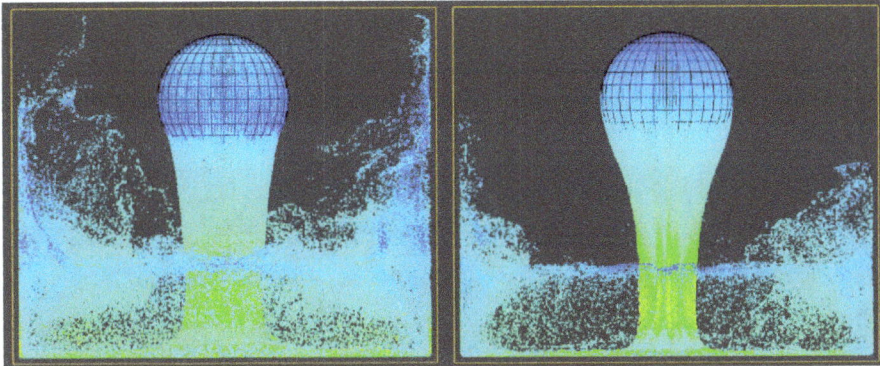

Figure 2.21 – FLIP (left) and APIC (right) examples

FLIP (left) will give you more splashes and fluid flying everywhere, while **APIC** (right) will be a little calmer and preserve a lot of those splashes.

- **FLIP Ratio**: This is for the **FLIP** method only. It controls how much velocity the particles will have. Higher values will result in larger splashes, while lower values will give smaller, more subtle splashes.

- **System Maximum**: This controls the number of particles in the simulation. With it set at 0, Blender will automatically add more particles when needed.

- **Particle Radius**: This is the space around each liquid particle. Sometimes, at a high resolution, the simulation will seem to gain volume. If this happens, you will want to turn this value down. If the opposite happens, and the fluid seems to disappear, try turning this value up!

- **Sampling**: This is like the upres factor for the smoke. It will add more particles to the simulation the higher you turn this value up. In the following figure, the values are 1 on the left and 5 on the right:

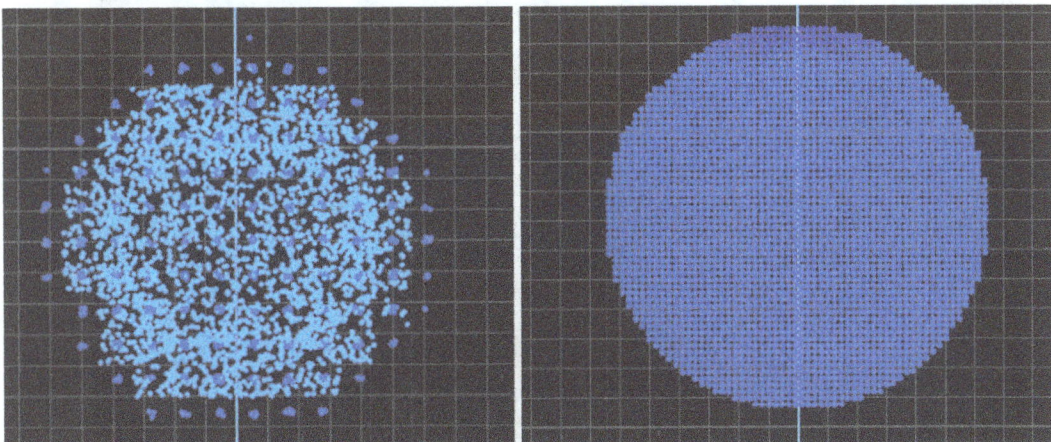

Figure 2.22 – Particle sampling example

- **Randomness:** This does exactly what it sounds like. When new particles are added to the simulation, they will have some randomness attached to their position. The higher you set this value, the more random it will appear. The following figure shows the result of a value of 0 on the left and 10 on the right:

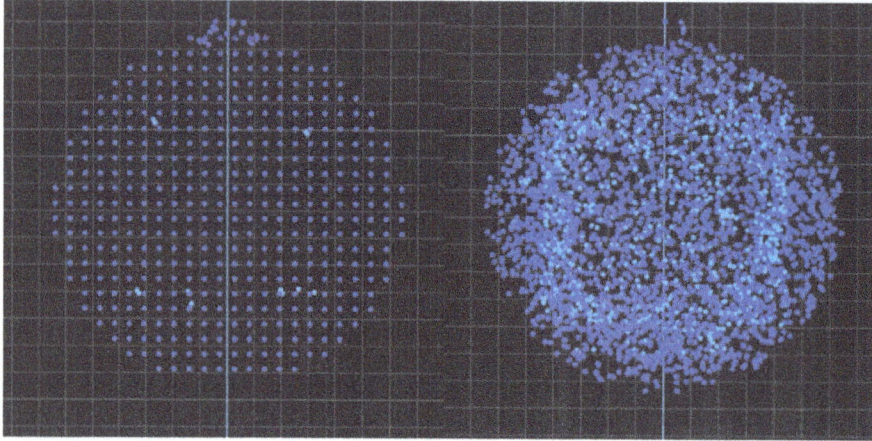

Figure 2.23 – Particle randomness

- **Particles Maximum** and **Minimum:** These control how many particles are going to be in each grid cell. Remember when we talked about voxels in the previous chapter? Just like smoke is broken into voxels, fluid is split up into what we call grid cells. The size of these cells is based on the resolution divisions. You can see the size by looking at the cube at the bottom-left corner of the domain. To visualize this option of **Particle Maximum** and **Minimum** better, take a look at the following figure, where both values are set at 1000:

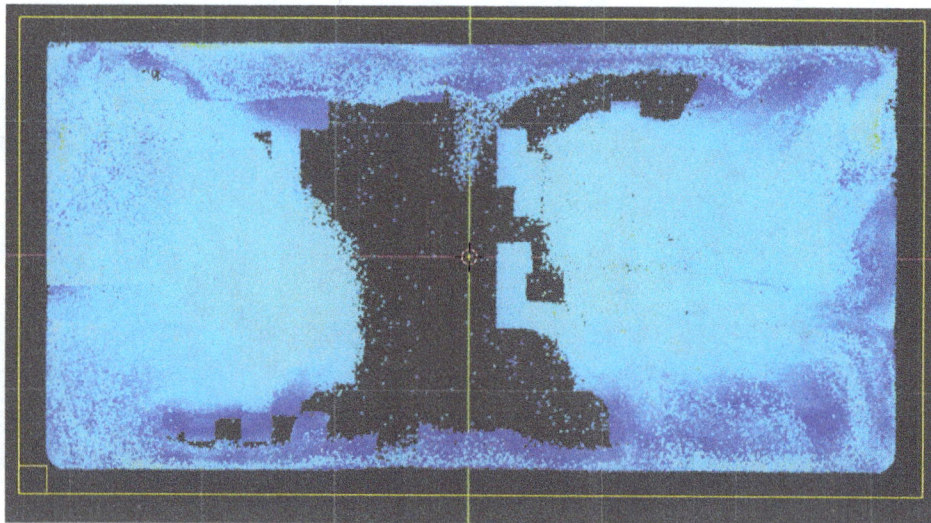

Figure 2.24 – Particles Maximum and Minimum

- **Narrow Band Width** is the thickness of the band of particles near the top of the fluid. Turning this value up can result in the entire simulation being filled with particles. This can be useful if that is what you are trying to create! Otherwise, it's recommended to not turn up this value because it will slow down the simulation. In the following figure, the values are 2 (top) and 15 (bottom):

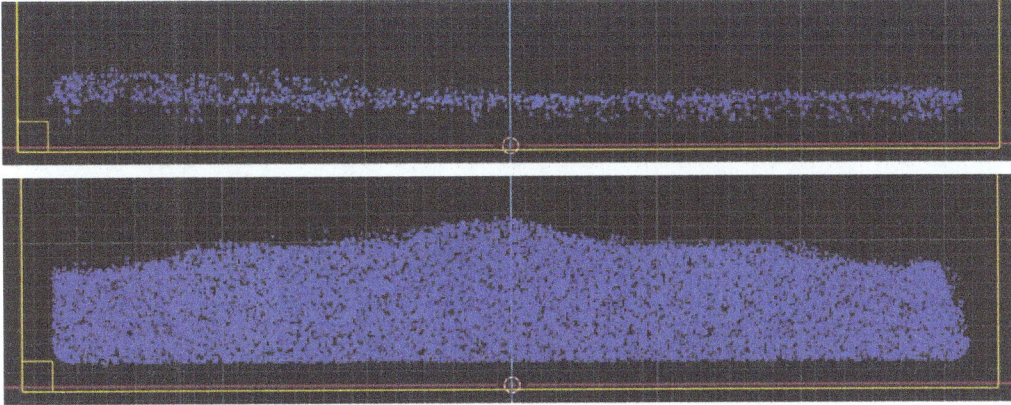

Figure 2.25 – Narrow Band Width

Increasing **Narrow Band Width** to 15 and assigning an object to each particle allows you to create very interesting simulations. For example, in the following figure, an *icosphere* has been assigned to be the particle, and the color changes based on the velocity of each particle! You can learn to create this by viewing the video at https://youtu.be/y2KvuDgRMS4:

Figure 2.26 – Narrow Band Width simulation

- **Fractional Obstacles**: This allows better-quality obstacle collisions. In some simulations, the fluid might stick to the obstacle. Enabling **Fractional Obstacles** will help prevent that and ensure smoother flow over collisions:

  - **Obstacle Distance** is the distance the fluid will be from the collision. In some situations, changing this value will help the fluid flow better, but in others, it will cause more problems with fluid disappearing or intersecting with the obstacle. Setting this value to a negative will allow some of the fluid inside the obstacle.

  - **Threshold** is how smoothly the fluid will travel over the obstacle. Lower values will result in some fluid sticking to the obstacle.

Now that we have covered the liquid particles, let's learn about all the other fluid options and values in Blender. Next up, we will discuss the **Diffusion**, **Particles**, and **Mesh** settings!

Diffusion

Diffusion is a way to add thickness and change the behavior of a fluid.

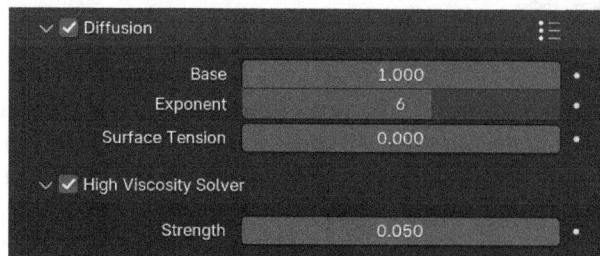

Figure 2.27 – Diffusion settings

The viscosity of the fluid in the real world is measured in **Pascal-seconds (Pa.S)**, or, more commonly, **centipoise (cP)** units. Instead of using cP, Blender uses kinematic viscosity, which is Pa.S divided by the density in kg.m³ of the fluid.

I'm going to give you two equations to help you understand how this operation works.

First, we need to understand how to convert cP into Pa.S. All you have to do is divide cP by 1,000 and you will have the Pa.S number. The cP of water is 1.002, so the Pa.S would be 0.001002; the density of water is about 1,000 kg.m³.

With all this in mind, we can set up the equation: 0.001002/1000 = 0.000001002, or in other words, 1.002×10^{-6}. In Blender, we need to set **Base** to 1 and **Exponent** to 6 to get the viscosity of water!

In the following example, we will use lava. There are different kinds of lava but the one we are creating has a cP of 3,500,000, or 3,500 in Pa.S, and the density is around 3,100 kg.m³. Our equation would be 3,500/3,100 = 1.129, which we can round to 1.0. In Blender, all we have to do is set **Base** to 1 and **Exponent** to 0 to get the thickness of lava!

Turning up **Surface Tension** will give the surface of the fluid more tension, making it look stiff. What we just talked about is technical but it's good to understand how diffusion works in Blender.

However, there is a much easier way to add thickness to fluid and that is by using the **High Viscosity Solver** option. This setting simplifies everything by adding a **Strength** value. This value makes it very easy to create things such as honey, oil, lava, or any other kind of liquid.

Keep in mind that enabling this will add some viscosity, even if the strength is set to 0. If you don't want any viscosity, make sure it is unchecked. In the following figure, the **Viscosity** values are 0 on the left, 0.1 in the middle, and 0.4 on the right.

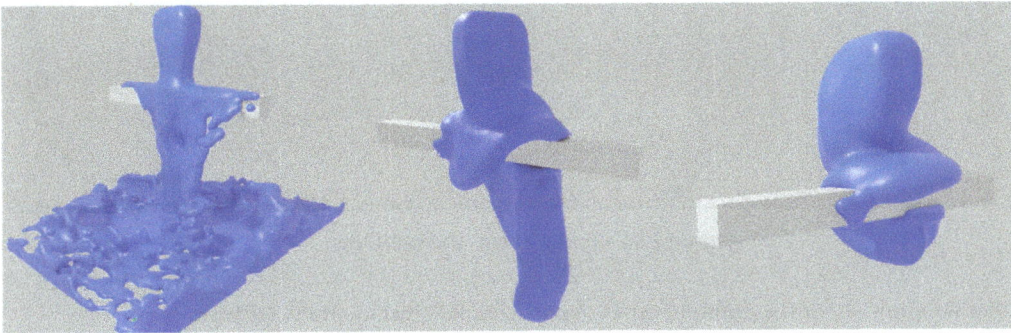

Figure 2.28 – Viscosity example

This setting can also be animated. For example, you could have the simulation start thick like slime, but then gradually turn into something thin such as water!

Particles

The next panel that we will look at is **Particles**.

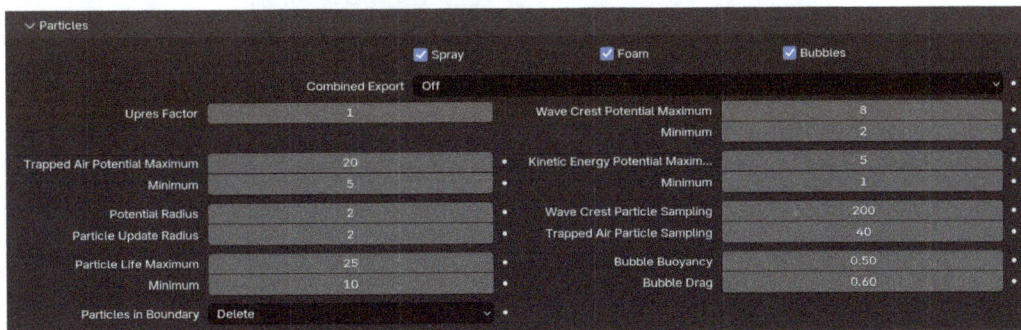

Figure 2.29 – Particle settings

These particles are different from the liquid particles we have already learned about. These deal with a certain part of the simulation. There are three particle types we can add:

- **Spray**: These particles are created when there is a big splash in the simulation.

- **Foam**: These particles lay on the surface of the fluid and move with it.

- **Bubbles**: These types of particles are created inside and move about beneath the surface of the fluid:

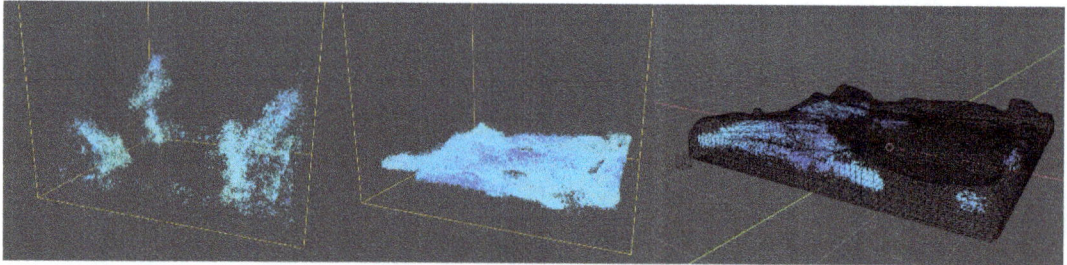

Figure 2.30 – Spray, Foam, and Bubbles

Now that we know about the different types of particles, let's discuss their settings:

- When checking either **Spray**, **Foam**, or **Bubbles**, a new particle system will be created. When **Combine Export** is set to **Off**, Blender will create three separate particle systems for each type you select; this setting allows you to combine multiple systems into one:

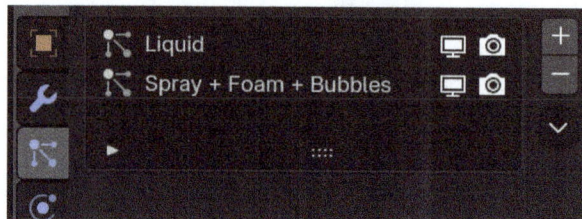

Figure 2.31 – Export examples

- **Upres Factor**: This works exactly as you'd expect: it will multiply the number of particles based on the resolution divisions. The higher you set this value, the more particles will be created.

- The next three settings are similar, so let's cover them all at once. Each of these values has the potential to create a particle at a certain place in the fluid. Here, you can control the maximum and minimum number of particles that will be created:

  - **Wave Crest**: This is for the particles at the top of the splash or wave.

  - **Trapped Air**: When fluid overlaps, sometimes, it will create an air pocket. This setting is for the number of particles in that space.

- **Kinetic Energy**: This takes the speed of the particles and determines whether particles should be emitted.

We have done a lot of testing with these three settings and all of them have a very minimal effect on the simulation. For most simulations, you could probably leave the maximum and minimum at the default values, and it will look just fine.

- **Potential Radius** and **Update Particle Radius**: These values determine how smoothly the particles will move. The difference between these two settings is that the **Potential Radius** will smooth out the grid cells, where as **Update Particle Radius** will smooth out the individual particles in the simulation. Lower values will result in particles flying everywhere, while higher values will minimize the movement, making it less chaotic. The following figure shows a value of 1 for both the **Potential Radius** and **Update Particle Radius** on the left and 4 on the right:

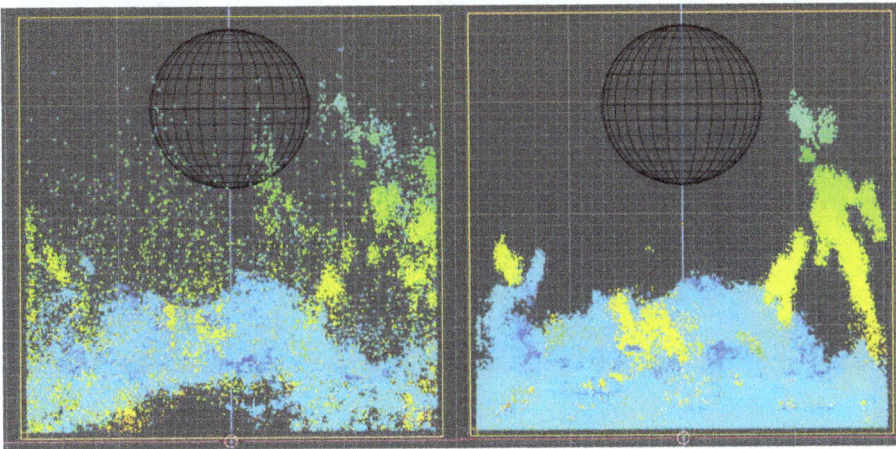

Figure 2.32 – Particle radius

- **Wave Crest Particle Sampling** and **Trapped Air Particle Sampling**: These work only with **Spray** particles. These two values determine the amount of particles that will be generated at the crest of the wave and wherever there is fluid flying through the air. Higher values will, of course, add more particles to those areas.

- **Particle Life Maximum** and **Minimum**: These control how long the particle will live in the simulation before it dies out and disappears.

- **Bubble Buoyancy**: This controls the force at which the particles will rise upward. Higher values will result in more particles hanging out on the surface of the fluid.

- **Bubble Drag**: This controls how strong the particles will move with the fluid. Higher values will result in the particles sticking very closely to the movement of the fluid.

- **Particles in Boundary**: This is for when the particles get stuck inside an obstacle. You can have them set to either **Push Out** or **Delete**.

These are all the settings for the particles in the fluid simulation! Next, let's look at the settings for the mesh.

Mesh

A mesh is another way to visualize a fluid simulation. With **Modular Cache Type** selected and the **Is Resumable** box checked, you can enable **Mesh** and be able to bake it in! Let's go through the settings and talk about each one:

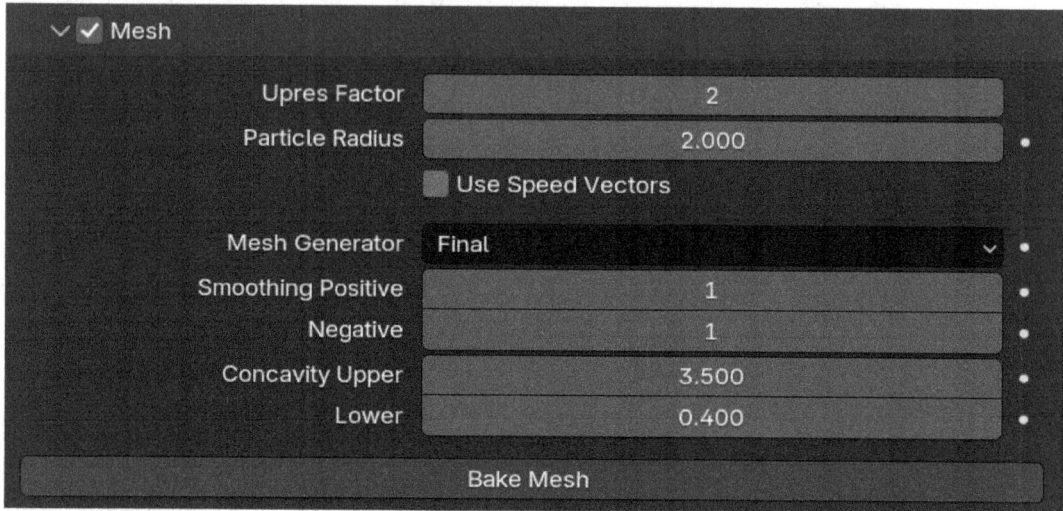

Figure 2.33 – Mesh settings

- **Upres Factor**: This will multiply the resolution of the mesh based on the value set for **Resolution Divisions**. The following figure shows the result of 1, 2, and 4 being used as values:

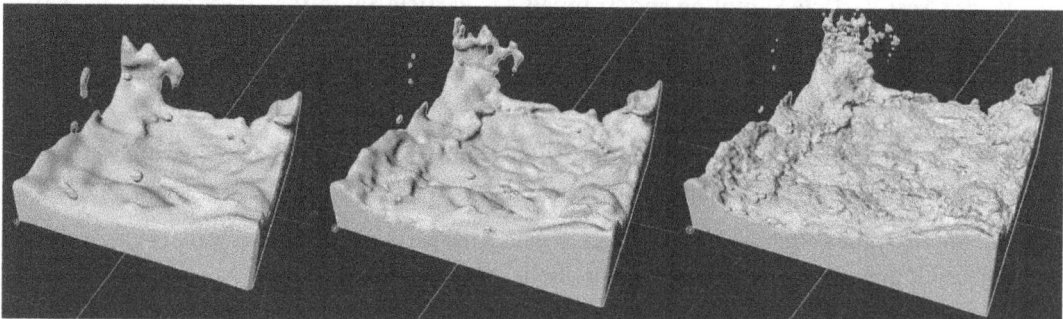

Figure 2.34 – Mesh Upres Factor example

- **Particle Radius**: This is very similar to **Particle Radius** in the **Liquid** panel. It controls the mesh size around each particle. Higher values will result in a blobby-looking simulation, while lower values will give a more realistic result. The following figure shows the result of 1 and 8 being used as values:

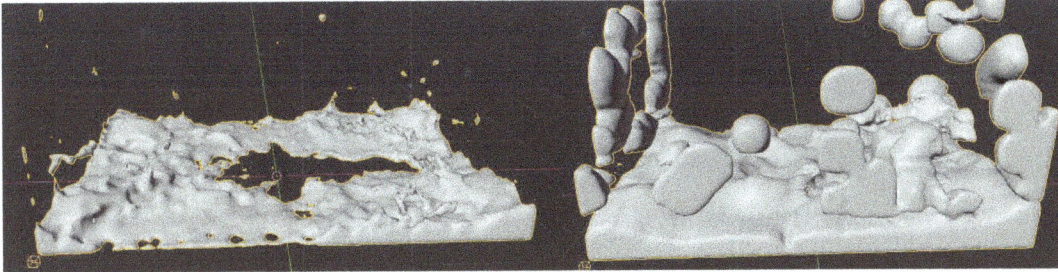

Figure 2.35 – Mesh Particle Radius

- **Speed Vectors**: This is used for adding motion blur to the fluid. With it checked, it will create data that is used in Blender's compositor (post-processing editor) for motion blur. There are three important things to note:

    - You need to be in Cycles, as EEVEE does not support this feature.

    - You also need to use the **Uni Cache** option under **Volume Format** in the **Cache** panel. **OpenVDB** will not work here.

    - Next, you need to enable **Vector** in the **Render Layers** panel:

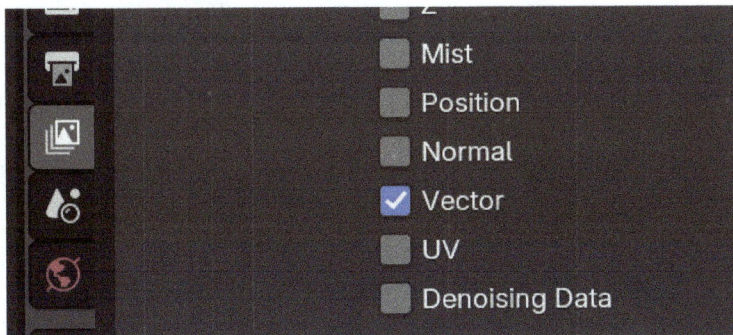

Figure 2.36 – Vector

After you render an image, you can jump over to the **Compositor** area and add a **Vector Blur** node. Take **Vector Output** from the **Render Layer** node and plug it into **Speed** input of the **Vector Blur** node. By doing this, you should get a result similar to the following:

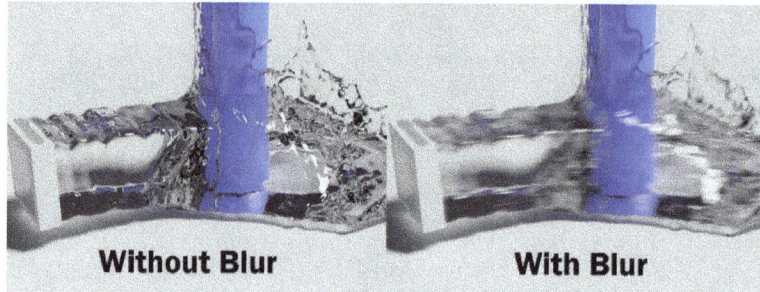

Figure 2.37 – Speed Vector example

This was a brief overview of how speed vectors work. Don't worry – we will learn how to use this in *Chapter 4*, when we create a waterfall.

- **Mesh Generator**: This controls how accurate the mesh will be. **Final** will give you the best results and provide a higher-quality mesh. **Preview**, on the other hand, is less accurate but faster when baking. For more realistic results, you should use **Final**.

- **Smoothing Positive**: This will smooth out the look of the fluid. Keep in mind that increasing this will also get rid of small details.

- **Negative**: This does the exact opposite. Instead of smoothing the surface, it will increase the sharpness of the fluid, making the edges look choppy and detailed.

If you take a look at the following figure, you will see that the left image's values are 1 for **Smoothing Positive** and 1 for **Negative**, the middle image's values are 8 for **Smoothing Positive** and 1 for **Negative**, and the right image's values are 1 for **Smoothing Positive** and 10 for **Negative**:

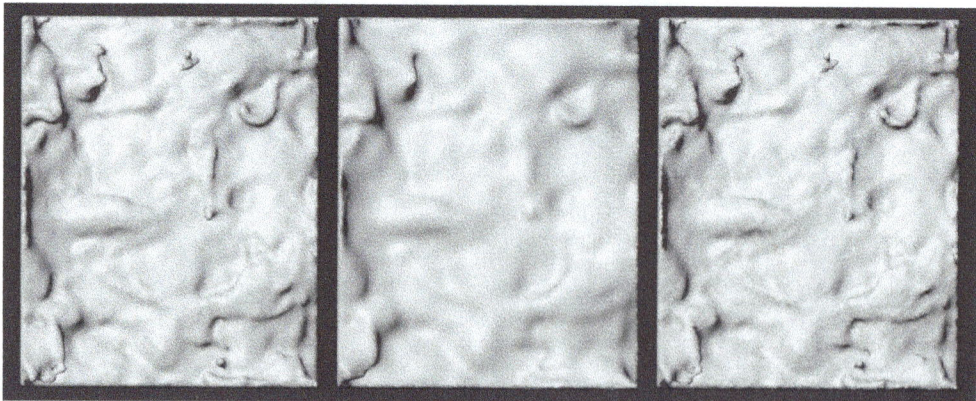

Figure 2.38 – Smoothing

- **Concavity Upper** and **Lower**: These determine how smooth the concave areas in the fluid are. Higher values tend to smooth out the fluid, while lower values might give sharper results.

  One thing to note is that if you set the **Lower** value between 0.5 and 1, this can result in some strange distortion in the mesh. If you go higher than 1, it will smooth out again:

Figure 2.39 – Concavity

To bake in the mesh, just set the cache type to **Modular** and click the big **Bake Mesh** button! If **Bake Mesh** is grayed out, make sure to turn on **Is Resumable** in the **Cache** panel as well. If you don't like how the mesh looks or want to change the settings, just click **Free Bake**.

That covers all the settings in the **Mesh** panel! Next, we will learn about guides.

Guides

Guides are another way to add force to your simulations. Unlike force fields, guides are used to help *guide* the flow of the simulation. This can be done with an effector object or another domain.

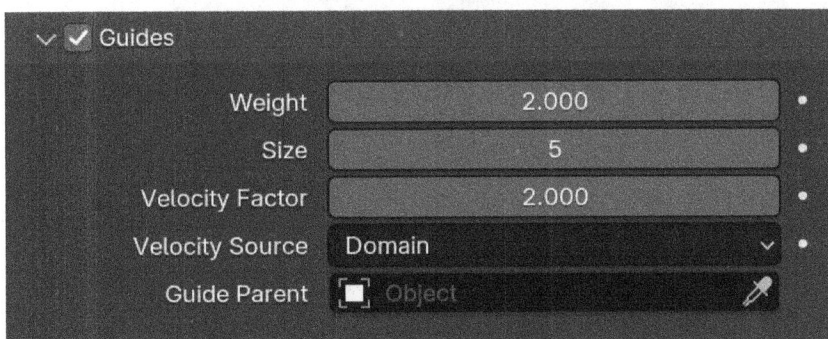

Figure 2.40 – Guides settings

One thing to note is that **Adaptive Domain** will not work properly with guides. Make sure that **Adaptive Domain** is off before baking; otherwise, you might end up with crashes.

Enabling guides adds a lot more computation to the simulation

Even if you don't use any guides, and if they are enabled, the simulation will still compute the algorithm. This will increase the bake time, so it's recommended to only enable guides when they are going to be used.

Guides work by taking the velocity of an object or simulation and adding it to the current simulation. It's similar to how a force field works. For example, if you set a cube to be a guide and it moves through the smoke, it will add some velocity and move the smoke with it, as shown in the following figure:

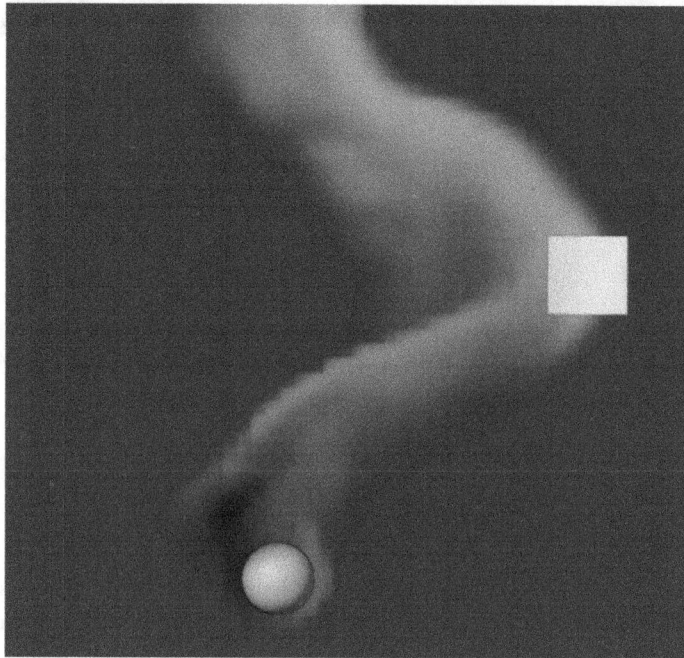

Figure 2.41 – Guides example

With the **Modular** cache type selected, you can enable guides by clicking on the respective checkbox in the **Guides** panel. From there, we have a couple of settings to go through:

- **Weight**: This controls the amount of "lag" the guide has. Higher values will make the guide not as strong, and the smoke will lag.

- **Size**: This determines how big the swirls and billows that are created from the guides are. The higher the value, the larger the vortices:

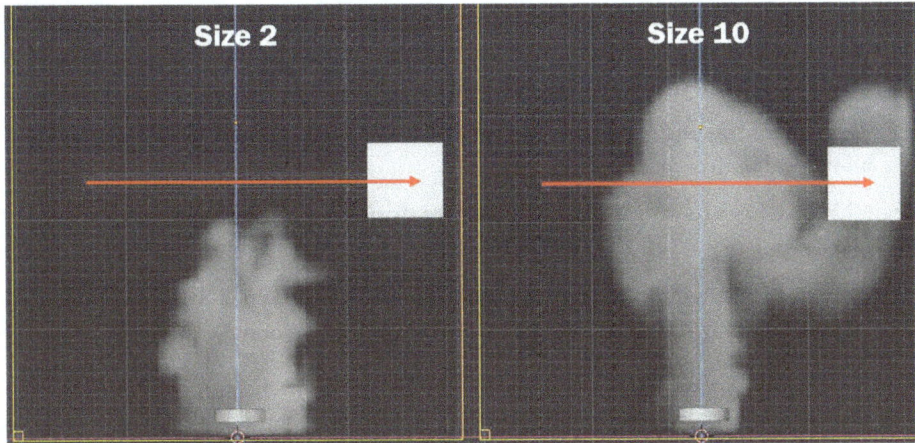

Figure 2.42 – Size example

- **Velocity Factor**: This takes the velocity of the guide and multiplies it by this value. The higher the number, the faster the smoke/fluid will move.

- **Velocity Source**: This can either be an effector object or another domain. If you select **Domain**, that means you will need to create another simulation to act as the guiding velocity and select it in the **Guide Parent** menu:

Figure 2.43 – Domain guide example

In the preceding figure, I set up a fluid simulation to be a guide for a smoke simulation. As you can see, the smoke is acting like fluid.

- For this, first, you need to create and bake in a fluid simulation. Then, you can create another simulation, this time using smoke. Make sure to use different domains and a different cache directory so that they don't overwrite each other.

    Finally, enable **Guides**, and for **Guide Parent**, select the fluid domain. Bake it in, and you will have a smoke simulation that acts like fluid!

    Bake and **Free Bake** are only available if you are using an **Effector** type and the cache type is **Modular**.

To add an object as an effector guide, select a mesh and choose **Fluid | Type | Effector | Effector Type | Guide**. You want to make sure the effector has some movement/velocity; otherwise, it won't have much of an effect on the simulation.

We will cover the first four settings in the **Effectors** section of this chapter, but for now, let's discuss **Velocity Factor** and **Guide Mode**:

- **Velocity Factor**: This is the strength of the guide. Higher values will produce faster-moving smoke. The reason there is a velocity factor value in the **Effector** settings and **Domain** settings is so that you can individually control each guide in the simulation.

- **Guide Mode**: This determines how the guide effector should influence the simulation's velocity based on the value of **Velocity Factor**:

    - **Maximum**: This takes the velocity from the previous frame and current frame and keeps the maximum value.

    - **Minimum**: This takes the velocity from the previous frame and current frame and keeps the minimum value.

    - **Override**: This is the option you will probably use most of the time. It will always write a new guiding velocity for every frame.

    - **Average**: This takes the velocity of the previous frame and current frame and averages it out.

Guides are pretty unique and can create some really interesting simulations! I recommend playing around with the settings and seeing what you can create.

Collections

The **Collections** panel allows you to select certain collections to act as flows or effectors in that domain. For example, if you have multiple flows in different collections and you only want to use one of those collections, you can select it here:

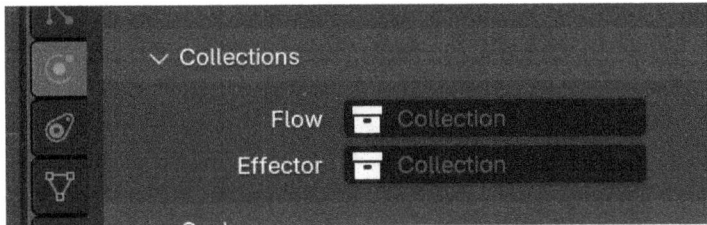

Figure 2.44 – Collections example

Now, only the flows in that collection will interact with the simulation. This works the same way with effector objects as well.

Field Weights

Field Weights allows you to change how much a force field will affect the simulation.

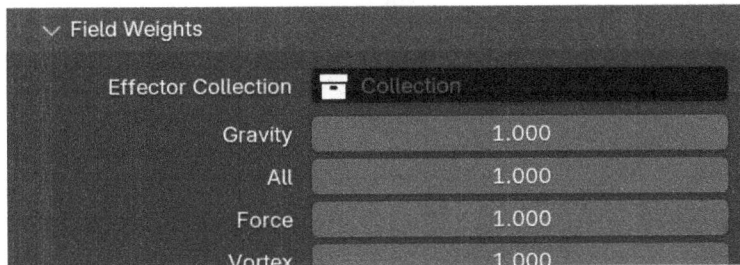

Figure 2.45 – Field Weights

If you have a wind force field in the scene, and you turn down the **Wind** value to 0, that force won't influence that domain. This is useful if you have multiple domains and don't want a force affecting all of them.

When you set **Effector Collection**, only the force fields in that collection will influence the simulation.

The **All** value will affect all the force fields in the simulation.

Viewport Display

Viewport Display is another way to view the simulation, and it only affects the viewport, not the render. **Viewport Display** allows you to visualize the velocity of the smoke, the density, the X, Y, or Z force, heat, fuel, and a bunch more.

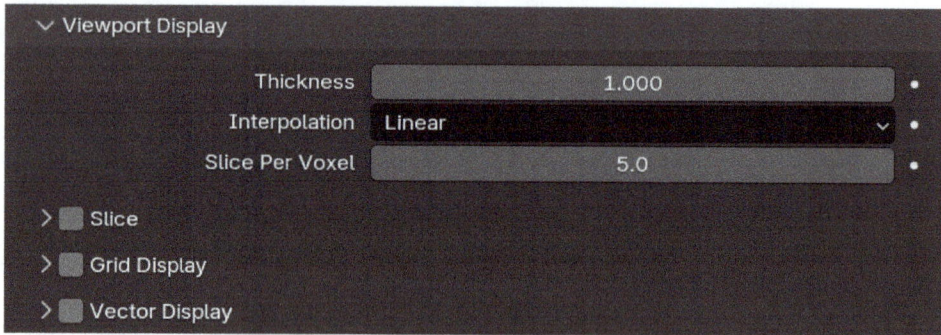

Figure 2.46 – Viewport Display

- **Thickness**: This will change the density of the smoke, allowing you to see what thick or thin smoke will look like.

- **Interpolation**: This determines how the smoke will be displayed. There are three options to choose from:

  - **Closest**: This displays raw voxels.

  - **Linear**: This is smooth and fast.

  - **Cubic**: This gives the best quality but will run a bit slower.

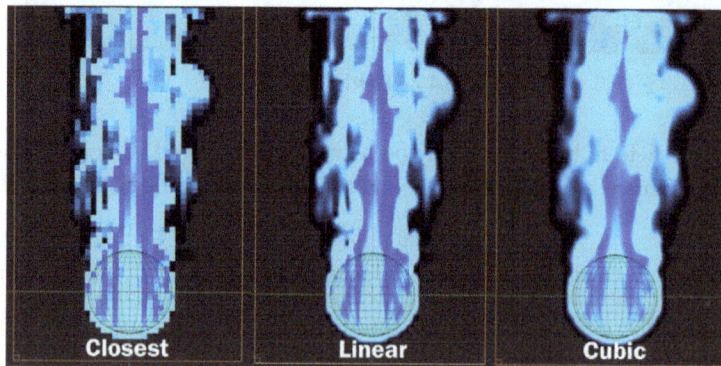

Figure 2.47 – Interpolation mode example

- **Slice**: This allows you to slice the simulation to see a flat version of it. You can change the **Axis** value of where it will be displayed, as well as its position!

- **Grid Display**: This shows different attributes of the simulation:

  - **Field**: This is the menu from where you can select attributes to visualize in the smoke. This includes **Density**, **Velocity**, and **Fuel**.

  - **Scale**: This controls how **ColorRamp** is displayed. Setting different colors in **ColorRamp** will give you some interesting results.

- **Vector Display**: This gives you information about the direction and velocity of the smoke. **Scale** will change how big the needles are that display the velocity:

Viewport Display is fun to play around with and it's a good tool to help visualize certain aspects of the simulation. Again, it only affects the viewport – it does not change how the render will look.

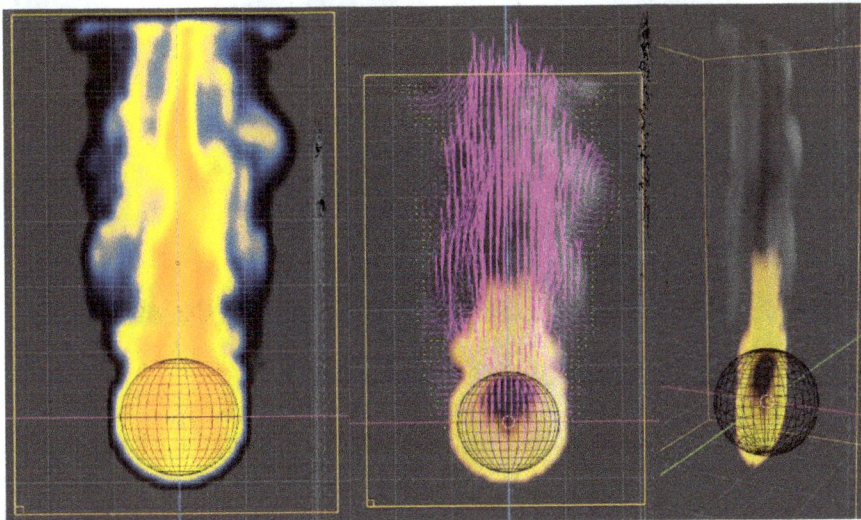

Figure 2.48 – Viewport Display example

Now let's take a look at the last setting in the domain!

Render

When using a gas-type domain, there is one more tab at the very bottom called Render.

Figure 2.49 – Render tab

Velocity Scale is a multiplier for the amount of motion blur that will appear for your fire and smoke. For this to work, you first need to enable motion blur by checking the **Motion Blur** box in the **Render** panel. Inside this tab, the **Shutter** value sets the strength of the blur for the scene, and the **Velocity Scale** value takes that value and multiples it for the fire or smoke. In the following figure, the **Shutter** amount is set at 0.5, and **Velocity Scale**, from left to right, is 0, 1, and 2.

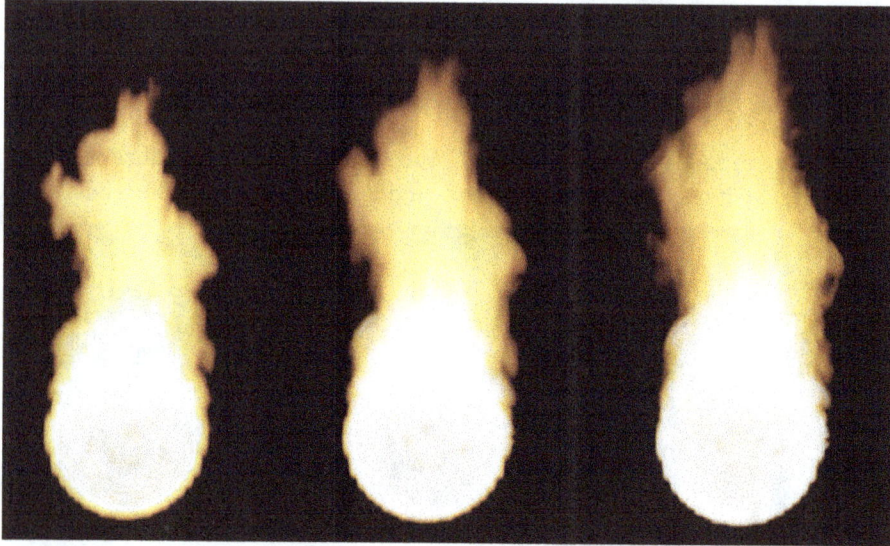

Figure 2.50 – Velocity Scale example

You'll see that with a value of 2, you lose a lot of detail in the fire and everything looks a bit stretched. In this case, you could turn down both the **Velocity Scale** and **Shutter** amount to reduce the blur. Another thing to keep in mind is that this setting only works in Cycles. EEVEE does not support motion blur for volumes at the current time.

And that's it – we have finished covering all the settings in the domain! It was quite a lot, but hopefully, you learned something new. If you ever forget what a setting does, just come back and reference this chapter. Finally, let's talk about flows and effector objects!

Flow objects

Flow objects are used to either add smoke/fluid to the simulation or remove it, and they must be within the domain bounding box to work properly. To add a flow object to the simulation, just select any mesh. Then, in the **Physics** panel, select **Fluid** | **Type** | **Flow**.

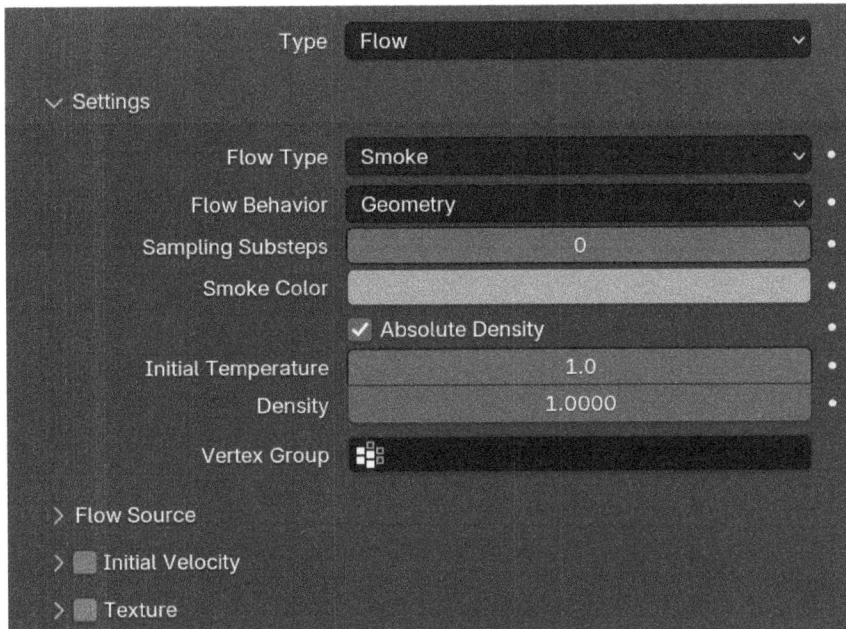

Figure 2.51 – Flow settings

Let's go through the settings for the flow object and learn about each one:

- There are four flow types we can add:

  - **Smoke**: This will only emit smoke into the domain.

  - **Smoke + Fire**: This will emit both smoke and fire into the domain.

  - **Fire**: This will only emit fire. Keep in mind that a little bit of smoke will be emitted from the burnt fuel. If you only want fire, set **Flame Smoke** in the domain to 0.

  - **Liquid**: This, of course, will emit fluid into the domain.

- **Flow Behavior**: This controls how the flow will interact with the simulation:

  - **Inflow**: This will constantly add fluid/smoke to the simulation.

  - **Outflow**: This will remove any fluid/smoke that touches the flow object from the simulation. This can be useful for creating a drain or vacuum or to prevent the entire domain from filling with fluid. You can also animate the movement of these objects to create interesting results.

  - **Geometry**: This takes the size of the mesh and adds that amount to the simulation.

- **Use Flow**: This is used to enable or disable flow objects. This value can also be animated. This is very useful for turning outflows or inflows off or on.

- **Sample Substeps**: This is used for fast-moving flows. If you have a flow object that is moving very fast, you will want to turn this up. If you don't, your smoke will look like it skipped some frames:

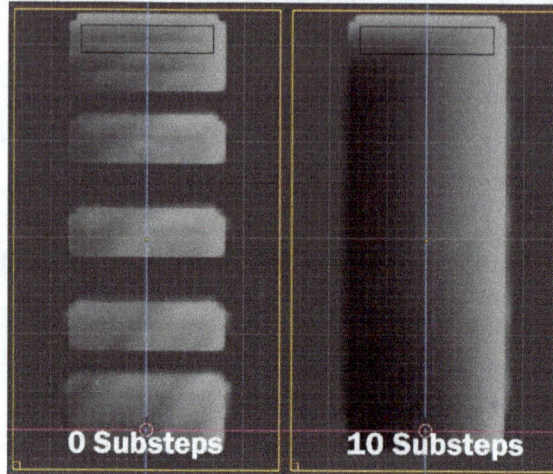

Figure 2.52 – Sample substeps example

- **Smoke Color**: This is useful for setting different colors of smoke for different flows. When mixed, it will create a combined color:

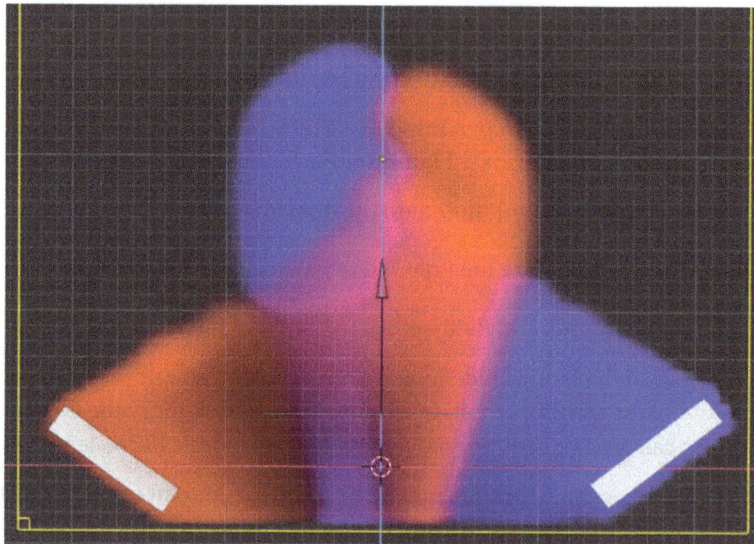

Figure 2.53 – Smoke Color example

- **Absolute Density**: When this is checked, the flow object will emit smoke, but only if there is room for it. If it's unchecked, the flow will continue emitting smoke into the domain, even if it's already filled.

- **Initial Temperature**: This controls whether the smoke will rise or fall. This value is also linked to the **Heat** value in the domain. If **Heat** is set to 1 and **Initial Temperature** is set to -1, the smoke will remain in the same spot, not moving much. But if **Initial Temperature** is set to -1.5, then the smoke will sink because the initial temperature has a higher value than the heat. Remember that if both values are negative, the smoke will rise, but if one is positive and the other is negative, the smoke will sink. This can be useful if you want different flow objects to rise or sink.

- **Density**: This is the amount of smoke that gets emitted and how dense it will be:

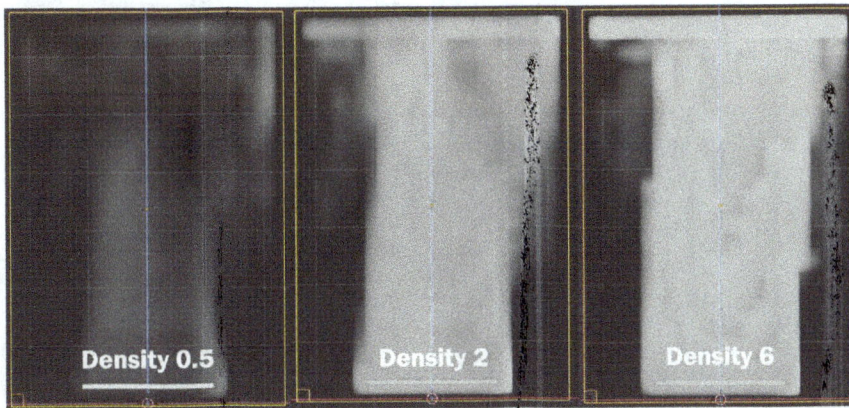

Figure 2.54 – Density examples

- **Fuel**: This controls the height and how crazy the flames will be. Higher values will produce taller and noisier flames:

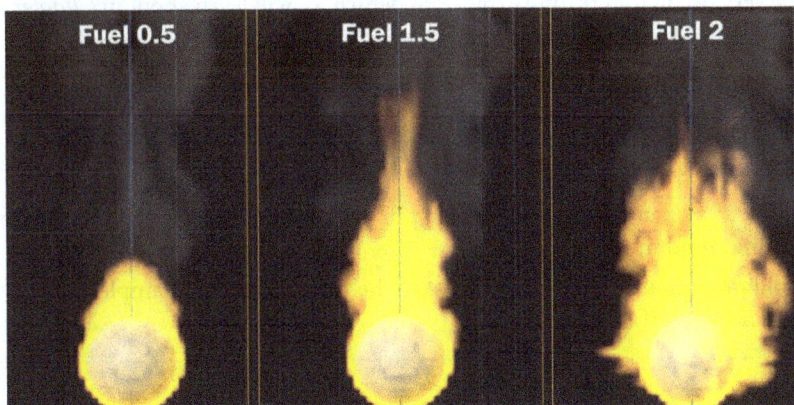

Figure 2.55 – Fuel examples

- **Vertex Group**: This allows you to pick a specific vertex group to determine where the fire or smoke gets emitted on the mesh. This can be very useful for creating a trail of fire or other cool effects. We will learn more about vertex groups in *Chapter 6*.

- **Flow Source**: This is where the flow is coming from. With smoke simulations, there are two options to choose from:

  - If you select **Mesh**, then the entire object will emit smoke.

  - If **Particle System** is selected, you will need to select a particle system from the dropdown menu. Now, each particle will emit smoke into the simulation. The following figure shows particles flying into the air and smoke trailing behind them:

Figure 2.56 – Particle system example

This can be very useful for creating explosions, which we will learn about in *Chapter 5*. You can also set the radius of smoke around each particle by changing the **Size** value.

When creating a fluid simulation, **Mesh** is the only option available.

- **Is Planar**: If your flow object is non-manifold, then make sure **Is Planar** is checked. This will help Blender get the most accurate results.

What is a non-manifold mesh?

A non-manifold mesh is a mesh that can't exist in the real world. For example, a plane would be considered a non-manifold mesh.

- **Surface Emission**: This is how far away from the surface of the mesh the smoke/fluid will be emitted.

- **Volume Emission**: This is the amount of smoke/fluid inside the mesh that will be emitted. 1 will fill up the entire object.

- If you change **Flow Source** to **Particle System**, you can also set the **Size** value at which the smoke/fire will be emitted from each particle.

- **Initial Velocity**: This, if checked, will enable the smoke/fluid to keep the momentum generated from the flow and apply it to the simulation. In the following figure, the top cube has **Initial Velocity** checked; as it moves across, the smoke will move with it:

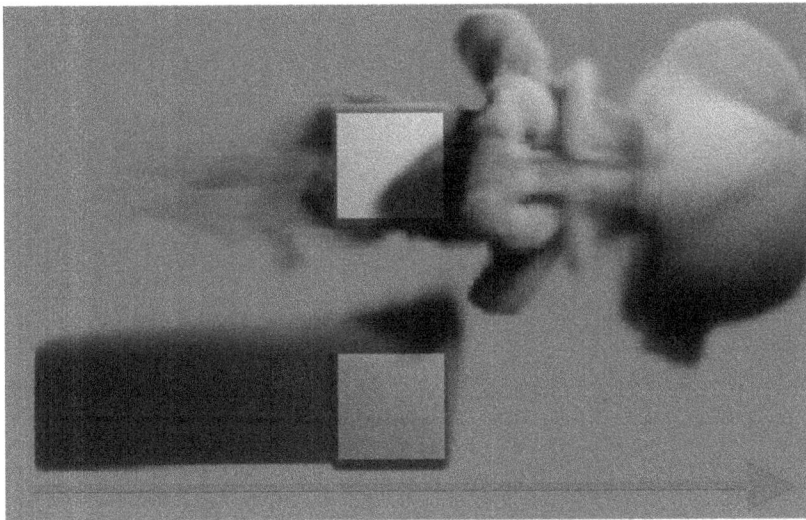

Figure 2.57 – Initial Velocity example

Inside the **Initial Velocity** panel, we have a couple more ways to control where the smoke/ fluid will emit:

- **Source**: This is the factor at which the smoke/fluid will inherit the momentum. 1 means it will have the same speed as the flow object. A value of 2 means it will move at double the speed as the fluid/smoke is being emitted.

- **Normal**: This is how much velocity the smoke/fluid will have along the normals of the mesh.

What are normals?

In geometry, normals are the direction in which the faces are pointed. For example, if you set a cube to emit smoke and bring up the **Normal** value, the smoke will shoot out along every face of the cube.

- **Initial velocity**: This can be set on a certain axis – be it **X**, **Y**, or **Z**. This is very useful for emitting fluids in a direction very quickly.

- **Texture:** This allows you to map a texture to the flow object (only for smoke/fire flows). To create a new texture, go to the **Texture Properties** panel and select **New**. You can either choose from a big list of generated textures or select your own by choosing **Image/Movie**. Once you are done, head back to the **Physics** panel and choose it from the dropdown menu!

You can set the **Size** and **Offset** values of the texture on the flow object. The **Offset** value can also be animated to give fire a realistic look:

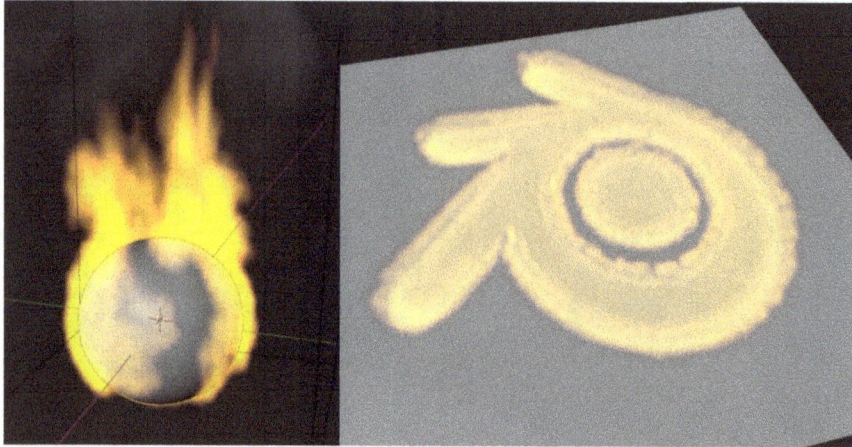

Figure 2.58 – Texture example

That is all the settings for flow objects. Before we end this chapter, let's look at the last object we can add to the simulation.

Effectors

Effector objects offer a way to add collisions to your simulation. These types of objects can be any mesh. To add an effector object, select any mesh. Then, in the **Physics** panel, select **Fluid | Type | Effector**.

Figure 2.59 – Effector settings

There are two types of effectors in Mantaflow: **collisions** and **guides**. We learned about guides earlier, so let's select **Collision**. Let's go over the four settings:

- **Sampling Substeps**: This is very similar to **Substeps** for the flow object. If you have a fast-moving collision, it's recommended to turn this value up; otherwise, you might get some inaccuracies.

- **Surface Thickness**: This is the area around the object that will be considered a collision. Higher values will result in fluid colliding further from the surface.

- **Use Effector**: This enables or disables the effector. This can be useful for animating the collisions and turning them off and on.

- **Is Planar**: Again, if your effector is non-manifold, then make sure **Is Planar** is checked. This will help Blender get more accurate collisions:

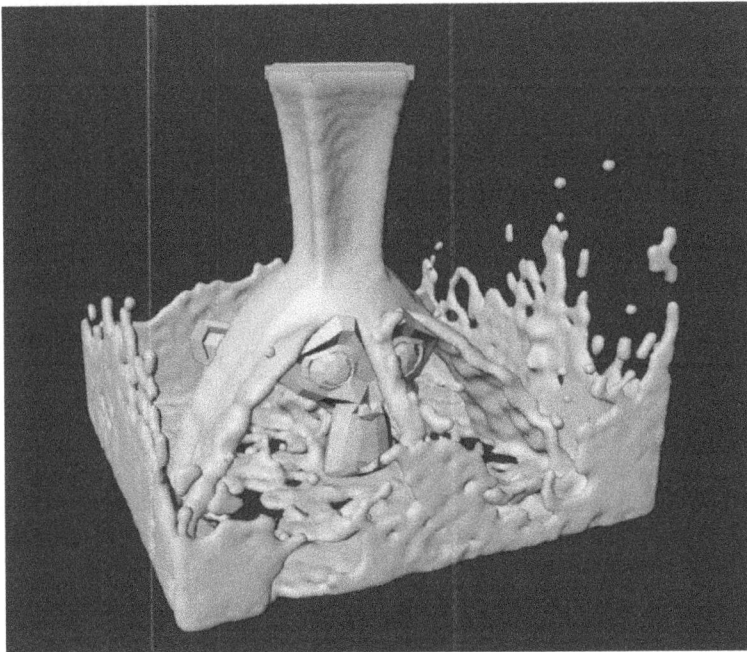

Figure 2.60 – Collision example

If you have multiple objects you want to add an effector collision to, the easy way to do that is to select all of them. Then, with an active object selected, click **Fluid | Type | Effector**. Then, press *Ctrl + L* or *Cmd + L* and select **Copy Modifiers**. That will copy the settings you have and apply them to all the objects selected.

And there you have it; those are all the settings in the effecter collision in Mantaflow!

Summary

We have covered quite a bit in this chapter, so let's take a quick recap. First, we learned about domains, some of the settings (resolution divisions and time steps), and the importance of the different cache modes, including **Replay**, **Modular**, and **Final**. We talked about the smoke settings, density, heat, vorticity, adaptive domain, and dissolving the smoke. We also covered how to easily add more detail to the smoke using **Noise** and how to change how the flames look in the **Fire** panel.

After that, we moved on to the liquid settings and talked all about liquid particles; meshes; foam, spray, and bubble particles; speed vector blur; and a bunch more options. Guides were another topic we covered, and we saw how you can add velocity from another object to your simulation. Finally, we covered flow objects and effectors and all the settings that come with those objects.

Hopefully, this chapter gave you an in-depth understanding of all the settings in Mantaflow. Remember to come back and reference this chapter if you forget what a setting does!

Before you move on to *Chapter 3*, I recommend jumping into Blender and creating a simulation from what you've learned in this chapter. This way, everything will sink in, and it will be easier to remember. You could create a torch that lights up a cave, a water fountain in a park, or something cool such as a meteor that falls from the sky! Use your imagination and go crazy with it!

We are done talking about settings. Now, let's create something with the knowledge we just learned. In the next chapter, I will show you how to make a realistic campfire using Mantaflow in Blender!

Join our community on Discord

Join our community's Discord space for discussions with the author and other readers:
`https://packt.link/learn-blender-simulations-discord-invite`

3

Creating a Realistic Campfire Simulation

It's time to put the skills we just learned to the test. In this chapter, we'll create a realistic campfire simulation and learn how to create sparks in Blender! Creating fire is easy but creating fire that looks realistic is a whole other story. You need to think about the settings for the domain, the flow object, any collisions you have, the lighting, and the materials. It takes a bit more than setting the resolution in the domain to 1,000 and hitting **Bake**. Remember, setting the resolution super high doesn't necessarily mean the fire will look good; plus, I'm pretty sure Blender would crash if you did that.

In this chapter, we'll be covering the following topics:

- Creating the campfire simulation
- Creating the fire materials
- Creating sparks using a particle system
- Creating the particle material
- Adding the final details

We have a lot of things to cover in this chapter, so let's jump right into it!

Technical requirements

This chapter requires that you have Blender version 4.2 or above installed. To download Blender, visit www.blender.org.

This tutorial is a bit more advanced, and we won't be covering everything. We're assuming you know the basics of Blender and how to render animations.

Make sure you download Campfire Setup.blend to follow along with this chapter. It can be downloaded from https://github.com/PacktPublishing/Learn-Blender-4-Simulations-the-Right-Way/tree/main/Chapter%203.

Creating the campfire simulation

As mentioned in the *Technical requirements* section, to get a head start on this chapter, make sure you download the 3D model of the campfire, called `Campfire Setup.blend`. This `.blend` file has some logs, rocks, and materials already in place; hence, we can jump straight into creating the simulation.

When you open the `Campfire Setup.blend` file, you'll notice that the campfire model is very large, at over 2.6 meters wide. If we were to scale the model down to a real-life size and try and simulate it, it wouldn't work very well. This is because Blender has a hard time simulating at a small scale. We've had problems where the fire fills the entire domain, which makes the fire look very noisy, and the bake will take a super long time. In general, it's usually a good idea to simulate at a large scale.

What if you already created a scene at a small scale? Well, a solution for that would be to create a simulation in another `.blend` file and then import that simulation as a volume object. Then, you'll be able to scale down the fire and move it anywhere in the scene.

For now, let's create the domain object and start setting up the simulation!

Setting up the domain

With the `Campfire Setup.blend` file open, let's create a domain object and change some of the settings to get the desired look:

1. First, add a cube object as our domain and scale it up to fit the campfire. You only need to scale it up to fit the logs, not the rocks. Then, double-check that the cube is tall enough for the flames that you want:

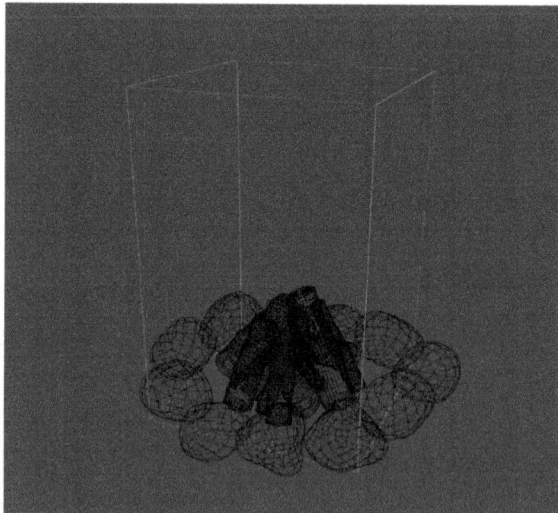

Figure 3.1 – Domain size

2. Once you're happy with it, head over to the **Physics** tab and select **Fluid**. Then, for **Type**, select **Domain**.

3. As for the domain settings, let's start by changing **Resolution Divisions** to 96. This will give us a nice high-quality fire.

4. With the current settings, the fire will move very quickly in the simulation, so let's counteract this by changing **Time Scale** to 0.5. This will slow down the fire.

5. Set **CFL Number** to 4. This will decrease the simulation steps, thus decreasing the bake time.

6. Check the box next to **Adaptive Domain** to help reduce the bake time.

7. In the **Gas** tab, set **Vorticity** to 0.1 so that we get a little bit of randomness with the smoke.

8. Open the **Fire** tab and change **Reaction Speed** to 0.50. With the default value of 0.750, the flames might be a bit too short for our scene. Remember that **Reaction Speed** controls the height of the flames. Lower values means taller flames and higher values means shorter flames. Feel free to customize this value however you like!

9. Now, let's set up the **Cache** panel so we can bake in the simulation:

    - First, change **Type** to **Modular** so that we can bake in the simulation.

    - Set **End Frame** to however long you want your simulation to be; 150 frames is a good length for this simulation.

    - Finally, check **Is Resumeable** just in case you need to stop the bake. We don't need any **Noise** in this simulation because we found that the fire looks too messy with it enabled.

10. Lastly, open the **Render** tab at the very bottom and set **Velocity Scale** to 0.1. This value controls how much motion blur will appear on the fire. Keep in mind that this value can be changed even after we've baked the simulation.

And there we go – we've set up the domain. Now, it's time to create all the **Flow** objects!

Setting up the inflows

Now that the domain has been set up and is ready to go, let's create the flow objects. If you take a look at real campfires, you'll notice that not all of the sticks and logs are on fire; only the ones that are near the bottom are:

Figure 3.2 – Real campfire example

Let's replicate this by only selecting the logs that are at the bottom of the fire and setting those as the inflow objects. The objects that we can select as inflows are **Cylinder.001** through **Cylinder.006**. You can view their names by looking at the **Outliner** area at the top right of Blender, as follows:

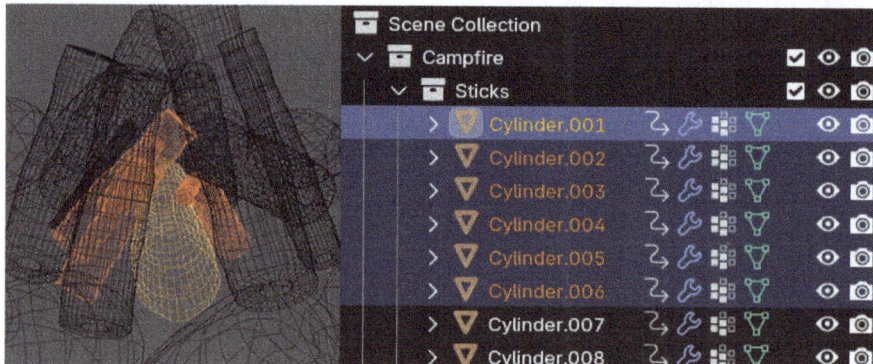

Figure 3.3 – Inflow selection

Once we've created the first inflow, we can apply those same settings to the rest of the objects. Let's get started:

1. Jump over to the **Physics** panel (if it's not already there, select **Fluid**).

2. For **Type**, choose **Flow**.

3. Set **Flow Type** to **Fire** and **Behavior** to **Inflow**.

4. Let's increase the **Fuel** value to 1.2, just to give the flames a bit more of a chaotic look.

5. In the **Source** tab, set **Surface Emission** to a lower value of 1. This will bring the fire closer to the surface of the mesh. For an example of this, view the following figure:

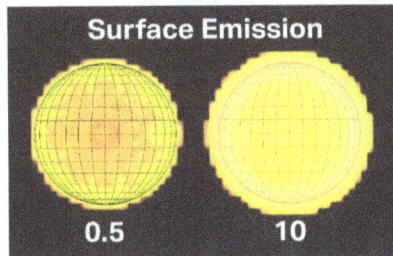

Figure 3.4 – Surface Emission example

6. Now, let's enable a texture. This will allow us to control where the fire will emit on our object. Check the **Texture** box, then head over to the **Texture** panel (it will look like a checkered pattern):

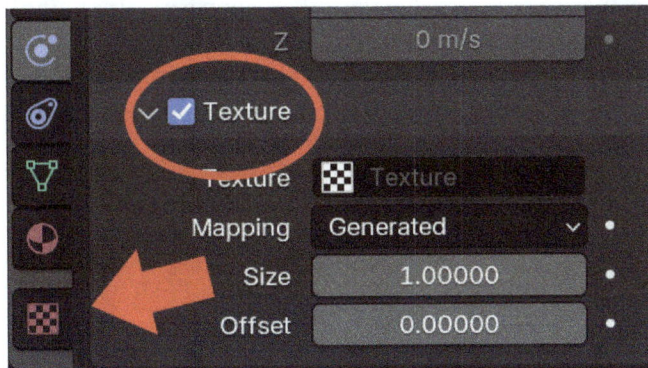

Figure 3.5 – Texture example

This is where we can create and set up textures for our objects:

I. Click the big **New** button to create a new texture.

II. To keep everything organized, let's name this new texture Inflow Texture.

III. For **Type**, choose **Clouds**. This will give us a very noisy pattern that will look nice when the fire emits from the **Inflow** object.

IV.   Currently, the texture is a bit too big for our object, so let's set **Size** to 0.1.

V.   When using textures for inflows, they act as a mask for where the fire will emit. The white parts of the texture will emit fire and the black parts won't. To get a bit more definition between the white and black parts of the texture, let's set **Contrast** in the **Color** tab to 2. This will give us sharper edges on the texture.

This is what your texture should look like now:

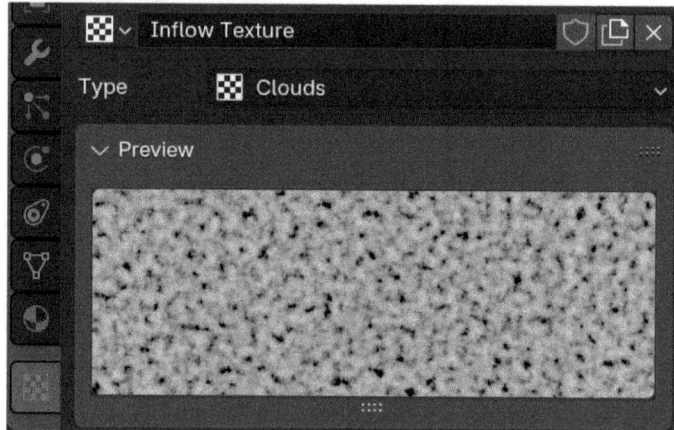

Figure 3.6 – Texture preview

7.   Let's assign the texture we just created to the inflow. Jump back over to the **Physics** panel and select the texture from the drop-down menu. You might see a lot of other textures – that's because of the rocks. Just type Inflow and our texture (**Inflow Texture**) will pop up!

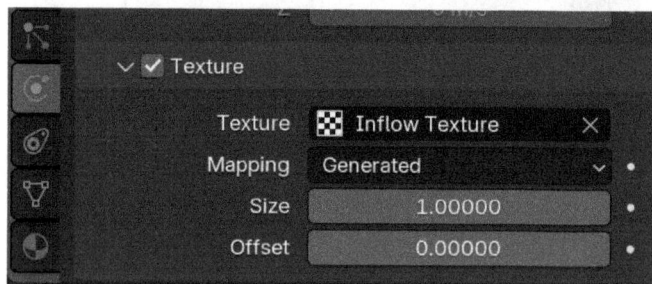

Figure 3.7 – Inflow Texture selection

8.   The other thing we want to do is move the texture around the object as it simulates. This will give us a random variation in the fire, making it look more realistic. We can achieve this by using **Offset** in the **Texture** tab. Instead of animating this value, let's just create a driver that does this for us automatically. Click on this **Offset** field, type #frame/250, and hit *Enter*!

Now, the texture will move around as the animation plays.

9. Now that we've created the first inflow, let's copy all of those settings and apply them to the rest of the objects. Make sure the objects you want to assign are selected and that the object with the inflow settings is selected *last*. If done correctly, the last object will be highlighted alone in a different yellow/orange color. This will make sure that it's the *active object*.

> **What's an active object?**
>
> When you have multiple objects selected in Blender, there will be one that has a yellow outline. This is your active object. The rest of the objects will have an orange outline.

Then, press *Ctrl + L* or *Cmd + L* and click **Copy Modifiers**. Now, all of those objects will have the same settings we just created! The other way to do this is by going to **Object | Link/Transfer Data | Copy Modifiers**.

10. The preceding step only copied the settings for the inflow – it didn't copy the driver we created in *step 8* for the texture offset. What we need to do is copy the animation data of the texture. Press *Ctrl + L* or *Cmd + L* and select **Link Animation Data**. Now, all of the objects will have the same driver we created earlier.

And there we go; we've successfully created all of the inflow objects. The next thing we need to do is assign some effector objects. We don't want the fire to go through the logs, so let's assign some collisions!

Adding effectors

This part is pretty simple – all we need to do is assign an effector collision to all the logs that aren't inflows, as follows:

1. Select **Cylinder.007** through **Cylinder.014** in the **Outliner** area (at the top right of the screen), as follows:

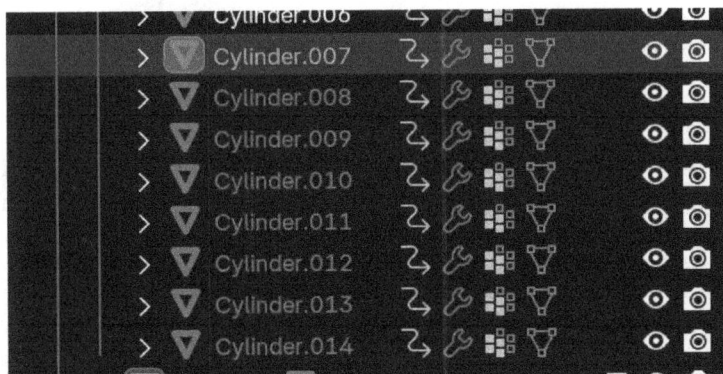

Figure 3.8 – Effector selections

2. In the **Physics** panel, select **Fluid**, and for **Type**, choose **Effector**.

3. Just repeat the process we did for the inflow objects by pressing *Ctrl + L* or *Cmd + L* and selecting **Copy Modifiers**. Now, each of those objects will have the effector collision assigned!

We don't need to assign the collisions to the rocks because the fire won't reach there! With that done, we're ready to bake in the simulation. To do that, select your domain object and click **Bake Data**. Look at the following figure to see what your simulation should look like so far!

Figure 3.9 – Baked simulation

Now that the simulation is complete, we're ready to create a nice fiery material!

Creating the fire materials

Now that the simulation is finished, we're ready to create the fire material. One thing we wanted to mention here is that for this scene, we'll be using Cycles to render the animation. There are a couple of reasons for this.

One of the main reasons is that when using EEVEE, volumetrics don't emit light. This means that the fire will look like it's just glowing and won't light up the rest of the scene. Since we're going for a realistic simulation, we want to use Cycles so that the fire emits light to the surrounding area.

Another reason is that there are a couple of features in the material that only work in the Cycles render engine. So, head over to the **Render** panel and switch the engine to **Cycles**. Once you've done this, you'll be good to go!

With that out of the way, let's create this fiery material:

1. Let's start by selecting the **Shading** workspace at the top of the screen. The following figure shows where you'll be able to create the fire material:

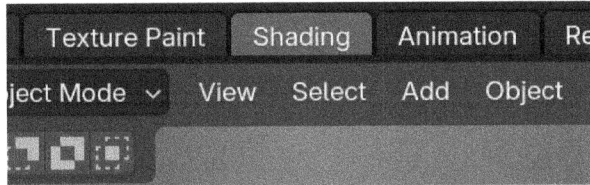

Figure 3.10 – The Shading workspace

2. To create a new material, click the big **New** button in the middle of the screen:

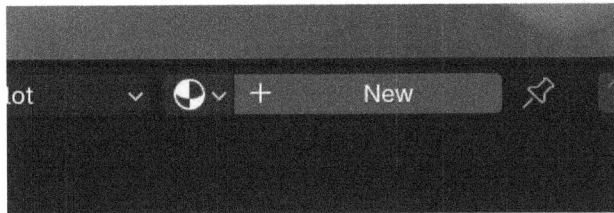

Figure 3.11 – New material

3. We don't need the **Principled BSDF** shader, so go ahead and delete it. Then, replace it with the **Principled Volume** shader. To add a new node, press *Shift + A*, then go to **Shader** and select **Principled Volume**. From there, take the **Volume** output and plug it into **Volume** in the **Material Output** node, as follows:

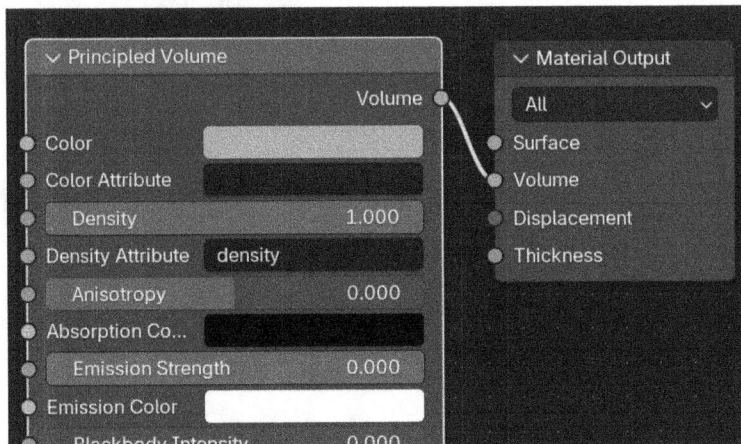

Figure 3.12 – Principled Volume

4. Set **Density** to a value of 5 or so to make the smoke denser.

5. In *Chapter 1*, we used **Blackbody Intensity** to add flames. While this does work, using this method will produce some sharp edges and give the fire a lower-quality look. Instead, we're going to be using the **Heat** attribute to add the flames.

Attributes

Heat, along with many other attributes, can be brought into the material and used however you like. For example, you could take the velocity attribute and plug that into the emission value. Then, you'll be able to see the values of the velocity in the simulation. *Flame, density, temperature,* and *velocity* are just a few of the attributes at your disposal. Also, the **Heat** attribute only works in the Cycles render engine.

For this to work, we need to add the **Attribute** node. To do this, press *Shift + A* and choose **Input | Attribute**.

6. In the **Name** field, type the word heat in lowercase. Then, plug the **Fac** output into **Emission Strength**.

7. To control this a bit more, let's add a **Color Ramp** node. To do this, click *Shift + A*, go to **Converter**, then select **Color Ramp** and place it in between the **Attribute** node and **Principled Volume**. If you slide the black handle of **Color Ramp** closer to the white handle, it will clamp down on those values, giving you the look of flames. You can also switch **Color Ramp** from **Linear** to **Ease** to get a smoother transition.

    If you go into **Rendered View**, you'll see what the node setup should look like so far:

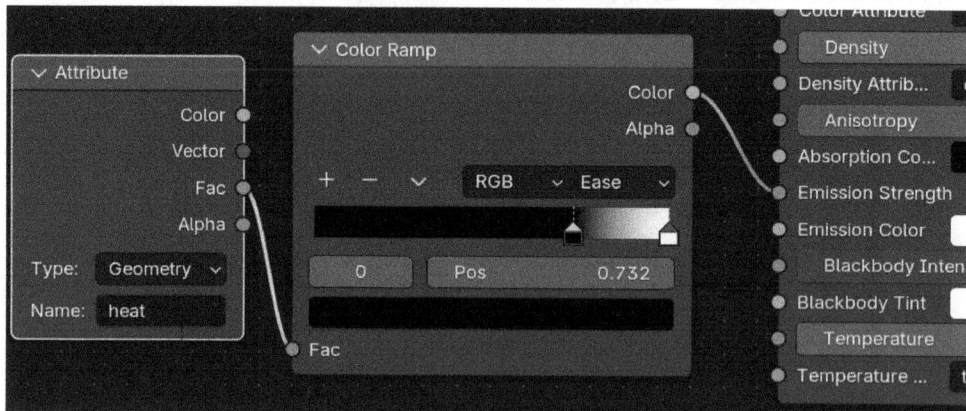

Figure 3.13 – Heat attribute

8. Let's brighten up our flames, shall we? To do this, add a **Math** node. Press *Shift + A*, go to **Converter**, and select **Math**. Then, place the node between **Color Ramp** and **Principled Volume**. If you set the mode from **Add** to **Multiply**, the bottom value will now control the strength of the emission. Let's set this to a value of 50.

9. Now, add some color. Duplicate **Color Ramp** by pressing *Ctrl + Shift + D*; this will keep the connection to the **Attribute** node (pressing just *Shift + D* will break the connection). Then, plug the new **Color Ramp** node into **Emission Color** in **Principled Volume**.

    If we look at real flames, you'll notice that the edges have this red tint, and as you travel closer to the bottom of the fire, it goes orange and then white:

Figure 3.14 – Real flame example

To get the same look, select the black handle of the **Color Ramp** node and set it to a red color, then set the white handle to an orange color. Play around with the positions until it looks good. You can always change the colors later to get different looks for the fire!

10. Finally, to give our flames more detail, let's jump back to the first **Color Ramp** node and add another handle by clicking the + button. Move the handle we just added to the far right-hand side and set the color to black. Double-check that the white handle is a little bit to the left. View the following figure for an example:

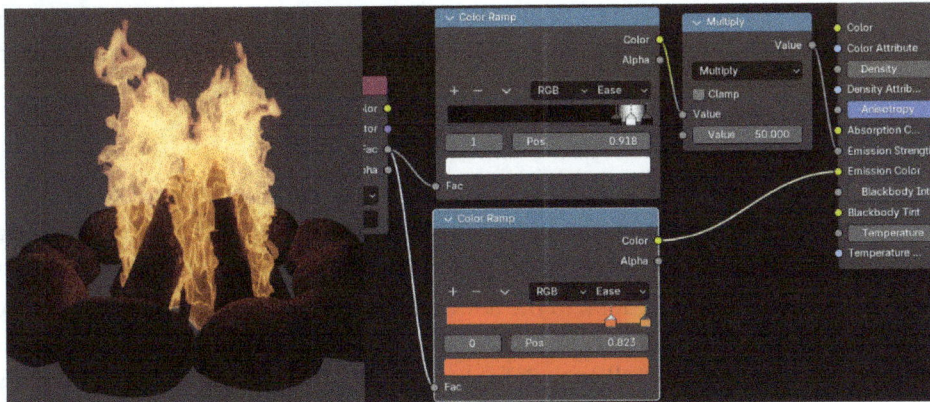

Figure 3.15 – Fire material example

Remember that with the **Color Ramp** node moving, the black handles around it clamp down on the fire values. With this in mind, adding a black handle to the right-hand side removes some of the fire at the very bottom. This, in turn, gives a much more detailed and interesting look to the fire. View *Figure 3.15*.

And there you have it! We've finished creating the fire material. And just in case you got confused in this section, the following figure provides a full preview of all of the nodes:

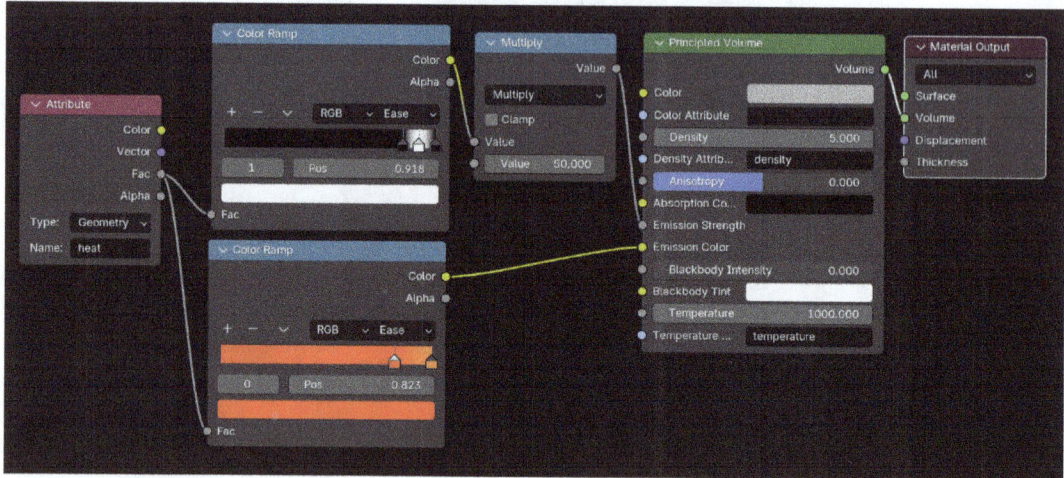

Figure 3.16 – Full material preview

In the next section, we'll learn how to add sparks to our flames using a particle system!

Creating sparks using a particle system

Now that the simulation is complete with a material, it's time to work on creating sparks that fly out of the fire. This is very easily done using a particle system. Using particle systems in Blender can be very useful and save a lot of time compared to adding the objects manually. The system works by emitting particles from a mesh object, normally in a great quantity. Things such as sparks, dust, hair, grass, and many more can easily be created using particles!

Now, let's create the sparks:

1. First, we need to add a new mesh object for the particles to emit from. For this scene, a circle would work great. Let's add one by pressing *Shift + A* and then going to **Mesh** and selecting **Circle**.

2. Once you've added the circle, look to the bottom left of the screen; you should see an **Add Circle** menu. Open it; this is where we set the properties for the circle. We need to make sure this mesh has a face and is small enough for the fire. Set **Fill Type** to **N-Gon** and **Radius** to 0.25. Then, place it underneath the fire:

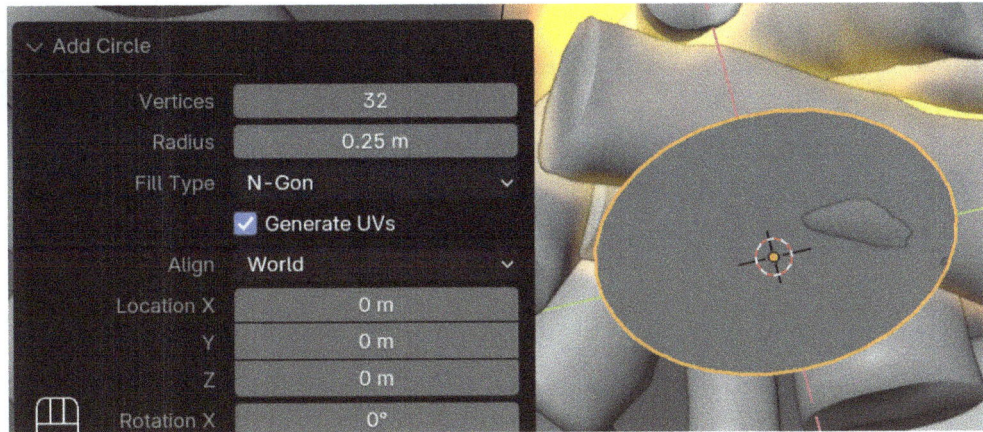

Figure 3.17 – Adding a circle

3.   Head over to the **Particle System** panel and create a new particle system by hitting the + button:

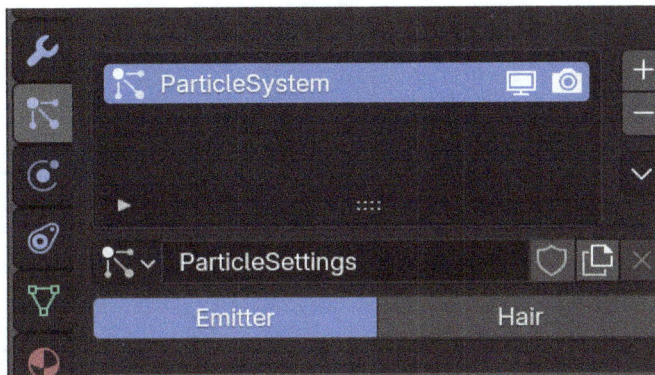

Figure 3.18 – Creating the particle system

4.   We don't need 1,000 sparks, so let's set **Number** to 50. Feel free to experiment with this value until you find something you like!

5.   Since the animation is only 100 frames long, set **End Frame** to 150 as well.

6.   If you play our animation, you'll notice that large white dots are appearing. These are called **halos**. These halos can be used in many ways, including emitting fire/smoke from each particle, something we'll learn about in *Chapter 5*. For this tutorial, we need to use an actual object instead. Let's add **Icosphere**, move it to the left of the campfire so it's out of the way, and scale it down to 0.5.

7.   Now select the Circle object again. To assign each particle as **Icosphere**, open the **Render** tab and set **Render As** to **Object**. Then, for **Instance Object**, select the **Icosphere** object we just added.

8. Play around with the **Scale** value until the particles are small enough. You can also increase **Random Scale** to give a random size to each particle.

9. We don't want this circle to show up in the render, so turn off **Show Emitter**:

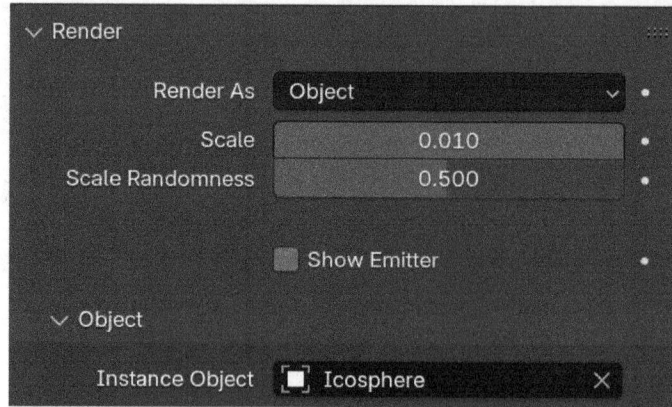

Figure 3.19 – Scaling the particles

10. Currently, the particles are falling, which isn't very good. Let's open **Field Weights** and set **Gravity** to 0:

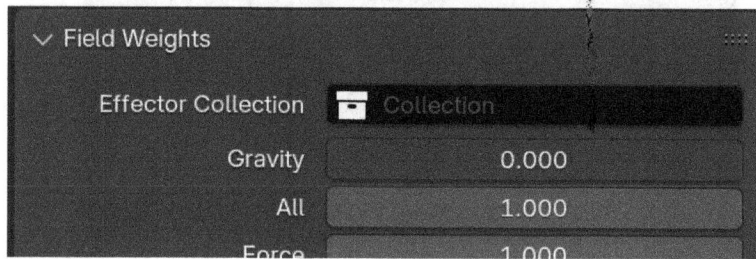

Figure 3.20 – Gravity

11. The next question is, how do we make the particles follow the flow of the fire? Well, there's a force field that does that exact thing! Let's add it by pressing *Shift + A* and then going to **Force Field** and selecting **Fluid Flow**.

With **Force Field** selected, we need to jump over to the **Physics** panel and set **Domain Object** as the domain in our scene, which in this case is the **Cube** object. Now, the particles will move with the flow of the fire! If you want the particles to move faster, you can increase the **Strength** value:

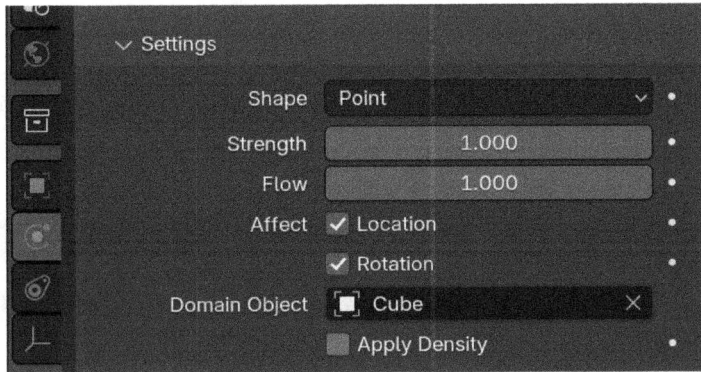

Figure 3.21 – Fluid Flow settings

With that, we've finished creating the particle system! Feel free to play around with the number of particles, the strength of the force field, and whatever else you like to get your desired look! Before we talk about rendering, we need to create a material for our sparks.

Creating the particle material

The next thing on the list is creating the particle material. In real life, right when sparks are emitted from a fire, they're very bright white. As they rise and cool off, they turn to more of an orange-red-ish color. We can create this same look by adding a couple of different nodes to the material:

1. Select **Icosphere** and open **Shader Editor** once again. Then, create a new material by clicking the **New** button.

2. Delete **Principled BSDF** and replace it with **Emission Shader**, then set **Strength** to a value of 20.

3. Plug the **Emission** output into **Surface** in **Material Output**.

4. Next, we're going to add a new node called **Particle Info**. To add this new node, press *Shift + A*, go to **Input**, and select **Particle Info**.

> **The Particle Info node**
>
> This node allows us to take certain data from the particle system and have it influence the material. For example, you could take the **Random** output and plug that into **Color Ramp** Now, each particle will have a random color based on **Color Ramp** One thing to note is that this node only works in the **Cycles** render engine.

5. We need to take the **Age** and **Lifetime** outputs from the **Particle Info** node and divide them together using a **Math** node. This will allow the color to change as the particle ages and rises into the air. To do this, press *Shift + A* and go to **Converter | Math**. Set the **Math** node to **Divide** and plug **Age** and **Lifetime** into the two inputs of the **Divide** node. Refer to *Figure 3.22* if you get confused.

6. Finally, just add **Color Ramp** and change the colors to a bright yellow and red color, then plug that into the **Emission Color** socket. The left-hand side of **Color Ramp** controls what color the particles are at the start. As the particle rises, it changes to the color shown on the right-hand side.

Play around with the handle positions to control when the particle will change colors. The following figure shows the full node setup:

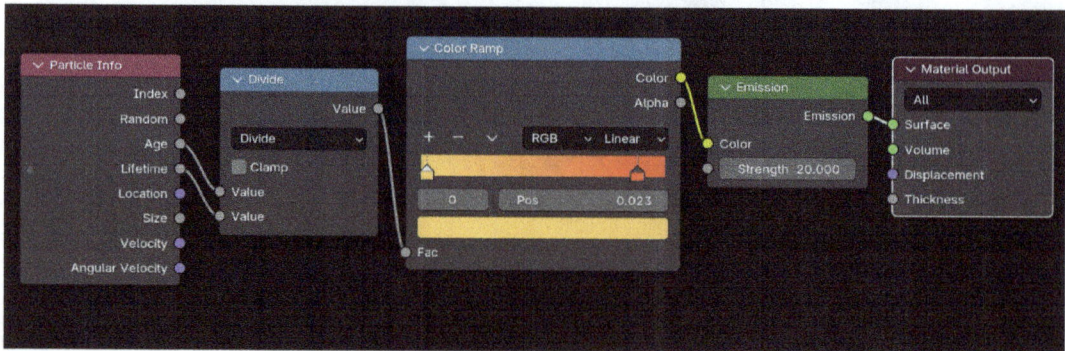

Figure 3.22 – Particle material

With that, we've nearly finished this tutorial. The last step is to place the camera and set up some render settings!

Adding the final details

Congratulations on making it to this part of the tutorial! Hopefully, you've learned some new tricks and techniques along the way.

In the last part of this tutorial, we'll be adding a ground plane and a lamp to help brighten the fire. We'll also enable motion blur. Let's get started:

1. Let's start by adding a **Plane** object; this will act as the ground floor. This way, the fire won't be floating in 3D space.

2. Next, let's jump to the **Render** panel and enable **Motion Blur**. This will give a much more realistic look to the sparks! The higher the **Shutter** value is, the more motion blur you'll have. A value of 0.2 works for most situations:

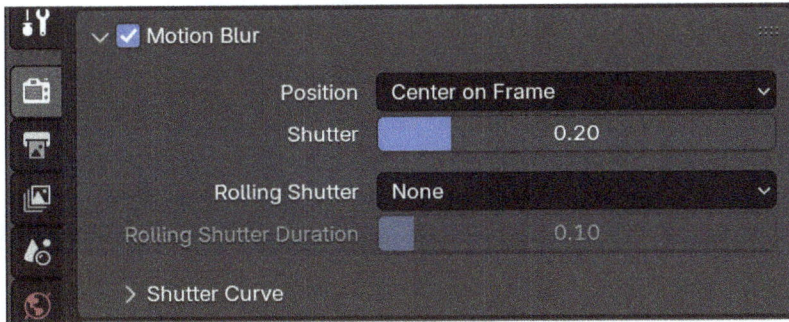

Figure 3.23 – Motion Blur

Remember that the **Velocity Scale** value in the **Render** tab in the domain settings also affects how much motion blur will appear on your fire. So, if you want to add more motion blur to the other objects in the scene but not the fire, you need to increase the **Shutter** value and decrease the **Velocity Scale** value. Before you render the animation, it's recommended that you do a couple of test renders to see what the motion blur will look like:

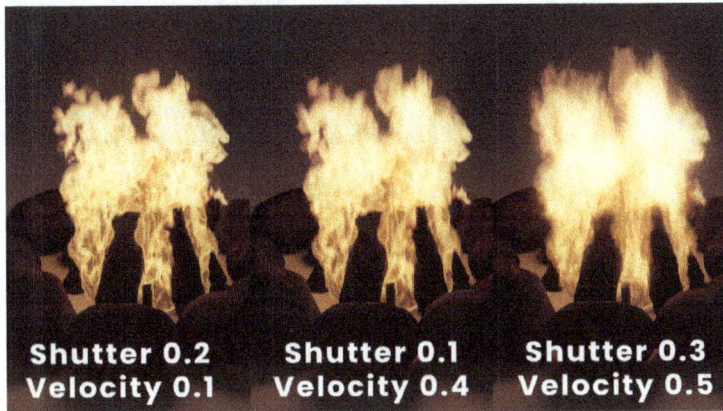

Figure 3.24 – Motion Blur examples

3. Next, open the **Render Sampling** tab and set **Max Sampling** to around 50. Make sure **Denoising** is checked as well; this will make your render look nice and clean without any noise!

4. To make the colors pop a bit more, open the **Color Management** tab and set **Look** to **High Contrast**.

5. Finally, change **End Frame** in the timeline so that it matches however long your simulation is. For this scene in particular, we chose 150.

That's all we need to do. We encourage you to add a bit more to the scene. Maybe scatter some leaves around the ground, set up a background, add a couple of sticks and logs around the fire, or even have a character sitting down – it's all up to you! If you want a bit of a glow around the fire, you could also add some **Glare** in **Compositor**.

Once you're happy with your scene, just set up the camera, choose an **Output** directory, and hit **Render Animation**! If you want a full breakdown of how to render animations properly in Blender, view the *Rendering animations* section at the end of *Chapter 4*.

The following figure shows a frame from our animation:

Figure 3.25 – Final scene frame

To view the final result or to download this scene's blend file, visit `https://github.com/PacktPublishing/Learn-Blender-4-Simulations-the-Right-Way/tree/main/Chapter%203`

Summary

That concludes this tutorial. We hope you learned a lot and made something cool along the way!

We covered quite a bit in this chapter, so let's do a recap. First, we learned how to create a fire simulation, add textures to flow objects to create variation in the fire, and apply those same settings to multiple objects at the same time. After that, we discussed how to add a lot of detail to the fire using the **Heat** attribute in **Shader Editor**. We also created a particle system and learned how to make the particles follow the flow of the fire using the **Fluid Flow** force field. Finally, we made a particle material so that it changes color as it rises into the air!

In the next chapter, we'll be moving away from smoke and fire. Instead, we're going to learn how to use the liquid simulation to create a nice waterfall in Blender 4.2!

Exercise

While it's great to follow a tutorial and learn how to do things, it's also important to try and create things yourself. Not only is it good practice, but it will help you remember everything we just learned! So, take a look at the following figure and try to think about how you would go about creating it:

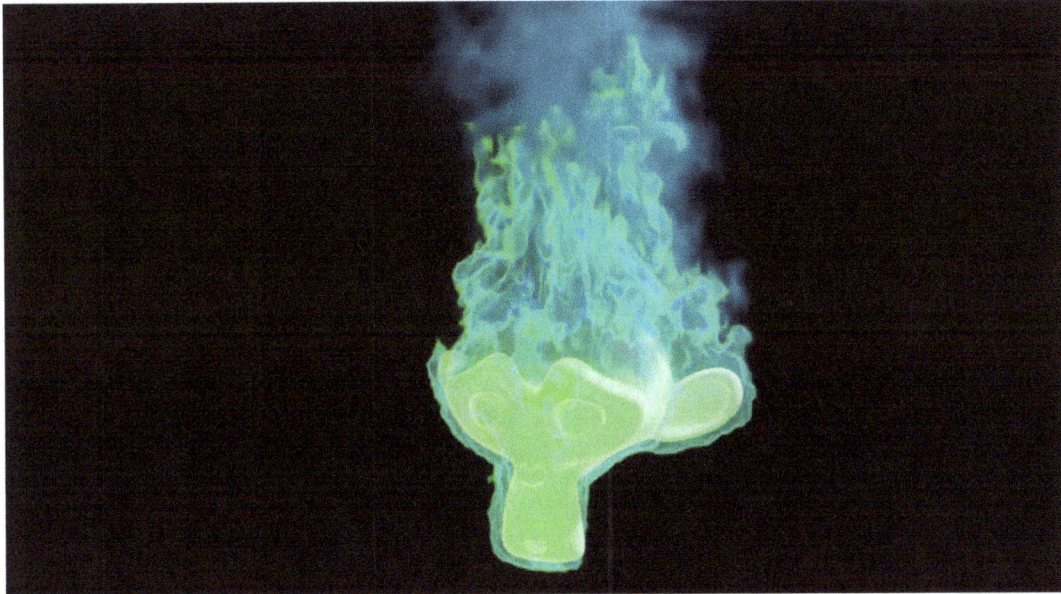

Figure 3.26 – Green fire example

4

Creating a Waterfall Using Mantaflow

If you have ever worked on creating a realistic liquid simulation, you will know how frustrating it can be – 95% of your time will be spent waiting for the simulation to finish baking. Then, when you finally get to rendering, you find out there is a problem with the simulation. You are back to square one and have to restart the whole process.

To help solve this problem of trial and error, we will learn about the entire process of creating a realistic waterfall in Blender using Mantaflow. You will also get an idea of which settings to use for your own simulations so that you don't have to spend hours (even days) testing out settings and figuring out what to do.

We will first start by adding a domain, creating **Flow** and **Effector** objects, and adding **Foam** particles. Then, we will create a realistic water material and learn how to add "fake" motion blur to fluid.

In this chapter, we'll be covering the following topics:

- Setting up the simulation
- Adding inflow and effectors
- Creating foam particles
- Creating materials
- Adding vector blur
- Rendering animations

Technical requirements

This chapter requires you to have Blender version 4.2 or above installed.

To download Blender, visit www.blender.org.

Also, make sure to download the `Waterfall Setup.blend` file to follow along with this chapter, at `https://github.com/PacktPublishing/Learn-Blender-4-Simulations-the-Right-Way/tree/main/Chapter%204`.

Setting up the simulation

Before we get started creating a simulation, make sure to download the `Waterfall Setup.blend` file. This file includes a basic waterfall model with a rock material, a sky texture, and some render settings already in place. If you want to create your own waterfall model, feel free to do that as well!

We will first start by adding a domain object and setting up all the fluid settings to get the best simulation result! Go ahead and open up the `Waterfall Setup.blend` file and let's get started. We'll follow these steps:

1. We have created a couple of simulations already in this book, and the process is similar. The first thing we need to add is a domain to fit the waterfall model. Press *Shift + A* and add a **Cube** object. Remember to make the domain just big enough to fit the waterfall model. The following screenshot shows the side view of the domain object:

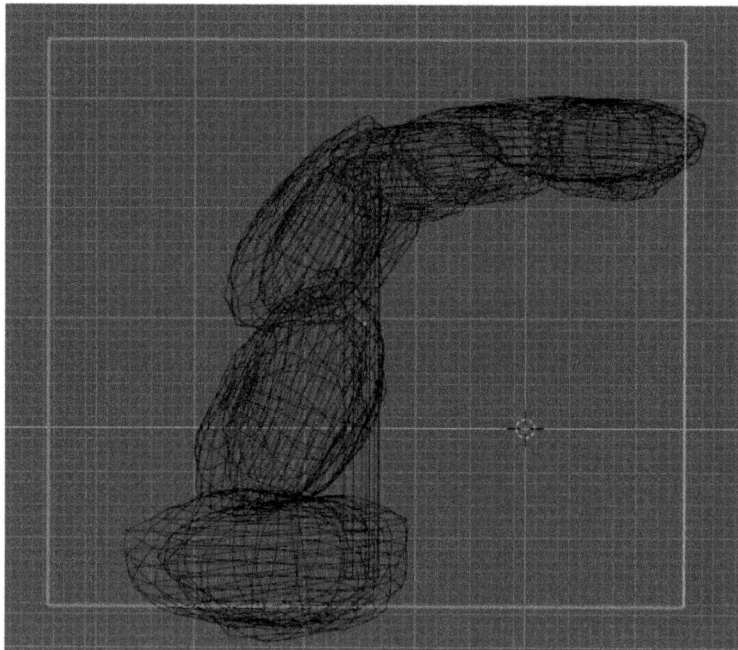

Figure 4.1 – Side view of domain

2. If we press *N* to open the **Properties** panel, you will notice the **Scale** values are proportionate to how much we scaled the cube initially to match the size of the waterfall.

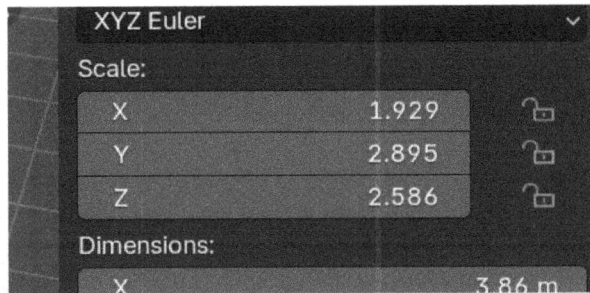

Figure 4.2 – Property scale

With the current values of **Scale**, this might cause problems with the simulation, so let's apply the **Scale** setting so that all the numbers go back to a value of 1. To do this, select the domain object, go up to **Object | Apply**, and select **Scale**, or press the *Ctrl + A* or *Cmd + A* shortcut and select **Scale**.

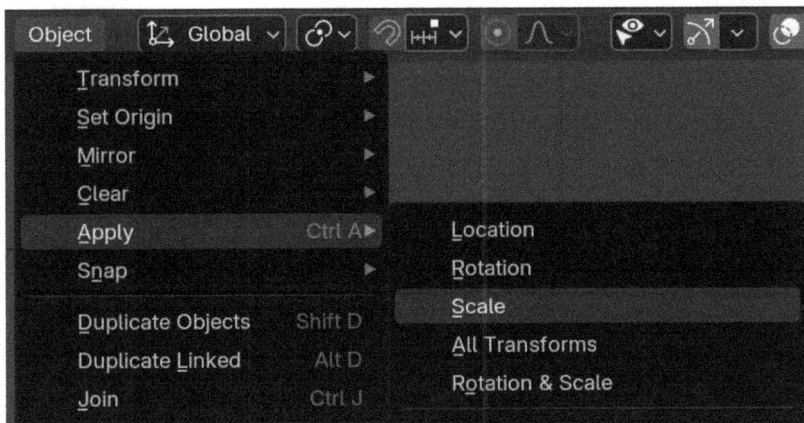

Figure 4.3 – Applying Scale

Why do we apply the Scale setting?

It's usually a good idea to apply the **Scale** setting after adding an object and changing its size. When this setting is not applied, modifiers, UV maps, and other operations can be a bit funky and will not work as intended because Blender stretches those operations based on the **Scale** values. Applying **Scale** sets all values back to the default value of 1, which means operations will be scaled in the right proportions.

3. Now, let's create a simulation! With the cube object selected, head over to the **Physics** panel and select **Fluid**. For the **Type** setting, choose **Domain**, and of course, set the **Domain Type** setting to **Liquid**.

4. Liquid simulations tend to take a long time to bake and can be computationally intensive. If you have a slow computer, I recommend only setting **Resolution Divisions** to 96 or 128. This will still give you a nice simulation. If your computer can handle it though, you can set **Resolution Divisions** to 160.

5. Let's change **Time Scale** to 0.6. Normally, fluid simulations tend to look very fast, so setting this value lower will slow down the simulation, making it look a bit more realistic.

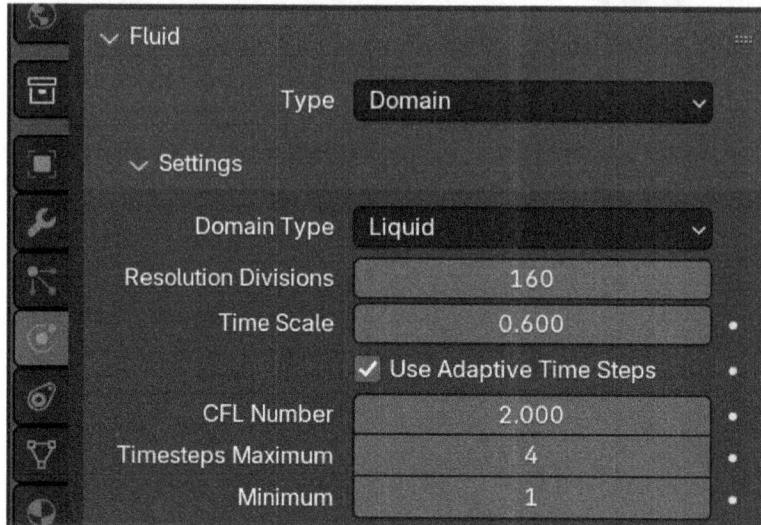

Figure 4.4 – Domain settings

6. Next up is the **Border Collisions** settings. Currently, all sides of the domain have collisions. This means fluid builds up and eventually fills the entire domain. Instead, we want the fluid to disappear when it reaches the bottom. Let's uncheck **Bottom** and **Front**, as illustrated in the following screenshot, so that fluid does *not* hit these edges but rather just disappears as if nothing is there:

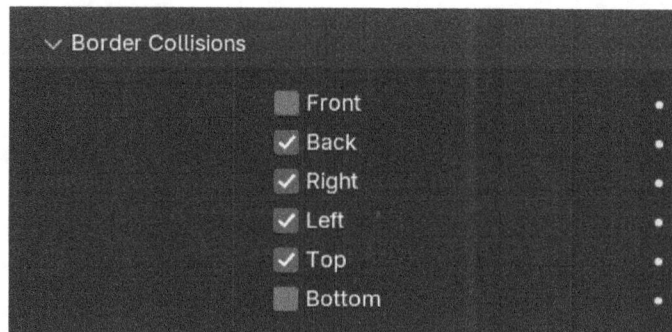

Figure 4.5 – Border Collisions

7. In **Liquid Settings**, set **Narrow Band Width** to 8. This will increase the number of particles in the simulation, giving us a better result. Also, enable **Fractional Obstacles**. This will make sure fluid doesn't stick to any **Effector** objects.

8. Now, let's add foam particles! Scroll down till you see the **Particles** panel and check **Foam**. We don't need **Spray** or **Bubbles** particles; I found that only using **Foam** works best for this simulation.

9. Set both **Potential Radius** and **Particle Update Radius** to 3. This will help smooth out the particle grids, giving us a better result. Sometimes, particles will flicker around, and setting this value higher will help prevent that.

10. Next, let's set **Wave Crest Particle Sampling** to 300. This will give us more particles in the crest of the wave. The following screenshot gives an overview of the settings:

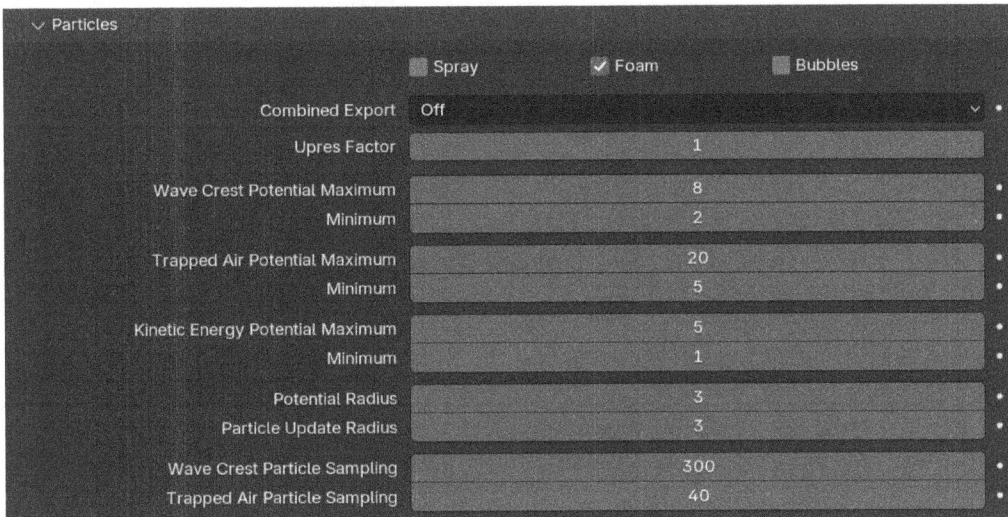

∨ Particles			
	▢ Spray	☑ Foam	▢ Bubbles
Combined Export	Off		∨ •
Upres Factor	1		
Wave Crest Potential Maximum	8		•
Minimum	2		•
Trapped Air Potential Maximum	20		•
Minimum	5		•
Kinetic Energy Potential Maximum	5		•
Minimum	1		•
Potential Radius	3		•
Particle Update Radius	3		•
Wave Crest Particle Sampling	300		•
Trapped Air Particle Sampling	40		•

Figure 4.6 – Foam particles

The remaining settings and values can remain at their default states.

11. Now, open up the **Mesh** panel and make sure **Upres Factor** has a value of 2. This will work nicely in this simulation, but if you find the mesh looks a bit **low polygon** (**low poly**), you can increase this value.

12. With the **Mesh** panel checked, a small mesh around each **Liquid** particle will be created. With a **Particle Radius** value of 2, the mesh will look a bit blobby and not very realistic. Let's bring this value down to 1.2. Now, the radius around each particle will be much smaller, and this will produce a much better result. View the following screenshot for an example. The left side has a **Particle Radius** value of 3 and the right has a value of 1:

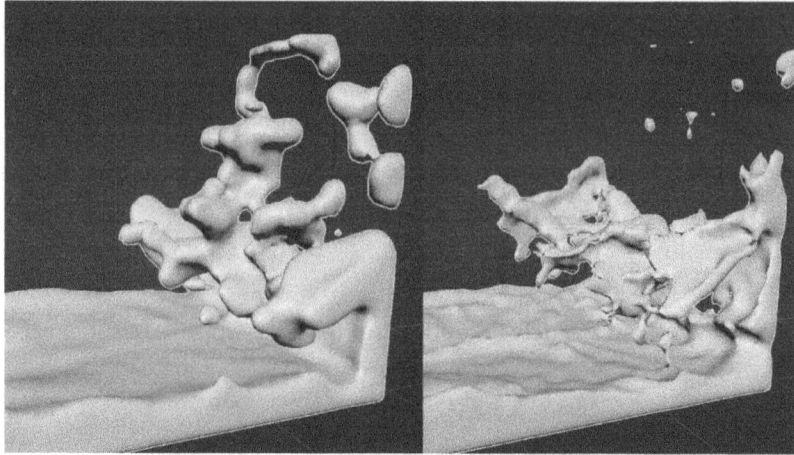

Figure 4.7 – Particle Radius example

13. Finally, check **Use Speed Vectors**. This will allow us to add motion blur later in this chapter! You can see this option checked here:

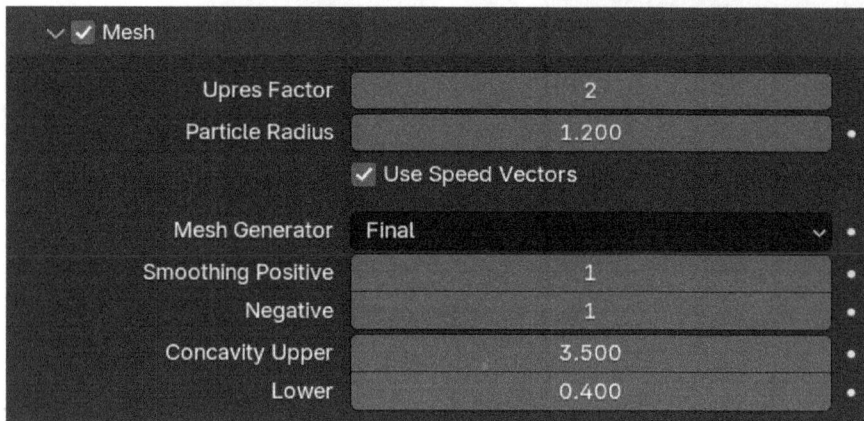

Figure 4.8 – Mesh settings

14. The last thing we need to do is open the **Cache** panel. Set **Type** to **Modular** and check **Is Resumable**, just in case we need to stop the bake. A very important step is to change **Format Volumes** from **OpenVDB** to **Uni Cache**. **Use Speed Vectors** only works with the **Uni Cache** format.

15. If you would like to increase or decrease the length of the simulation, you can change the **End** frame. For this simulation, we'll go with 200 frames. The settings are shown in the following screenshot:

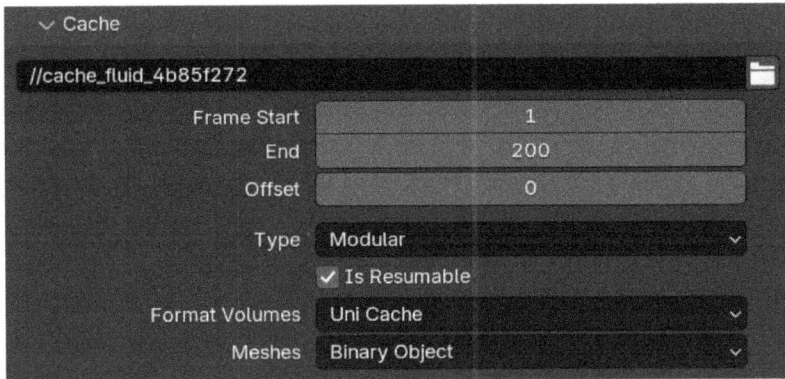

Figure 4.9 – Cache settings

And there we go! We have created a domain with all the settings we need. Next up, we will add **Inflow** and **Effector** objects and bake out the simulation!

Adding inflow and effectors

The domain is now completely set up and ready to go! We now need to add an **Inflow** object to emit fluid into the simulation. We also need to set up all the rocks and ground objects to have collision effectors, or the fluid will just fall right through them.

Let's start with the **Inflow** object:

1. First, add a **Plane** object and place it on top of the waterfall.
2. Rotate it 90° along the **X** axis and scale it to match the width and height that you need. You can see an example here:

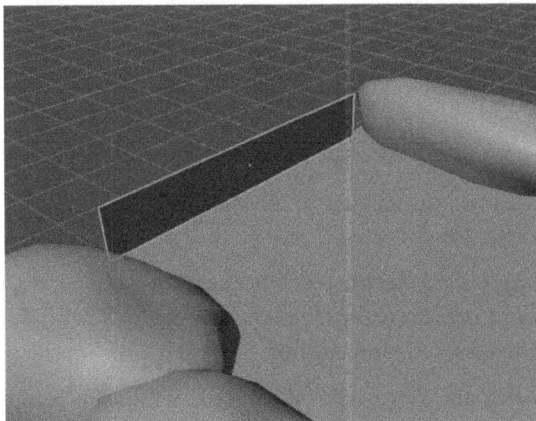

Figure 4.10 – Inflow scale

Changing the shape and size of the flow object will change how the fluid looks. You could have two smaller flows that collide with each other or move the flow up so that fluid drops down and creates a splash. Feel free to get creative here and get different looks for the river!

3. Since we have now rotated and scaled the plane, let's apply both the **Rotation** and **Scale** settings to make sure the simulation works correctly. Press *Ctrl + A* or *Cmd + A* and select **Rotation & Scale**.

4. Now, let's set this object to be an inflow. Head over to the **Physics** panel and select **Fluid**. For **Flow Type**, choose **Liquid**, and for **Behavior**, choose **Inflow**.

5. Next, open the **Flow Source** object. Since this object is a plane, we need to make sure **Is Planar** is enabled. This tells Blender to treat this inflow as an unclosed mesh, meaning it will emit fluid even though it doesn't have any thickness.

6. Now, enable **Initial Velocity**. To give more velocity and fluid to the simulation, let's set **Source** to 1.5. We also want the fluid to move in the direction of the waterfall. In this case, it's the **-Y** direction, so let's set the **Initial** value for the **Y** axis to -6. The higher you go with this value, the faster the fluid will move.

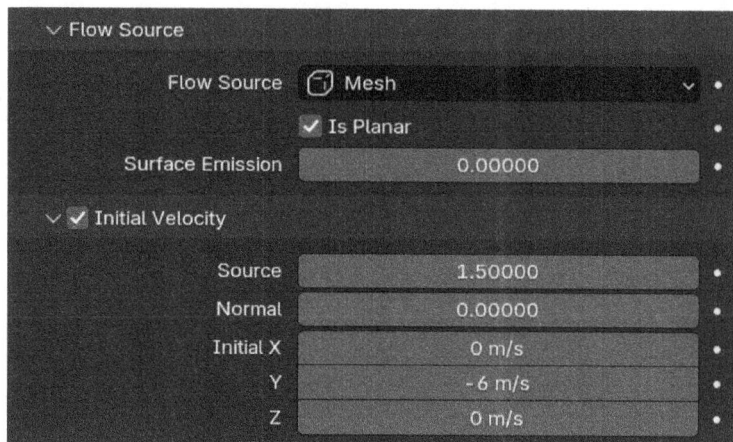

Figure 4.11 – Inflow settings

With that done, let's add collisions for the rocks and the middle part of the waterfall.

7. Select both the rocks and the middle part of the waterfall. Click on **Fluid** in the **Physics** panel and for **Type**, choose **Effector**.

8. Doing this will only apply the **Effector** value to the **active object**. So, press *Ctrl + L* or *Cmd + L* or go up to **Object | Link/Transfer Data** and select **Copy Modifiers**. Now, each of those objects will have the **Effector** collision applied.

9. Finally, select the middle part of the waterfall. Since this object is technically a plane, we need to make sure **Is Planar** is enabled in the **Effector** settings. You can see an overview of the settings here:

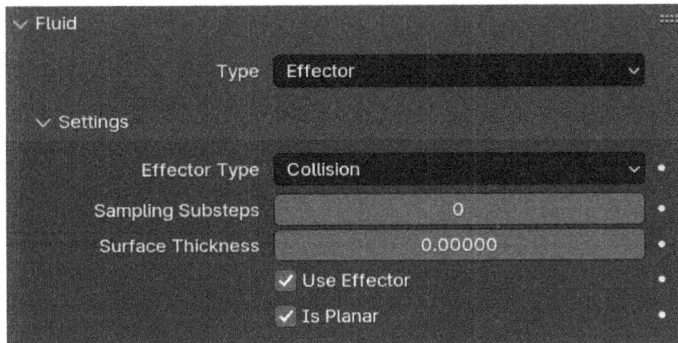

Figure 4.12 – Effector settings

With that done, we are now ready to bake in the simulation! Head back over to the **Domain** settings and click on **Bake Data** at the top. Remember—if you want to save the cache from being deleted, make sure to set a custom directory in the **Cache** panel.

Once the initial bake has finished, you will need to scroll down to the **Particles** panel and **Mesh** panel and bake both of those as well. After all three bakes are done, make sure to play the animation a little bit and double-check that everything looks good. If it does, continue by baking in the particles and the mesh. When everything is done baking, we will create foam particles! Also, don't forget to save the Blender file by pressing *Ctrl + S* or by going up to **File | Save**!

Adding foam particles

Now that the simulation is done baking, we can set up the foam particles. Foam particles add another level of detail to the simulation. These particles will be added near the top of the fluid, acting like foam or whitewater. Just like in real life, foam or whitewater is created in the midst of rapids or turbulence in the fluid and that is what we will be replicating.

At the moment, the particles are just halos, which means they are just points in **three-dimensional (3D)** space and won't show up in the render. You can see an example of this here:

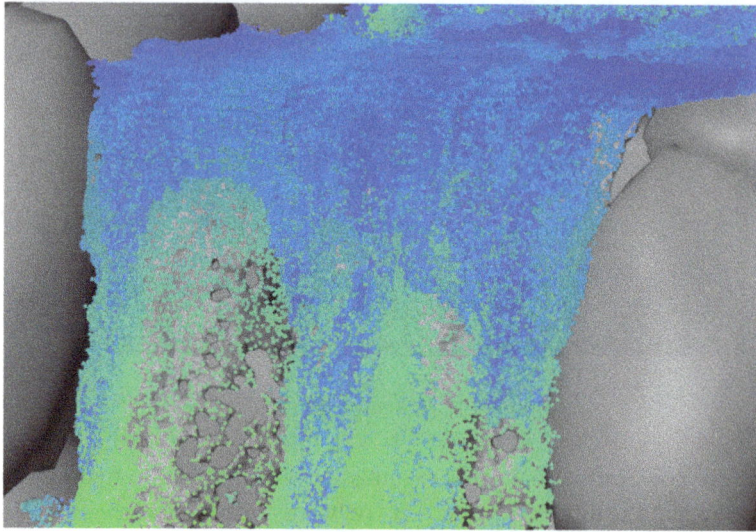

Figure 4.13 – Halo example

However, we need an actual object to be the particles. We also want to make sure whichever object we choose has as little geometry as possible, or it will slow down Blender a lot. A UV sphere has a lot of geometry on it, so that will not work. Instead, let's use a cone with a very low subdivision. Here's how we can achieve that:

1. First, select your domain object, right-click, and select **Shade Smooth**. This will shade the surface of the mesh in a smooth way so that we don't see individual faces.

2. Add a **Cone** object, then open the **Add Cone** menu at the bottom left and set **Vertices** to 3, as illustrated in the following screenshot. This will give us a very low-poly mesh:

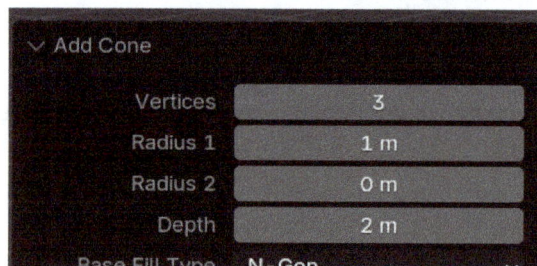

Figure 4.14 – Adding a cone

3. The cone is currently way too big, so let's use **Scale** to scale it down to a value of 0.02.

4. Now, we are ready to assign that **Cone** object to be the particles. Select your domain and head over to the **Particle System** panel. You should see two systems: **Liquid** and **Foam**, as illustrated in the following screenshot. Before assigning the particle, I recommend turning off

the visibility in the viewport by clicking on both monitor icons. Now, your viewport should be nice and smooth:

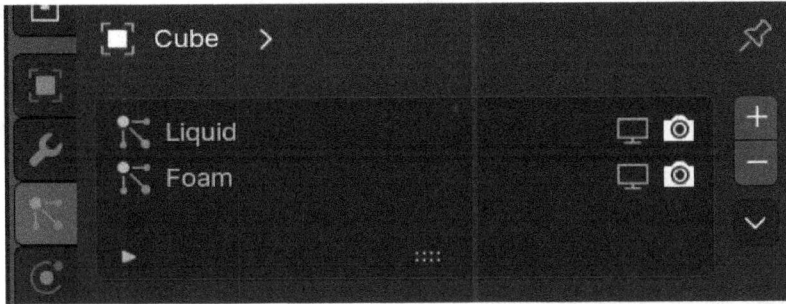

Figure 4.15 – Particle systems

5. Next, select the **Foam** particle system, and underneath **Render As**, choose **Object**. For **Instance Object**, select **Cone** in the dropdown menu! Now, each particle will be that cone that we added a couple of steps back! Remember—you won't be able to see it because we turned off the visibility of the particle system; it will still show up in the render, though.

6. Next, let's scale up the particles just a little bit so they show up in the render a bit more. To do this, set the **Scale** value to 0.075.

    Optional: If you would like some random variation in the size, you can increase **Scale Randomness**. We suggest not setting **Scale Randomness** to anything above 0.5 or some of the particles will be too small to see.

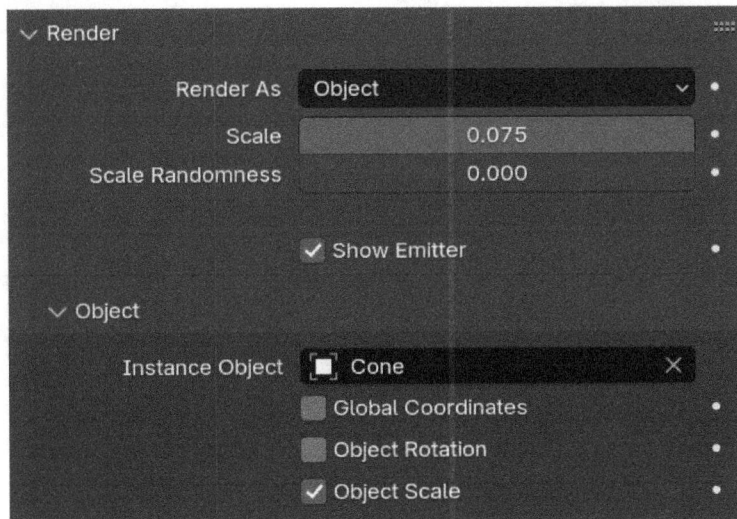

Figure 4.16 – Render tab

If you want to check the size of the particles and make sure they are small enough, you can do that by turning the monitor icon back on. This might lag the scene quite a bit, so make sure to open the **Viewport Display** panel and set the **Amount** value to 1%. Now you should be able to see some of the particles without the scene slowing down a lot.

When you are done, turn off the visibility (monitor icon) and set **Amount** back to 100% or you will only get 1% in the render as well. The settings are shown in the following screenshot:

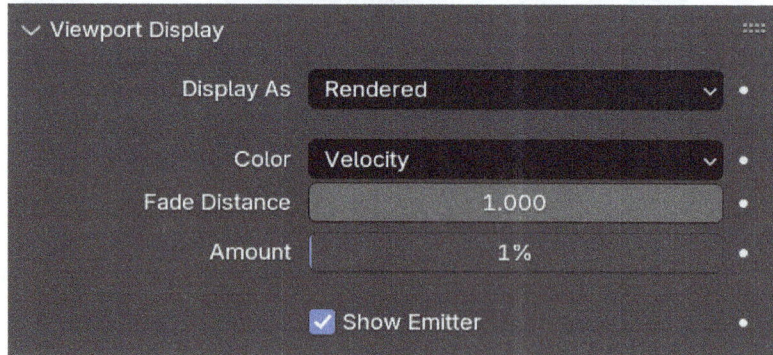

Figure 4.17 – Viewport Display

And there we go—we have now added foam particles to the simulation. Here is what the particles should look like when they are all visible. Since there are thousands of particles, this will really slow down your blend file, so we suggest keeping them invisible (as per *step 4*):

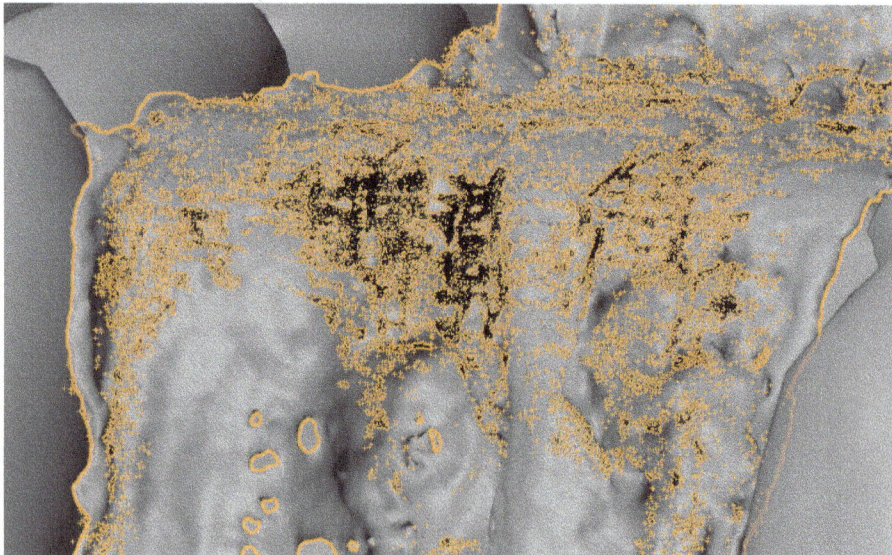

Figure 4.18 – Foam particles

The next step in this chapter is to set up the materials for both the particle and the fluid itself.

Creating materials

We have covered a lot in this chapter so far. We've learned how to create realistic settings for the domain, added flow objects, and created foam particles! Before we create materials, we need to decide which render engine to use. For this scene, I recommend sticking with Cycles, and the reason for this is EEVEE is limiting when it comes to transparent materials and particles and when there is a lot of geometry in the scene.

For most scenes, EEVEE will render much faster than Cycles because it's a real-time engine. For this scene, though, I found that Cycles renders about 80% faster than EEVEE. This is because there are so many particles, and EEVEE has a hard time computing all of them. If you were to turn off the particles, then EEVEE would be faster. Since we are rendering the particles, I recommend switching to Cycles for rendering. Plus, Cycles will give you much better reflections and shadows.

With that out of the way, let's jump into creating materials:

1. Let's create the water material first. Select your domain, jump over to the **Material** panel, and create a new one by clicking the big **New** button.

2. We don't need the **Principled BSDF** shader, so select it and change it to a **Glass BSDF** shader.

3. For the **Color** setting of the glass, choose a very slightly blue color. Don't go overboard with the **Color** setting or it might look a bit strange. If you want to use the same color I am using, the **hexadecimal (hex)** code is F8FFFF.

4. The **Roughness** setting controls how rough the glass will appear. We want to set this to 0 so that the glass looks nice and smooth.

5. **IOR** (which stands for **Index of Refraction**) basically controls how light will pass through the glass. The IOR of water is 1.333, so let's set that for this value. The settings are shown in the following screenshot:

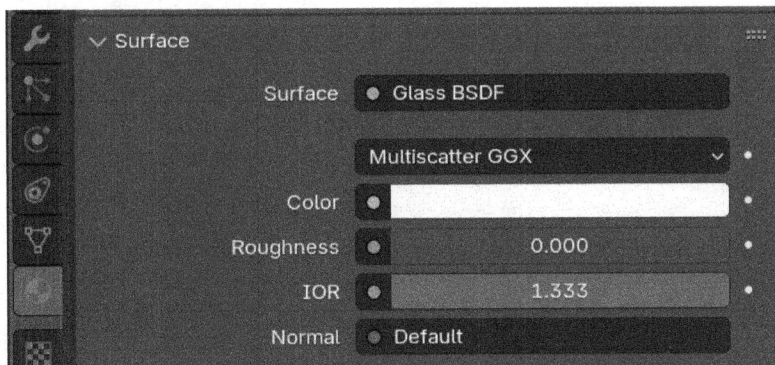

Figure 4.19 – Glass material

> **IOR**
>
> IOR indicates how fast light will pass through an object. The higher this value, the slower light will pass through. For example, air has an IOR value of 1.000277 and ice has an IOR value of 1.31. Light will pass through ice much slower than it passes through air, thus causing the light to bend more and giving it that distorted look. You can find a big list of IOR values for different real-world materials here: `https://pixelandpoly.com/ior.html`.

6. Finally, let's give the water a bit of volume. Rivers are not completely clean—they have dirt, rocks, and other stuff that gets picked up. To do this, go to the **Volume** tab, click on **None**, and choose **Principled Volume**.

7. Set **Color** to a blueish color and set **Density** to 0.5, as illustrated in the following screenshot:

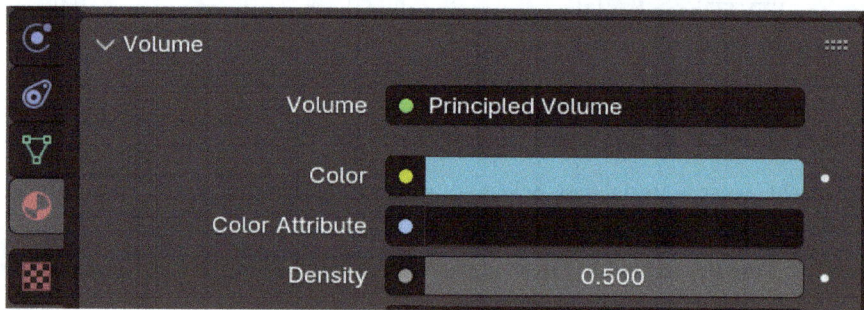

Figure 4.20 – Volume shader

The water material is now done! Let's quickly create the foam material; then we can move on to adding motion blur to the fluid.

8. Select the **Cone** object in **Outliner** and give it a **New** material.

9. Set the **Roughness** value in **Principled Volume** shader to 0.1. This will give us a nice reflective material. Technically, this isn't completely accurate. Foam is supposed to have a more transparent look. If we add that in though, it will slow down the render quite a bit. So, let's just leave it as it is, and it will still look really good!

And there we go! All the materials are now done and we are ready to start the rendering process. In the next section of this chapter, we will learn how to add motion blur to our fluid with a very simple trick in the **Compositor**!

Adding vector blur

Motion blur really adds a nice touch to your render. It can make your animation stand out from the rest and look much more realistic. It gives the fluid a sense of motion, which can make the simulation look much better! All cameras have a bit of blur when an object is moving very fast, and if it's not added, the animation can look a bit strange. Now, we could go over to the **Render** panel and check the **Motion Blur** box, but that's not what we are going to be doing. Instead, we will be adding **vector blur**!

Here, you can see an example of an animation with and without blur:

Figure 4.21 – With and without blur examples

Vector blur is a fast way to simulate motion in the render using the **Compositor**! It uses vector data from **Render Passes** to blur the image in 2D, giving a look of motion. So, technically, it's a *fake* blur, but it still looks great and can render much faster than a real motion blur.

To add vector blur to the render, we first need to tell Blender to give us that speed vector information from the fluid. Remember earlier when we checked **Use Speed Vectors** in the domain? That is the vector information we will be using to blur the fluid. Let's get straight into it:

1. Head over to the **Render Layers** panel and enable both the **Vector** and the **Z** passes, as illustrated in the following screenshot. These are the passes we need to add blur:

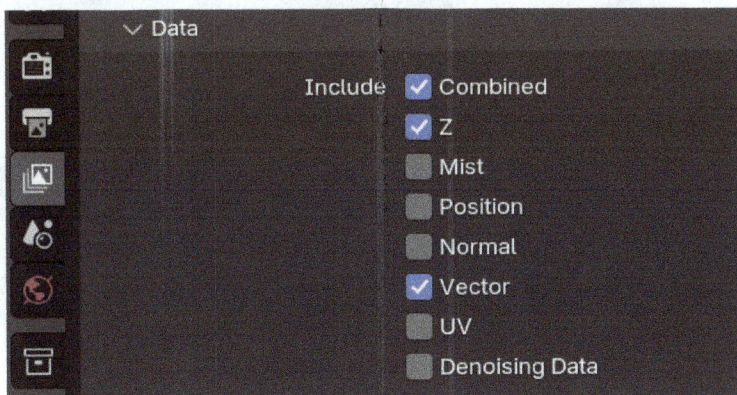

Figure 4.22 – Vector passes

2.   Next, let's render an image. The render settings should already be in place if you are using the `Waterfall Setup.Blend` file. Feel free to change the render, background, or lighting to your liking, then choose a frame in the **Timeline** that looks good. Once you have a good frame, head up to the **Render** setting and select **Render Image** or press the *F12* shortcut.

When the render has finished, jump over to the **Compositing** workspace at the top of the screen, as illustrated in the following screenshot:

Figure 4.23 – Compositing

3.   Select **Use Nodes**. You should see **Render Layers** and **Composite** nodes appear, as illustrated in the following screenshot (if not, then just add them in):

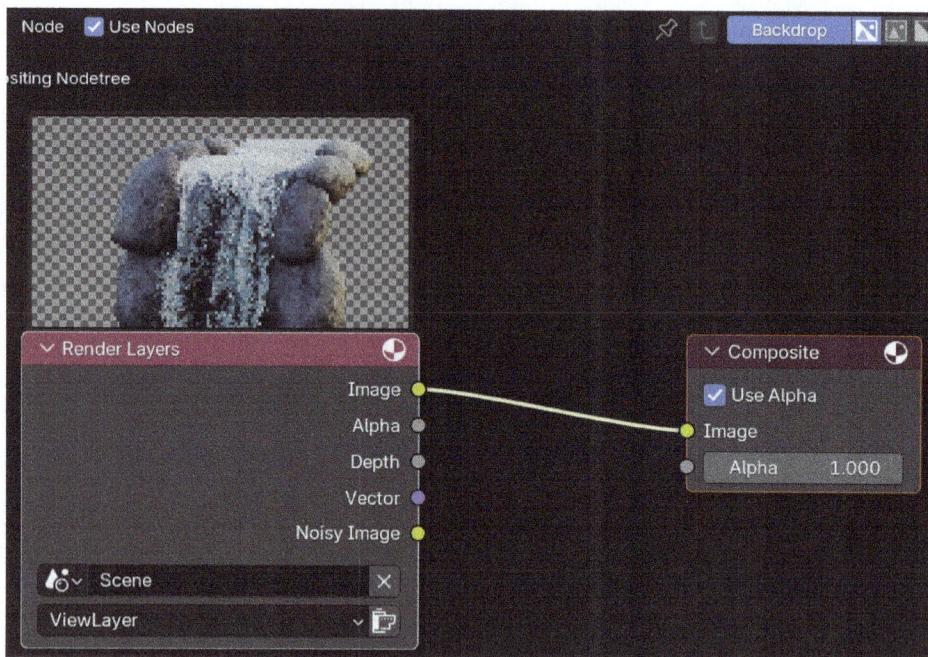

Figure 4.24 – Use Nodes and Render Layers

4.   To see what we are doing, add a **Viewer** node by pressing *Shift + A* under **Output | Viewer**. Then take **Image** from the **Render Layers** node and plug it into the **Image** socket in the **Viewer** node.

Another way to do this automatically is to hold *Shift + Ctrl* or *Shift + Cmd* and left-click on the **Render Layers** node. This will automatically add a **Viewer** node and allow us to see the render. To zoom the image out, press *V* and *Alt/Option + V* to zoom back in.

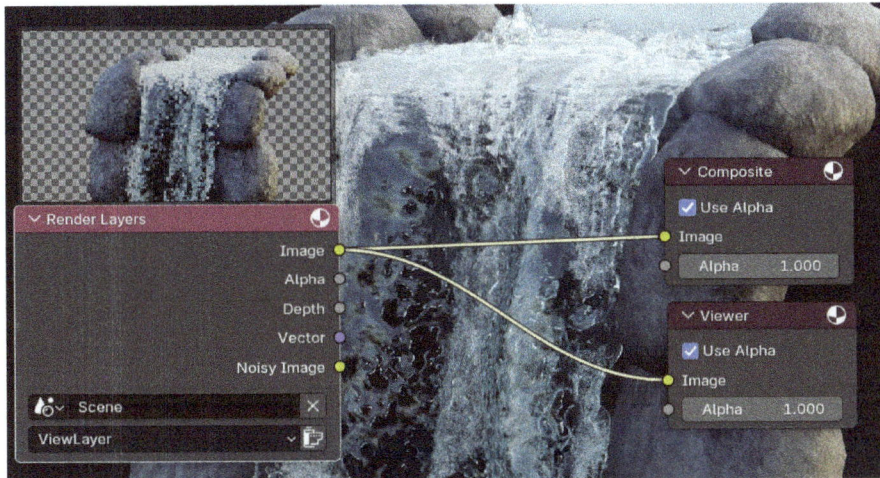

Figure 4.25 – Viewer node

5. Currently, the background is transparent, so let's add an **Alpha Over** node to fix that. Press *Shift + A* and go to **Color**, and then choose **Alpha Over**. This node allows you to add transparent images on top of other images.

    Place it in between the **Render Layers** and the **Composite** nodes and make sure the **Render Layers** node is plugged into the bottom **Image** socket. View the following screenshot:

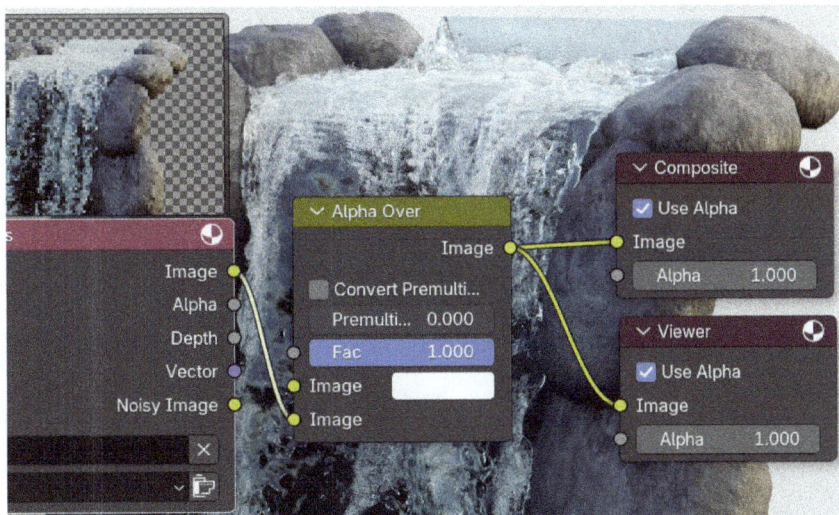

Figure 4.26 – Alpha Over example

6. The top **Image** color socket in the **Alpha Over** node now controls the color of the background. Let's set it to a nice dark gray color!

    Now, the moment you have been waiting for… let's add in vector blur!

7. Press *Shift + A*, go to **Filter | Blur**, and select **Vector Blur**. Place it in between the **Render Layers** and the **Alpha Over** nodes.

8. Take the **Vector** output from the **Render Layers** node and plug it into the **Speed** input. This will give us the information to add motion blur! Sometimes when using vector blur, you will get some bleed in areas of the image. This is because we don't have **Depth** information yet. So, take the **Depth** socket and plug it into the **Z** input. Now, it should look much better. View the following screenshot:

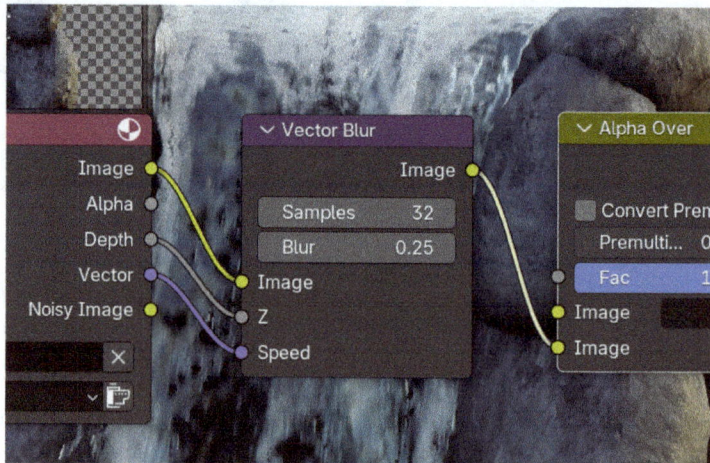

Figure 4.27 – Vector Blur

9. The **Samples** setting relates to the quality of the blur. Higher values will give better quality blur at the cost of render time. A value of 32 will be perfect for this scene.

10. **Blur** controls how much blur is there in the scene. A value of 0.25 might be a bit much, so let's bring it down to 0.15.

11. One final thing before we render—make sure to turn off the visibility of the inflow object, or you will get a white plane in the render that won't look very good. You can do this by toggling the **Eye** icon and **Camera** icon in the **Outliner**.

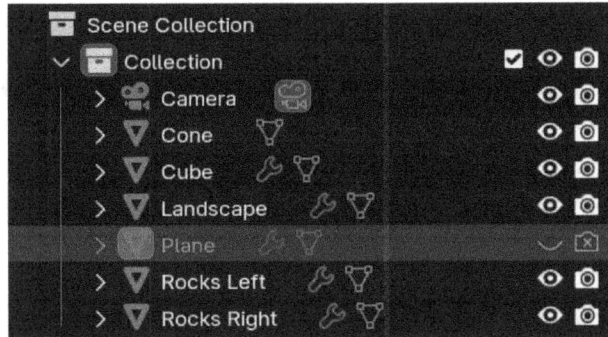

Figure 4.28 – Inflow visibility

Before this tutorial ends, let's go through the proper way to render animations in Blender!

Rendering animations

Everything is now set up, and we are now ready to render the waterfall animation! Whenever you render any type of animation in Blender, you should always export it as an image sequence and not a movie file.

The reason for this is that if you are rendering the animation into an MP4 file and for some reason Blender crashes or something happens, the file could get corrupted, and you would have to re-render the entire thing. Rendering as an image sequence allows you to stop the render at any point without having to worry about restarting or something getting corrupted.

Once the animation has finished rendering, you can then import all those images and turn them into a movie file. Let's get started:

1. In the **Timeline** set the **End** frame to match how long the simulation is. In this case, it's 200 frames.

2. Head over to the **Output** panel and choose a folder where you want the image sequence to render. View the following screenshot:

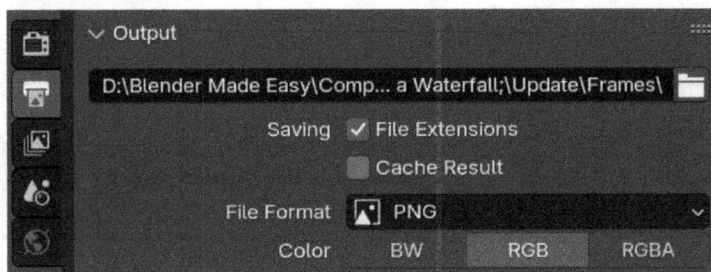

Figure 4.29 – Output

3. Once a folder has been set, head up to **Render** and select **Render Animation** or press the *Ctrl + F12* or *Cmd + F12* shortcut! Now, all we have to do is wait for it to finish! If for some reason you decide to stop the render, make sure you uncheck **Overwrite** in the **Output** panel when you resume it. This way, it doesn't restart, but the render resumes at the frame it left off.

4. When all the images have been rendered out, let's jump back into Blender. At the top of the screen, you should see a + sign next to the workspaces. Click on that and then select **Video Editing | Video Editing**, as illustrated in the following screenshot. This will open the **Video Sequence Editor** workspace:

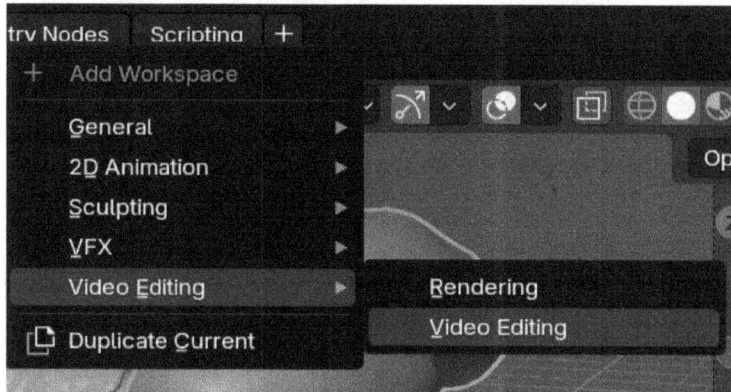

Figure 4.30 – Workspaces

5. Now, we need to import all the images we have rendered. Make sure the blue cursor is on **Frame 1**, press *Shift + A*, and choose **Image/Sequence**. Navigate to where your images are saved, press *A* to select everything, and import them.

6. If for some reason the animation is playing backward, that probably means animations were sorted by **Date** rather than **Name** when they were imported. An easy fix for this is to go to the **Properties** panel on the right side. You can press *N* to open this panel if it isn't already open and, under the **Strip** tab, select **Reverse Frames** in the **Video** tab, as shown in the following screenshot:

Figure 4.31 – Reverse Frames

7. Finally, the last step is to make sure the **End Frame** value in the **Timeline** matches the length of the animation, and then head over to the **Output** panel once again. If you want to render it as an MP4 file, choose **FFmpeg Video**, and for the **Container** type, select **MPEG - 4**. The settings are shown here:

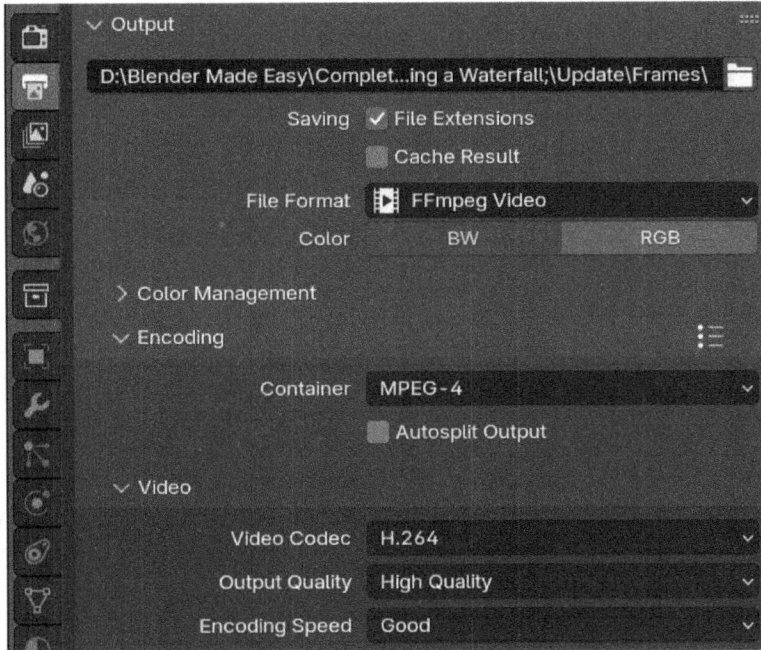

Figure 4.32 – Output file format

Then, just render the animation once again, and this time, it will take those images and turn them into an MP4! The file should be in the same directory as all your rendered images! The following screenshot is a frame from my animation! (If you want to download my project file for this chapter, just visit this link: https://github.com/PacktPublishing/Learn-Blender-4-Simulations-the-Right-Way/tree/main/Chapter%204)

Figure 4.33 – Rendered waterfall

Congrats on making it all the way to the end of this tutorial! I hope you learned something new and made something really cool in the process! This scene also doesn't need to end here—feel free to add more to this waterfall, maybe adding a second layer, creating an environment, and adding trees! You could also add another waterfall that splashes into this one! It's all up to you! If you don't want to create your own trees or assets, there are many websites where you can get models for free. *CGTrader* (`https://www.cgtrader.com/`) and *Poly Haven* (`https://polyhaven.com/`) are two great websites for models and other resources! Here is some inspiration for something you could create:

Figure 4.34 – Real-life waterfall

That brings us to the end of this chapter!

Summary

And there we go! We have completed this chapter and created a nice, realistic waterfall simulation. We have covered a lot, so let's do a quick recap.

First, we learned about the domain settings for creating realistic fluid, added an inflow object, and set obstacles for the fluid to collide with. We then learned how foam particles work and how to add them to the simulation. We covered realistic water materials in Blender and how to add motion blur in the **Compositor**! Finally, we learned how to properly render out animations in Blender and sequence them together in the **Compositor**. For the rest of the tutorials in this book, I won't be covering how to render animations, so just remember to reference this chapter for a quick recap!

Fluid simulations are quite complicated and can take a long time to create, but hopefully, this chapter gave you an understanding so that you can go out and create your own realistic simulations! I hope you like explosions because, in the next chapter, we will be blowing up some stuff in Blender using the particle system and gas simulations!

Join our community on Discord

Join our community's Discord space for discussions with the author and other readers:
`https://packt.link/learn-blender-simulations-discord-invite`

5

Creating a Realistic Explosion

To get an explosion to look right, there are a lot of factors to think about. First, you need to decide what kind of explosion you are creating. There are three main types: chemical, mechanical, and nuclear. A **mechanical explosion** occurs when gas rapidly expands and causes pressure that is stronger than its current container. A **nuclear explosion** happens when there is a fusion or fission reaction; this explosion creates the iconic mushroom cloud look. Finally, there's a **chemical explosion**, which is the one we will be creating in this chapter. These kinds of explosions happen when there is a decomposition or combination of certain gases.

Figure 5.1 – Explosion examples

Whatever kind of explosion you are trying to make, I recommend looking at reference images of such explosions before you even open Blender. This will help you to know what objects, particle systems, simulation settings, and materials to add to your explosion to achieve the look you're going for.

The goal of this chapter is to help give a baseline for you to understand how to simulate an explosion in Blender and how to customize it to get the look you want. We will also provide some troubleshooting tips along the way!

In this chapter, we'll be covering the following topics:

- Creating the particle system
- Creating the simulation

- Creating the material
- Rendering in Cycles and EEVEE

Technical requirements

This chapter requires you to have Blender version 4.2 or above installed.

To download Blender, visit www.blender.org.

To view the final result or to download this project's .blend file, please visit https://github.com/PacktPublishing/Learn-Blender-4-Simulations-the-Right-Way/tree/main/Chapter%205.

Creating the particle system

There are a couple of methods to simulate an explosion. The simpler approach would be to rapidly scale up a flow object, causing the fire or smoke to expand quickly. While this can produce decent results, it often looks too uniform and lacks realism. A more effective method, which we will be using, involves a particle system. This system will define the initial shape of the blast, making it crucial to get the setup right for a more dynamic and realistic explosion. If you have never used a particle system, don't worry. We will go through creating the particle system step by step and learn exactly how it all works! So, open Blender and let's get started:

1. First, let's delete all the default objects so that we have a blank scene to work with. Next, we need an object for the particles to emit from. Press *Shift + A*, select **Mesh | Icosphere**, and scale it down to 0.125. Make sure that you apply the scale as well. To do so, press *Ctrl + A* or *Cmd + A* and choose **Scale**.

2. To create a particle system, head over to the **Particle System** panel and click on the + icon:

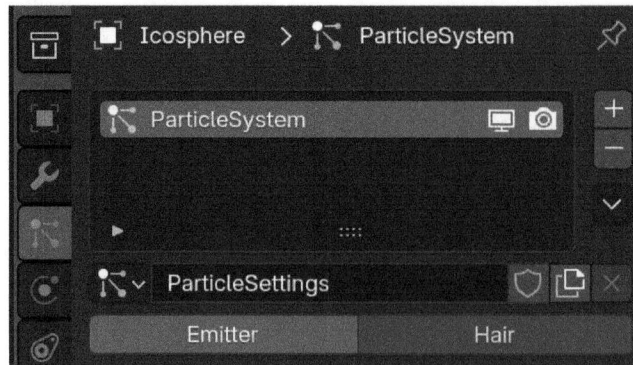

Figure 5.2 – Creating a particle system

3. If you press the spacebar to play the animation, you will notice all the particles emitting and falling straight down. To fix this, go to the **Velocity** tab and set **Normal** to 7 m/s. This will increase the velocity of the particles along the normals of the faces. To make it less uniform, set **Randomize** to 6.000. Now, the particles should be shooting out everywhere:

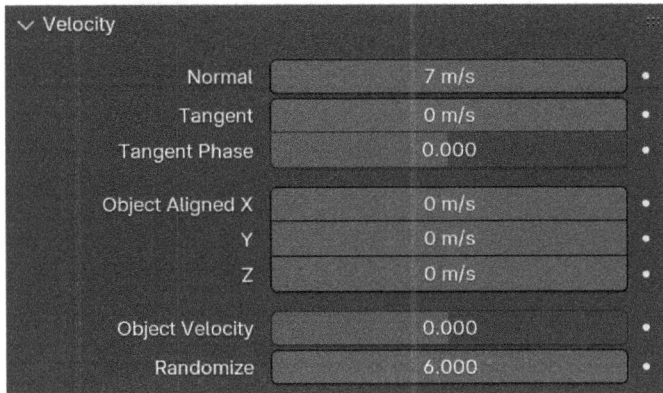

Figure 5.3 – The Velocity tab

4. This is starting to look like an explosion, but it is still not perfect. Now, we need to set when the particles will emit and how long they will last. Go to the **Emission** tab and set **Frame Start** to 10 and **End** to 14. This means that over 4 frames, 1,000 particles will be emitted. ButBut we want way more particles than this, so let's set the **Number** to 5000.

5. The particles are also lasting way too long in the animation. Let's set **Lifetime** to 5. This way, they only last for five frames and then disappear.

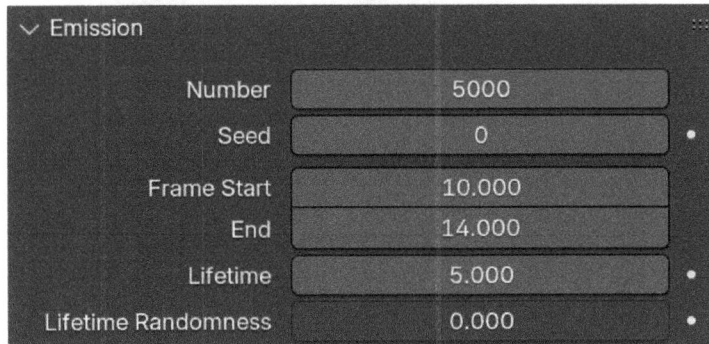

Figure 5.4 – Emission settings

Here is what the simulation looks like now on frame 15:

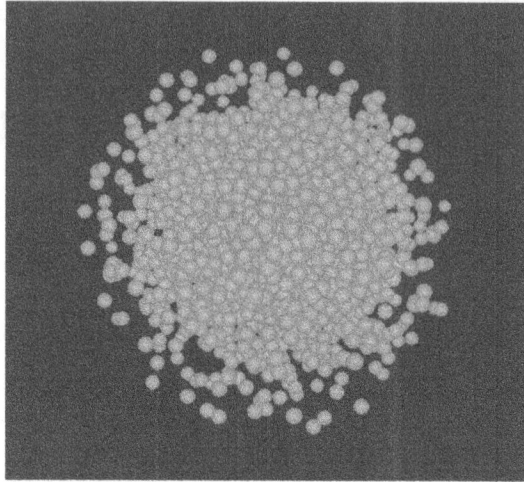

Figure 5.5 – Particle system example

6. If we were to add the smoke simulation to this particle system, it wouldn't be that interesting. The reason is that right now, we have a perfect circle of particles. We need more randomness and variation. To achieve this, let's add a new object with another particle system. Press *Shift + A*, then go to **Mesh** and select **Circle**. Before you do anything else, open the **Add Circle** menu at the bottom. Set **Fill Mode** to **N-Gon**; this will make sure the circle has a face.

7. Scale the circle down, rotate it about 90 degrees, and place it on the right-hand side of the icosphere.

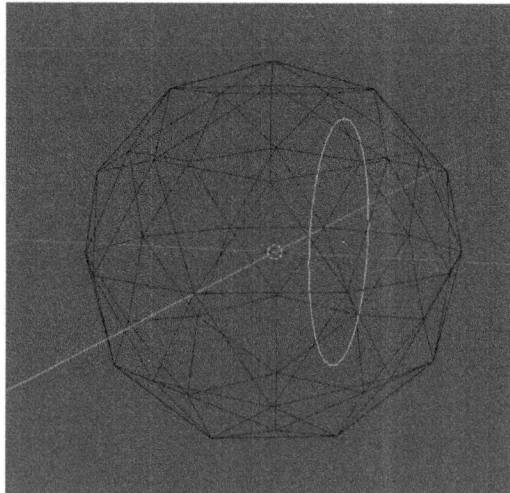

Figure 5.6 – Adding the circle

8. Now, let's give it a new particle system by clicking the + sign in the **Particle System** panel just like before.

9. We are going to be doing something very similar to the previous system. Set **Number** to 2000, **Frame Start** to 10, **End** to 14, and **Lifetime** to 5.

10. In the **Velocity** tab, set **Normal** to 7 once again, but set **Randomize** to 3. This will give a tighter spread of particles. It might be hard to see what this looks like with the first particle system, so you can hide the icosphere temporarily by clicking the *eye* icon in the **Outliner** at the top right:

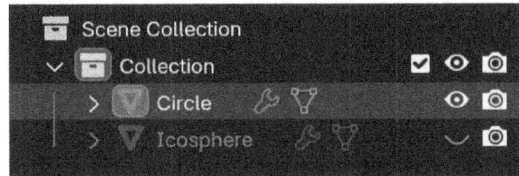

Figure 5.7 – Hiding objects

The circle particle system should look something like this now:

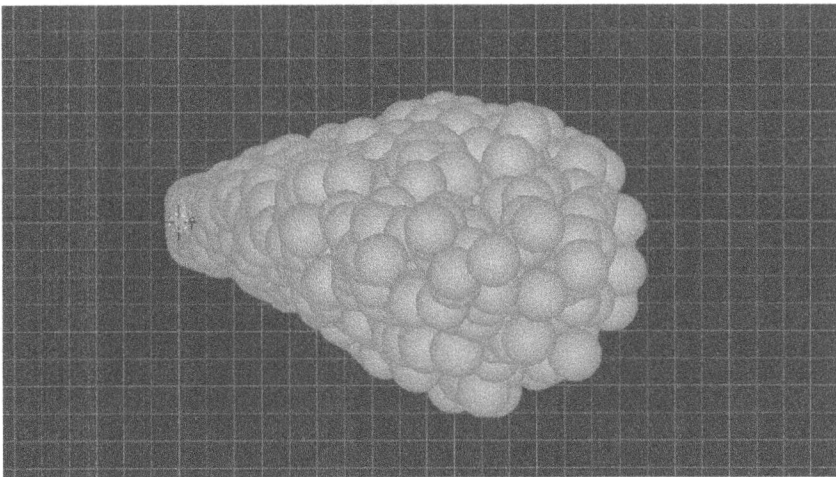

Figure 5.8 – Circle particle system

11. Let's duplicate the circle twice (*Shift* + *D*) and place one rotated upward and the other rotated left of the icosphere. Feel free to play around with the position, rotation, and scale of these circles to get more variation.

12. Unless you are creating an explosion in the air, we need a floor for the particles to hit. Press *Shift* + *A* and add a plane. Scale it up pretty big and make sure it's below all the objects.

13. To add collision to this plane, head over to the **Physics** panel and choose **Collision**. In the **Particle** tab, set **Friction** to 0.9; this will make sure the particles don't slide around the plane.

Also, set **Damping** to 0.9; this value controls the bounciness of the collision. Higher values will equal less bounce. For more variation, you can set **Randomize** for both settings to 0.3:

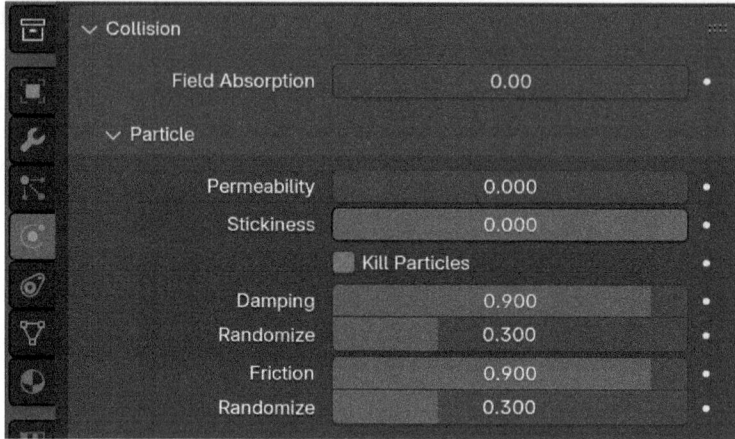

Figure 5.9 – Collision settings

14. Finally, let's bake in the particle system! Select the icosphere and head back over to the **Particle System** panel. Under the **Cache** tab, click on **Bake All Dynamics**. This will bake in all four particle systems automatically!

Here is what the particles should look like so far:

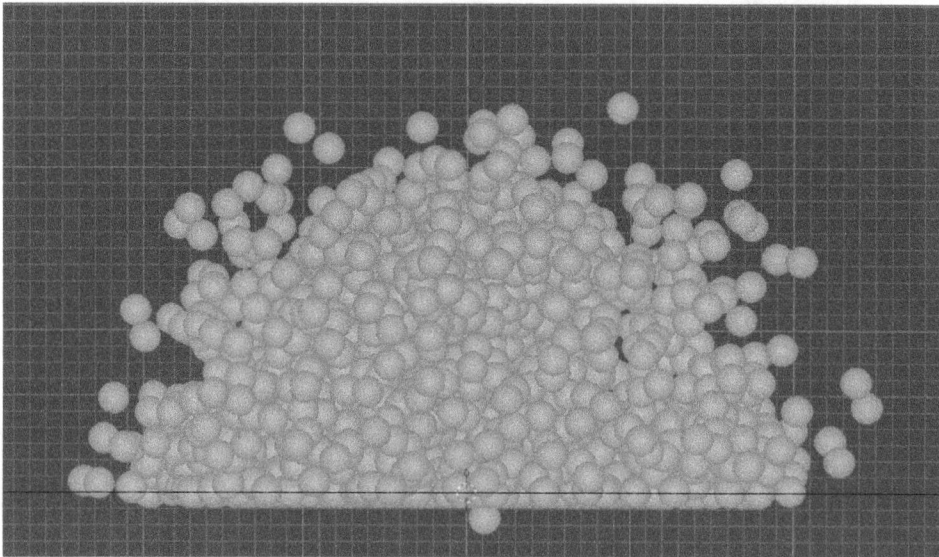

Figure 5.10 – Front view of particles

We have now finished creating the particles for our explosion! If you want to change any of the settings for the particles, make sure to click on **Delete All Bakes** in the **Cache** tab. This will free all the settings, and you can change what you like.

Feel free to play around with the velocity and randomness to get different results. You can also add more emitter objects for a bigger explosion! Once you are happy with your results, we can start creating the smoke and fire simulation!

Creating the simulation

Now, we need to use the particle system we just created as an inflow for the simulation. This means that every particle is going to emit smoke and fire into the scene. Let's set up all the settings and values for the simulation and bake it out!

Setting up the domain

Follow these steps:

1. Of course, we need a domain object. A quick and easy way to do this is to select the icosphere and choose **Object | Quick Effects | Quick Smoke**:

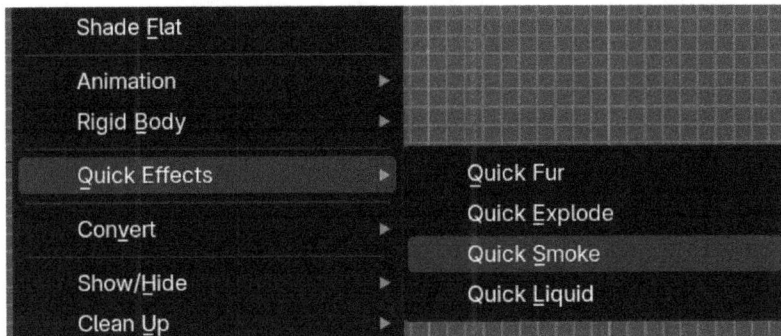

Figure 5.11 – Quick Smoke

This will automatically add a domain for us with the default smoke settings!

2. The domain is currently the wrong size and in the wrong place. Let's move it up so that it's on top of the plane and scale it up. Since we are creating an explosion, we want the domain to be pretty large:

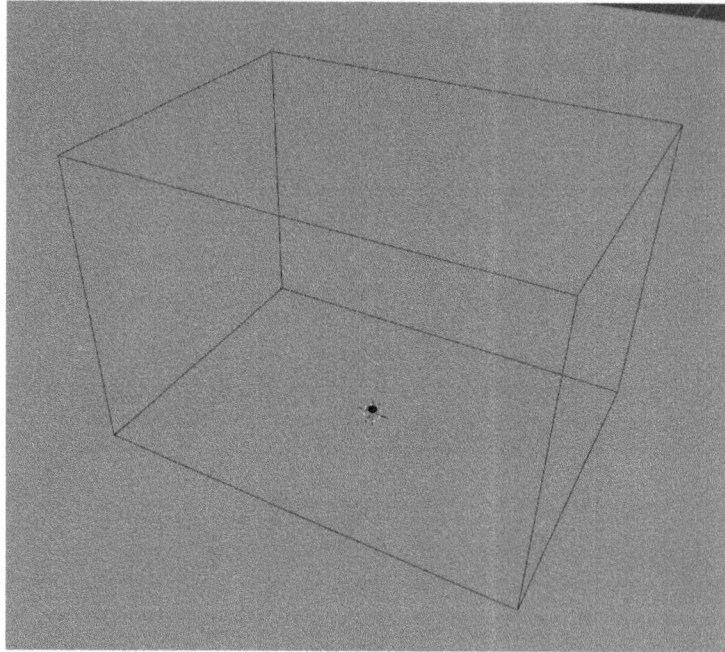

Figure 5.12 – Domain size

Here are the dimensions I used:

Dimensions:	
X	12 m
Y	9 m
Z	9 m

Figure 5.13 – Domain dimensions

3. Now, we can set up the simulation settings! With your domain selected, head over to the **Cache** panel and set **Type** to **Modular**. Also, enable **Is Resumable**. As for **End Frame**, set it to 150 or however long you want the simulation to be.

4. Scroll up to the top and set **Resolution Divisions** to 256. Keep in mind that this is a high resolution. If you have a computer that is a little bit slower, I recommend setting this to 128 instead, or you might spend a very long time baking and rendering the animation.

5. Next, let's set **CFL Number** to 4. This will help improve bake times and give a slightly better look to the simulation, in my opinion.

6. Moving on, let's head to **Border Collisions**. Check the **Bottom** box so that the smoke will collide with the floor of the domain.

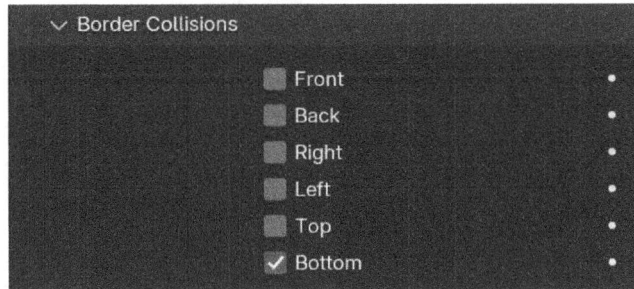

Figure 5.14 – Border Collisions

7. After that, enable **Adaptive Domain**. This will improve the baking time by quite a bit. Be careful, though – sometimes, this setting will delete smoke when you don't want it to. If this happens, you may want to turn down the **Threshold** value in the **Adaptive Domain** settings.

8. In the **Gas** tab, set **Vorticity** to 0.1. This will add more swirls and randomness to the smoke.

9. Now it's time to enable **Noise**. This is going to give the smoke much more detail. Again, if you have a computer that can handle it, set **Upres Factor** to 2, but if it can't, I recommend leaving it at 1. The rest of the settings can be left as is.

With that done, we are now ready to start working on the Inflow objects!

Adding the inflows

Now that the domain is ready to go, let's start setting up the inflows for the simulation:

1. Select the icosphere. Since we used the **Quick Smoke** feature, it should already have the basic flow settings. The first thing we need to change is **Flow Type**. Set this to **Fire + Smoke**.

2. Since the particles are moving very quickly, it's also a good idea to turn up **Sampling Substeps** to 5.

3. Right now, the smoke is coming from the icosphere itself and not the particles. To fix this, open the **Flow Source** tab, set **Flow Source** to **Particle System**, and select the one we created from the dropdown menu. View *Figure 5.15* for a reference.

4. The last, very important step is to check **Initial Velocity**. This will keep the momentum of the smoke when the particles shoot out. If this is not checked, the smoke will just stop moving right when the particles reach the maximum distance. This will look very strange and not realistic, so make sure **Initial Velocity** is checked!

5. The **Source** value multiplies the current velocity. A value of 1 means the smoke will move at the same speed as the particle. This also means that the higher you set this, the more velocity the smoke will have. Let's bring it up to a value of 15. If you find the smoke is moving too fast, bring this value back down.

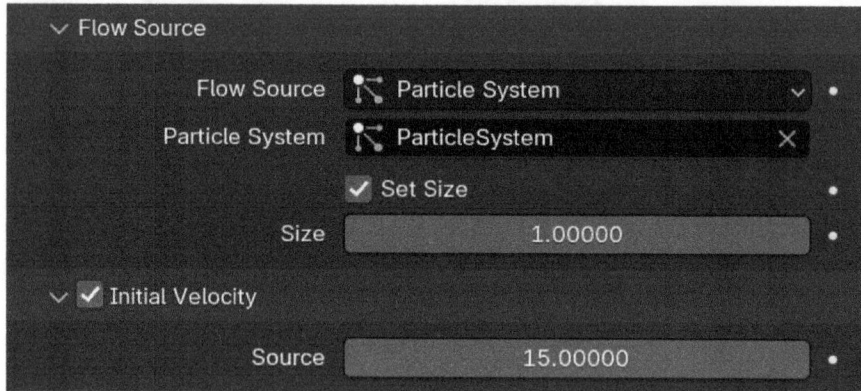

Figure 5.15 – Flow Source

6. Now, let's select the rest of the inflows (the three other circles we've added), and then select the icosphere last so that it's the **active object**. Press *Ctrl + L* or *Cmd + L* and select **Copy Modifiers**. Now, each of those circles will have the same settings as the icosphere! You can also go to **Object | Link/Transfer Data | Copy Modifiers** to do this.

7. With that done, we are ready to bake the simulation! Remember that if you haven't saved your project, the cache data will be put in a temp folder. This means it will get deleted once you close this .blend file. You can set a custom folder for the cache, or if you saved your project before doing the Quick Smoke, , the cache will automatically be put into the same folder as your .blend file:

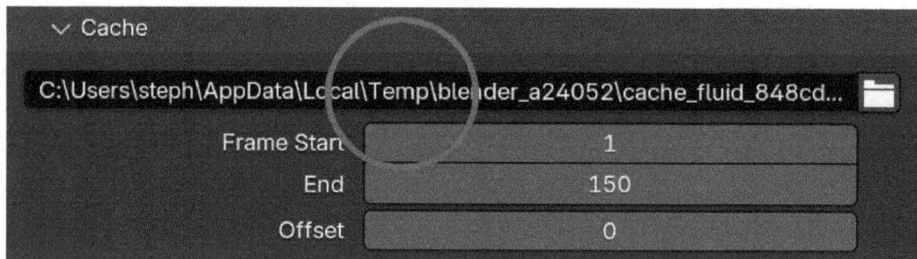

Figure 5.16 – Temp cache folder

Once you have saved your project, select your domain object and click **Bake Data**. This might take a while, but once it has finished, go to the **Noise** tab and click **Bake Noise** as well!

Now, just wait for the baking to finish. At this point, we can start creating the material for our explosion!

Creating the material

Now that the simulation is done, we are ready to set up the material for our smoke and fire! This is where you would want to look at reference images again. When you look at chemical explosions, you will notice that the smoke is very dark and dense. The fire is a very bright orange and yellow color, so let's replicate that in the material!

Creating the smoke

Let's start creating the smoke:

1. To see what our explosion looks like, go to frame 25 and press *Z*, and then select **Rendered View**. The scene lighting is also a bit boring, so add a sun lamp by pressing *Shift + A* going to **Light | Sun**. Place and rotate it so that it's facing the front. In the **Object Data** panel, under the **Light** tab, set **Strength** to 10:

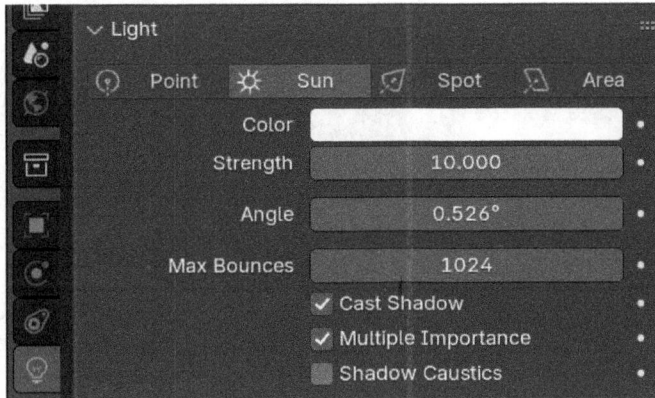

Figure 5.17 – Lamp properties

2. Next, let's head over to the **Shading** workspace at the top.

3. With your domain selected, you should see a basic material already in place since we used the **Quick Smoke** feature. Before we start working on the material, you need to decide which rendering engine to use. When working with smoke materials, I like to use Cycles, just because it looks better and allows us to see the smoke and fire more clearly. Later in this chapter, we will learn how to use both engines to render, but for now, select **Cycles** in the **Render** panel.

4. Now, let's start creating the material. Let's add three nodes so that we can plug everything in. The first node we will add is a **Volume Info** node. This node allows us to take attributes from the smoke simulation and plug them into the material. Press *Shift + A* and select **Input | Volume Info**. Place it to the left of the **Principled Volume** shader for now.

5. Next, let's add a **Color Ramp** node by pressing *Shift + A* and going to **Converter | Color Ramp**. This node is fantastic, and it will enable you to do so many things in the material. In this case, it's going to allow us to control the falloff of the density. Place it between the **Principled Volume** and **Volume Info** nodes.

6. Finally, let's add a **Math** node to control how dense the smoke will be. Press *Shift + A* and go to **Converter | Math**. You can place this in between **Color Ramp** and **Principled Volume**.

7. Change the **Math** node mode from **Add** to **Multiply**. Once we plug everything in, the bottom **Value** will control the density of the smoke.

8. Now, to connect everything, let's take the **Density** output from the **Volume Info** node and plug it into **Color Ramp**. Then, take the **Color** output from the **Color Ramp** node and plug that into the top input of the **Math** node. Finally, plug the **Math** node into **Density** of **Principled Volume**. To see the whole setup, view the following figure:

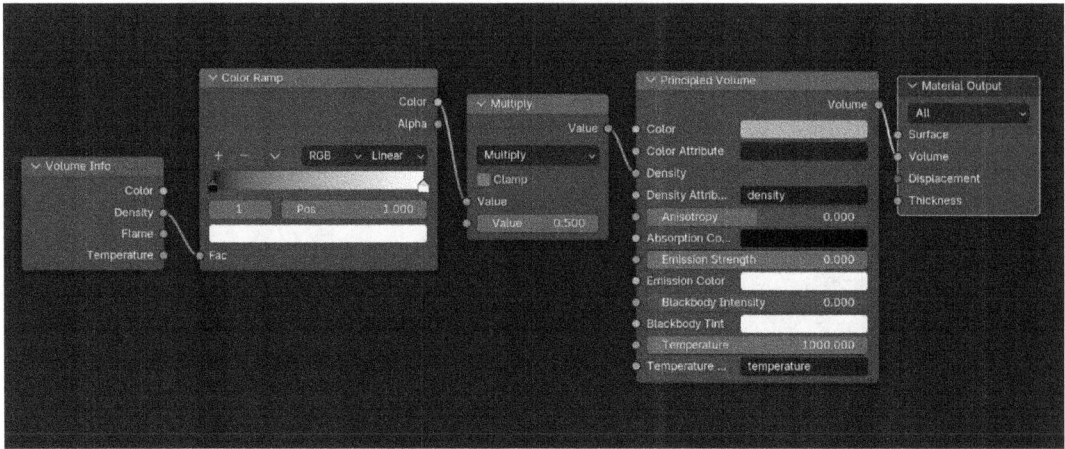

Figure 5.18 – Smoke density node setup

9. Now, let's change some values to get the smoke looking a lot better! First, set the bottom **Value** in the **Math** node to 100. This will make the smoke much denser. Currently, the smoke becomes less dense as it gets closer to the edge. We can change this by taking the white handle of **Color Ramp** and dragging it much closer to the black handle. Now, the edges of the simulation will be much more dense, giving it the look of very thick smoke.

10. Finally, let's set the **Color** property of **Principled Volume** to a darker gray to get the look of smoke from an explosion. Make sure to go into **Rendered View** in the **3D Viewport** area to see what your smoke looks like. Here is what the scene should look like so far:

Figure 5.19 – Frame 48 of the explosion

Now that the smoke is looking good, let's continue working on the material and creating the fire!

Creating the fire

The next step in this tutorial is creating the fire from the explosion. Let's do the same process by adding all the nodes, plugging everything in, and then changing the values:

1. To get fire into the smoke, we will be using the **Emission** values in the **Principled Volume** area. If we drag **Strength** up, it's not going to work because we need to tell Blender where to put the fire.

2. Let's create the color of the fire first. Add a new **Color Ramp** node and place it below the first **Color Ramp**.

3. In the **Volume Info** node, there is a **Flame** output, but that is not what we will be using because I found that it doesn't look as good. Instead, we will be using the **Heat** attribute, as we did in *Chapter 3*.

    Press *Shift + A*, add an **Input | Attribute** node, and place it on the left. In the **Name** field, type the word heat (no caps) and plug **Fac** into the **Fac** property of **Color Ramp**. Then, take **Color Ramp** and plug that into **Emission Color**.

    One thing to keep in mind is that the **Heat** attribute does not work in EEVEE. If you decide to use EEVEE, take the **Density** output from **Volume Info** instead. It will work very similarly to the **Heat** attribute.

4. Now, let's make this fire look good! Set **Emission Strength** to 100 so that we can see what we are doing.

5. Next, take the black handle of the **Color Ramp** node and drag it about a quarter of the way to the right. This will clamp down on the amount of emission in the smoke.

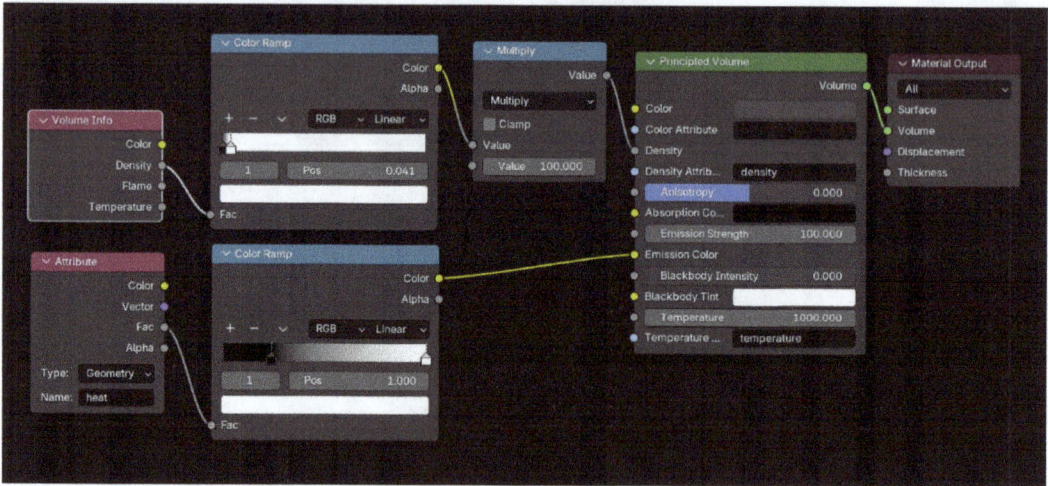

Figure 5.20 – Fire node preview

6. As for the color, let's add a new handle by clicking the + sign in **Color Ramp**. Set this handle to a nice red/orange color. Then, select the white handle and set it to a bright yellow color. Play around with the position and colors until you are happy. You can add more handles if you want; this way, you will be able to play around with the color even more! Here is the full node setup if you want to take a look:

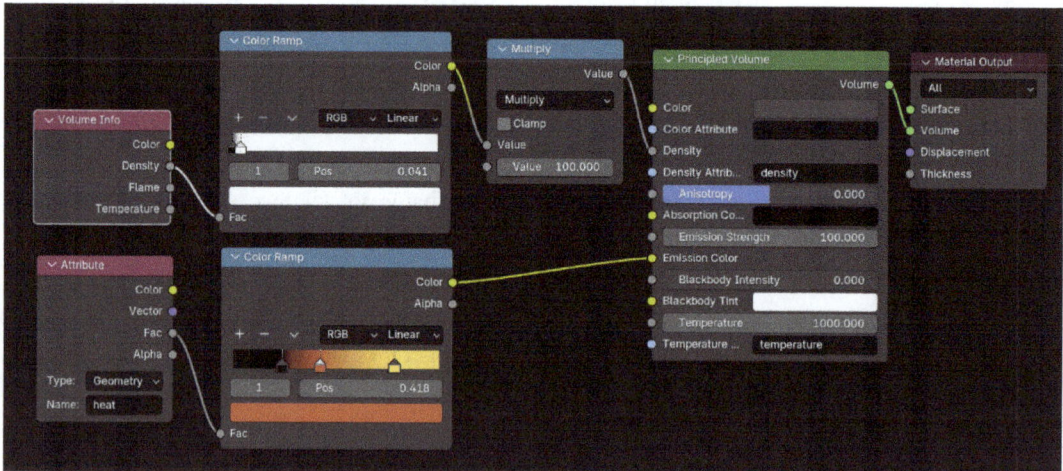

Figure 5.21 – Full material preview

With that, the material is done! Feel free to play around with the values, colors, and handles to get your desired look. The following figure shows the result of the explosion so far:

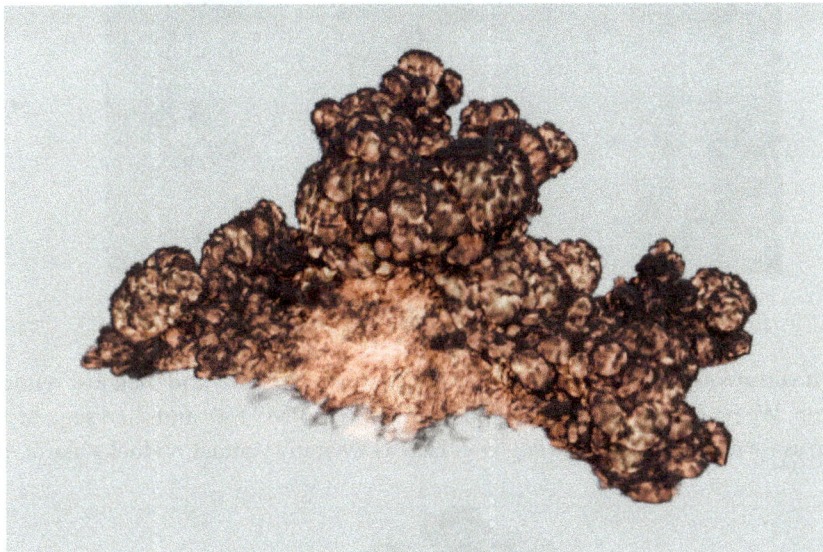

Figure 5.22 – Explosion result

If the colors look a bit dull and not saturated, don't worry; we will fix that in the next section, where we will learn how to use Cycles and EEVEE to properly render fire!

Rendering the explosion in Cycles and EEVEE

The last step in this tutorial is to set up the camera and render settings.

Rendering in Cycles

So, let's get started by setting up the camera and rendering the explosion with Cycles first:

1. Firstly, in the Timeline, set the **End** frame to match however long your simulation is. In this case, ours is 150.

2. Since we deleted the camera at the beginning, we need to add a new one. Press *Shift + A* and select **Camera**. Place it where you want to view the explosion. We think a high-up angle looking down looks pretty nice.

3. Next, go to the **Render** panel and scroll down to the **Color Management** tab. Set **View Transform** to **Filmic** and **Look** to **High Contrast**. This will make your colors pop:

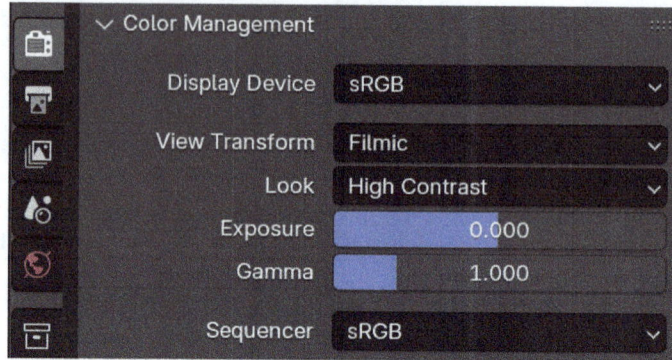

Figure 5.23 – The Color Management tab

4.   Finally, if you are using Cycles, set **Render Max Samples** to 100, and then just render out the animation. We recommend exporting the animation as PNG files and then sequencing them together, as we did at the end of *Chapter 4*. Here is what my simulation looks like at frame 35:

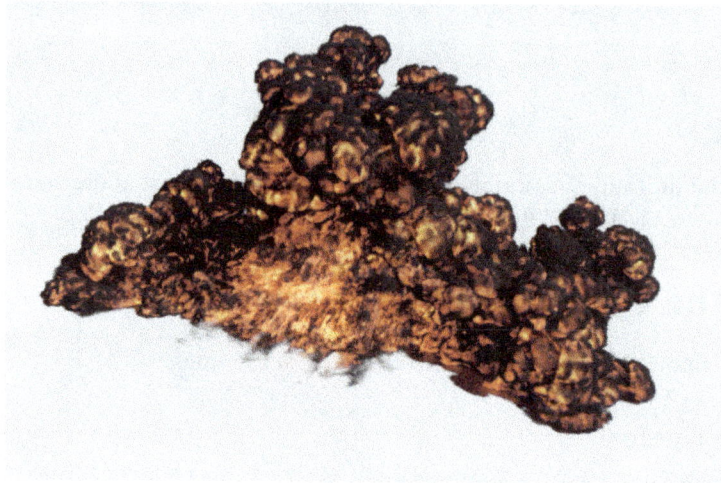

Figure 5.24 – Cycles render preview

If you would like to add some motion blur to the render, you can set **Velocity Scale** in the domain settings to 0.1 and check the box next to **Motion Blur** in the render settings. This is very similar to what we did in *Chapter 3*. However, the downside to adding motion blur is the render time will significantly increase by around 300%. It will look better in the end, but you will pay for it in the render time.

That is all you have to do when rendering with Cycles. EEVEE, on the other hand, is a bit different and requires more setup. Let's go ahead and switch the engine to EEVEE and discuss how this works!

Rendering in EEVEE

Right when you switch to EEVEE, you will notice the smoke looks terrible. It's way too pixelated and the fire has now disappeared. The reason for this is that the **Heat** attribute doesn't work in EEVEE. So, instead, we need to jump back over to the material and switch it to the **Density** attribute. Let's get started:

1. The first three steps here are the same as rendering in Cycles. In the Timeline, set the **End** frame to match however long your simulation is. In this case, ours is 150.

2. Since we deleted the camera at the beginning, we need to add a new one. Press *Shift + A* and select **Camera**. Place it where you want to view the explosion. We think a high-up angle looking down looks pretty nice.

3. Next, go to the **Render** panel and scroll down to the **Color Management** tab. Set **View Transform** to **Filmic** and **Look** to **High Contrast**. This will make your colors pop. Refer to *Figure 5.23*. Open the **Shading** workspace again and take the same **Density** output from **Volume Info**, then plug that into the bottom **Color Ramp**. You may need to play around with the black handle if too much fire is coming in.

Figure 5.25 – EEVEE material nodes

4. Now, let's get back to the detail in our smoke. Open the **Volumes** tab in the **Render Properties** panel. Here is where we will add back all the detail. Let's start by setting **Resolution** to 1.1. This will bring back a lot of the detail and it will make the next step a bit easier to see.

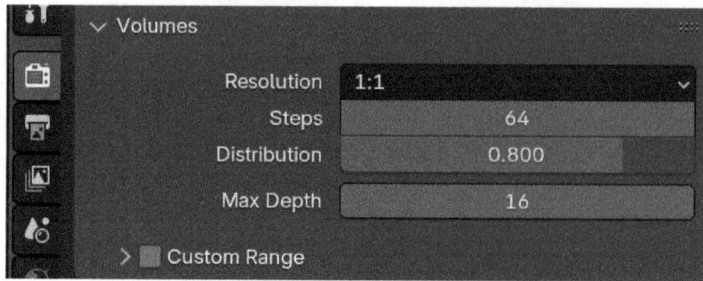

Figure 5.26 – Volumes

5. Now, our simulation should have much more detail. The next step is to enable **Volume Shadows**. This will give the smoke shadows and make it look a lot more realistic. To do this, scroll up to the **Shadows** tab and check the box next to **Volume Shadows**, then turn **Steps** up to 32 for more detail.

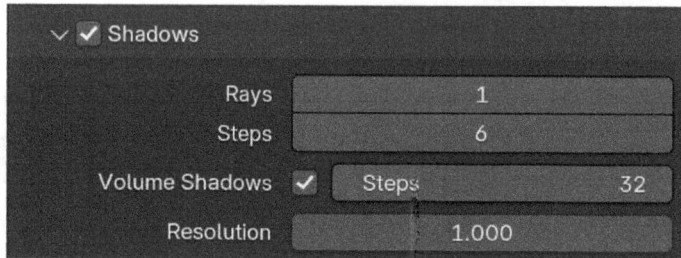

Figure 5.27 – Shadows

6. Finally, if you think the smoke looks too bright from the sun lamp, you can open the **Lamp Properties** panel by selecting the sun, and under the **Influence** tab, set **Volume Scatter** to around 0.3. This will make the smoke look darker and not have as many light bounces.

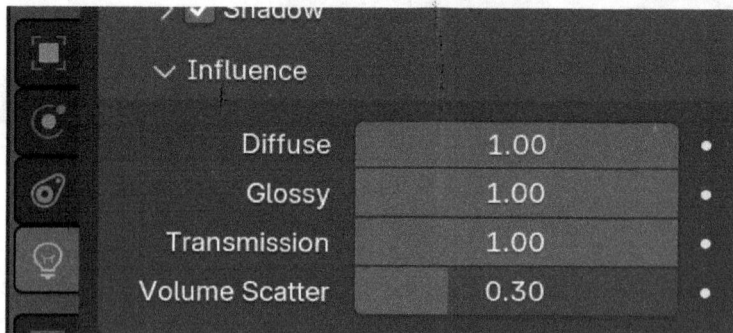

Figure 5.28 – Volume Scatter

One thing to note about using EEVEE is that you won't be getting any shadows underneath the smoke from the sun lamp. That is one of the limitations of EEVEE – you can get shadows in the volume itself, but it's not going to cast shadows on other objects in the scene.

So, if you want to get a realistic result with shadows, you are going to have to render this scene in Cycles. But if you don't care too much about that, EEVEE will be faster at rendering!

7. The last step is to set an output and render out the animation. As mentioned earlier, it's recommended to render the animation as a PNG or another image format and then sequence it out later. Refer to *Chapter 4* to see how to do that. The following figure shows one frame after using the EEVEE render engine:

Figure 5.29 – EEVEE final result

As you can see, it does look pretty good in EEVEE, but again, you will notice that there are no shadows underneath the smoke. So, whichever rendering engine you use is up to you. They both have their advantages and disadvantages but the result will still look great!

This scene doesn't have to end here. You can also add a lot to it! For example, you could create an environment and have the explosion come from barrels filled with oil. You could also have a rainy sky to set the atmosphere. It's all up to you!

Summary

And there we go! We have successfully created an explosion in Blender using a particle system and Mantaflow. Hopefully, you learned something new along the way and created something cool!

We covered a lot of topics in this chapter, so let's recap. First, we created the initial shape of the explosion using a particle system. Then, we added three more particle systems to give variation and randomness to the simulation.

After that, we started working on the smoke and fire. We used the **Quick Smoke** feature to automatically add a domain and then set up all the settings for the inflow objects. We learned about creating a dense smoke material and how to add fire to the smoke. Finally, we discussed how to render in both Cycles and the real-time render engine EEVEE.

This concludes the first part of this book! We have covered four Mantaflow tutorials so far, and now, it's time to move on to a different simulation. In *Part 2* of this book, we will be diving into soft body and cloth simulations and learning how to use those simulations efficiently.

Get This Book's PDF Version and Exclusive Extras

UNLOCK NOW

Scan the QR code (or go to `packtpub.com/unlock`). Search for this book by name, confirm the edition, and then follow the steps on the page.

Note: Keep your invoice handy. Purchases made directly from Packt don't require an invoice.

Part 2: Simulating Physics with Soft Bodies and Cloth

Using soft bodies and cloth is a great way to easily create certain objects that would otherwise be quite difficult to model by hand. In this part, we will dive deep into the Soft Body and Cloth simulations and learn all there is to know about them. We will create some nice, satisfying animations along the way!

This part has the following chapters:

- *Chapter 6, Getting Started with Soft Bodies*
- *Chapter 7, Creating a Soft Body Obstacle Course*
- *Chapter 8, An Introduction to Cloth Simulations*
- *Chapter 9, Creating a Realistic Flag*

6

Getting Started with Soft Bodies

What is a **soft body simulation**? A soft body simulation is a way to visualize the motion or deformation of a *soft* object. This could be a pillow and cushions, a beach ball, jello, swinging rope, clothing, or anything else that can deform from its original shape. You can even use the soft body simulation to create a car crashing! Even though a car isn't technically a "soft body," you can use this system to create the deformations that would occur in a crash.

Soft body simulation is also used to add secondary motion to something. If you have a character walking, you may want to add a soft body simulation to give some physics to the body. This way, the character doesn't look as stiff, with the character's muscles, fat, hair, and clothing moving as well while they walk. While you could use a soft body simulation for clothing, it's usually better to use a cloth simulation. This is because that is what it is specifically designed for, and the results are usually more accurate and realistic.

In this chapter, we will be learning how a soft body simulation works in Blender, and we will be covering all the settings for it. In the following chapters, we will get more into the practical ways to use this system to create unique and satisfying animations.

In this chapter, we'll be covering the following topics:

- Introduction to soft body simulations
- Understanding collision objects
- Understanding soft body settings and values
- Interacting with multiple soft bodies

Technical requirements

This chapter requires you to have Blender version 4.2 or above installed.

To download Blender, visit www.blender.org.

The supporting files for this chapter are available here: https://github.com/PacktPublishing/ Learn-Blender-4-Simulations-the-Right-Way/tree/main/Chapter%206.

Introduction to soft body simulations

As we mentioned at the start of this chapter, soft bodies are used to deform objects and make them look soft. A soft body simulation calculates gravity, force fields, and the strength of the interior force connecting the vertices and applies deformations accordingly. This gives a realistic look as if the object were filled with something. Think of a water balloon, for example.

To add a soft body simulation to an object, you need to head over to the **Physics** panel and select **Soft Body**, as illustrated in the following screenshot:

Figure 6.1 – Creating a soft body simulation

Unlike a Mantaflow simulation, you can use any object with control points or vertices for a soft body simulation. This includes meshes, curves, surfaces, and lattices. The number of vertices on the object also correlates to how the simulation will look. If you try to simulate a cube, for example, with only eight vertices, that's not going to work very well because it's so **low polygon** (**low poly**).

On the other hand, when you simulate a soft body object with a high vertex count, Blender will slow down quite a bit. So, it's usually best to have an object with a lower number of vertices when working with a soft body simulation. This also applies to collision objects. If your collision is very high poly, the simulation will take a long time to bake and calculate. What if you don't want to lower the vertex count of your collision object? The solution for that would be to create an invisible low-poly version of that collision and use that instead. This way, you still have your high-poly object, but it won't interact with the simulation.

Once you add the soft body simulation to an object, you can head down to the Timeline and play the animation to view it in real time. You can even add other objects and collisions and interact with the simulation as it's playing, which is useful for quick testing.

One thing that you will find common with soft body and cloth simulations is that you want to have an even distribution of geometry for that object. For example, if you have an object with a high number of vertices in one area and not very many vertices in another, a soft body simulation will act differently for those two areas. The high vertex area might be loose, while the low vertex area would be very stiff. So, unless you are specifically going for that sort of animation, it's generally best to have even geometry throughout the object.

The following diagram illustrates good and bad geometry:

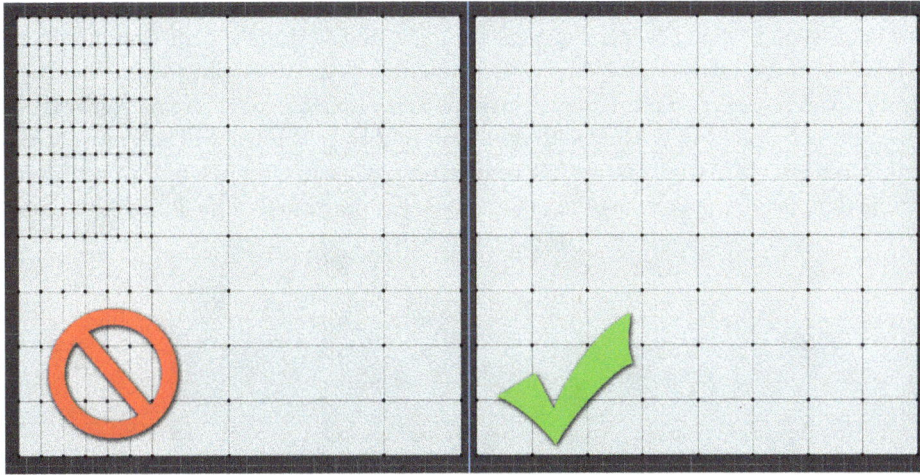

Figure 6.2 – Good versus bad geometry

A soft body simulation is great and can save you a lot of time from trying to animate an object deforming or interacting with collision, but it can also waste time if you try to make it work in the wrong scenario. Therefore, only use a soft body simulation when it works for your scene. You can see an example of one here:

Figure 6.3 – Soft body example

Before we jump into all the settings for soft bodies, let's take a moment and talk about collision objects!

Understanding collision objects

If you want a soft body object to collide with another mesh, you need to add collision to that mesh. Otherwise, the soft body will just pass right through that object, and it will not interact with the simulation.

You can enable collision by going over to the **Modifier** panel and adding the **Collision** modifier or by selecting **Collision** in the **Physics** panel. These collision objects are used quite often when working with soft bodies, clothes, or even particle systems! You can even add collision to a soft body object itself; this way, the soft body will interact with other soft bodies as well (we will talk more about this at the end of the chapter). To disable the **Collision** setting, you can either click **X** to get rid of it or you can disable it in the viewport by toggling the eye icon, as illustrated in the following screenshot:

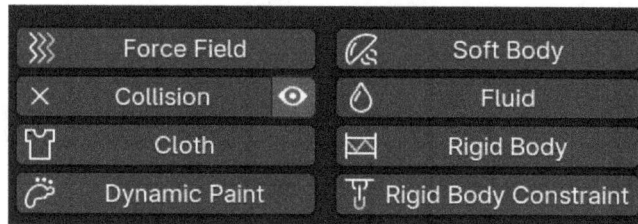

Figure 6.4 – Enabling and disabling collisions

When you first add collision to an object, you will see two tabs in the settings: **Particle** and **Softbody & Cloth**, as illustrated in the following screenshot:

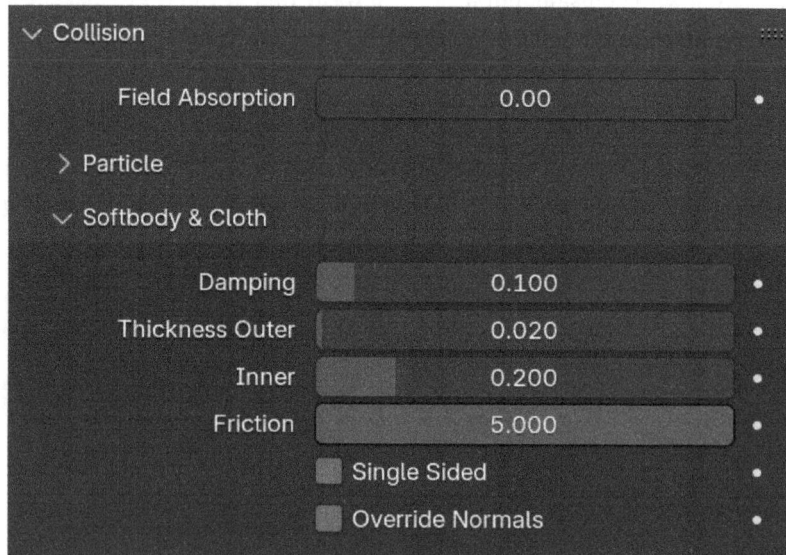

Figure 6.5 – Collision objects

The **Particle** settings are for how particles will interact with the collision; this has no effect on soft bodies, so let's skip it for now. The settings in the **Softbody & Cloth** tab do have an effect, so let's go through each and discuss how they change the simulation! They comprise the following:

- **Field Absorption**: This allows you to absorb a percentage of a force field's strength. For example, if a wind force field is going through a collision with a **Field Absorption** value set at 0.2, it will absorb 20% of the force field's strength. If the value is set at 1, it will absorb 100% of the force field, and no wind will be able to get through. Note that to get this setting to work, you also need to enable the **Absorption** checkbox in the **Force Fields** physics panel.

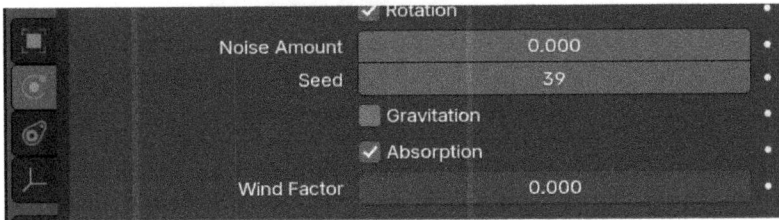

Figure 6.6 – Field Absorption

- **Damping**: This is the amount of bounciness a soft body will have on collision. 0 means no damping, so there will be a lot of bounce. 1 means maximum damping, and there will be very little bounce.

- **Thickness Outer**: This is the size of the area on the outside of the collision. With a value of 0.5, there will be a pretty large gap between the collision and the soft body. This setting also acts as padding for the collision. Instead of hitting it and bouncing up, it will seem as though the soft body is hitting a pillow. In some situations, this can be good to help prevent clipping between objects. You can see a representation of this here:

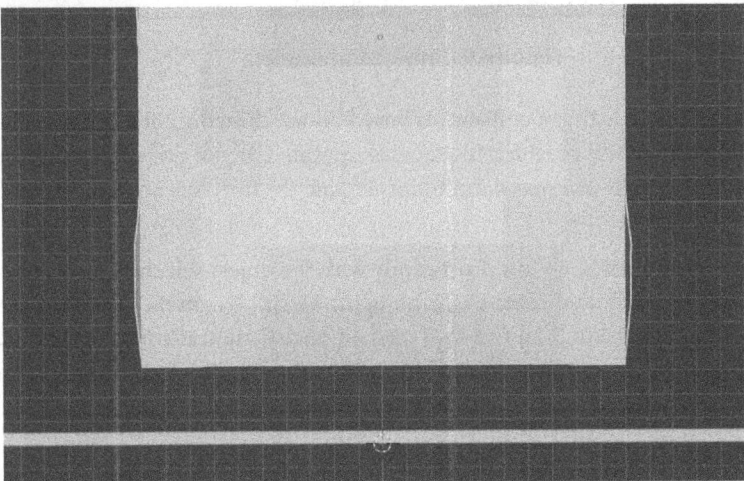

Figure 6.7 – Thickness Outer example

- **Inner**: This is the collision area for the inside of the object. This is basically the padding distance, and if a soft body enters this area, it will try to force it out. You can see an illustration of this here:

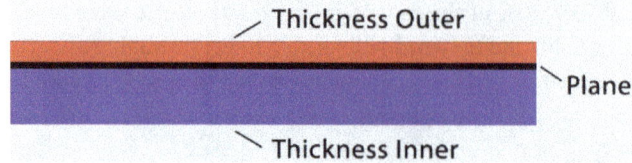

Figure 6.8 – Plane collision area

An example of this would be to place a soft body in the middle of a plane. Since half of the soft body is inside the **Inner** zone, it will push it up and out. Keep in mind that this does not work for a cloth simulation, only for soft bodies. Here's a visual example of this:

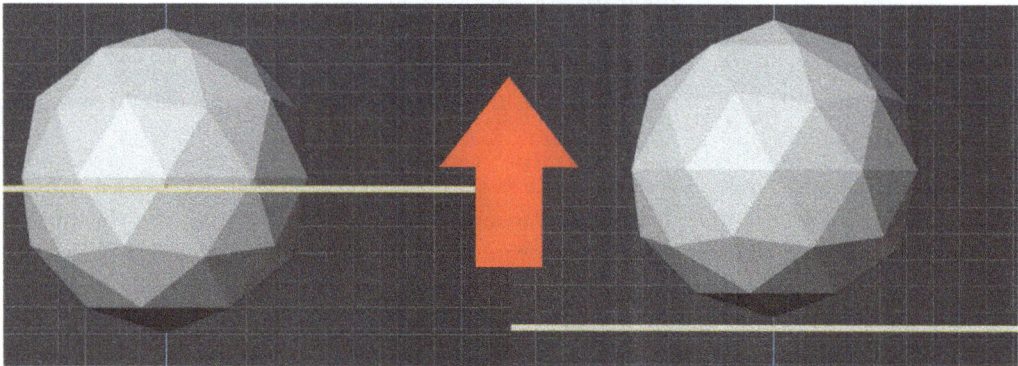

Figure 6.9 – Inner zone example

Another thing to note is that a collision is based on the direction of **normals**. The normals of an object are the direction in which the faces are pointed. If you notice that the collision object is not working properly, you may want to recalculate the normals and see which direction the normals are pointed in.

To recalculate the normals, go into **Edit Mode** with the object selected. Then, press *A* to select all vertices on the mesh, and from there, go up to **Mesh | Normals | Recalculate Outside** or press the *Shift + N* shortcut. You can also turn on **Face Orientation** in the **Overlays** menu to see which direction the faces are pointed in, as illustrated in the following screenshot:

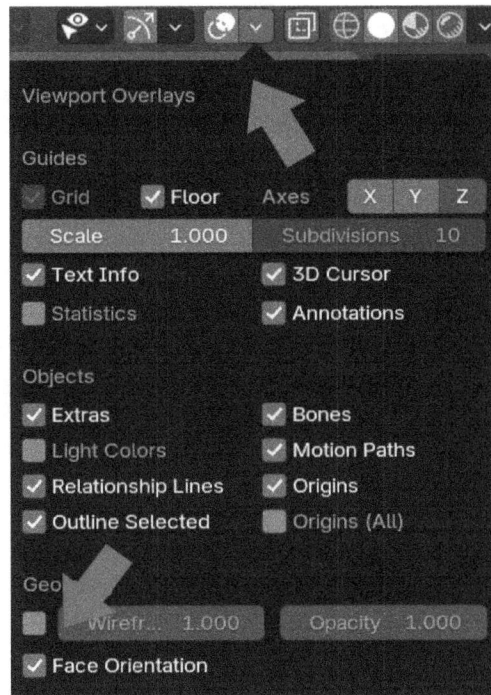

Figure 6.10 – Overlays menu

The **Friction, Single Sided,** and **Override Normals** settings are used only for cloth simulations, which we will learn about in *Chapter 8*.

With that out of the way, let's jump into a soft body simulation and learn all about the settings and the nitty-gritty details!

Understanding soft body settings and values

Now that you know how a soft body simulation and collision objects work in Blender, it's time to get into the technical details and learn about all the settings and values and how they can affect the simulation. While going through this chapter, I suggest you test out the settings for yourself so you can visualize how they work. You can download a basic .blend file that I have created for that exact purpose from https://github.com/PacktPublishing/Learn-Blender-4-Simulations-the-Right-Way/tree/main/Chapter%206. When you open this file, you will find just a basic scene with an icosphere and a collision object.

Now, let's talk about the settings!

Object settings

When you first select **Soft Body** in the **Physics** panel, you will see a lot of settings on the right side, as we can see here:

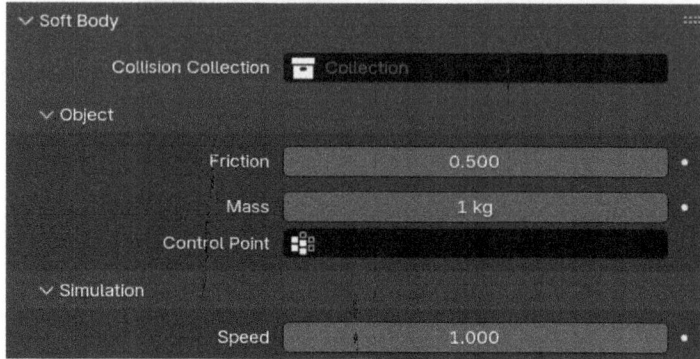

Figure 6.11 – Object settings

Let's start out from the top and work our way down, as follows:

- **Collision Collection**: This allows you to control which collections interact with the simulation. With it set to **none**, every collision in every collection will interact with the soft body.

- **Friction**: This works a little differently than you would expect. This is the overall friction of the entire area. If you increase this value, it will dampen the movement of the soft body, making it look like it's moving in slow motion.

- **Mass**: This controls the weight of each vertex on the object. In the following screenshot, the left example has a **Mass** value of 1 kg, while the right has a **Mass** value of 10 kg. You will notice that it's collapsing in on itself because the weight is too heavy to maintain the structure of the object:

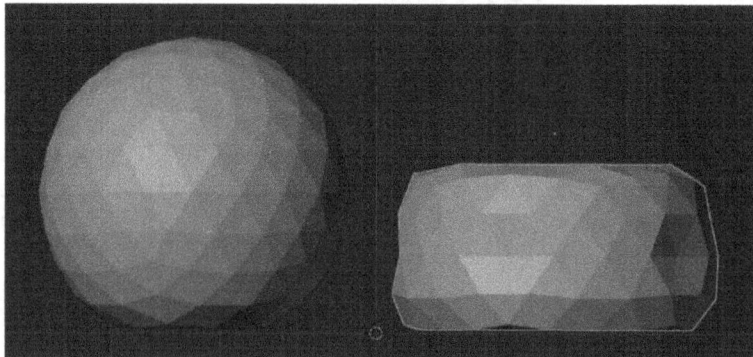

Figure 6.12 – Mass example

- **Control Point**: This allows you to use a **vertex group** to control the **Mass** value of the object. If you have never used a vertex group before, it basically allows you to paint values from 0 to 1 on each vertex. In this example, I have set the left side of the cube to a value of 1, which is red, so it's using the full mass. The right side is set to blue, which is 0, so it weighs nothing. As you can see here, it is collapsing in on itself because the left side weighs more (we will talk about vertex groups in more detail later in this chapter):

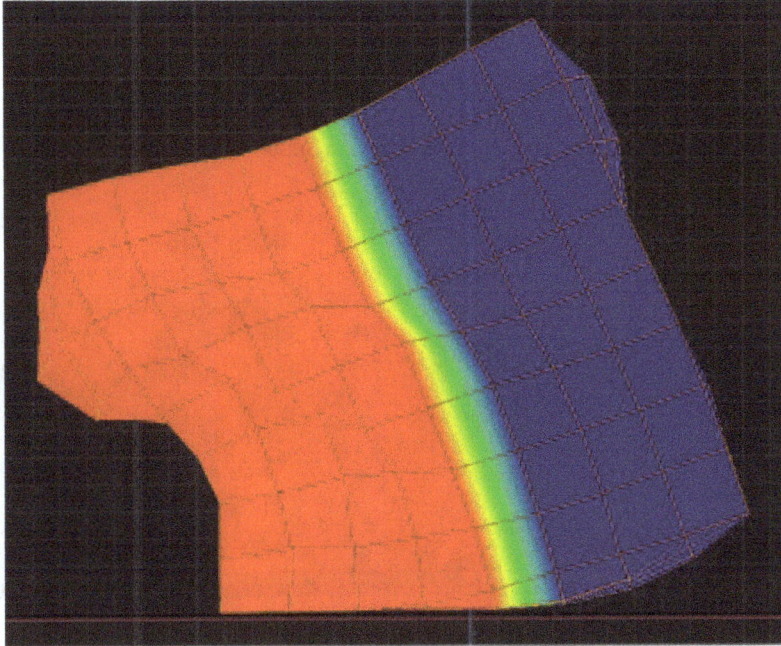

Figure 6.13 – Control Point example

- **Speed**: Finally, we have the option to control the speed of the simulation. This value is based on the **frames per second** (**FPS**) of the scene. For example, if you have the frame rate set to 60 and the **Speed** value set to 1, it's going to look like the simulation is playing at twice the speed, so you would need to slow the speed to match the frame rate. Consider what you are trying to make, the scale of your scene, and your frame rate, and adjust the speed accordingly.

With that done, let's move on to the **Cache** tab and learn how to bake in the simulation!

Cache

Below the **Object** settings, we have the **Cache** tab. This is where you bake in the simulation. Some of these options should be familiar because they are the same as with a Mantaflow simulation.

One thing that is different, though, is the ability to have multiple caches. For example, you can click the + button to create another cache, as shown in the following screenshot. Double-click the cache to rename it. You can then select one of them, change the settings as you wish, and bake it in, and it won't affect the other caches:

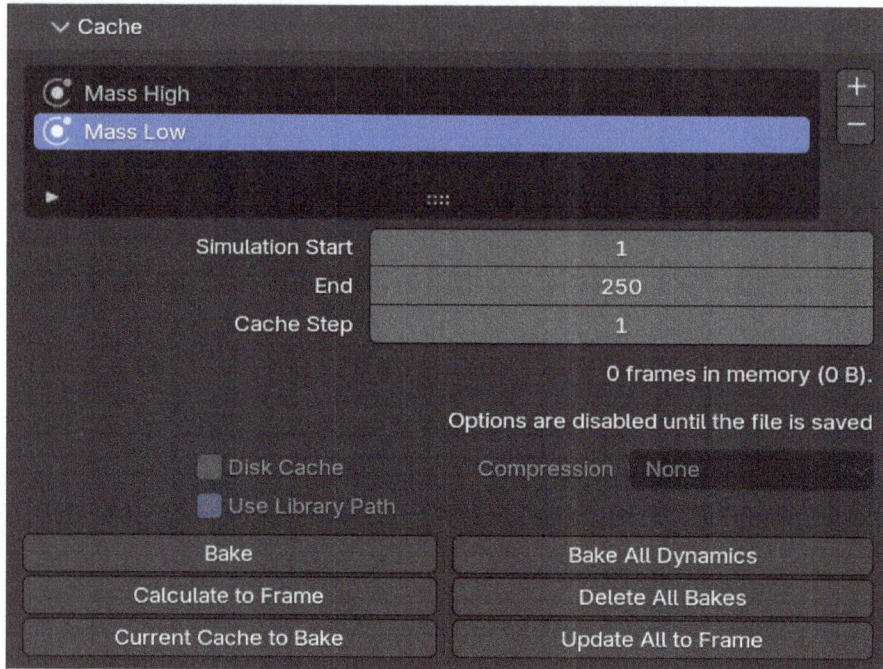

Figure 6.14 – Multiple caches example

This can be very useful for quickly previewing certain settings in the simulation. To switch between two caches, make sure to restart the Timeline, then select the one you want to preview and hit **Play**.

We should also discuss the difference between a **cache** and a **bake**. The cache is the result of the animation as it's being played. In the following screenshot, you see an orange line at the bottom of the Timeline—this is the cache:

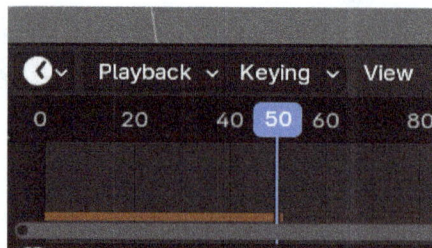

Figure 6.15 – Cache example

Whenever you change a setting in the simulation, the cache will disappear, and you will have to replay the animation to get it back. When you bake, then the result of the simulation is locked in, and you won't be able to change the settings unless you click **Free Bake**. The Timeline will also be filled with that orange line at the bottom. The following screenshot provides an example of this:

Figure 6.16 – Bake example

That is the difference—the cache is a temporary result, which will reset if you make any changes, and the bake is the locked-in result. Now, let's look at the rest of the settings for the **Cache** tab:

- **Simulation Start** and **End**: These just allow you to set the frame range of the simulation for baking.

- **Cache Step**: This allows you to skip frames of a simulation when baking. Instead of baking every frame, it will bake every other frame if this value is set to 2. This can save on storage, but you might end up with a less accurate simulation.

- **Bake**: This bakes in the simulation.

- **Calculate to Frame**: This allows you to select any frame in the **Timeline**, and Blender will calculate the animation up to where you selected.

- **Current Cache to Bake**: This allows you to take the temporary cache and use that as the bake.

- **Bake All Dynamics**: This will bake in every simulation in the scene. If you have multiple soft bodies, particle systems, or cloth simulations, all of them will be baked at once.

- **Delete All Bakes**: This is pretty self-explanatory. It deletes every bake in the scene.

- **Update All to Frame**: This will update all simulations to the current frame you have selected.

Sometimes, a simulation will not work properly if you try to render an animation without baking. So, it's usually a good idea to bake in the simulation before rendering; this way, everything works correctly and there are no problems.

Soft Body Goal

You might notice that right when you create a soft body object and play the animation, the object just floats and bobs up and down. This is because **Goal** is checked in the settings. The Goal option is basically a way to pin vertices in place. This can be useful when trying to create blankets hanging from a line, corners of a flag pinned to the pole, or characters walking. You can see an example here:

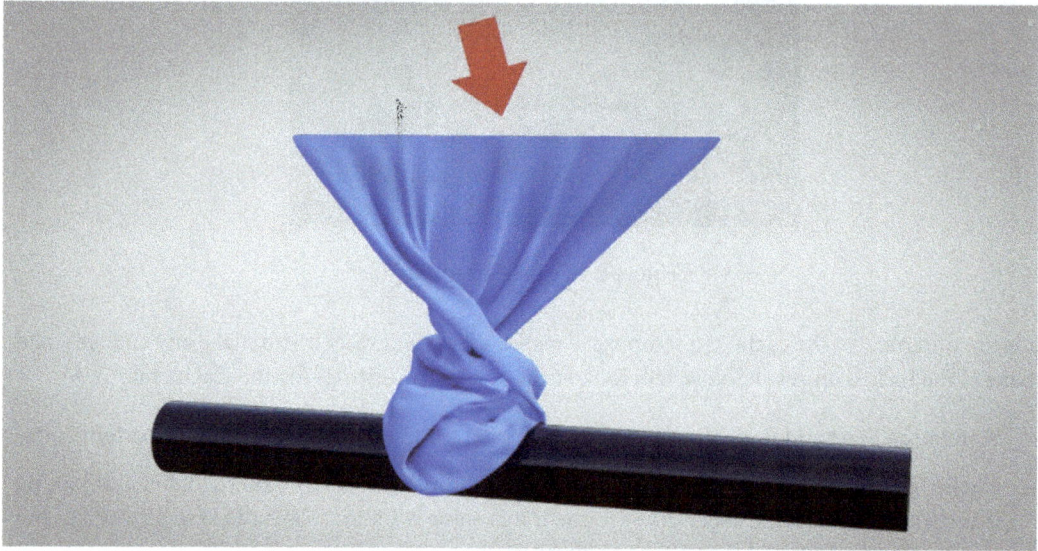

Figure 6.17 – Goal example

Since **Goal** is trying to pin the vertices in place, this means any animation data will work for the soft body simulation. You could have an object fly across the scene but still have soft body physics! When **Goal** is enabled, the entire object is going to be *pinned*. If you only want some parts of the object to use **Goal**, you can create a vertex group and paint where you want the pinning to happen.

Let's learn about vertex groups a bit more and how they work in Blender. As mentioned earlier, vertex groups are used to assign a value to a vertex from a range of 0 to 1. To create a new vertex group, you can manually paint vertices by pressing *Tab* and selecting **Weight Paint**. Now, you can select the value you want at the top and start painting on the mesh.

Just as when creating a soft body simulation, you need to have geometry to use weight paint. If you try to paint on a plane with only four vertices, this won't work very well because there is no geometry in the middle to paint on. So, make sure you have enough geometry when painting on an object. You can see an example of a high polygon plane in the following screenshot:

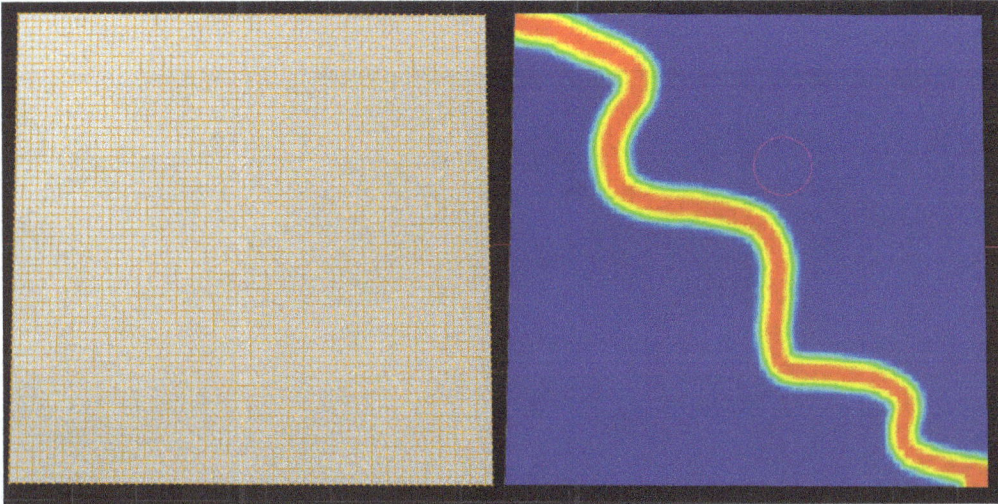

Figure 6.18 – Weight paint geometry

Another way to create a vertex group is by going over to the **Object Data Properties** panel and clicking + next to **Vertex Groups**, as illustrated in the following screenshot:

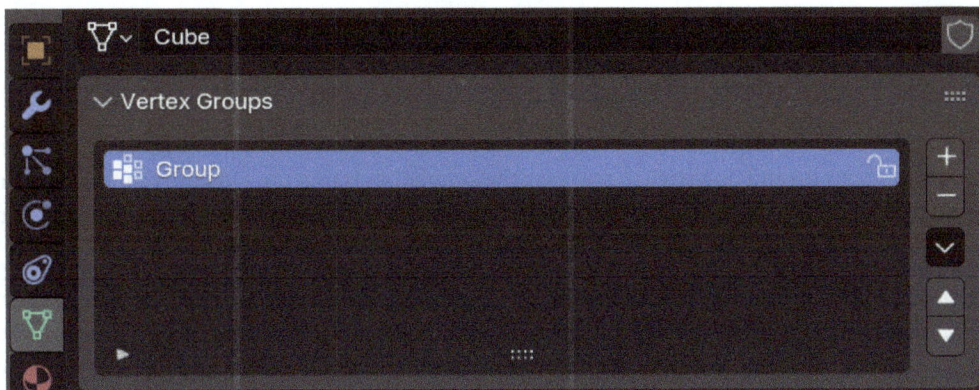

Figure 6.19 – Vertex Groups

At this point, you can go into **Edit Mode** and select the parts of the mesh that you want to be a part of the vertex group. Choose your **Weight** value from a range of 0 to 1, then click **Assign**. You can also remove a vertex group by selecting parts of the mesh and clicking on **Remove**. If you want to delete a vertex group, just click on the – sign. Once you have created your group, you can assign it to the soft body simulation by selecting it in the **Vertex Group** dropdown menu, as illustrated in the following screenshot:

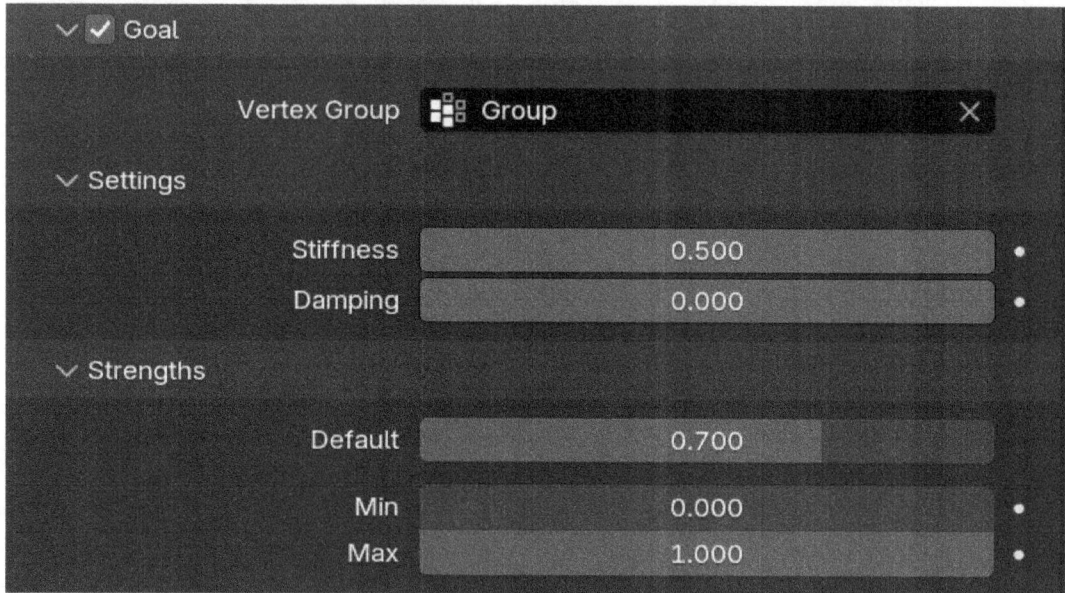

Figure 6.20 – Soft body Goal

Let's jump back into the settings and learn what each one does, as follows:

- **Strengths**: Let's skip **Stiffness** and **Damping** for a second and talk about **Strengths**. The reason the object bobs up and down when you play the simulation is that the **Default** value of the goal is set at 0.7, so it's only pinning the vertices at about 70%. If this value is set at 1 instead, then the entire object/pinned vertices will be stuck in place and won't be able to move.

- **Min** and **Max**: These values offer a way to fine-tune how the vertex group affects the simulation. The **Min** value is going to be the minimum strength for the lowest vertex weight. Let's say you assign the entire object with a vertex group weight of 0 and you set the **Min** value to 1. What do you think is going to happen? The object is going to be completely stuck because it's now using a strength value of 1 for the goal. After all, that is the minimum. **Max** works the same way—it controls the pinning strength of all vertices with a weight of 1.

- **Stiffness**: Jumping back up to **Stiffness**, this setting controls how stiff the pinning will be. In the following screenshot, **Stiffness** on the left is set at 0.2, and on the right, it is set at 0.999 (which is the highest value). As you can see, the left side is very loose and the pinning is not very stiff:

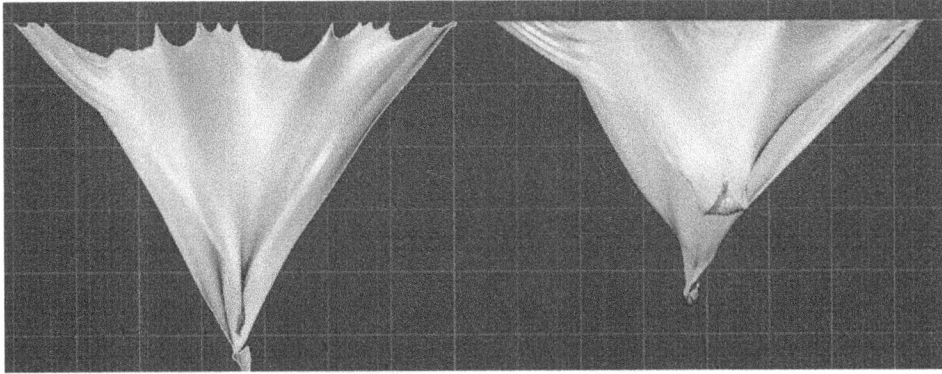

Figure 6.21 – Stiffness example

- Finally, the **Damping** value will dampen the movement of the soft body until it stops moving. The higher you set this value, the faster the object will stop moving.

Goal is very useful and can come in handy when trying to create certain simulations, such as flags and anything else that you need to pin. Next up, we are going to discuss the **Edges** tab.

Edges

The **Edges** option is what gives the soft body object some structure. So instead of collapsing in on itself, it will retain its shape. Basically, when **Edges** is enabled, it adds virtual springs to all edges of the object. You can see an example here:

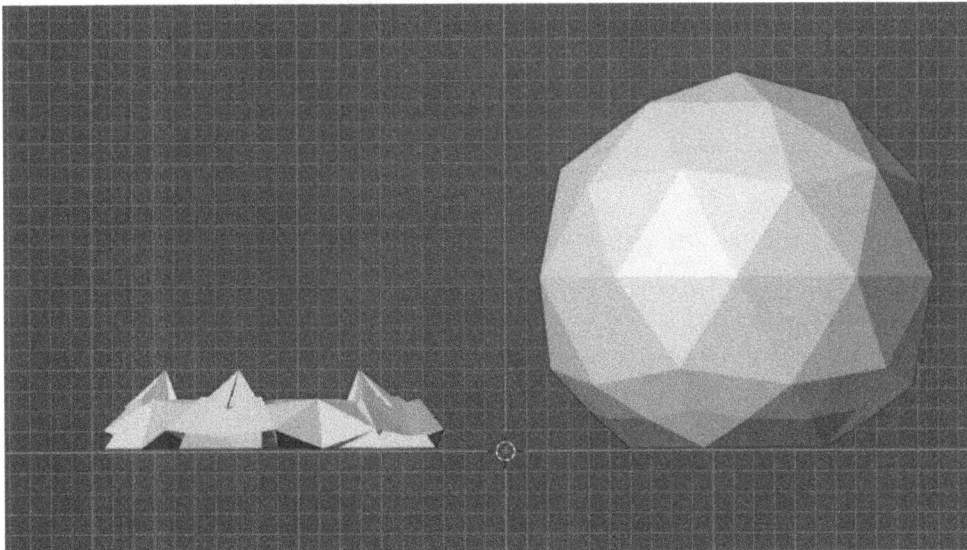

Figure 6.22 – Edges example

Here, you can see the **Edges** settings:

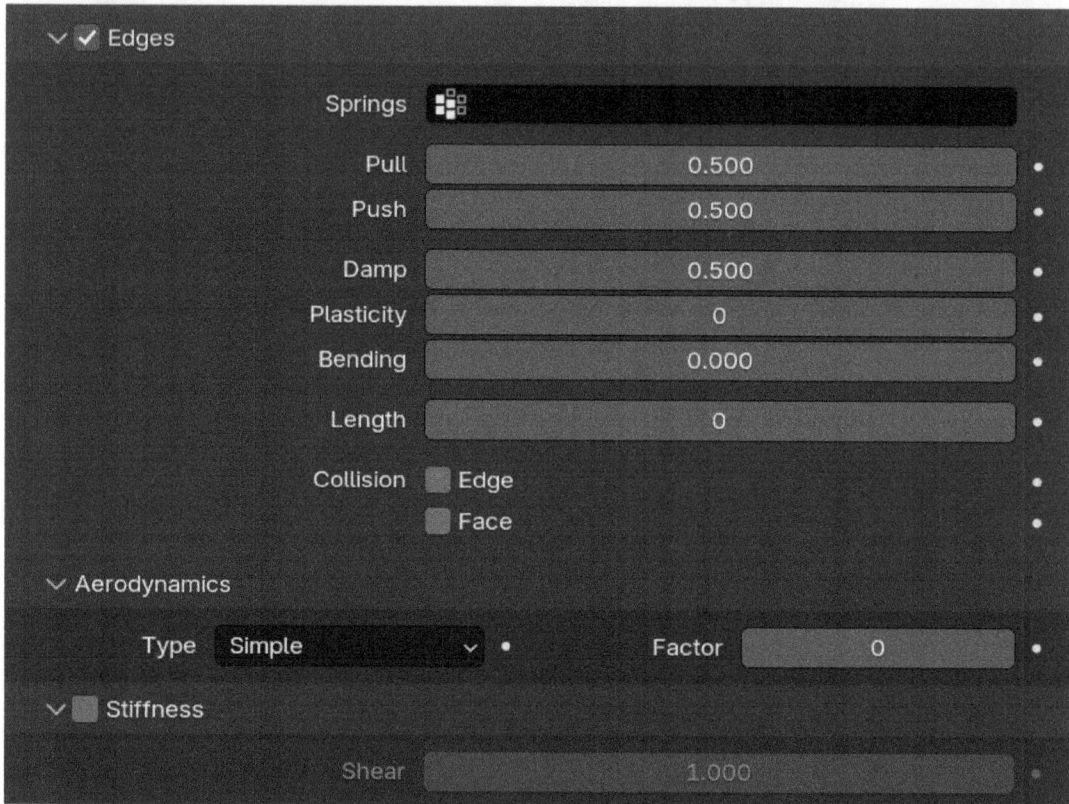

Figure 6.23 – The Edges tab settings

Let's go through the settings now, as follows:

- **Springs**: Just as in the **Goal** tab, we have the **Springs** option to assign a vertex group to control where these are and how strong they will act.

- **Pull**: This value basically acts as a rubber band for the simulation. The higher this value, the stronger the *rubber band* is, which means the edges will stick together rather than being stretched out. In the following screenshot, the left image has a **Pull** value of 0.1, and the right has a value of 0.999. As you can see, the left example is being stretched out a lot more:

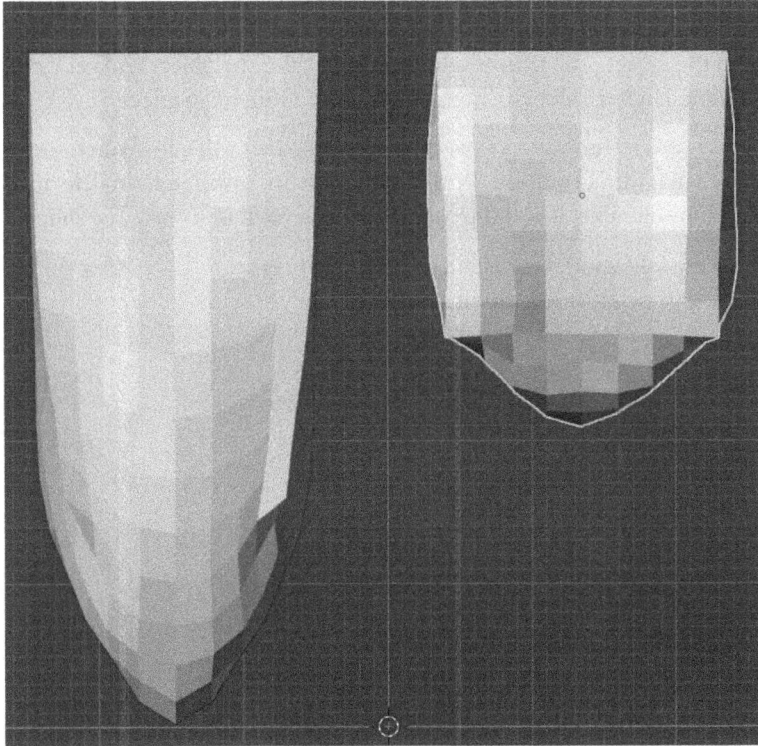

Figure 6.24 – Pull example

- **Push**: This value, on the other hand, controls how much the soft body resists being crushed. You can think of it as how strong the springs inside something are. Higher values will result in higher resistance. In the following screenshot, the **Push** value is set at 0.6 on the left and 0.9 on the right:

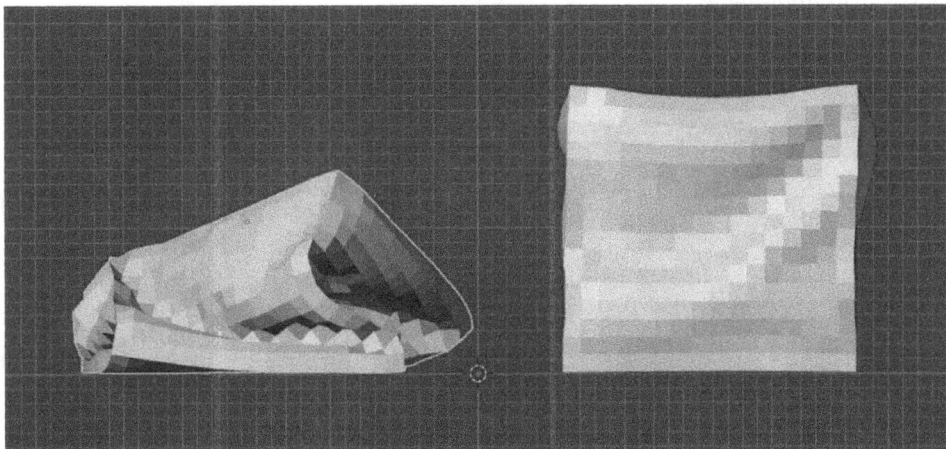

Figure 6.25 – Push example

- **Damp**: Sometimes, when creating a soft body simulation, there will be a lot of little movements and jiggling in the object. The **Damp** value will help calm the object and get rid of a lot of that subtle movement. Higher values, of course, will have more of an effect.

- **Plasticity**: This is a very fun value to play around with. This will allow you to deform the mesh permanently when it hits a collision. With a value of 100, it will remain deformed forever, but if you set it to a lower value, it will then slowly morph back to its original shape.

  You can see, in the following screenshot, that **Plasticity** is set to 100. After the sphere collides with the cubes, it gets deformed, and it stays that way:

Figure 6.26 – Plasticity example

- **Bending**: This controls how much bending there will be in the simulation. At a value of 0, the mesh will just collapse in on itself, but at higher values, the mesh will retain its structure. You can see an example here:

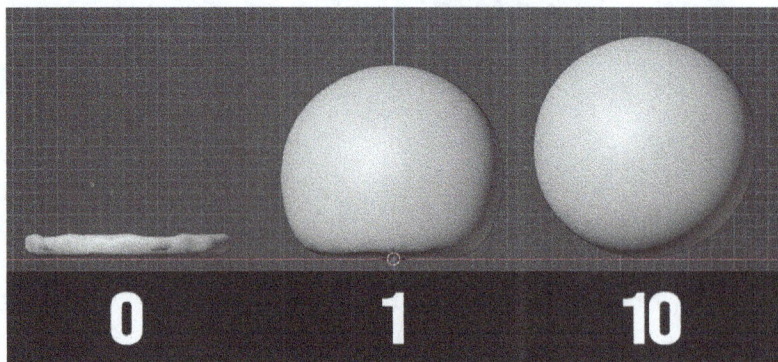

Figure 6.27 – Bending example

- **Length**: This value will either shrink or expand your mesh according to the value you set. For example, if **Length** is set at 70, then the mesh will shrink down to 70% of its size. If the value is set at 150, then the mesh will expand 50% past its original size.

- **Collision**

  - **Edge** and **Face**: These checkboxes will allow the soft body simulation to collide with the edges or the faces. Normally, vertices are the only thing that collide with collisions, but enabling either **Edge** or **Face** will allow them to collide as well. When you enable **Face**, keep in mind that it can be pretty computational, and you might get a lot of jittering on the object because the **Damp** setting does not affect it.

- **Aerodynamics**: This value allows the soft body object to have some air drag in the scene. The **Factor** value controls how much air drag there will be. To see this in effect, you will need to set the **Factor** value quite high, such as a value of 2000 or so. This will make the air around the object very dense, which will make the object fall slower and deform.

  There are two different types of aerodynamics: **Simple** and **Lift Force**. **Simple** is faster to calculate but less accurate. **Lift Force** is slower to calculate but the simulation will be closer to a real-world scenario.

- **Stiffness**: This adds virtual springs to the edges of a face, and the **Shear** value controls how stiff those springs are. With **Stiffness** enabled, a cube is prevented from collapsing in on itself. In the following screenshot, the cube on the left does not have **Stiffness** enabled, but the one on the right does:

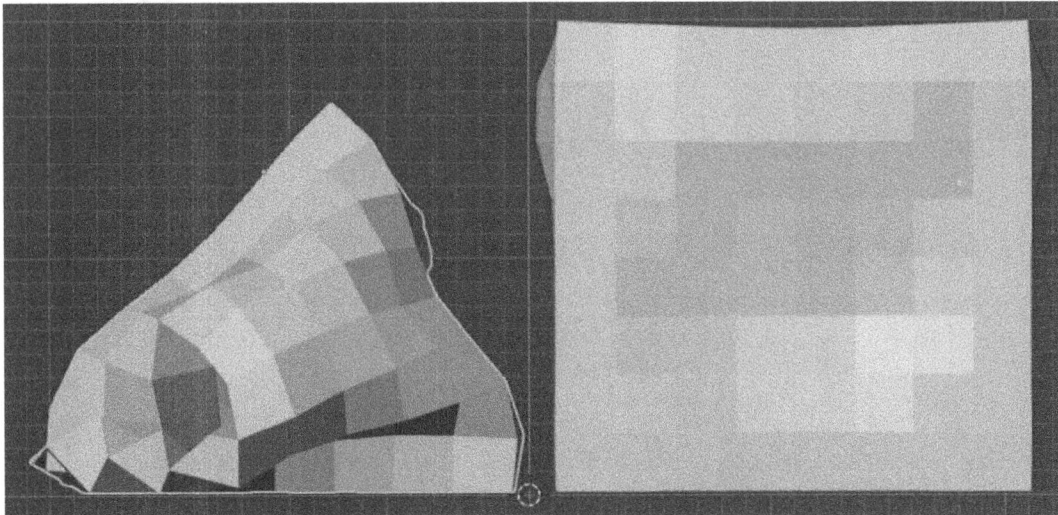

Figure 6.28 – Stiffness example

One thing to note is that **Stiffness** only works with quad faces. A quad face is a face with four vertices. A face with three vertices will not work, and the **Stiffness** setting won't have any effect.

And that is all the settings in the **Edges** tab. Next up, let's discuss how you can have the soft body collide with itself using **Self Collision**!

Self Collision

Self Collision is exactly what it sounds like. If enabled, the soft body will collide with itself. This is useful when creating blankets or clothing. If it's not enabled, the soft body will just pass through itself and not collide. In the following screenshot, you will see, on the left, an example with a soft body and **Self Collision** enabled. As you can see, it's colliding with itself as it swings down, unlike the example on the right, in which **Self Collision** is not enabled:

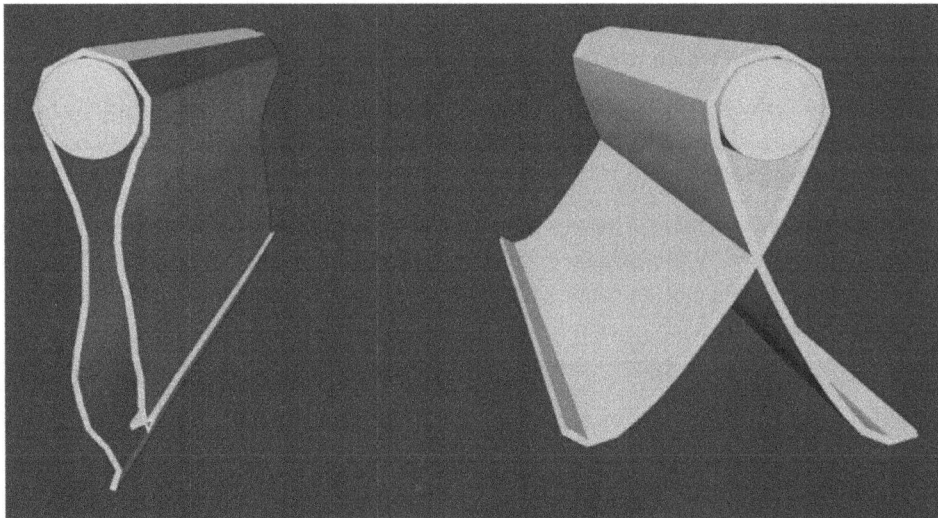

Figure 6.29 – Self Collision example

Now, let's jump into the settings of **Self Collision** and understand how it works. You can see these here:

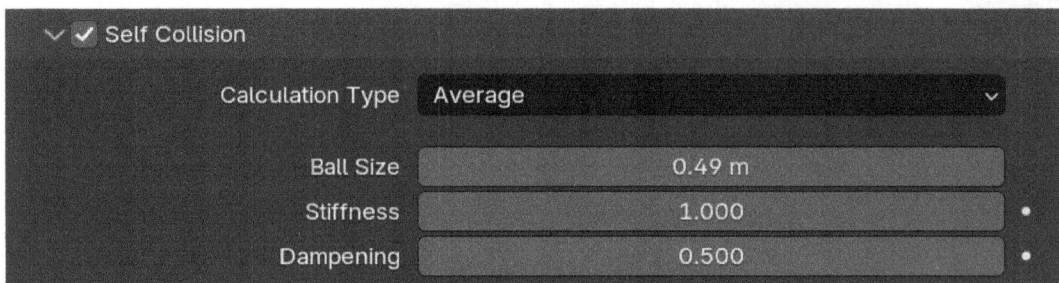

Figure 6.30 – Self Collision settings

Self Collision works by creating a small virtual ball around each vertex and using that for the collision. The size of that virtual ball can be controlled by the **Ball Size** setting in the **Self Collision** tab. When this value is set to high, a vertex collision area might intersect with another. This causes the soft body to stretch out to compensate for the collision area. If you find your soft body object expanding when you enable **Self Collision**, you probably need to lower the **Ball Size** value.

In the following screenshot, you will see an example of what the **Ball Size** collision would look like if it were visible:

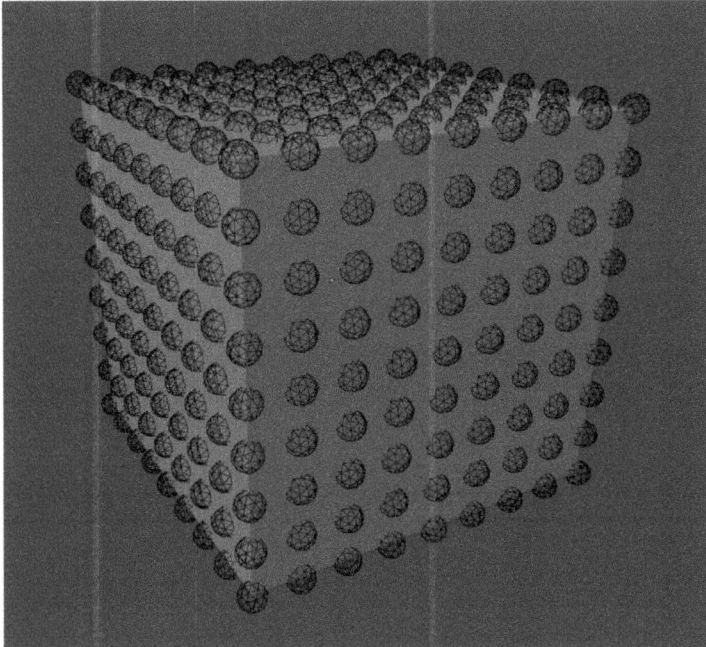

Figure 6.31 – Ball collision example

Now, let's talk about the settings!

- **Calculation Type**: This determines how the size of the collision ball size will be set. You can choose from the following options:

  - **Manual**: You manually set the size of the collision ball.

  - **Average**: Takes the average length of each edge and multiplies it by the **Ball Size** value.

  - **Minimal**: Takes the smallest edge on the object and multiplies that by the **Ball Size** value.

  - **Maximal**: Does the opposite. It takes the largest edge and multiples it by the **Ball Size** value to figure out the collision.

  - **Average Min & Max** adds both, divides by 2, and multiplies the result by the **Ball Size** value.

For most situations, you don't need to change these settings, so just stick with **Average**.

- **Stiffness**: This controls how **Self Collision** works when a vertex enters another vertex collision ball. With it set at a high value, it will push the vertex out very quickly. When it's set at a lower value, it will push the vertex out slowly.

- **Dampening**: This is used to slow down a vertex as it gets close to another vertex collision ball. High values will slow it down very quickly.

Most of the time, all you have to do is enable **Self Collision** and all the default settings will work just fine. Keep in mind the simulation will take longer to calculate, so only enable **Self Collision** when it's needed.

Solver

The **Solver** tab helps the simulation be more accurate. Sometimes, with fast-moving collisions, the simulation will have a hard time calculating, and you may get a couple of errors and issues with collisions. However, in this tab, you will be able to change the settings in order to get a more accurate simulation. You can see these settings in the following screenshot:

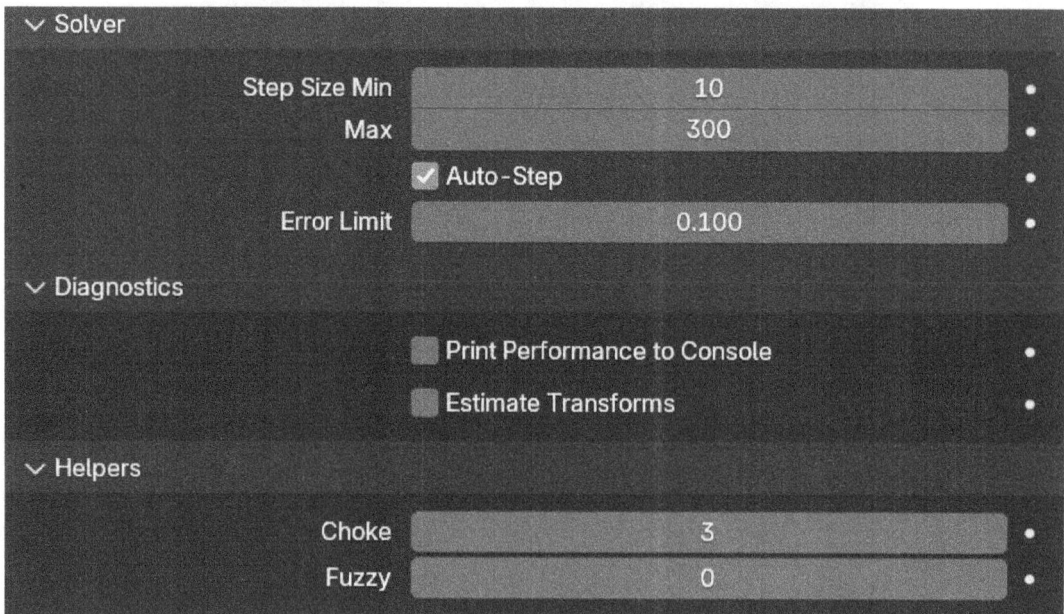

Figure 6.32 – Solver settings

Let's go through each option and talk about how they can help improve the accuracy of the simulation:

- **Step Size Min**: When the simulation gets errors or if collisions aren't working properly, you will want to turn up this setting. This value is how many times the simulation will be calculated per frame. Increase this if you are having collision problems.

- **Max**: This is the maximum number of steps that will be calculated per frame.

- **Auto-Step**: With this enabled, Blender will automatically set the number of steps per frame based on the velocity of the object.

- **Error Limit**: This value determines the quality and accuracy of the simulation. If you see a lot of errors in the simulation, you may want to turn this setting lower.

- **Print Performance to Console**: This is exactly what it sounds like. It prints out the performance of the simulation to the Blender console and gives you the number of steps the simulation needs to be accurate. To bring up the console, you can go to **Window | Toggle System Console**. To close the console, use the same option.

- **Estimate Transforms**: This option allows you to store all the transformations the soft body object has (movement, rotation, and scale) in the simulation settings.

- **Choke**: If a soft body object penetrates through a collision, the simulation will try to push it out. When it does this, the soft body object will have some velocity. This velocity is controlled by the **Choke** values. Higher values will slow down the soft body as it passes out of a collision.

- **Fuzzy**: This value sets the accuracy of a collision. High values are faster but less accurate, and lower values will give you more accurate results but will run slower.

The **Solver** tab is great and can help solve a lot of errors in the simulation.

Field Weights

The last tab in the soft body simulation is **Field Weights**. This works exactly how it did with the fluid simulation. You can set certain strengths for certain force fields and customize which force fields will work in your simulation.

If you have multiple force fields in your scene, you can choose which collection to use in the **Effector Collection** menu. Now, only the force fields in that collection will affect the simulation.

Before this chapter ends, let's quickly talk about how to make multiple soft body objects interact with each other.

Interacting with multiple soft bodies

For some simulations, you may want multiple soft bodies to interact with each other. If you add multiple objects and try to simulate them just using soft body simulation, they will just pass right through each other. The reason for this is that you need to make sure each soft body also has a **Collision** modifier applied to it—that way, they will collide. It's also important to make sure the **Collision** modifier is below the **Softbody** modifier in the modifier stack, as depicted in the following screenshot:

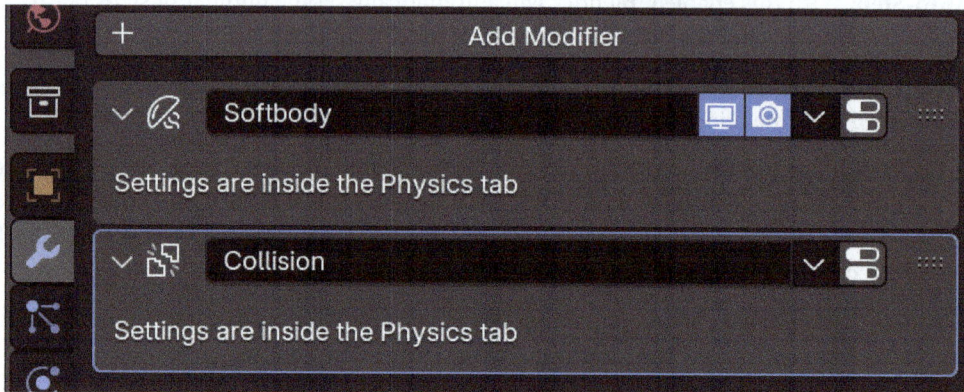

Figure 6.33 – Modifier stack example

If you try to simulate with the **Collision** modifier above the **Softbody** modifier, the collision will be at the original position at the start of the simulation, rather than where the soft body object is. You can move modifiers up and down by dragging the dots on the right side of the modifier.

If done correctly, you should see your soft bodies colliding and interacting with each other, like so:

Figure 6.34 – Interacting soft bodies

And there it is! We have covered every single setting for soft body simulations!

Summary

The goal of this chapter was to give you an understanding of soft body simulations so that you can go out and create your own without having to test every setting to see what it does! We have learned quite a bit, so let's do a quick recap!

First, we discussed how a soft body simulation works and what you need to get started. Then, we learned about collision objects and how they interact with the simulation. Next up were all the settings for soft body objects. We talked about vertex groups and how they interact with **Goal**. We went over all the settings for **Edges**, **Self Collision**, **Solver**, and **Field Weights**, and finally, we ended by learning how to make multiple soft body objects interact with each other.

A soft body simulation is very useful and can save a lot of time when animating and modeling. Be sure to use it in the right way, though, because it is sometimes simpler to do a quick animation rather than a full soft body simulation.

In the next chapter, we will be putting what we learned to the test by creating a full obstacle course for a soft body object to go through!

Join our community on Discord

Join our community's Discord space for discussions with the author and other readers:
`https://packt.link/learn-blender-simulations-discord-invite`

7

Creating a Soft Body Obstacle Course

In the last chapter, we covered everything there is to know about soft body simulation. In this chapter, we will put those skills to the test while creating an obstacle course for a sphere to go through. Knowing what a setting does can be good, but we should also know how to use it properly in our projects. So, the goal of this chapter is to give you a practical understanding of how to use soft body simulation while creating a nice, satisfying animation in the process.

We will start by opening the setup file and getting familiar with the scene. After that, we will start creating the simulation and adding all the physics properties to each of the objects. Next, we will create a glass material and learn how to render it properly in EEVEE. We will be covering a lot of tricks and techniques throughout this chapter, and by the end, you will have created a nice obstacle course animation! You will also be able to apply what you learned here for your own future soft body simulation projects!

In this chapter, we'll be covering the following topics:

- Creating the simulation
- Using Soft Body Goal
- Creating a glass material in EEVEE
- Setting up camera tracking

Technical requirements

This chapter requires you to have Blender version 4.2 or above installed.

To download Blender, visit www.blender.org.

Make sure to also download the setup file, which includes some basic modeling of the obstacle course: `https://github.com/PacktPublishing/Learn-Blender-4-Simulations-the-Right-Way/tree/main/Chapter%207`

Creating the simulation

The first thing to do is to download the `Obstacle Course Setup.blend` file. This includes a basic obstacle course scene, with lighting and materials already in place. Feel free to change or add any more obstacles you would like the sphere to go through!

Once you have downloaded the file, open it up and get familiar with the scene and all the objects in it. There are a total of 17 objects, and each of them is named so it's easy to follow along. You can view the name of each object by looking at the **Outliner** in the top-right corner. Be sure to look at the **Outliner** throughout the chapter so you know what objects to select and work on.

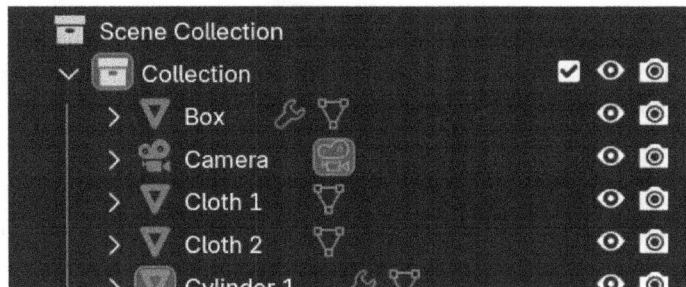

Figure 7.1 – Outliner

Once you are familiar with the scene and all the objects in it, let's start working on creating the simulation! Let's start at the very top and work our way down the objects. Be sure to constantly restart and play the simulation while we are working on it to make sure everything is working properly.

Adding the soft body

The object that will be going through the obstacle course is an icosphere called **Soft Body Sphere**. Let's start here:

1. Select the sphere, head over to the **Physics** panel, and choose **Soft Body**.
2. Set **Mass** to 2 so it's a bit heavier.
3. On the **Cache** tab, let's set **End Frame** to 600. This way, the physics will simulate for much longer when we play the animation. If you decide to add more obstacles, you may need to change this value.

4. For now, uncheck **Goal** so the object doesn't float. Later in this chapter, we will re-enable it and then animate some of the settings and values to control how **Goal** operates in the simulation.

5. On the **Edges** tab, let's change a few settings. To give the sphere some structure, set the **Push** and **Pull** values to 0.6. When the sphere collides with something, it's going to have a lot of movement and jitteriness. To calm it down a bit, let's set **Damp** to 40. To prevent the sphere from collapsing and losing its structure, set **Bending** to 2.5.

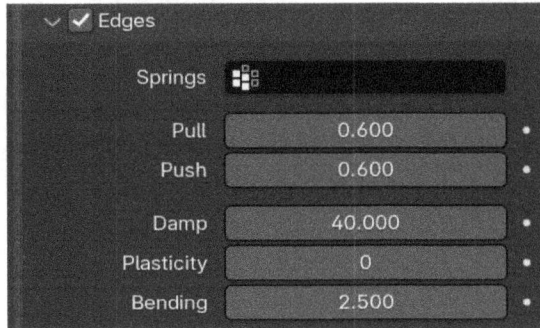

Figure 7.2 – Edges settings

With that done, let's move on to collision objects!

Adding collisions

If we play the animation, the sphere will pass through all the objects. This is not what we want, so let's add collisions to everything in the course:

1. Select **Cylinder 1**, which is the top cylinder that the sphere is inside of, and give it collision by selecting **Collision** in the **Physics** panel.

2. Next, head over to the **Modifier** panel and make sure the **Collision** modifier is *above* the **Solidify** modifier or you will get some clipping issues. You can move modifiers up or down by dragging the dots on the right side. You will have to do this for most objects in this obstacle course:

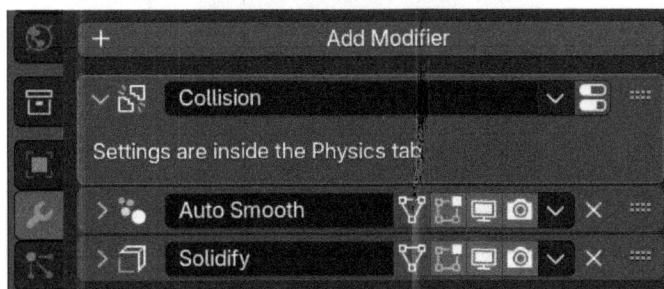

Figure 7.3 – Modifier stack

It's also important to note that the normals on the **Cylinder 1** object are pointing toward the inside of the mesh rather than the outside.

Figure 7.4 – Direction of the normals

This is because the collision is based on the direction of the normals. If they were pointing to the outside of the mesh, the soft body would not collide but simply fall through. View the previous chapter on collision objects for more of an explanation.

If you want to see the direction of the normals of your object, you can go into edit mode and, in the **Mesh Edit Mode** menu, turn on the **Vertex**, **Edge**, or **Face** normals and change the size. This will bring out the blue lines in your mesh (*Figure 7.4*) and show which direction the normals are facing.

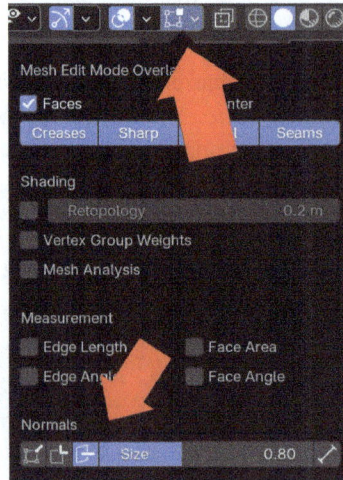

Figure 7.5 – Mesh Edit Mode menu

3. We don't need collision on **Cylinder 2** as the sphere will not interact with it, so let's skip to **Cylinder 3**. Select it and add collision. If we play the simulation, you will notice that this happens:

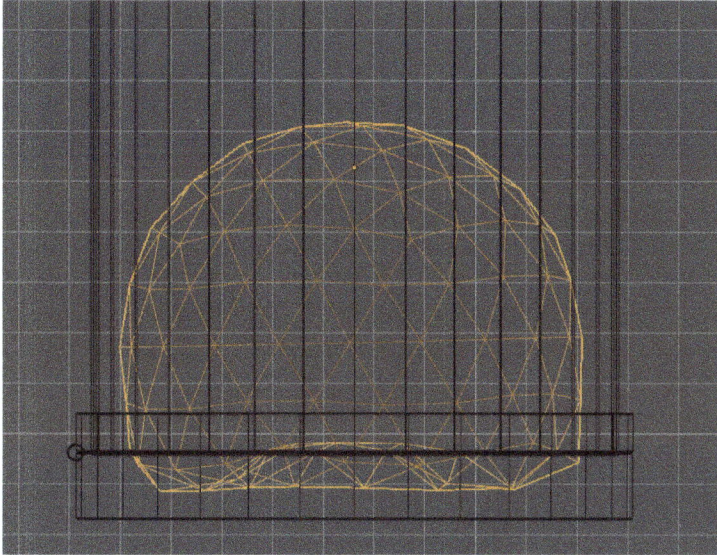

Figure 7.6 – Collision example

The reason this is happening is that the **Inner** and **Outer** thickness zones are overlapping. Remember in the last chapter when we went over the **Outer** and **Inner** zones? In this case, the **Cylinder 3** object is thin enough that the collision boundaries on the outside and inside of the mesh are overlapping. This causes the soft-body object to get stuck.

4. To fix this, set the **Inner** thickness of **Cylinder 3** to the lowest value, 0.001. Now it should collide properly without getting stuck.

To save time in this chapter, there is already some basic animation of **Cylinder 3** opening and closing. This will cause the sphere to fall out and go down the obstacle course.

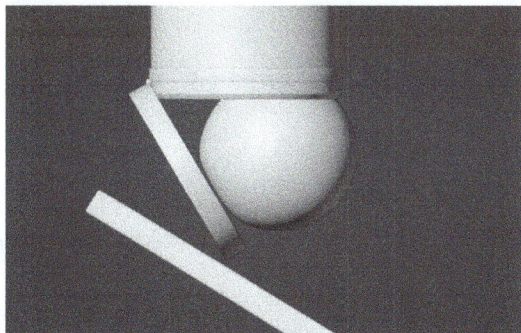

Figure 7.7 – Cylinder opening

5.   Next, let's work on the platforms! Select **Platform 1** and add a **Collision** modifier, and again, make sure it's at the top of the modifier stack. We don't need to change the **Inner** value because this object is a plane with a **Solidify** modifier.

6.   Repeat *step 5* for **Platform 2** as well!

7.   Select the **Gear Left** and **Gear Right** objects, and let's give them the **Collision** modifier as well. Let's also make these gears rotate as the animation plays.

To do this, select **Gear Right** and open the **Properties** panel by pressing *N*. On the **Rotation** tab, for the **Y** rotation, type #frame/-25. This will add a rotation driver to the gear, and now it will rotate to the left as you play the animation! The value -25 sets the speed of the rotation. If you want it to go faster, reduce this value, and if you want it to go slower, increase this value.

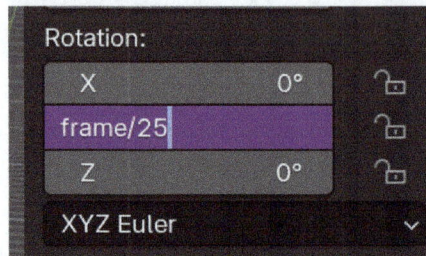

Figure 7.8 – Driver example

Do the same thing for **Gear Left**, except this time, type #frame/25. Now **Gear Left** will rotate to the right as the animation plays.

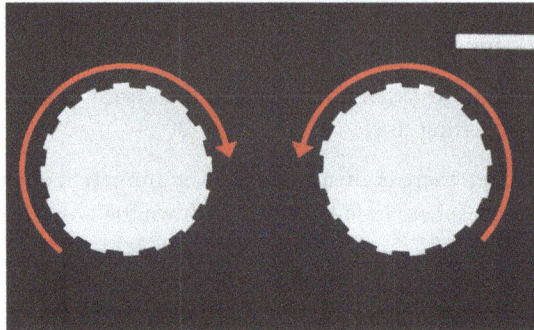

Figure 7.9 – Gears rotating

8.   Add collision to the rest of the objects, except for **Goal Guide**, and make sure to move the **Collision** modifier to the top of the stack for each object. This will ensure the simulation collisions works properly.

There we go! We now have collision for all the objects in the scene. Next, let's add the cloth simulation to both **Cloth 1** and **Cloth 2**.

Creating the cloth simulation

The cloth simulation works very similarly to the soft body simulation. It adds physics to a mesh object and simulates the behavior of cloth. You can change the type of cloth you want to simulate and much more. We will be diving deep into this simulation in the next chapter!

For now, let's just add the cloth simulation to our current simulation. What we are going to do is add the cloth physics to both **Cloth 1** and **Cloth 2**. This will give us a very nice look when the soft body collides with it. So, let's get started:

1. Select the object called **Cloth 1**, then head over to the **Physics** panel and select **Cloth**.

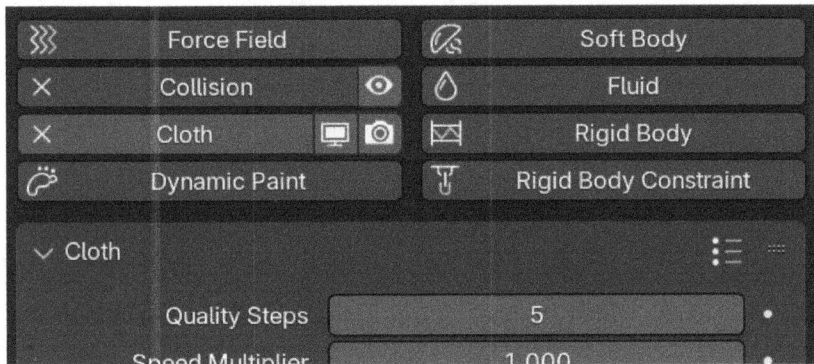

Figure 7.10 – Cloth physics

2. Scroll down to the **Cache** tab and set **End Frame** to 600 to match the length of the animation.

3. If we play the animation, the cloth will just fall straight down. What we need to do to fix this is use the **Pin Group** option on the **Shape** tab.

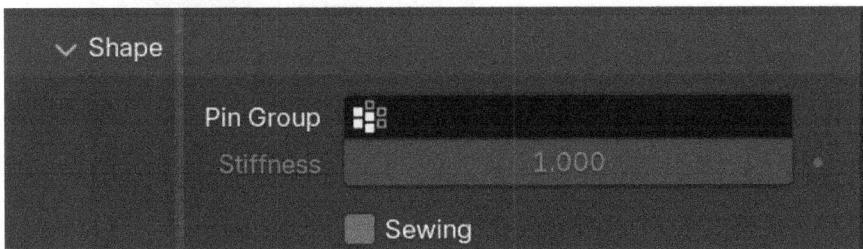

Figure 7.11 – Pin Group

This is the same process as **Soft Body Goal**. We first need to create a vertex group and assign the corners to it. Go into **Edit Mode** and select the faces on each corner.

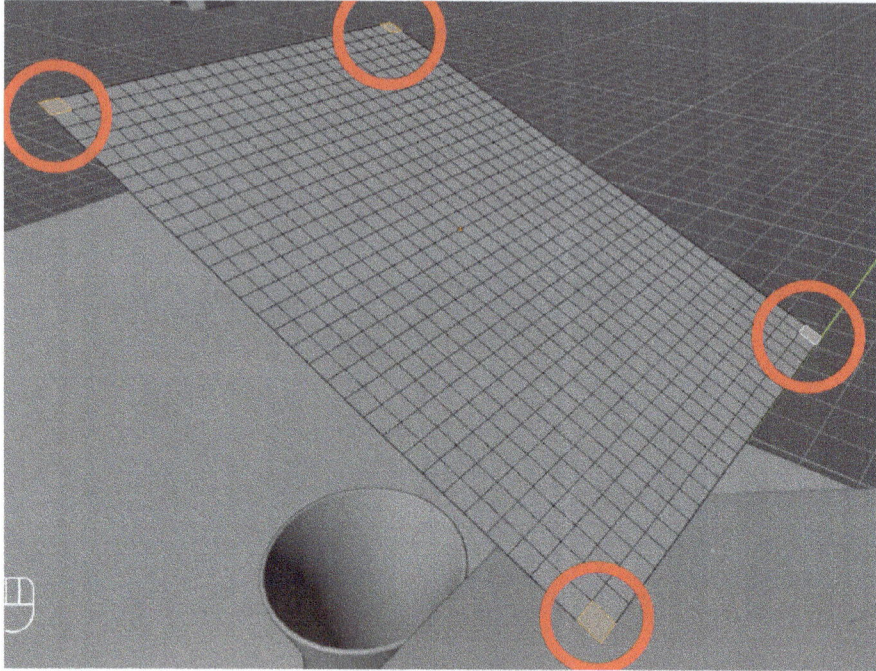

Figure 7.12 – Selected corners

4. Jump over to the **Object Data** panel (it looks like a triangle with dots) and create a new vertex group by hitting +. Then hit **Assign** with those faces selected. View the following figure:

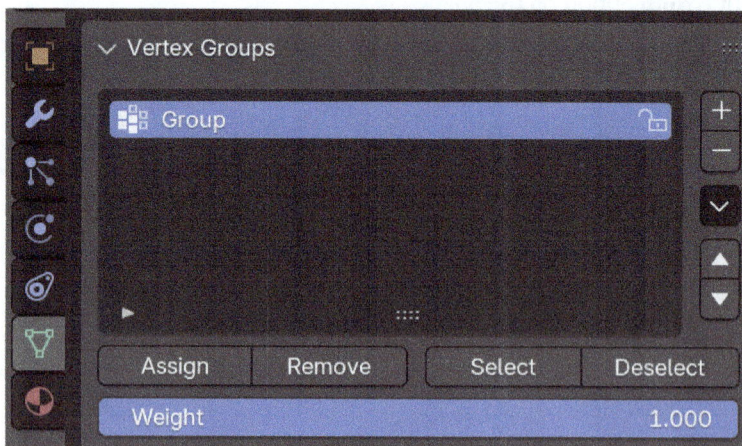

Figure 7.13 – Vertex groups

5. Next, head back to the **Physics** panel and select the new vertex group in the **Pin Group** menu.

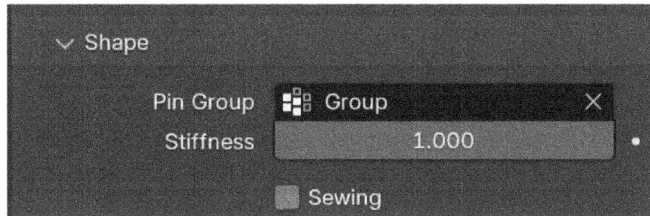

Figure 7.14 – Cloth Pin Group

6. Make sure you move the **Cloth** modifier *above* the **Collision** modifier. This will make sure that the soft body collides with the cloth, and it will take the cloth deformation into account.

7. Finally, select the **Soft Body Sphere** object, and add a **Collision** modifier as well. Now the cloth and the sphere will interact with each other. Again, make sure the **Soft Body** modifier is above **Collision**.

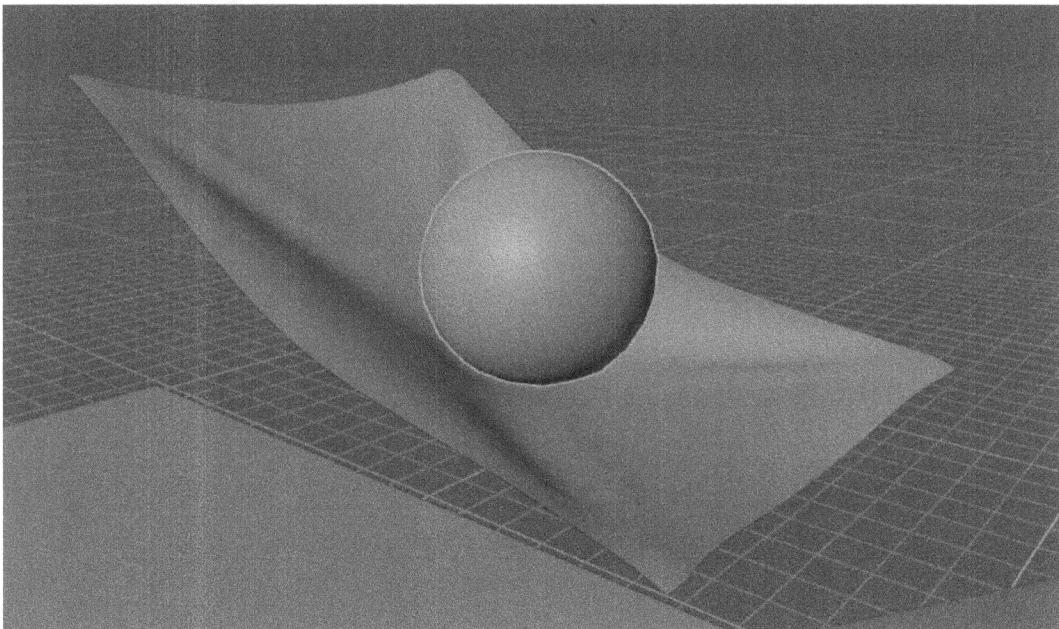

Figure 7.15 – Cloth collision

8. Instead of repeating all the steps we just did for the **Cloth 2** object, let's just delete it and duplicate the **Cloth 1** object. You can duplicate an object by selecting it and pressing *Shift + D*. Then rotate and place the duplicated object where the **Cloth 2** object used to be.

Now let's move on to using **Soft Body Goal**!

Using Soft Body Goal

In the last step, before we bake in this simulation, we will learn how to use **Soft Body Goal** to make the sphere follow a curve. If you remember the previous chapter, **Goal** allows you to pin and animate a soft body. The soft body's "goal" is to try and get back to its original position, or where the origin point is. This is why, when you enable **Goal**, the object will just bob up and down: it's trying to get back to the origin point.

So, what we are going to do is turn on **Goal** when the soft body sphere enters the **Glass Tube** object. Then the sphere will follow the curve that is inside, bouncing and hitting the walls until it falls out the other side. Let's go ahead and get started:

1. First, we need to find when the sphere enters the glass tube. Play the animation from the start to figure that out. For my simulation, it was at around **Frame 420**. Yours may be slightly different.

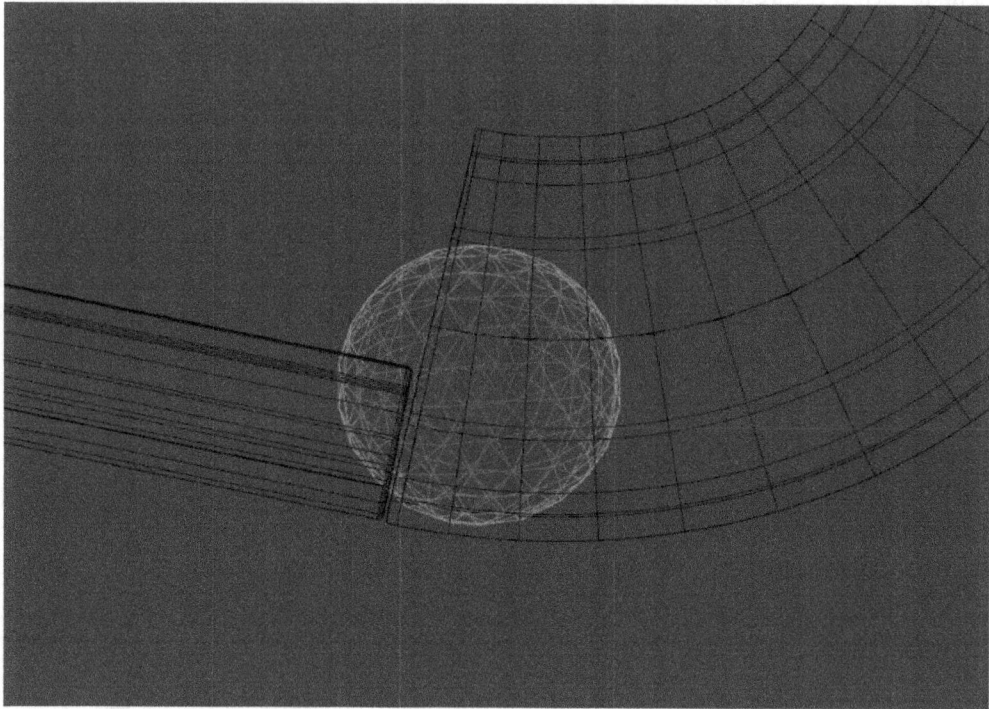

Figure 7.16 – Frame 432

2. Enable **Goal** for the **Soft Body Sphere** object in the **Physics** panel.

3. Unfortunately, Blender does not allow the **Default** strength value to be animated. (You can see there is no animation button next to the setting in *Figure 7.17*.) So instead, we will be using the **Min** and **Max** values:

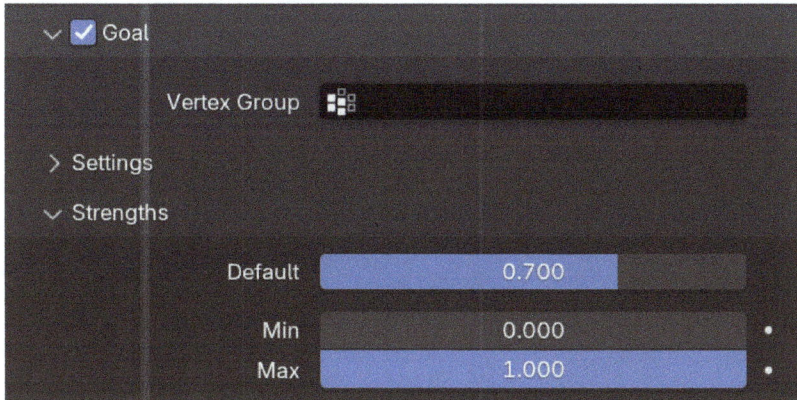

Figure 7.17 – Goal strength settings

Let's set both values to 0 for **Frame 419** and add a keyframe to each of them. You can do this by clicking that little dot next to the value or by hitting *I* while hovering your mouse over the value. This should turn the setting into a highlighted yellow color.

4. Jump to the next frame, that is, **Frame 420**. Set both the **Min** and **Max** values to 0.5 and add another keyframe:

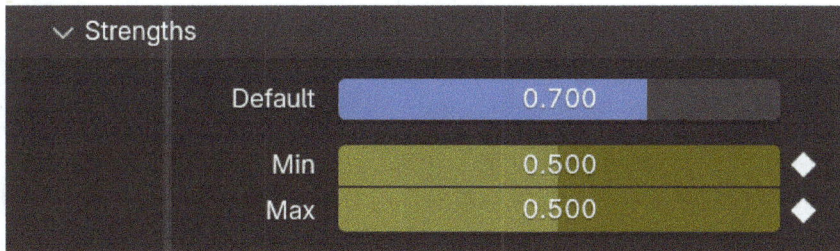

Figure 7.18 – Animated Min and Max values

5. Now we can set up the sphere following a curve! To do this, head over to the **Constraints** panel and add a **Follow Path** constraint.

6. In the **Target** menu, select **Goal Guide**, which is the curve inside **Glass Tube**. **Offset** controls when the object will start following the curve. We need to set this to 420. Then click on **Animate Path**.

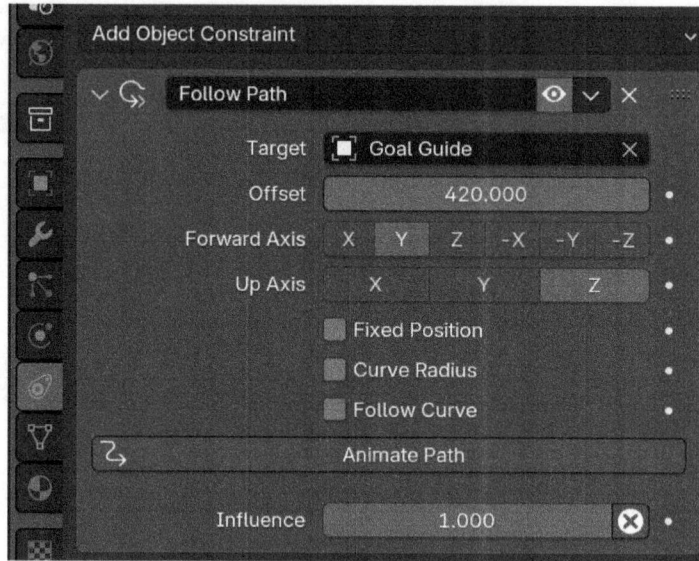

Figure 7.19 – Follow Path constraint

7. One issue that you might see is the sphere has moved very far away! This is due to the **Follow Path** constraint. Don't worry, it's an easy fix!

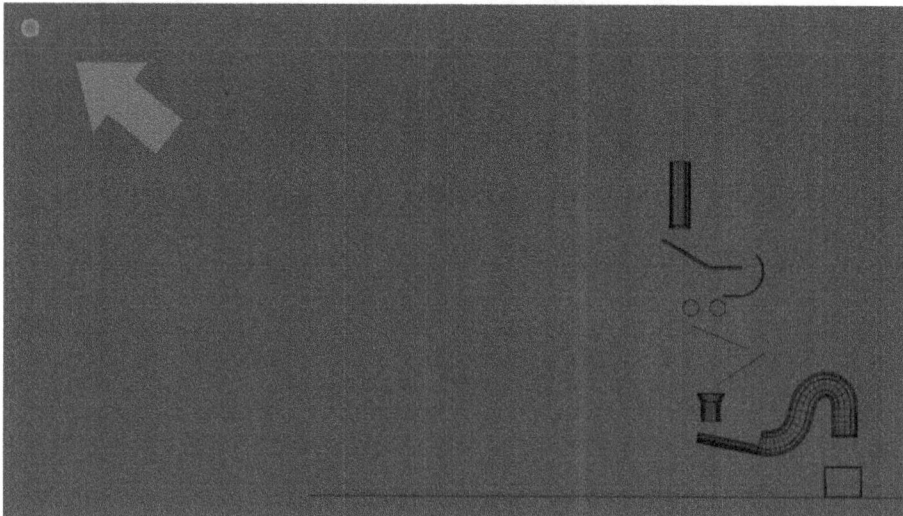

Figure 7.20 – Sphere position

We need to set up some **Location** keyframes on the **Soft Body Sphere** object. When we animate it following the curve, the origin point of the sphere needs to be at the start of the curve to work properly:

8. First, make sure you are on **Frame 1**; then hide the **Follow Path** constraint by clicking the **Eye** icon at the top of the constraint. View *Figure 7.19*. This will make the sphere snap back to its original position.

9. Next, let's place our cursor at the location of the sphere. We can do this by having the sphere selected, pressing *Shift + S*, and choosing **Cursor to Selected**.

10. Re-enable the **Follow Path** constraint by clicking the **Eye** icon. The sphere should have moved far away again. To bring it back, press *Shift + S*, and this time, choose **Selection to Cursor**. This will snap the sphere back to its original position.

    The reason we did this method instead of just moving the sphere manually is because it might not end up in the exact same position as when we started this chapter. Even the tiniest bit of position difference could change the outcome of the simulation, resulting in the keyframes we added in *step 4* not lining up properly.

11. Now let's add a **Location** keyframe! On **Frame 1** with the sphere inside the starting tube, let's press *K* and add a **Location** keyframe.

12. Next, let's jump to **Frame 420** and move the sphere all the way down to the start of the curve. Then add another **Location** keyframe.

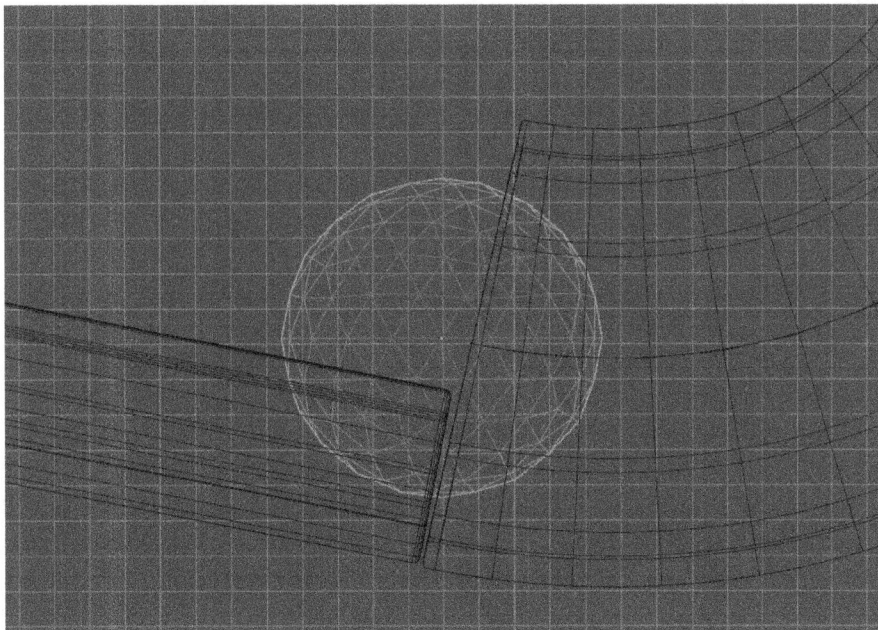

Figure 7.21 – Start of the curve

13. With all that done, the **Soft Body Sphere** object should follow the curve at **Frame 420** and make its way through the **Glass Tube** object. However, we also want to turn off **Goal** when it reaches the end. To do this, play the animation until the sphere is about to exit the tube.

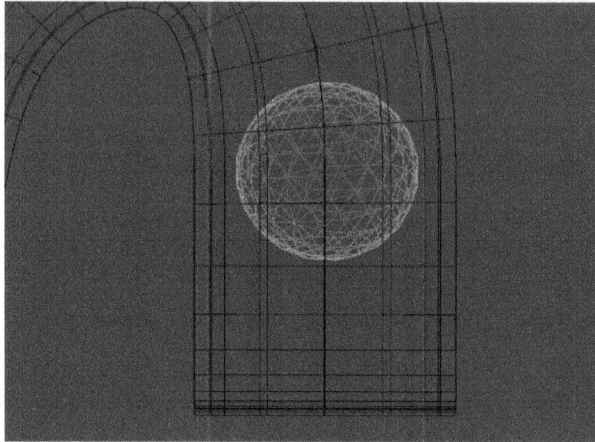

Figure 7.22 – End position

Add a keyframe to both **Min** and **Max** with a value of 0.5.

14. Then, on the next frame, let's set the **Min** and **Max** values to 0 and add another keyframe. Now the **Goal** will turn off, and the sphere will act like a normal soft body.

15. You may notice that when we play the animation, the sphere jumps to the right just slightly. This is because the origin point is moving right at the start of the simulation.

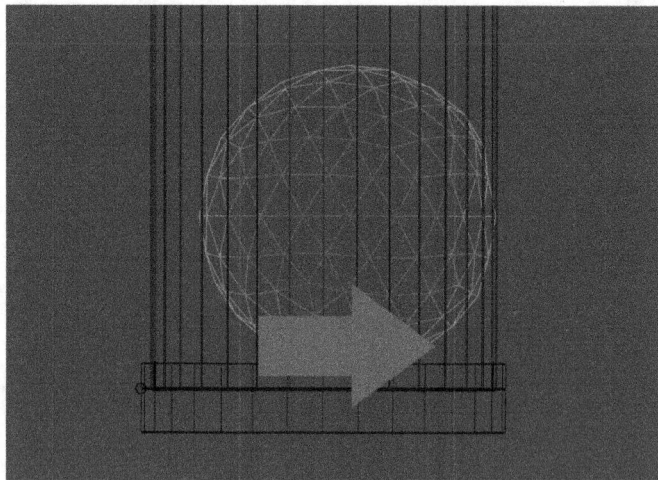

Figure 7.23 – Sphere start

To fix this, all you have to do is set the **Simulation Start** value in the **Cache** tab to 0 instead of 1.

With that done, click on **Bake All Dynamics**, and that will bake in everything, including the cloth simulations. There we go, the simulation is done! Make sure to play through it and double-check whether there are any issues. Once you are happy with it, we can move on to creating a nice glass material in EEVEE!

Creating a glass material in EEVEE

If you go into rendered view, you will see some materials already in place. These are just basic metallic materials with a dark color. Feel free to change them however you like. What we are going to do now, though, is learn how to create a glass shader in EEVEE!

Creating a nice glass material in EEVEE is a bit more complicated than just adding a glass shader. We need to set up some render settings and then add a few nodes to the material to get it to look good! Let's get started:

1. First, head over to the **Render** panel and turn on **Raytracing**. This is going to allow the objects to reflect off each other, and it's what we need to create glass. Also, set **Resolution** to **1:1** for better results!

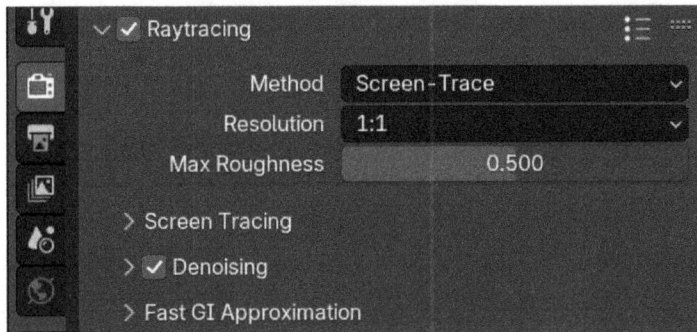

Figure 7.24 – Raytracing

2. In the **Color Management** tab, set **Look** to **High Contrast** to give more contrast to the scene.

    Now let's create the material!

3. Select **Cylinder 1** and head over to the **Shading** workspace at the top of the screen.

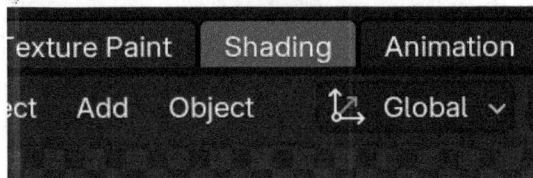

Figure 7.25 – Shading workspace

4. Click **New** to create a new material. Name the material `Glass` so it's easy to find later.

5. In the **Material** panel, scroll down to the **Settings** tab, check **Raytraced Transmission**, and set **Thickness** to **Slab**. This will help the glass look much better.

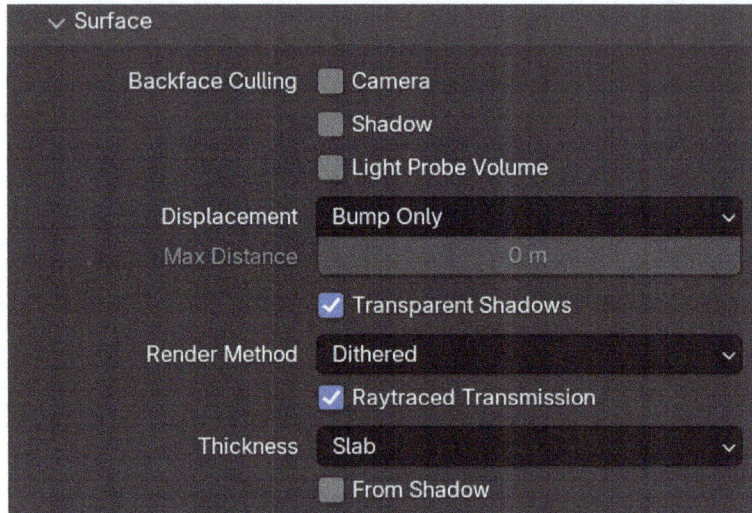

Figure 7.26 – Material settings

6. In the **Node Editor** workspace, let's delete the **Principled BSDF** shader and add a **Glass** shader. To do this, press *Shift + A* and then go to **Shader | Glass BSDF**.

We are starting to get reflections, but we still can't see through the glass so let's fix that!

Figure 7.27 – Basic glass material

7. We are going to do this by making the front of the glass transparent, but the sides will still have reflections. Add a transparent shader by pressing *Shift + A* and going to **Shader | Transparent BSDF**.

8. Next, add a **Mix Shader** node so we can mix the **Transparent** and **Glass BSDF** shaders together. View the following figure:

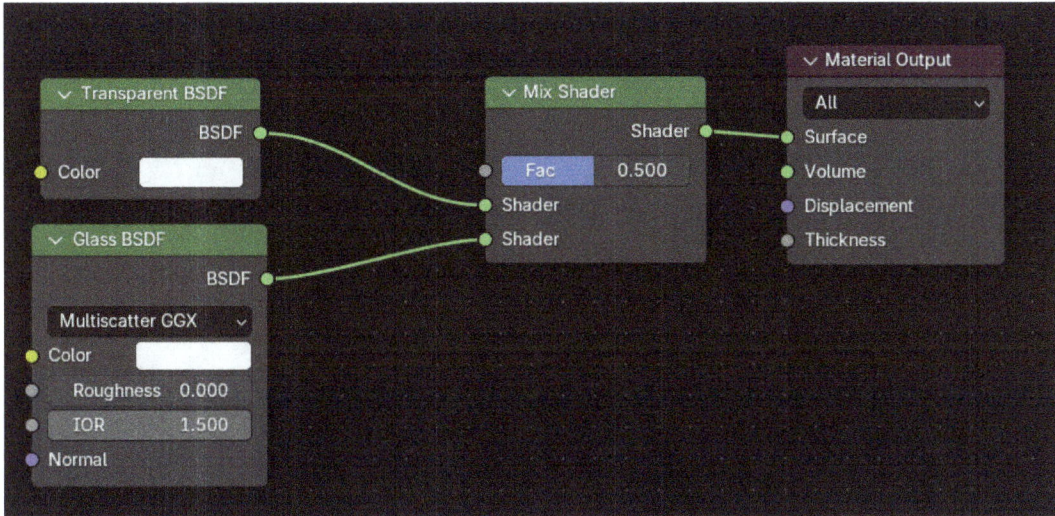

Figure 7.28 – Node setup

9. To control where the transparency is on the object, let's add a **Fresnel** node and plug it into the **Fac** input of **Mix Shader**. Press *Shift + A*, then click on **Input | Fresnel**. A **Fresnel** node basically lightens up the edges of a surface while keeping the middle dark. You can control this by changing the **IOR** value. Let's set this value to 1.100. You can see an example of this in the following figure:

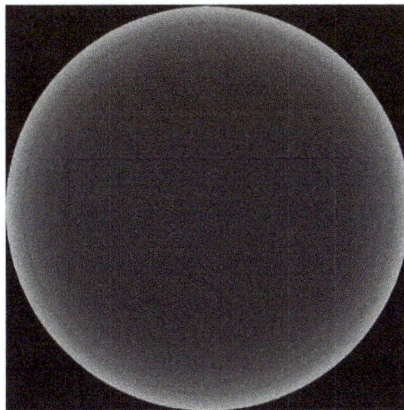

Figure 7.29 – Fresnel on a sphere

In this case, we are adding transparency to the middle of **Cylinder 1**, but the edges will still have that glass shader.

10. Finally, to control how much transparency there is in the glass, add a **Color Ramp** node and place it between the **Frensel** node and the **Mix Shader** node.

11. The left side of the **Color Ramp** node controls the transparency in the middle of the glass and the right side controls the edges. Since the left side is completely black at default, this means the glass is 100% transparent. We do want a little bit of reflection, so let's set the left handle to be more of a gray color. View the following figure to see the full node setup.

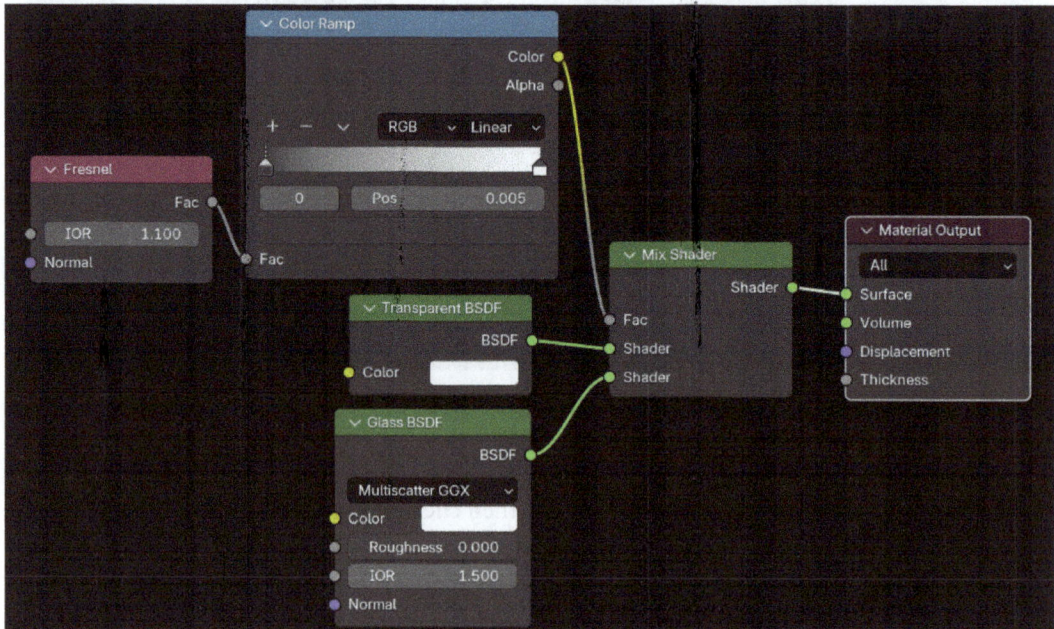

Figure 7.30 – Glass material node setup

12. Now that the glass material is finished, let's apply it to the **Glass Cylinder**, **Glass Tube**, and **Box** objects! To do this, select each one, then select **Cylinder 1** last so it's the active object.

13. Go up to **Object | Link/Transfer Data | Link Materials**. Alternatively, you can press the *Ctrl + L* or *Cmd + L* shortcut and click **Link Materials**. Now, each object you had selected will have that same glass material applied!

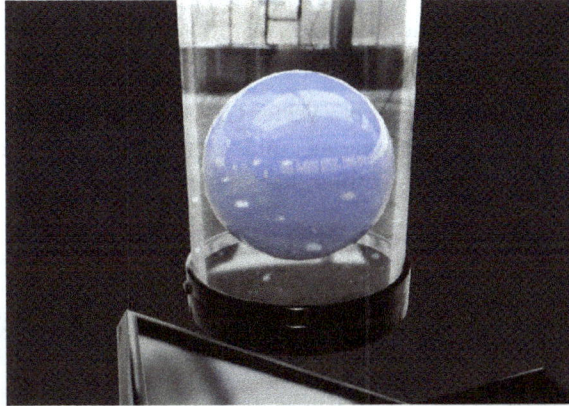

Figure 7.31 – Glass preview

The **Soft Body Sphere** object is already made of a nice reflective blue material, but feel free to change it however you like! With that done, let's set up the camera and render this animation!

Setting up camera tracking

The last step in this tutorial is to set up the camera so that it follows the sphere as it goes through the obstacle course. This is pretty easy to do:

1. Select the **Camera** object. We are going to be adding another constraint. This time, it's the **Copy Location** constraint.

2. In the **Target** menu, select **Soft Body Sphere** and uncheck **Y Axis**. We only want to follow the Z and X locations.

3. Next, check **Offset**. This will allow you to offset the camera's position to wherever you like, but it will still follow the sphere when you play the animation.

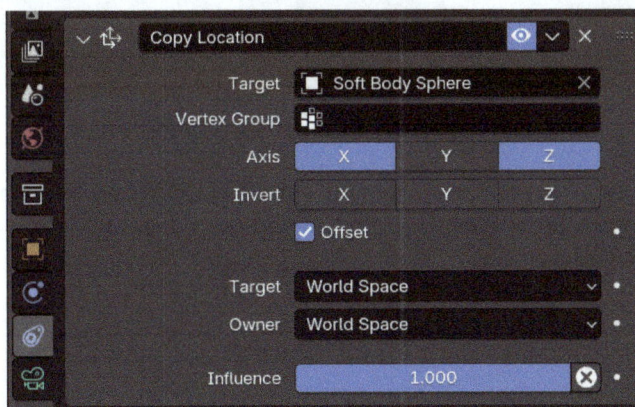

Figure 7.32 – Copy Location constraint

4.   You may notice when you play the animation that it's not really working. That's because the camera is following the origin point of the sphere rather than the position of the mesh.

In the **Copy Location** constraint, there is a **Vertex Group** option. You can probably guess what we are going to do! Let's create a new vertex group for the sphere and then select it here. This way, the camera will follow the mesh rather than the origin point.

To do this, select **Soft Body Sphere** and create a new vertex group in the **Object Data** panel.

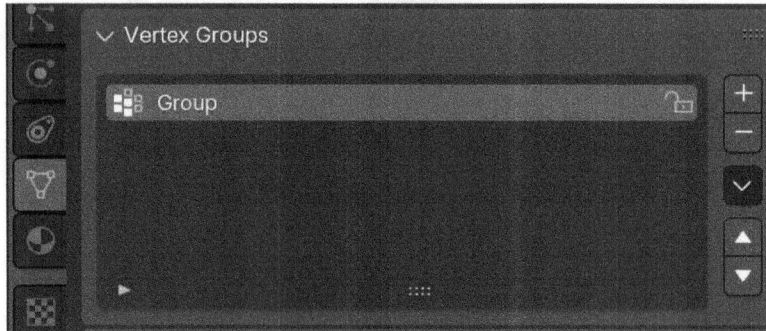

Figure 7.33 – Vertex groups

5.   Go into **Edit Mode** with **Soft Body Sphere** selected and assign all the vertices to **Vertex Group** with **Weight** set to **1**.

6.   Finally, in the **Copy Location** constraint, select the group in the **Vertex Group** menu.

Figure 7.34 – Copy Location vertex group

You can go into the camera view by pressing *0* on the number pad or by going up to **View | Viewport | Camera**. From there, you may need to move the camera around to the correct position facing the sphere.

7. The background of the scene is currently set to a gray color. If you would like to change the color of the background, head over to the **Compositing** workspace at the top. The top **Image** input of the **Alpha Over** node will change the background color of the scene.

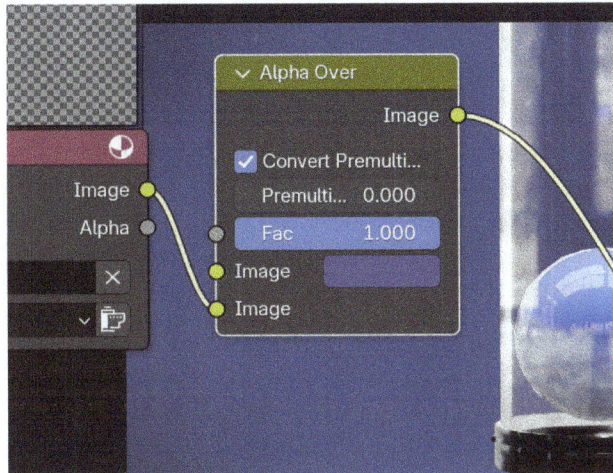

Figure 7.35 – Alpha Over node

From here, just set up the **Output** settings and hit **Render Animation**! If you forgot how to render animations, just look at *Chapter 4*. The following figure is one frame of my result!

Figure 7.36 – Frame 163 result

There it is! We have now completed this project! I encourage you to change the obstacles and add your own twist to it. Maybe add a spinning cube? Or something to carry the sphere around? Or even a wrecking ball to swing and hit the soft body? There are endless possibilities, and it's all up to you!

Summary

Creating soft body simulations can be super fun, and there are a lot of things you can do with them! Hopefully, by now, you have a good understanding of soft body simulations so you can go out and create your own animations!

We have covered quite a bit in this chapter, so let's do a quick recap once again! First, we discussed the obstacle course and how to get familiar with the objects. From there, we started working on the simulation by creating the soft body, and then we added collision to the objects. We learned about the **Inner** and **Outer** thickness zones for collisions and how to use them properly. After that, we started working on **Soft Body Goal**, and we learned how to get the sphere to follow a curve using it. We also created a nice glass material in EEVEE and learned how to set it all up. Finally, we talked about constraints and how to make the camera follow the sphere throughout the obstacle course.

Earlier in this chapter, we briefly discussed cloth simulation and how to pin vertices. If you enjoyed that bit, you will definitely like what's coming next! In the next chapter, we are taking a closer look at the cloth simulation and all of the settings and properties, as well as how to use this simulation effectively!

8

An Introduction to Cloth Simulations

The next type of simulation we will discuss is a cloth simulation. This is one of the easier simulations to work with, but it is also quite complex due to the amount of internal and external interactions it will have. Such a simulation makes things that would otherwise be very difficult to model—such as tablecloths, flags, and blankets—super simple and easy to create! Normally, we use cloth simulations to create **two-dimensional** (**2D**) things like the examples mentioned earlier, but they can also be used to create **three-dimensional** (**3D**) objects such as pillows, stuffed animals, and even balloons!

The goal of this chapter is to give you an understanding of how cloth simulations work in Blender and what all the settings and values do. Just as with the previous chapters, we will start by learning what a cloth simulation is, following which we will jump straight into the settings and values. In later chapters, we will be using what we learned here in this chapter to create practical animations with the cloth simulation.

In this chapter, we'll be covering the following topics:

- What is a cloth simulation?
- Understanding collision objects
- Understanding cloth simulation settings and values

Technical requirements

This chapter requires you to have Blender version 4.2 or above installed.

To download Blender, visit www.blender.org.

What is a cloth simulation?

A cloth simulation in Blender is used to simulate the behavior and interactions of cloth in the real world. It is great for creating things such as fabrics, blankets, pillows, flags, and much more. While you can get similar results using a soft body simulation, a cloth simulation is designed and better suited for this type of thing, and you will generally get better results. You can see an example of a cloth simulation here:

Figure 8.1 – Cloth simulation example

Blender simulates cloth by calculating its physical properties and creating virtual springs that are connected to each vertex of the object. These springs control how stiff the cloth will be, how much it will bend, or how much it will resist collapsing. There are four types that you need to remember, as outlined here:

- **Tension springs**: These are used to control how stiff the cloth will be and how much it will resist stretching.

- **Compression springs**: These are used to control the overall structure of the cloth.

- **Shear springs**: These are used to control angular deformations.

- **Bending springs**: These are used to control how much the cloth will bend and fold.

We will be covering these springs in a bit more depth, and you will see examples of how they work later in this chapter!

To add a cloth simulation to your object, first head over to the **Physics** panel, then select **Cloth**, as illustrated in the following screenshot:

Figure 8.2 – Physics cloth simulation

One thing to keep in mind before you start simulating is the amount of geometry on your object. You need to have enough geometry on the mesh for the cloth to simulate and deform. If you try to add a cloth simulation to a plane with only four vertices, that's not going to work very well. Likewise, if you have too much geometry, the simulation will slow down and take longer to calculate and bake.

A good idea would be to have enough geometry to get a nice simulation and then add a **Subdivision Surface** modifier on top. This will smooth out the cloth and make it look much better while not impacting the performance. You can view the differences by looking at the following screenshot:

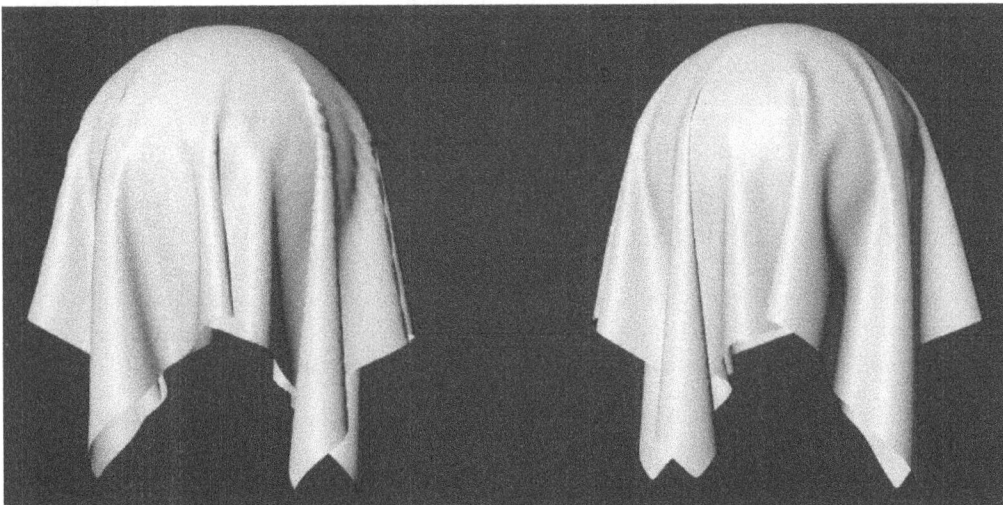

Figure 8.3 – Without subdivision (left) with subdivision (right)

If you add the **Subdivision Surface** modifier above the **Cloth** modifier, the simulation will take that extra geometry into account when simulating. Therefore, make sure to add the **Subdivision Surface** modifier below the **Cloth** modifier, as shown in the following screenshot:

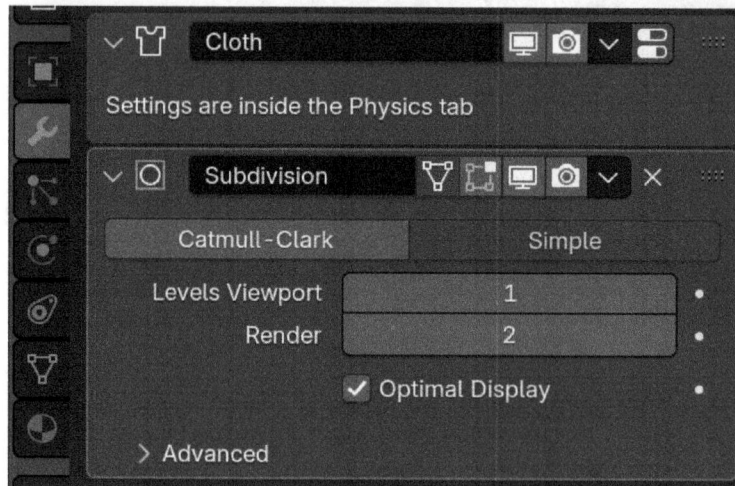

Figure 8.4 – The Cloth and Subdivision Surface modifiers

Another thing to note is when you apply the **Cloth** modifier, it will lock the cloth in place, and from here, you will be able to go into **Edit Mode** and see the geometry. This will also remove the modifier and you won't be able to simulate anymore. Why would you want to apply a modifier? Well, this can be very useful when you want to create an animation but you want the cloth to remain still, such as a blanket draped over a couch or a towel hanging from a hook.

Now, before we jump straight into the settings of the cloth, it's important to discuss collision objects and how they can interact with the simulation!

Understanding collision objects

We discussed collisions in *Chapter 6*, and they work basically the same way with cloth objects. You first need to select a mesh you want to add collision to, then head over to the **Physics** panel and select **Collision**. This will also add the **Collision** modifier in the **Modifier** panel.

Keep the modifier stack in mind when working with collisions. You need to make sure that the **Collision** modifier is at the very bottom of the stack; this way, Blender will accurately calculate the collision boundaries when simulating. In the following figure, both objects are cubes with a **Subdivision Surface** modifier, which rounds them out into spheres:

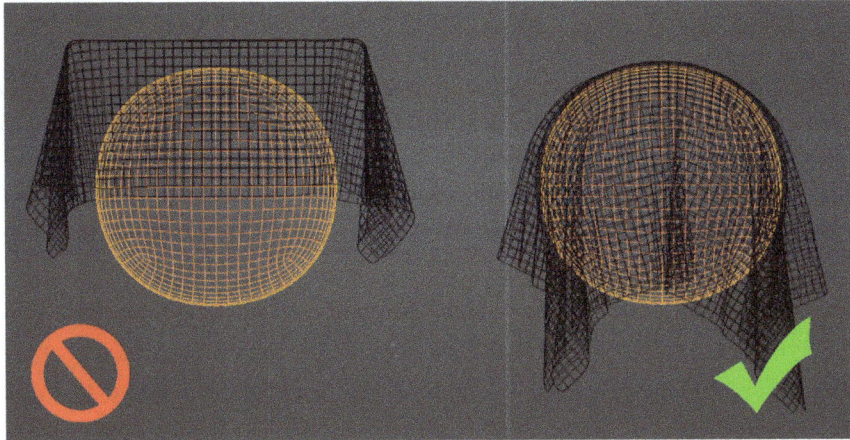

Figure 8.5 – Collision modifier stack

The left example has the **Collision** modifier above the **Subdivision Surface** modifier. This means that the collision boundary is going to be the original shape of the mesh, ignoring the **Subdivision Surface** modification. So, make sure that the **Collision** modifier is always at the bottom of the stack unless you want to specifically ignore certain modifiers, which can be beneficial in some cases. For example, the **Bevel** modifier rounds the edges and corners of a mesh, which in turn adds more geometry to the object. If the **Collision** modifier is below the **Bevel** modifier, the simulation will take longer to bake because of that extra geometry. In this case, the simulation outcome will pretty much be the same regardless of the **Collision** modifier above or below. So, it might be better to have the **Collision** modifier above the **Bevel** modifier to save on bake time.

With the collision object selected, you will be able to see the settings in the **Physics** panel, like so:

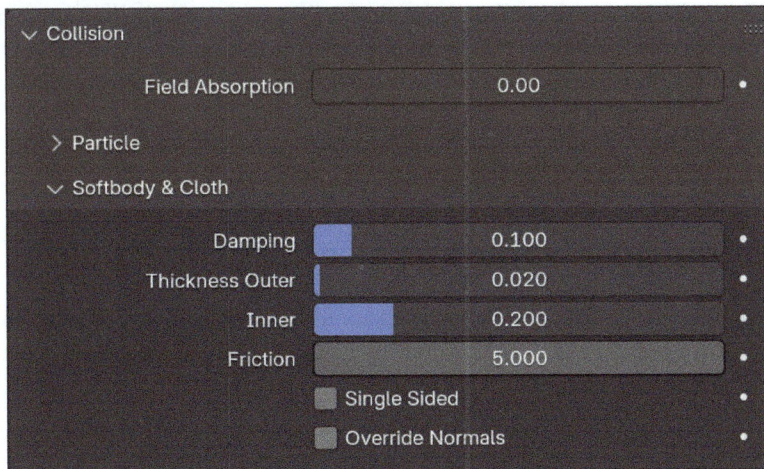

Figure 8.6 – Collision settings

Let's go through each one and talk about them:

- **Field Absorption:** This allows the collision object to absorb a percentage of a force field's strength. For example, if a wind force field is going through a collision object with the **Field Absorption** value set to 0.2, only 20% of the force field's strength will be able to pass through the collision. If the value is set to 1, it will absorb 100% of the force field, and no wind will be able to get through. It's also important to make sure, in the **Force Field** objects settings, that **Absorption** is checked for this to work properly.

- **Particle**: This tab only deals with particle systems and does not affect the cloth, so let's skip that for now.

- **Damping**: This option does not affect the cloth simulation either. It is only used for soft bodies.

- **Thickness Outer**: This option represents the boundary of the collision. Increasing this value will extend the collision boundary past the object's surface.

- **Inner**: This option represents the collision boundary for the inside of the object. If the cloth enters this zone, it will be pushed out.

- **Friction**: This denotes how slippery the cloth will be to the object. A value of 0 will make the collision behave like ice, and the cloth will slide around. A higher value will prevent sliding and increase the stickiness of the collision.

- **Single Sided**: When this is turned on, the collision will be based on the direction of normals. When it's turned off, normals will be ignored and the collision boundary will be over the entire object. This means that if you were to flip a plane upside down with **Single Sided** turned off, the cloth would collide with the underside of the plane rather than pass through, like it would with **Single Sided** turned on.

- **Override Normals**: This works with fast-moving collisions. When this setting is enabled and a collision hits the cloth, the cloth will shoot out in the direction of the normals of the collider. With a lot of testing, this setting seems to have very little effect on the outcome of the simulation.

Remember—if your collision seems to be acting strange, double-check the modifier stack and make sure it's at the very bottom! With that out of the way, let's jump straight into the **Cloth** settings and properties!

Understanding cloth simulation settings and values

Now that we understand what a cloth simulation is all about and how collision objects work, it's time to jump into all the settings and values. You can see an overview of the **Cloth** settings here:

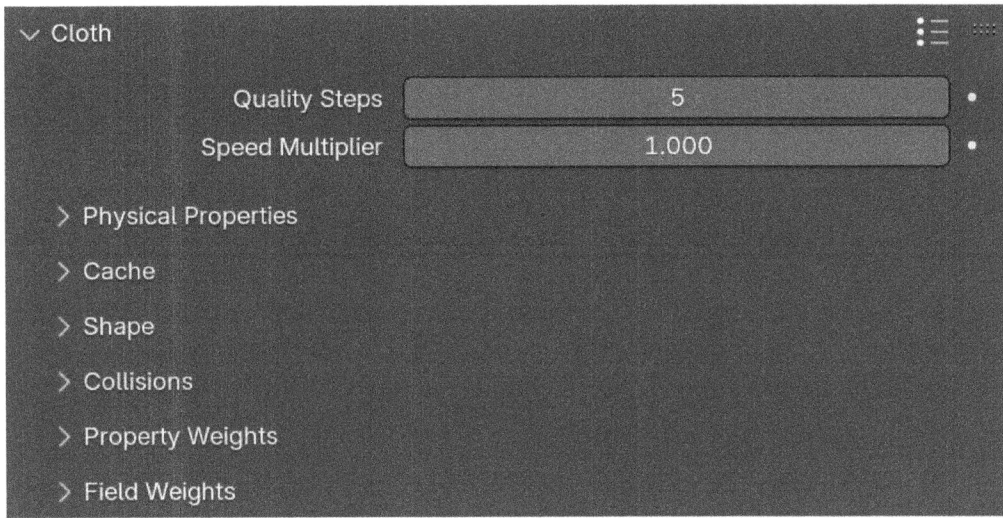

Figure 8.7 – Cloth settings

We are going to start at the very top and work our way down:

- If you click on the icon with three dots and lines above **Quality Steps**, you will see a list of presets to choose from, as shown in the following screenshot:

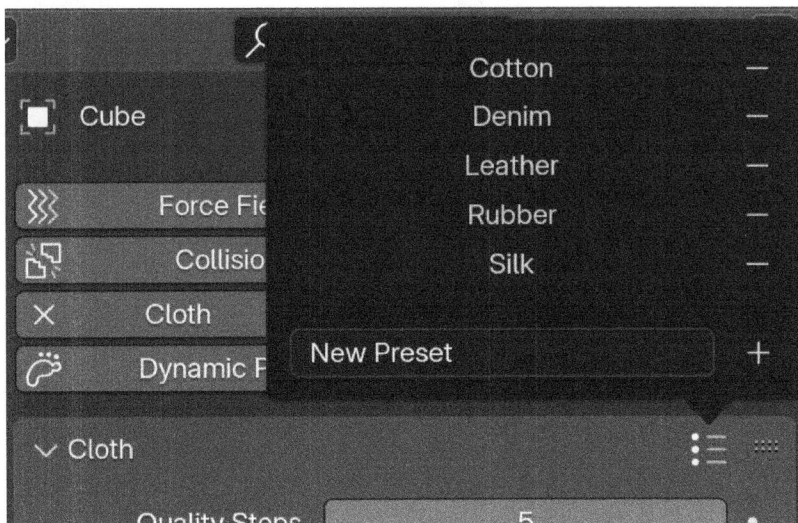

Figure 8.8 – Presets

This is a quick and easy way to create different types of cloth. You can also create your own presets by giving them a name and hitting the + button.

- **Quality Steps**: This option controls how many simulation steps per frame Blender will calculate. The higher the value, the more accurate the simulation will be, but in turn, this will take longer to bake. If cloth or collision objects aren't working properly or if you have very fast-moving collisions, it's recommended to turn this value up.

- **Speed Multiplier**: This option, of course, controls how fast the cloth will simulate when you play the animation. Higher values will increase the speed, while lower values will slow the simulation.

Now, let's move on to the different submenus of the cloth simulation, starting with **Physical Properties**! Here is where we will learn how the cloth behaves and interacts with collisions!

Physical Properties

The **Physical Properties** settings of the cloth are exactly what they sound like. These settings and values change how stiff the cloth will be, how much it will weigh, and much more. When you are changing these settings, you need to think about what kind of cloth you are trying to create (leather, for example, will have a much higher stiffness than silk, and a comforter for a bed will weigh more than a thin blanket). You can see an overview of the settings here:

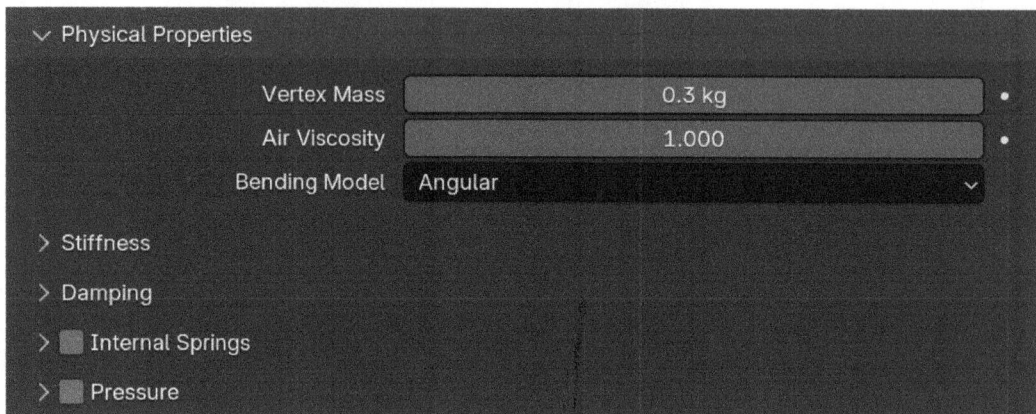

Figure 8.9 – Physical Properties

Again, let's start at the very top, work our way down, and talk about each value, as follows:

- **Vertex Mass**: This controls the weight of the cloth. Every single vertex will weigh the amount you set here. This is important because if you have a lot of geometry, the cloth is going to weigh more. The weight also impacts how a force field will interact with the cloth. If the **Vertex Mass** value is high, you will need a much higher strength value for the force field to interact and push the cloth around. Generally, it's a good idea to have this value set low.

- **Air Viscosity**: This option sets the thickness of the air around the object. Increasing this value will make the cloth fall through the air more slowly.

- **Bending Model**: This basically sets how the springs in the cloth will bend and deform. There are two options for **Bending Model**: **Angular** and **Linear**. The differences between these two are minimal, but I've noticed **Angular** looks a bit better in most cases. In the following screenshot, **Angular** is on the left and **Linear** is on the right:

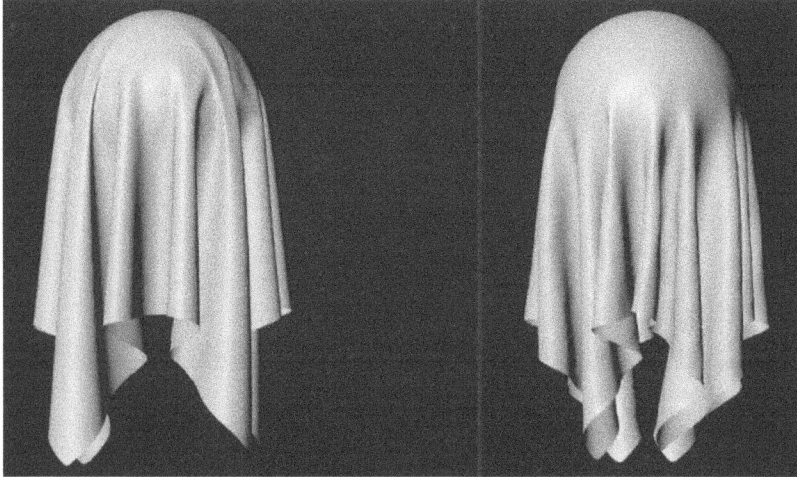

Figure 8.10 – Bending models

Next up, let's discuss the other tabs in the **Physical Properties** submenu, starting with **Stiffness**!

Stiffness

Below **Bending Model**, we have the **Stiffness** tab, as shown here:

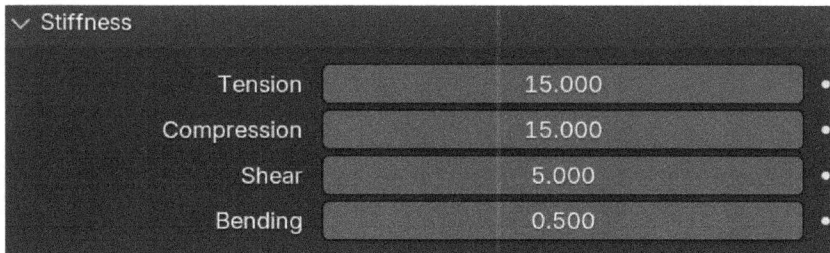

Figure 8.11 – Stiffness settings

There are four options that we can change here:

- **Tension**: This controls how much the cloth will resist stretching. Higher values will make the cloth a bit stiffer and less stretchy. If you have a high **Vertex Mass** value but a low **Tension** value, you may see some stretching because the cloth weighs so much; this can be very useful for creating rubber bands and stretchy fabrics!

- **Compression**: This is how much the cloth will resist collapsing. Higher values will help the cloth keep its structure, while lower values will make the cloth collapse. The values in the following screenshot are 1 (left) and 25 (right):

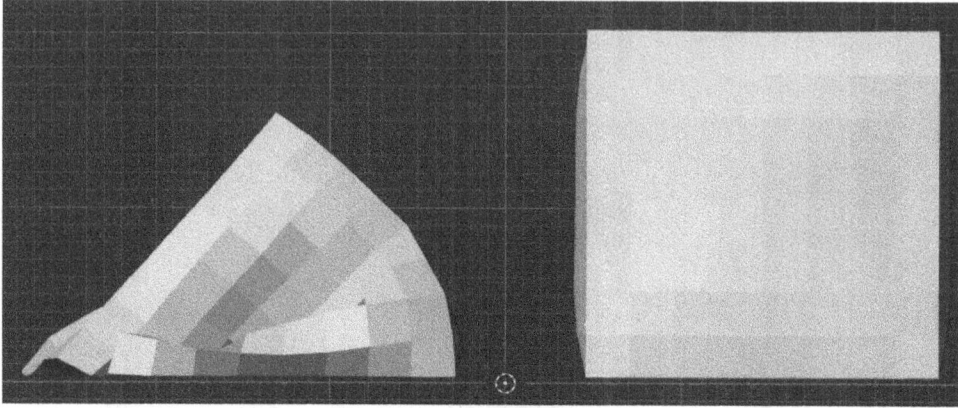

Figure 8.12 – Compression example

- **Shear**: This works similarly to **Compression**. It helps prevent the cloth from collapsing on itself. Higher values will help keep the structure of the cloth, while lower values will let the cloth bend and lose its structure.

- **Bending**: This sets how much the cloth will bend and wrinkle. A higher value will make the cloth stiffer and produce bigger folds, and lower values will create smaller wrinkles and make the cloth a lot looser. Setting this value higher can be very useful for creating fabrics such as leather and rubber. The values in the following screenshot are 0.5 (left) and 50 (right) so that you can see the difference:

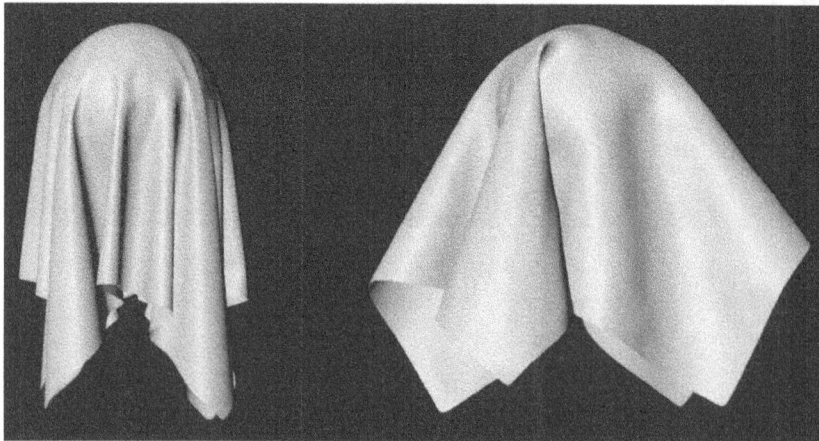

Figure 8.13 – Bending example

Finally, if you set **Bending Model** to **Linear**, the **Tension** and **Compression** settings will disappear and be replaced with **Structure**. This setting controls both the structure of the cloth and how much it will stretch.

Damping

The **Damping** tab has all the same settings listed in the **Stiffness** menu: **Tension**, **Compression**, **Shear**, and **Bending**. These values basically slow down the effect of each setting in the **Stiffness** tab.

For example, if the **Compression** option in the **Stiffness** tab is set to 0 but **Compression** in the **Damping** tab is set to 50, the cloth will still collapse but it's going to take longer. If the **Compression** option in the **Damping** tab is also set to 0, then the cloth would collapse instantly and lose all its structure. So, again, these settings slow and dampen the effect of each option in the **Stiffness** tab.

Internal Springs

Checking the **Internal Springs** box will basically turn your cloth into a soft body.

Remember that earlier in this chapter, we talked about springs for a cloth simulation? Well, normally, springs can only be applied to 2D surfaces, but when **Internal Springs** is enabled, 3D springs will be created inside the object, and now, it will behave very similarly to a soft body.

When you check the **Internal Springs** box, these options will be available:

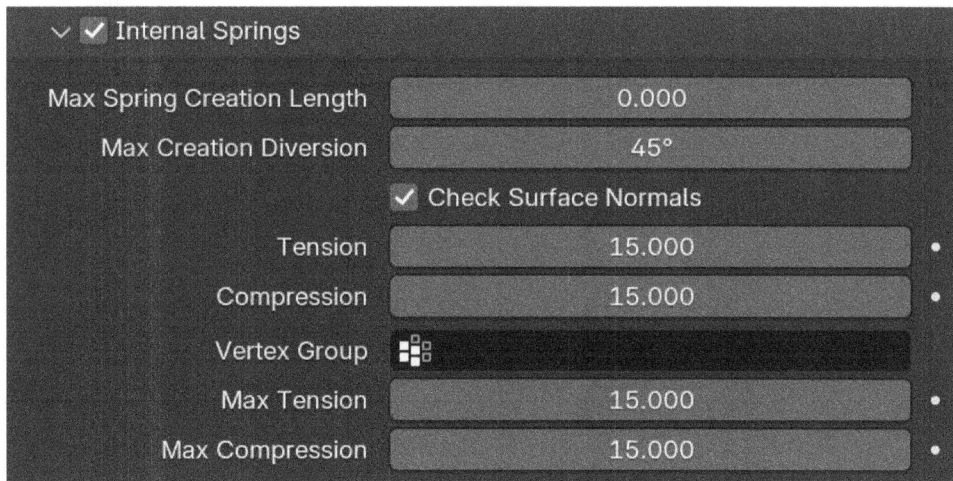

Figure 8.14 – Internal Springs settings

Let's go through each of them:

- **Max Spring Creation Length**: This sets the maximum distance for a spring. If the spring distance exceeds this length, no spring will be created. For example, in the following screenshot, there is a big cube and a small cube. **Max Spring Creation Length** is set to 0.5 for each. Since the distance inside the big cube is longer than 0.5, no springs are created, and it collapses. However, the small cube is within that 0.5 distance, so springs are created, and it retains its structure:

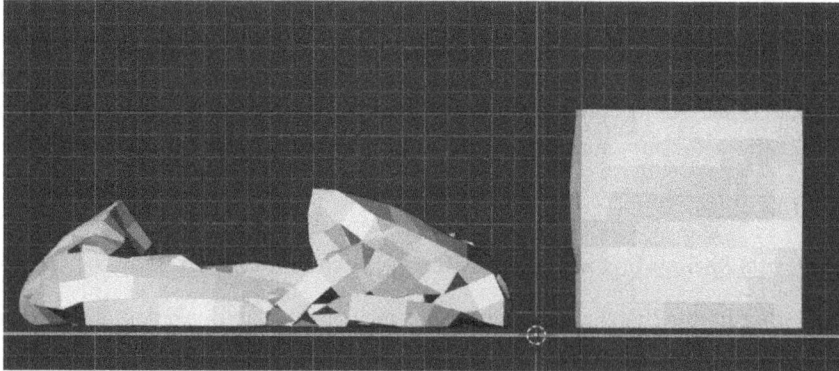

Figure 8.15 – Max Spring Creation Length

- **Max Creation Diversion**: This sets the maximum angle at which a spring will be created. If the angle of the normals exceeds this value, no springs will be created.

- **Check Surface Normals**: This checks and sees whether normals are pointed in opposite directions. If normals are not pointed in opposite directions, no springs will be created. In the following screenshot example, the top of the cube has normals pointed toward the inside of the mesh. That means no springs will be created on that top face. When this setting is unchecked, it will ignore the normals and add springs everywhere:

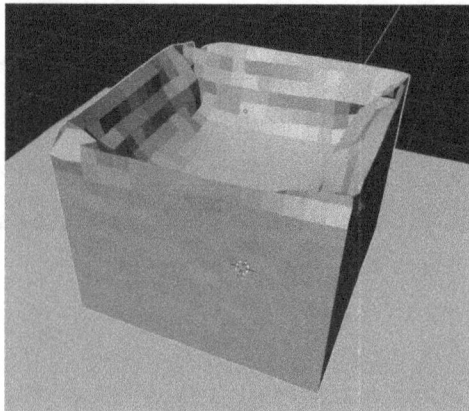

Figure 8.16 – Check Surface Normals example

- **Tension** and **Compression**: Higher **Tension** values will have the cloth resist stretching, and higher **Compression** values will keep the cloth from collapsing.

- You can also create a vertex group and assign internal springs to it. This gives you finer control over where you want springs to be created. The **Max Tension** and **Compression** values control how the vertex group will be applied.

With that done, let's take a look at **Pressure**!

Pressure

Enabling **Pressure** will allow you to inflate your cloth, which can be very useful for creating things such as pillows or balloons. You can see an overview of the settings here:

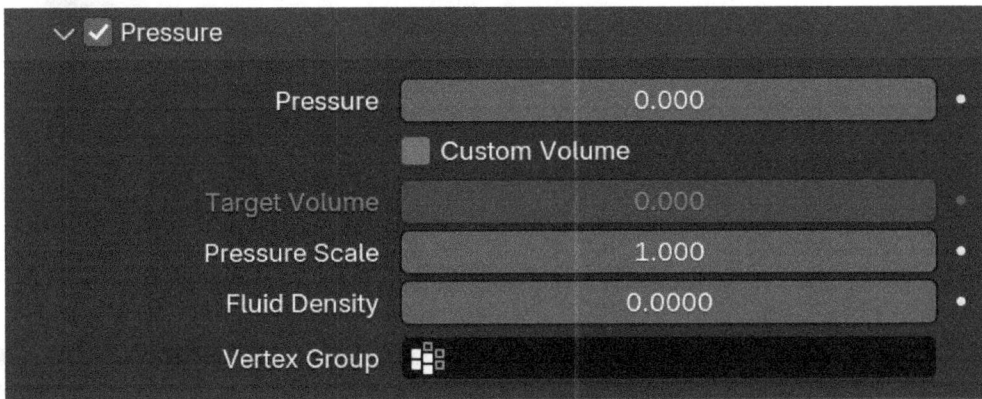

Figure 8.17 – Pressure settings

Let's discuss the settings:

- **Pressure**: This controls how inflated the cloth will be. Positive values will expand the mesh out, and the higher you set this value, the more the cloth will expand. You can also set a negative value, which will deflate the object, causing it to shrink. The following screenshot provides an example of text with the **Pressure** value set to 15:

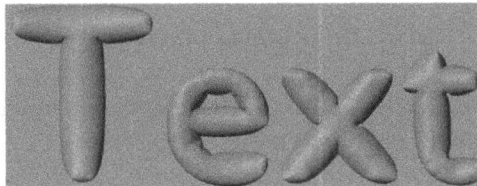

Figure 8.18 – Pressure example

- **Custom Volume**: When this is checked, you will be able to set a target volume. This means that the pressure is going to be calculated based on the volume of the object rather than the mesh itself. Normally, when **Custom Volume** is unchecked, the pressure will be the same for all objects regardless of size, as you can see in the following screenshot:

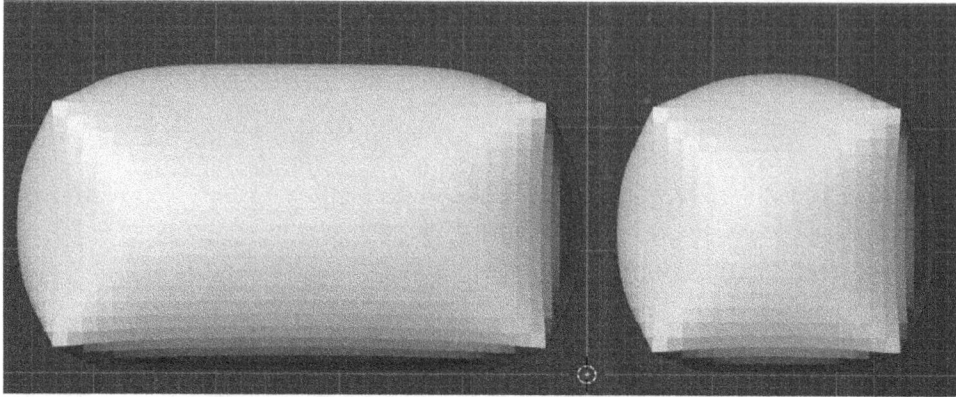

Figure 8.19 – Pressure volume example

When **Custom Volume** is checked, the size of the mesh will be calculated when applying pressure. In the following screenshot example, **Target Volume** is set to 15 for each cube. Since the bigger cube has a larger volume, the pressure is not going to be as strong as for the smaller cube:

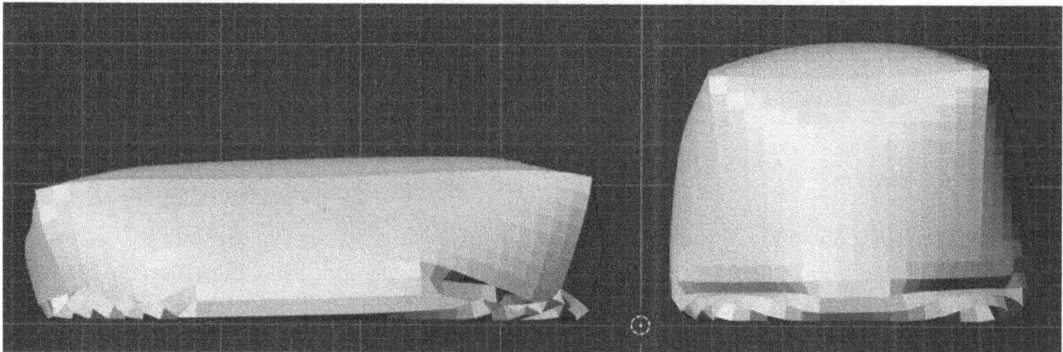

Figure 8.20 – Target Volume example

- **Pressure Scale**: This is the ambient pressure on the outside and inside of the object. Increasing this value tends to expand the mesh even more.

- **Fluid Density**: This is the density of the fluid (air) inside the object. When you increase this value, the air inside will become denser, thus making the cloth weigh more. Setting this value to a negative number will do the opposite and make the object rise and float into the air (this is a good way of creating a balloon).

- **Vertex Group**: You can create a vertex group to fine-tune where you want the pressure or inflation to happen, as illustrated in the following screenshot:

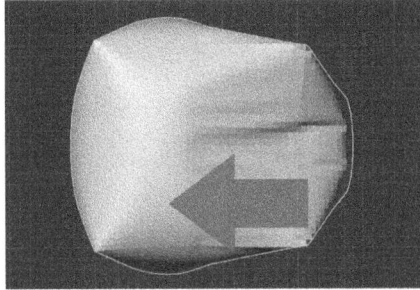

Figure 8.21 – Pressure vertex group

When selecting a vertex group to determine where the mesh has pressure, you may experience some strange movement. Due to the pressure on one side of the mesh, the inflated side will force the cloth to fly off in that direction. This may not be how it's intended to work but keep that in mind in case you decide to use this feature!

Now, let's move on to the **Cache** tab and learn how to bake the simulation!

Cache

The **Cache** tab is where you bake in the simulation. It's usually a good idea to bake in the simulation before you render it, just to make sure everything works correctly, but it's not necessary.

The **Cache** tab may look familiar; that's because it's the same as the **Soft Body Cache** tab, as we can see here:

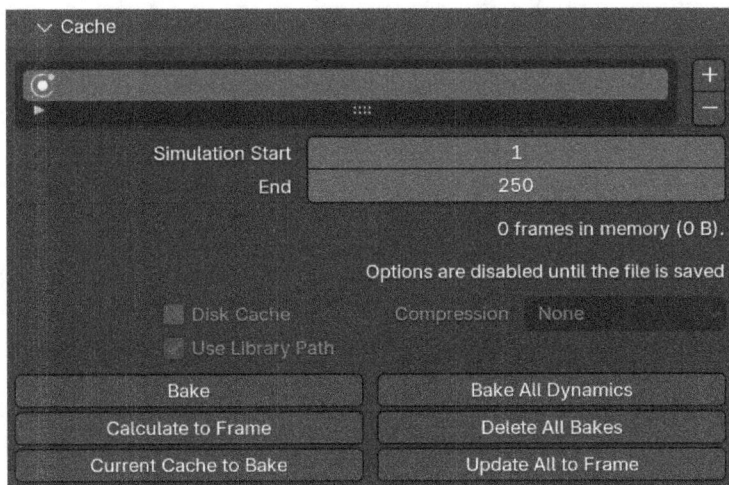

Figure 8.22 – Cache

You should already know how all this works because we went over it in *Chapter 6*, but here are some quick notes just in case you wish to recapitulate:

- **Simulation Start** and **End** control the frame range of the simulation.

- To bake in the cloth, all you have to do is click on **Bake**. This will gray out all the settings, and you won't be able to change them unless you click **Free Bake**.

- If you have multiple clothes, soft bodies, or even particle systems and you want to bake everything at once, just click **Bake All Dynamics**. This will then bake every simulation in the scene at once.

- The great thing about baking in the simulation is that you can skip to any frame in the Timeline and preview what the cloth will look like in that frame. Without baking the cloth simulation, you won't be able to skip any frames; rather, you will have to play the simulation from the start.

As for the rest of the settings, since we have already discussed them in *Chapter 6*, let's go ahead and move on to the **Shape** tab!

Shape

The **Shape** tab allows you to pin vertices in place. This can be very useful for creating things such as flags, a towel hanging from a hook, a hammock, or anything where cloth is pinned to something.

To get the cloth to be pinned in a certain place, first go into **Edit Mode** and select the parts of the mesh you want to pin, as illustrated in the following screenshot:

Figure 8.23 – Selected vertices

Next, head over to the **Object Data** panel and create a new vertex group by clicking the + button. Make sure the **Weight** value is set to 1 (a value less than 1 will result in the vertices only being partially pinned based on the weight value; this will basically make it look like your cloth is attached to a bungee cord) and click **Assign**. You can see an overview of this in the following screenshot:

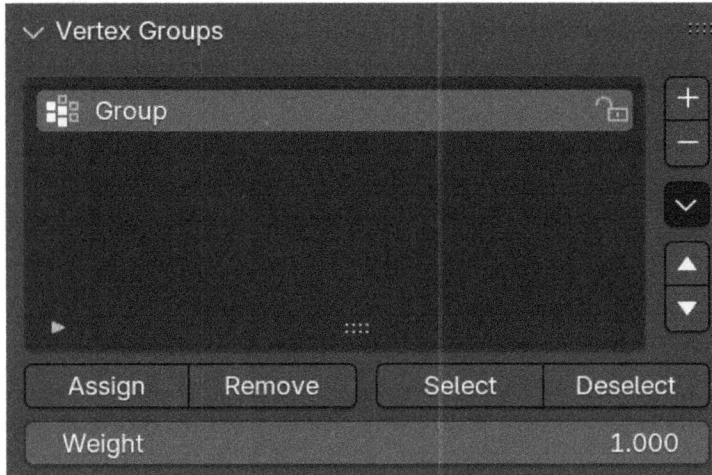

Figure 8.24 – Assigned vertex group

Over in the cloth simulation, select that vertex group in the **Pin Group** menu, as illustrated here:

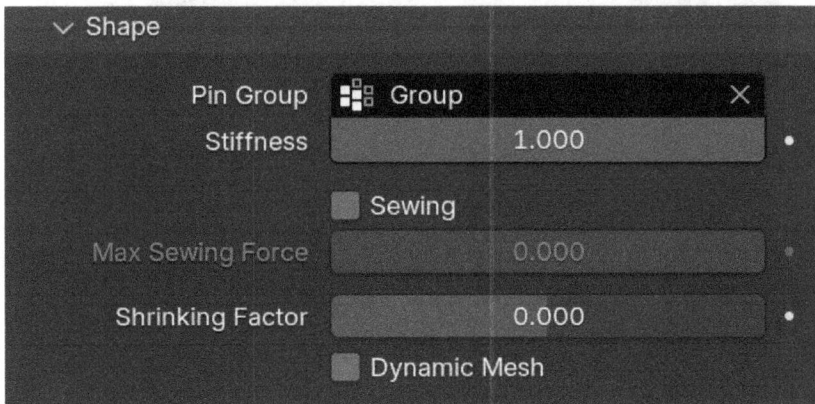

Figure 8.25 – Pin Group

Now, when you play your animation, those vertices you assigned will be stuck in place!

Your cloth will now be pinned in those places you assigned. Let's talk about the rest of the settings:

- **Stiffness**: This simply controls the stiffness of pinned vertices. For example, when the **Stiffness** value is at 0, only vertices with a **Weight** value of 1 will be pinned. However, if you set the **Stiffness** value to 50, then a lot more vertices will be pinned, even though the **Weight** value is less than 1. You can see an example of this in the following screenshot:

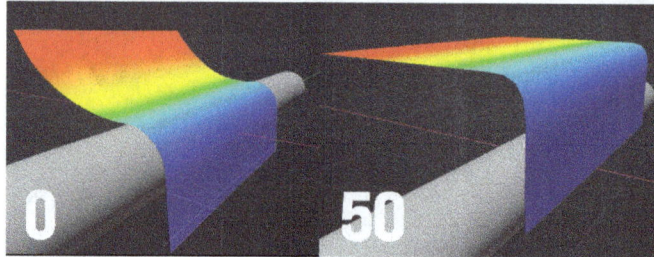

Figure 8.26 – Shape stiffness

- **Sewing**: This allows you to create virtual strings on the mesh and pull them together, just as in real-life sewing. This is a fast way to create clothing for your character or to have a cloak tied around their neck. How this works is that you need to have the parts you want to be pulled together connected by an edge and not a face, as shown in the following screenshot:

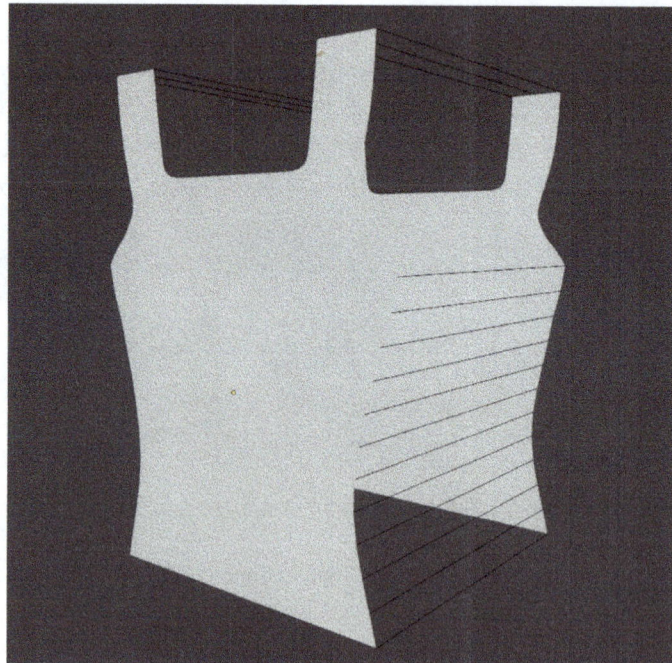

Figure 8.27 – Sewing edges example

You can create an edge between two vertices by selecting them in **Edit Mode** and pressing *F*. You can see this in the following figure:

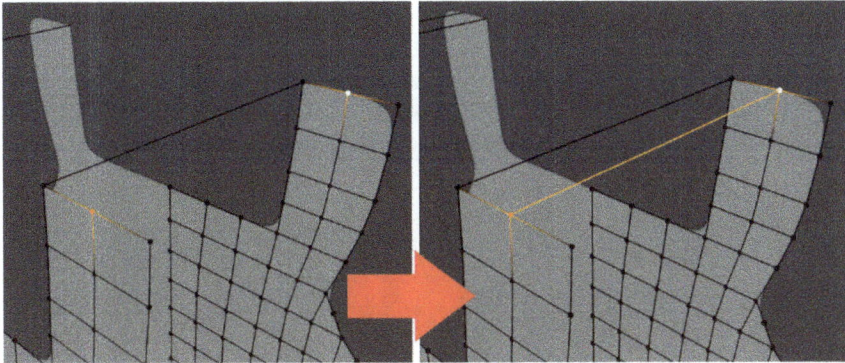

Figure 8.28 – Connecting vertices

After that, enable **Sewing** and play the animation. Your cloth should now close together where those edges are connected, as shown in the following screenshot:

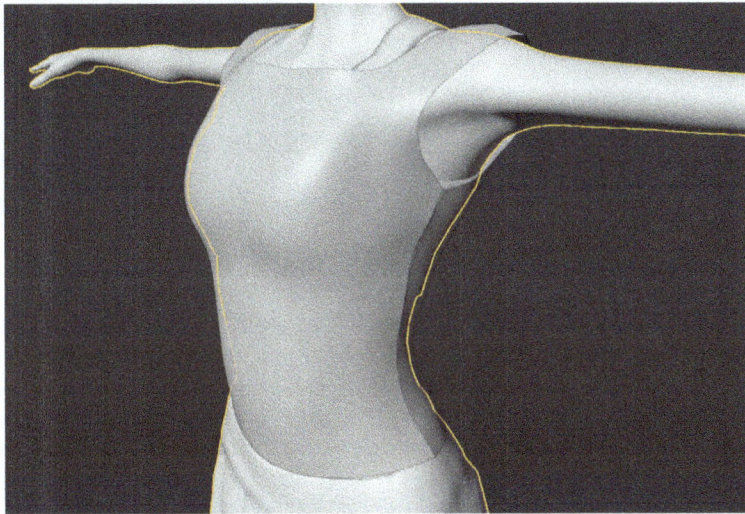

Figure 8.29 – Sewing example

- **Max Sewing Force**: This controls how strongly and quickly those edges will be pulled together. If it is set to 0, that means there is no max force, and the edges will be pulled extremely quickly. This may cause issues in the simulation, so it's recommended to turn this value up.

- **Shrinking Factor**: This will either shrink or grow the mesh when the edges are pulled. Negative values will make the cloth grow, while positive values will shrink the mesh; in the following screenshot, it is set to -0.2, and as you can see, the cloth has now expanded due to being set to a negative value:

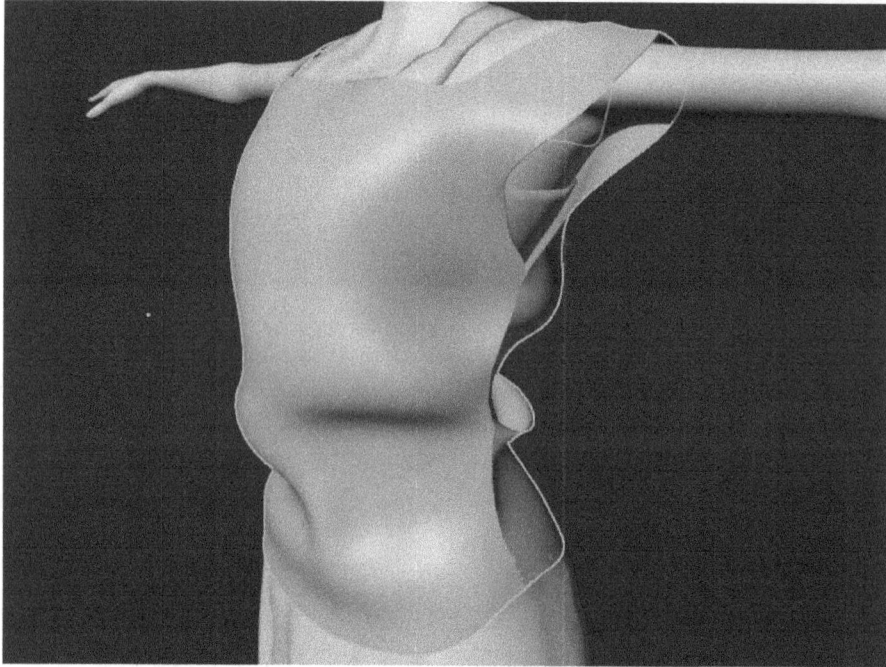

Figure 8.30 – Shrinking Factor example

- **Dynamic Mesh**: This enables **Sewing** to allow any animation or deformation modifiers to be applied to the mesh (this could be an armature, lattice, and so on). When enabled, every frame of the simulation is recalculated to give more accurate results when those modifiers are in use.

Now that we understand the **Shape** tab, let's move on to the **Collision** tab and learn about how the cloth collides with other objects!

Collisions

Now, it's time for all the **Collision** settings and values. Here is where we set up the quality and distance and determine whether we want the cloth to collide with itself.

As mentioned earlier in the chapter, to get the cloth to collide with something, we need to give that object collision in the **Physics** panel. Then, in the **Cloth** settings, make sure the **Object Collisions** box is checked (it should already be checked by default; unchecking it will mean the cloth will just pass through any collisions).

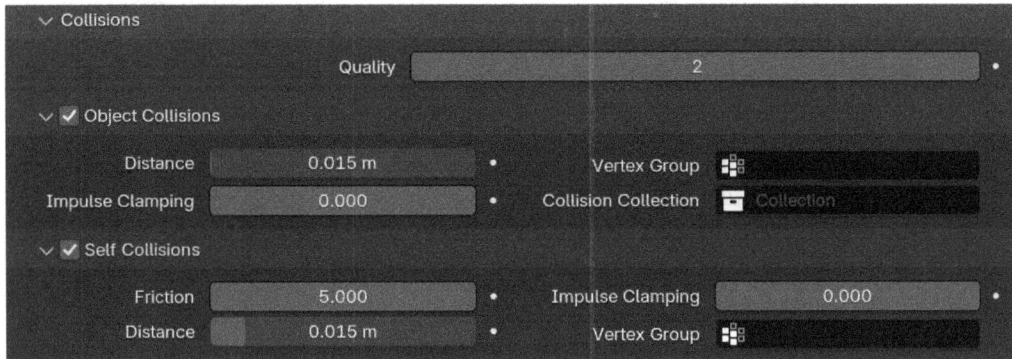

Figure 8.31 – Cloth collision settings

Let's go through the settings and talk about each one, as follows:

- **Quality**: This controls how accurately and well the collisions will happen. Higher values will produce better collisions and fewer errors but will take longer to simulate. If the collisions are not working as intended, try turning this value up.

- **Distance**: This is how far away the cloth will collide. If this value is set too low, you might get some errors and the cloth might clip through the collider. Generally, the default value of 0.015 works well for most scenes.

- **Impulse Clamping**: Sometimes, in tight, complicated collisions, the cloth may experience some errors and explode out. **Impulse Clamping** helps prevent any explosions from happening by restricting the movement of the cloth after a collision. So, if your collision is not working properly, try turning this value up.

- **Vertex Group**: You can select a **Vertex Group** type to be the collision area. This can be useful if you want only half of the cloth to collide.

- **Collision Collection**: This will allow you to limit which collection will interact with the cloth. This is also useful if you have multiple simulations and don't want them interacting with each other.

- **Self Collisions**: Normally, the cloth will not collide with itself unless you check **Self Collisions**. If you create a pillow using **Pressure**, you don't necessarily need **Self Collisions** because the cloth won't overlap itself. On the other hand, if you are creating a blanket falling on the couch, you probably want **Self Collisions** turned on. This will take longer to calculate, so only enable it when it's needed or if you want realistic results.

- **Friction**: This option within the **Self Collisions** menu relates to how slippery the cloth will be when it collides with itself. The value you set here depends on the type of cloth you are trying to create. For example, a cotton blanket will have much higher friction than a silk one.

We have already discussed the rest of the settings, and they are used in the same way, except that they apply to self-collision.

Property Weights

Remember when we discussed the different spring types earlier in this chapter? Well, the **Property Weights** tab allows you to fine-tune those springs for the cloth using vertex groups. This can be very useful if you want some parts of the cloth to have different physical properties. For example, you can set some parts of the cloth to have more tension using the **Structural Group** type or shrink down using the **Shrinking Group** type.

Another example would be creating a blanket with different materials. If some parts of the blanket bend and wrinkle more than others, you can use the **Bending Group** type. Of course, if you want some parts of the cloth to collapse and shear less, you can use the **Shear Group** type.

You can see the different group types in the following screenshot:

Figure 8.32 – Property Weights

To use **Property Weights**, you first create a vertex group and assign vertices to it. In this example, we have assigned half of the vertices on this plane a weight of 1 (left):

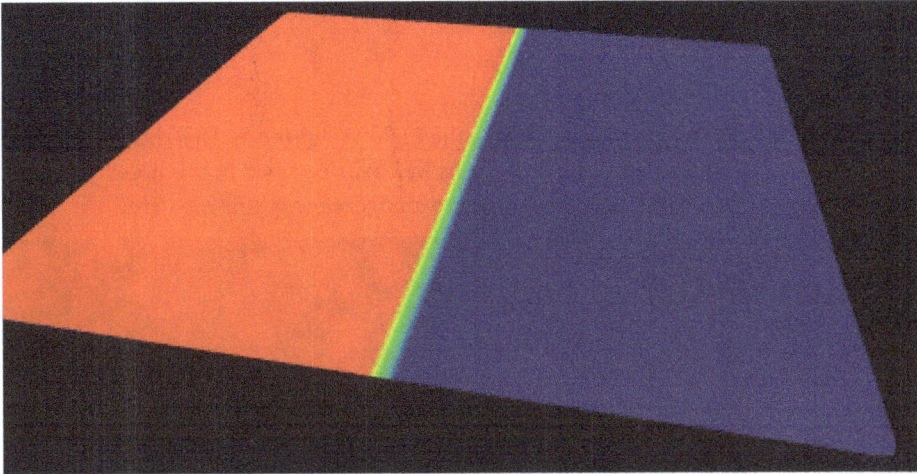

Figure 8.33 – Plane vertex group

Then, in the **Property Weights** tab, we set **Max Tension** and **Max Compression** to 100. We also set **Max Bending** to 15 and assigned that vertex group to each of the four **Property Weight** groups. Now, when we add a sphere underneath the plane to collide with the cloth, you can see that half of the plane is very stiff and the other half is loose, as depicted here:

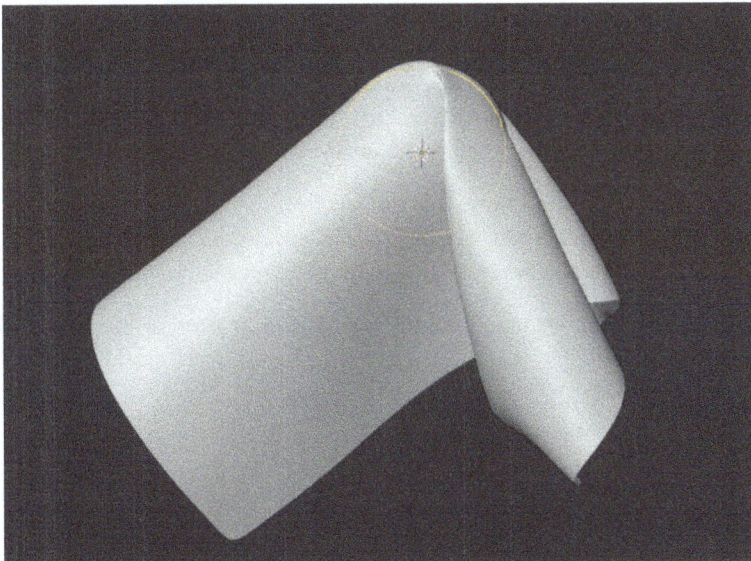

Figure 8.34 – Property Weights example

So, again, the **Property Weights** tab allows you to fine-tune certain areas on your cloth to have certain physical properties with vertex groups. Now, before this tutorial ends, let's quickly discuss the **Field Weights** tab!

Field Weights

Finally, the last tab in the cloth simulation settings is the **Field Weights** tab. This should look familiar, as it works exactly the same as for the other simulations we have discussed in this book. Here, you can fine-tune how force fields affect your cloth. You can see an overview of this tab here:

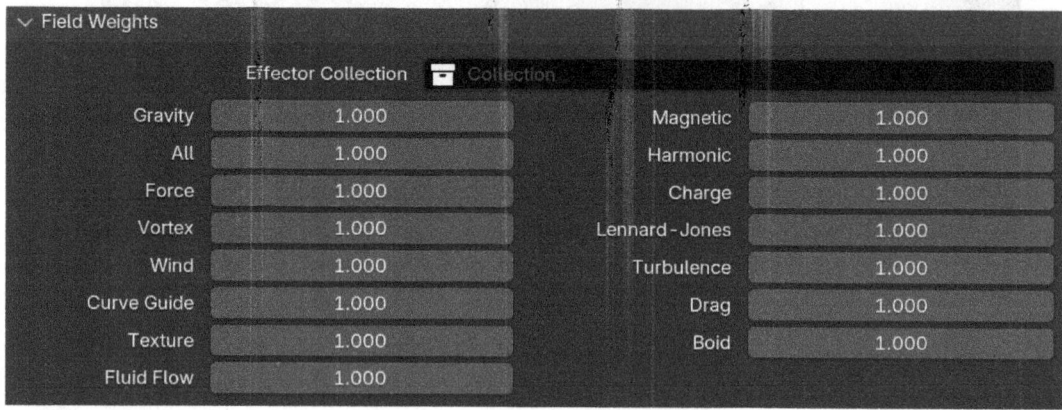

Field Weights				
Effector Collection	Collection			
Gravity	1.000	Magnetic	1.000
All	1.000	Harmonic	1.000
Force	1.000	Charge	1.000
Vortex	1.000	Lennard-Jones	1.000
Wind	1.000	Turbulence	1.000
Curve Guide	1.000	Drag	1.000
Texture	1.000	Boid	1.000
Fluid Flow	1.000		

Figure 8.35 – Field Weights

The **Effector Collection** allows you to limit which collection will affect the cloth. If no collection is set, then every force field in the scene will interact with the simulation.

You also have the option to change the **Gravity** value of the simulation. Do you want your cloth to float like it's in space? Just set the **Gravity** value to 0 and you're good to go!

As for the rest of the values, they control how strong of an effect the force fields will have. For example, if **Wind** is set to 0 . 5, then only half of any wind force field's strength will affect the cloth. This can be useful if you have multiple cloths and you want the wind to affect each one differently!

There we go! We have covered every single setting for a cloth simulation in Blender. With that done, let's do a quick summary!

Summary

We have discussed around 60 settings and values in this chapter so far. This can be quite a lot to remember, so you can always reference this chapter if you forget what something does. As for right now, let's do a quick recap to go over what we learned!

First, we talked about what a cloth simulation is, the importance of the modifier stack, and how the cloth simulates using different springs. After that, we learned about collision objects and how they interact with the simulation. Then, we went over every setting for the cloth simulation. We discussed the physical properties, internal springs, pressure, pinning, cloth collisions, and property weights.

Modeling a tablecloth with realistic wrinkles and folds can be challenging and take a long time. Thankfully, a cloth simulation can save you many hours of work. Hopefully, this chapter gave you a good understanding of this simulation and how it works. In the next chapter, we will be putting those skills to the test by creating a realistic flag using this system!

Join our community on Discord

Join our community's Discord space for discussions with the author and other readers:
`https://packt.link/learn-blender-simulations-discord-invite`

9

Creating a Realistic Flag

Creating a flag cloth simulation seems easy; however, there are many aspects to simulating a flag that you may or may not have considered. If you look at real flagpoles, there are many different parts to them. For example, the hoist is the part of the flag that attaches to the halyard. The halyard is the rope that raises and lowers the flag from the ground. There are also snap hooks that attach the flag to the halyard. In this step-by-step tutorial, we will be simulating a flag in Blender and adding all those different parts to our flag to create a realistic result!

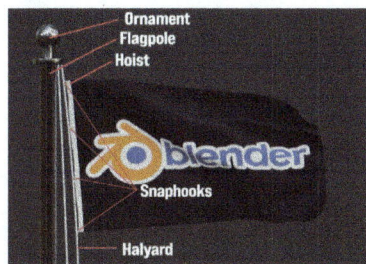

Figure 9.1 – A flag diagram

We will start by adding all the objects we need for the scene, such as the flag, the flagpole, the rope, and the hooks. Then, we will move on to creating the simulation and attaching the flag to the rope. Finally, we will create the materials and render them out. The goal of this chapter is to give an understanding of how to use the cloth simulation in Blender in a practical way while creating a satisfying animation in the process. By the end of this project, you should be able to apply what you learned here to your own projects in the future!

In this chapter, we'll be covering the following topics:

- Adding the objects
- Creating the simulation
- Making the materials
- Rendering the animation

Technical requirements

This chapter requires you to have Blender version 4.2 or above installed.

To download Blender, visit www.blender.org.

There is also a texture that we will be using later in this chapter. To get the texture, visit https://github.com/PacktPublishing/Learn-Blender-4-Simulations-the-Right-Way/tree/main/Chapter%209.

Adding the objects

First, we need to decide how big we want the flag to be. The size of the flag also depends on the height of the flagpole. For example, a pole that is 6 meters or 20 feet would have a flag that is about 91 x 152 centimeters or 3 x 5 feet. The taller the flagpole, the bigger the flag should be. With that in mind, let's go ahead and get started with this tutorial.

Creating the flag

For this tutorial, we are going to be creating a flag that is 91 x 152 cm. To create it, follow these steps:

1. Open a brand new scene in Blender. You can also go ahead and delete the default cube; we won't need that for this scene.

2. Press *Shift + A* and add in a plane object. Next, set the dimensions by opening the **Properties** panel by pressing *N* and then setting **Dimensions** to 1.52 m for the **X** axis and 0.91 m for the **Y** axis.

Figure 9.2 – Flag dimensions

3. Let's also rotate this plane by 90 degrees so that it's standing upright. Make sure to apply the scale and rotation by pressing *Ctrl + A* or *Cmd + A* and select **Scale** & **Rotation**. This way, all the values are correct, and the simulation will work properly!

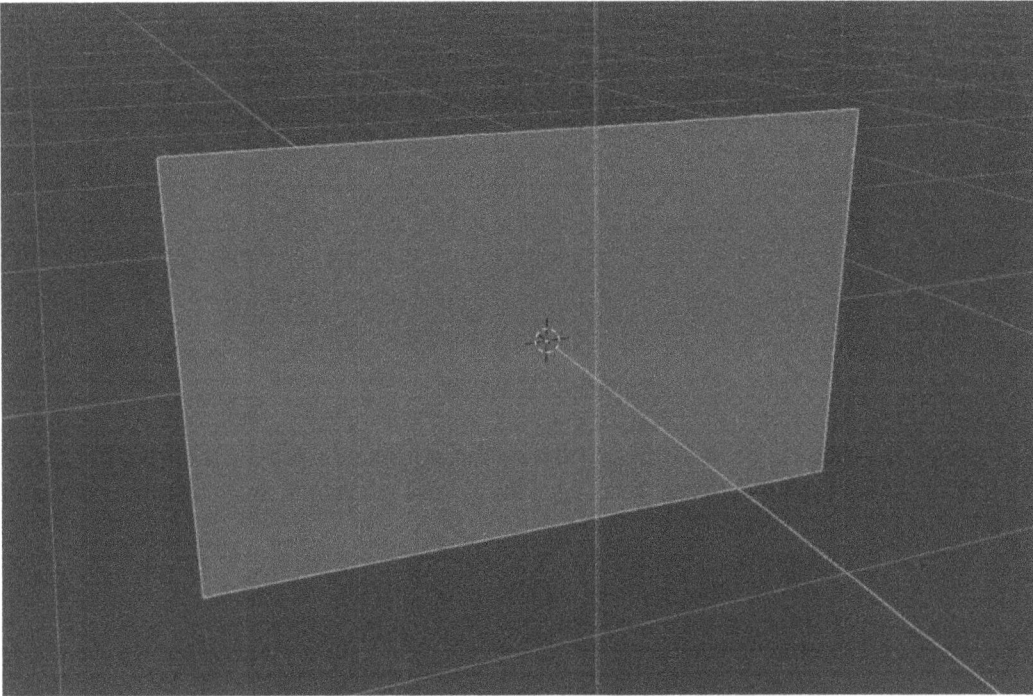

Figure 9.3 – Flag example

4. The next step is to add more geometry to our plane; this will help simulate the cloth properly and give us more detail. Since our plane is a rectangle, if we subdivide the whole thing, we will also get rectangle faces. However, we want square faces instead. As mentioned in *Chapter 6*, to simulate soft bodies properly, even geometry through the whole object is key. This works the same with the cloth simulation. While rectangle faces will work, square faces give us an even length on each edge of the faces. This, in turn, gives a more realistic result and will simulate better overall.

To get square faces, you need to manually add two vertical loop cuts and one horizontal one. You can do this by going into **Edit Mode**, pressing *Ctrl + R* or *Cmd + R*, and hovering your mouse over one side of the plane. Then, use the scroll wheel to add multiple loop cuts.

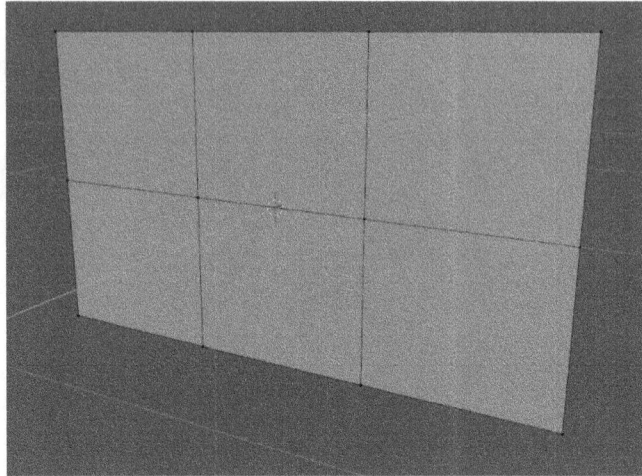

Figure 9.4 – Loop cuts

5.   Now, we can subdivide the whole thing, and we will get square faces. Press *A* to select everything, right-click, and select **Subdivide**. Then, open the panel at the bottom and set **Number of Cuts** to 15.

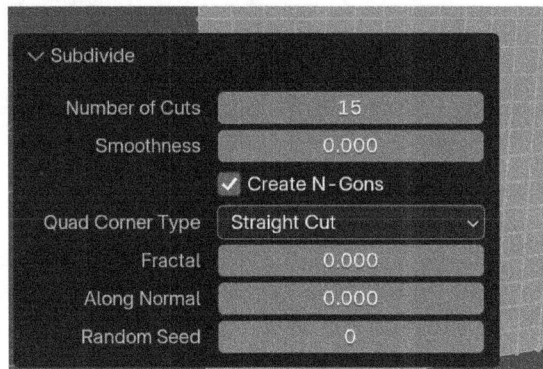

Figure 9.5 – Number of Cuts

And that is it for the flag! Next up, let's create the flagpole!

Creating the flagpole

At this point, it's a good idea to look at some reference images of real-life flagpoles so that you can get an idea of what yours should look like. The main part of the flagpole is the cylindrical shape, and normally, at the very top sits a brass or silver ball. One of the main purposes of the ball at the top is to give the flagpole a more aesthetically pleasing design, and it prevents the flag from sliding off the top of the pole. With that in mind, let's start modeling:

1. To start, press *Shift + A*, go to **Mesh**, and add a **Cylinder** object to the scene. Open the **Add Cylinder** menu at the bottom left of the viewport, and let's change a couple of settings. The **Radius** value of the cylinder should be around 0.05 m and **Depth** (which is the height) should be set to 6 m.

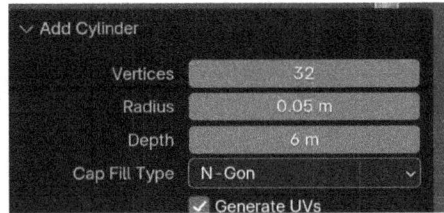

Figure 9.6 – Flagpole dimensions

2. Next, we are going to extrude and scale the top face to add a bit more interest to the look of the flagpole. Select the top face and press *E* to extrude, and then you can press *S* to scale out that face. Keep extruding and scaling until you get something that looks like the following figure!

Figure 9.7 – Extruded face

3. Let's also add a UV sphere to the top of the flagpole. This is going to represent the ornament that sits at the very top!

Figure 9.8 – UV sphere added

4. To round the edges of the pole so that they don't look as sharp, you can add a **Bevel** modifier. To do this, head over to the **Modifier** tab and click **Add Modifier | Generate | Bevel**. Looking at the **Bevel** modifier settings, **Amount** controls how round the edges will be; let's set this value to something very low, such as 0.002 m. Then, set the **Segments** option to 3; this will increase the resolution of the bevel and give us more geometry on the edges.

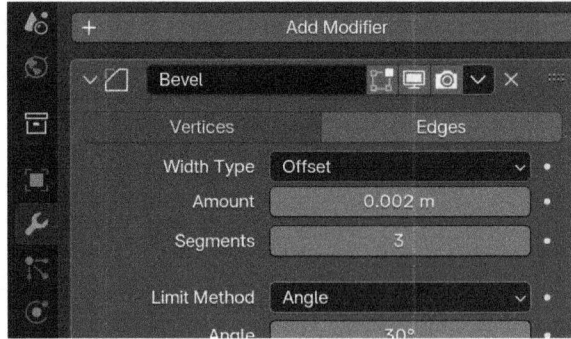

Figure 9.9 – The Bevel modifier

5. And, of course, right-click and select **Shade Smooth** for both objects to make sure everything looks good. Here is what the pole should look like so far:

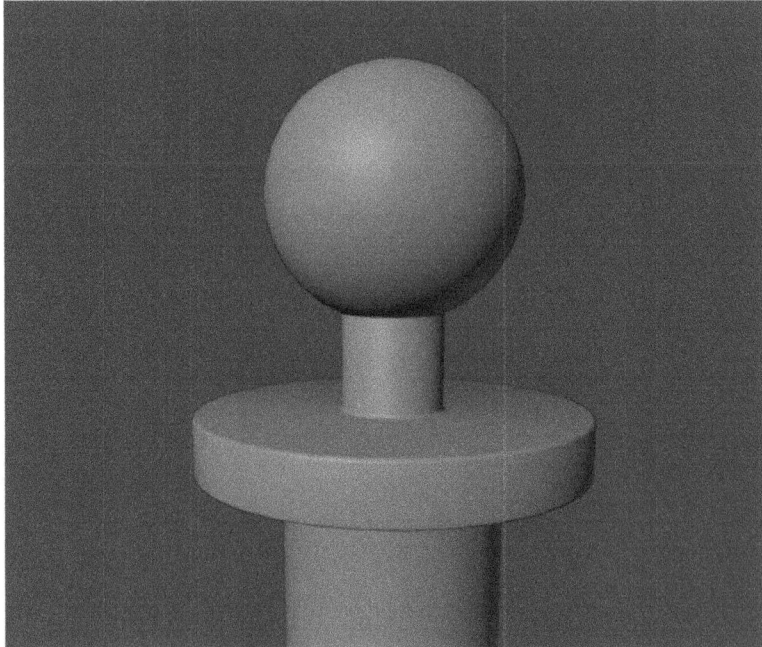

Figure 9.10 – The finished flagpole

6. Finally, let's move the flag object to the right side and a little down on the flagpole object. View the following figure.

Figure 9.11 – The flag position

Great! Now, we can work on creating the rope to hold the flag to the pole!

Creating the rope

The next thing that we will be creating is the rope that attaches the flag to the pole:

1. Add in a new **Cylinder** object. Then, set **Vertices** to 4, **Radius** to 0.008 m, and **Depth** to 6 m to match the height of the flagpole.

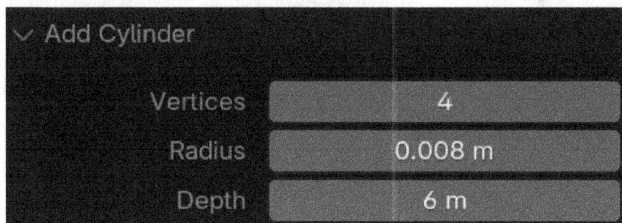

Figure 9.12 – Rope values

2. This rope object is also going to have the cloth simulation applied to it. This way, it will swing and move around with the flag. For this to work, we need more geometry, so let's go into **Edit Mode** and add some loop cuts.

    Press *Ctrl+ R* or *Cmd + R* and then type 200 to add 200 horizontal loop cuts.

3.   Normally, the rope goes through a pully system. This allows the flag to be raised and lowered. To simulate this, let's duplicate the rope (*Shift + D*) so that there are now two ropes.

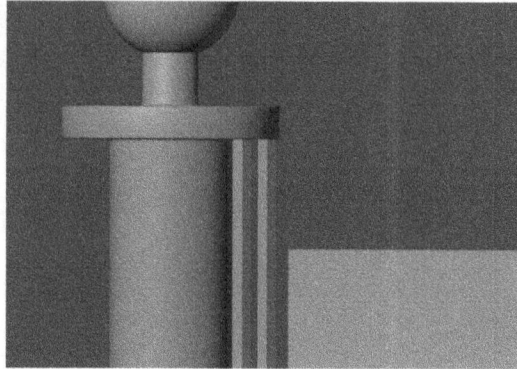

Figure 9.13 – Rope position

Place the ropes in between the pole and the flag, as you can see in *Figure 9.13*, and then we can move on to creating the hooks!

Creating the hooks

With real-life flags, depending on the size, there are usually two to four hooks that attach the flag to the rope. For this tutorial, we will be adding four hooks:

1.   Press *Shift + A* and add a **Torus** object.

2.   Scale it down to be around 0.03 m and place it in the top-left corner of the flag.

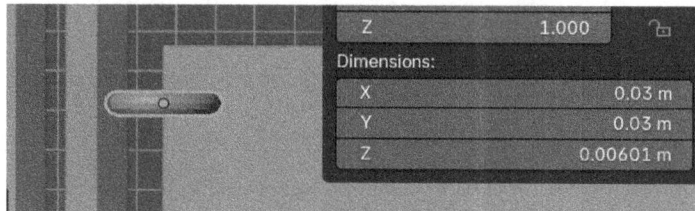

Figure 9.14 – The hook position

3.   Now, we need to make sure the torus object moves with the flag as it's simulating. To do this, we are going to parent the torus to the top-corner vertex of the flag. So, go into **Edit Mode** with the flag and torus objects both selected.

4. Now, select the entire torus first, and then hold *Shift* and select the top-left corner vertex.

Figure 9.15 – Vertex selection

5. Press *Ctrl + P* or *Cmd + P* or go up to the **Vertex** menu and select **Make Vertex Parent**. Now, the torus will be parented to that vertex, and wherever it goes, the torus will follow!

6. Repeat *steps 1–5* for the remaining hooks you want to add.

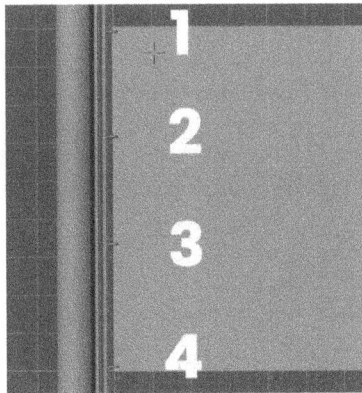

Figure 9.16 – Rings added

After you have added the rest, we can move on to the cloth simulation!

Creating the simulation

Now that all the objects in the scene are here, we can create the simulation. Before we do that, though, we have to do a few things:

1. Select the two rope objects and then the flag object. Then, press *Ctrl + J* or *Cmd + J* or go to **Object | Join**; this will join those two objects together as one so that our simulation will work properly.

2. Next, let's add a **Wind** force field to the scene. To do this, press *Shift + A* | **Force Field** | **Wind**.

3. Head over to the **Physics** panel and set **Strength** to 5000. We need quite a high strength value for the cloth to move around. Next, set **Flow** to 0 and **Noise Amount** to 5, which will give us more variation in the wind!

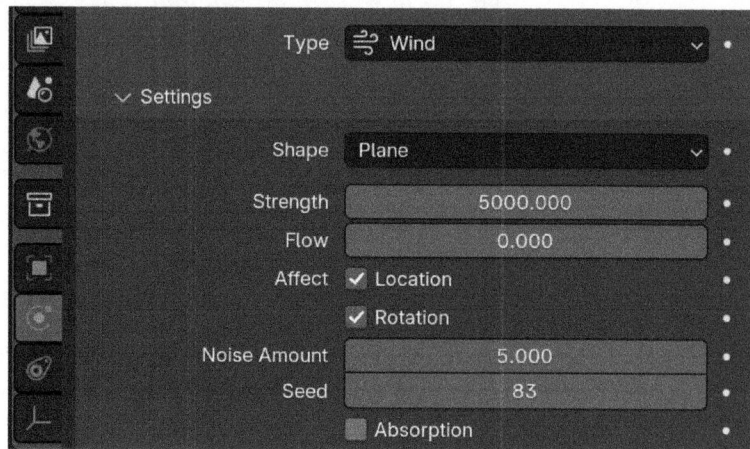

Figure 9.17 – Wind settings

4. Rotate the wind force field 90 degrees so it's pointed in the direction of the flag.

Figure 9.18 – Wind force field direction

Now, let's create the cloth simulation!

5. Select your flag and head over to the **Physics** panel.

6. Now, select **Cloth**. We are going to start at the top and work our way down the settings, changing them as needed. The first thing we'll change is **Quality**. This will increase the accuracy of the simulation and help prevent any errors. Since the ropes and the flag will be interacting with each other, we need to set **Quality** to a high value so that we get a nice simulation. Let's go with a value of 30.

7. Our cloth currently weighs way too much, and the wind is hardly going to affect it. To fix this, let's set **Vertex Mass** to 0.03 kg.

8. Since the wind strength is so high, let's set **Tension** in the **Stiffness** tab to 25 to make sure that the cloth doesn't stretch.

9. As for **Bending** in the **Stiffness** tab, set this value to 0.4 so that we get slightly smaller wrinkles and bends.

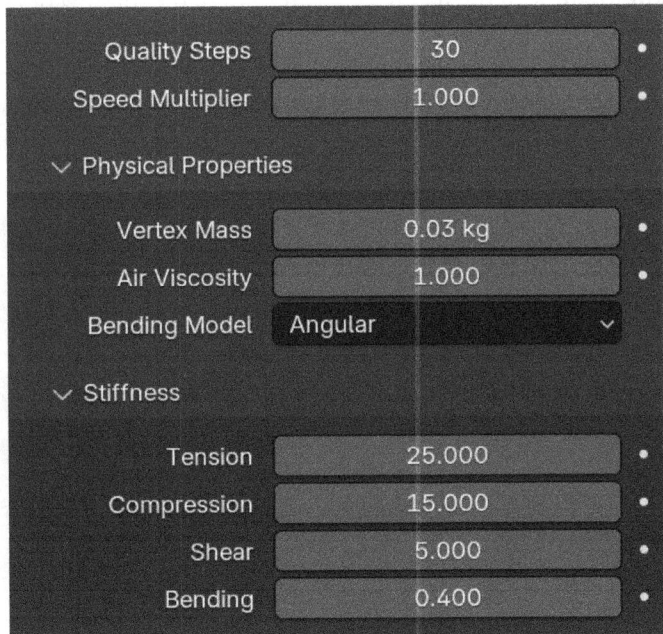

Figure 9.19 – Stiffness values

10. Now, let's create the pin group so that the flag stays in place and doesn't just fall straight down. For this, we need to create a vertex group and assign some of the vertices to it.

Head over to the **Object Data** panel and create a new vertex group by hitting + on the right side.

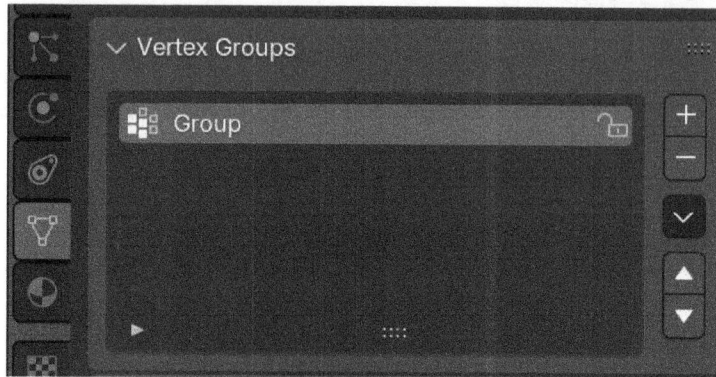

Figure 9.20 – Vertex Groups

11. Now, go into **Edit Mode** with the flag selected and assign the top row of faces of the ropes to that vertex group with a **Weight** value of 1. View the following figure to see which row of faces to select!

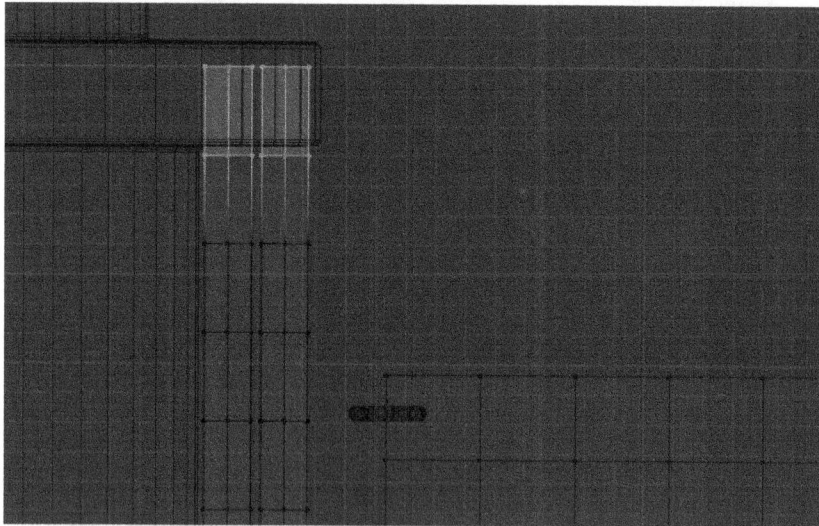

Figure 9.21 – Top faces on the rope

12. Select the bottom row of faces of the rope and assign those vertices as well.

The other thing we are going to be doing is tightening up this rope. If we play the simulation right now, the rope is going to arch far away from the flagpole because the wind is pushing it. We want it to be a little tighter and closer to the flagpole.

To achieve this, we will essentially be shrinking the rope using another vertex group to make it tighter.

13. First, go into **Edit Mode** and select both rope objects by hovering over them and pressing *L*. This shortcut will select the entire object automatically.

14. Next, hit the + button in the **Vertex Groups** tab and click **Assign** with a **Weight** value of 1.

Figure 9.22 – Two vertex groups

Essentially, we now have two vertex groups assigned to the flag. **Group** is assigned to the top and bottom faces of the ropes and **Group.001** is assigned to the entire rope objects. We will put both of these vertex groups into the cloth settings, so they actually affect the simulation in just a couple of steps! Now, we need to use the **Sewing** feature to attach the flag to the ropes!

We discussed how **Sewing** works with the cloth simulation in the last chapter, but if you need a refresher, it basically works by tightening the connecting edges of two meshes. In this case, we will be creating an edge between the flag and the rope objects. This way, when **Sewing** is enabled, that edge will automatically be tightened together! Here is how we do that!

15. In **Edit Mode**, find the vertices you want to attach between the rope and the flag, and press *F* to fill in an edge:

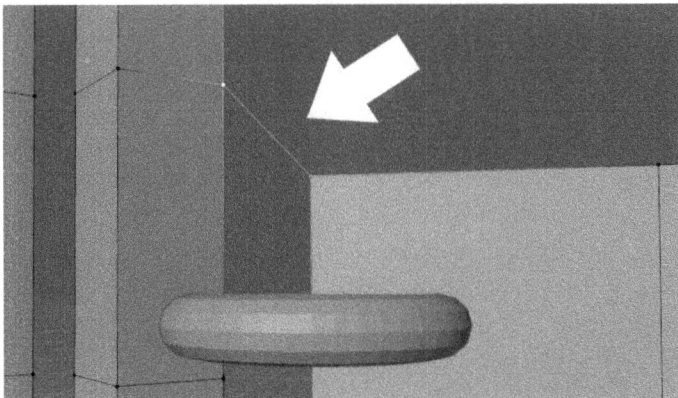

Figure 9.23 – The flag attachment

16. Do the same thing for the remaining hooks on the flag. Don't worry if the edge is not straight; this will actually give the flag some randomness and make it look better!

17. Back over in the **Physics** panel, jump down to the **Shape** tab, and in the **Pin Group** option, select **Group**. Then, enable **Sewing** and set **Max Sewing Force**, which sets how strong those edges will be pulled together, to 15!

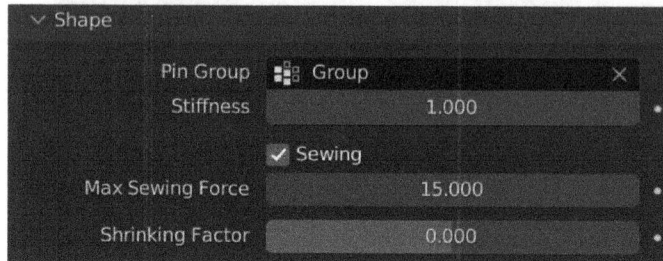

Figure 9.24 – Shape settings

18. Now to tighten the rope, scroll down to the **Property Weights** tab. From the **Shrinking Group** option, select **Group.001**. As for the strength of this shrinking effect, let's go with a value of 0.02 for **Max Shrinking**.

    Now, when we play the simulation, the rope should tighten, and the flag should be hooked to the rope at the top!

19. The last step before we bake the simulation is to set up the collisions! Open the **Collision** tab and set **Quality** to 4. This will give us more accurate results. Turn on **Self Collision** and lower the distance to 0.005.

20. With that done, we can bake in the simulation! Head up to the **Cache** tab and set **End Frame** to 200, or however long you want your animation to be, and then click **Bake**!

All the settings we just talked about are just a baseline to create a nice-looking flag. Feel free to change and customize anything to your liking. For now, we are ready to move on to creating the materials!

Making the materials

In this section, we will be creating all the materials for our scene! Starting out with the flag, we will be learning how to UV unwrap an object and assign a texture to it. After that, we will also create the materials for both the flagpole and the hooks! Let's get started!

Creating the flag material

Follow these steps to create the flag material:

1. The first thing we need to do is decide what texture we will be using for our flag. You could use your country's flag or the Blender flag that I have created for this chapter. Here is the link to download that texture: `https://github.com/PacktPublishing/Learn-Blender-4-Simulations-the-Right-Way/tree/main/Chapter%209`.

2. Once you have a texture ready to go, add it to the material. To do so, head over to the **Material** panel and create a new material by selecting **New**.

3. Next, click on the yellow dot next to the base color of the **Principled BSDF** shader, choose **Image Texture**, and open the flag texture you have downloaded.

Figure 9.25 – The flag texture

4. Now that the texture is added, we need to UV unwrap our flag so that the texture can be applied correctly. Skip to **Frame 1** and go into **Edit Mode** on the flag. Select the entire flag by pressing *A* followed by *U*, and select **Unwrap**.

5. If you press *Z* and go into **Material Preview**, you might notice that the texture is not in the correct spot. To fix it, jump over to the **UV Editor** workspace at the top. Then, in **Edit Mode**, select everything with *A*, and scale and move until you fill out the image with the UV map of the flag. View the following figure:

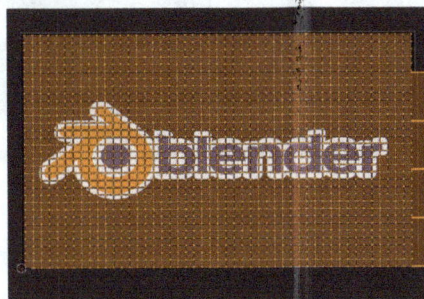

Figure 9.26 – UV map placement

6. Back in the **Principled BSDF** shader, let's set **Roughness** to 0.9 so that it's not as glossy!

7. The other thing that we need to do is create a new material for the rope. Right now, since the rope and flag are one object, they are sharing the same material. To fix this, hit the + button on the right side to add a slot material. Then, click **New**:

Figure 9.27 – A slot material

8. Give it the color of your choice and set **Roughness** to 0.9 so it's not glossy.

9. Then, to assign the new material to the rope objects, go into **Edit Mode**, select the ropes, and hit **Assign**!

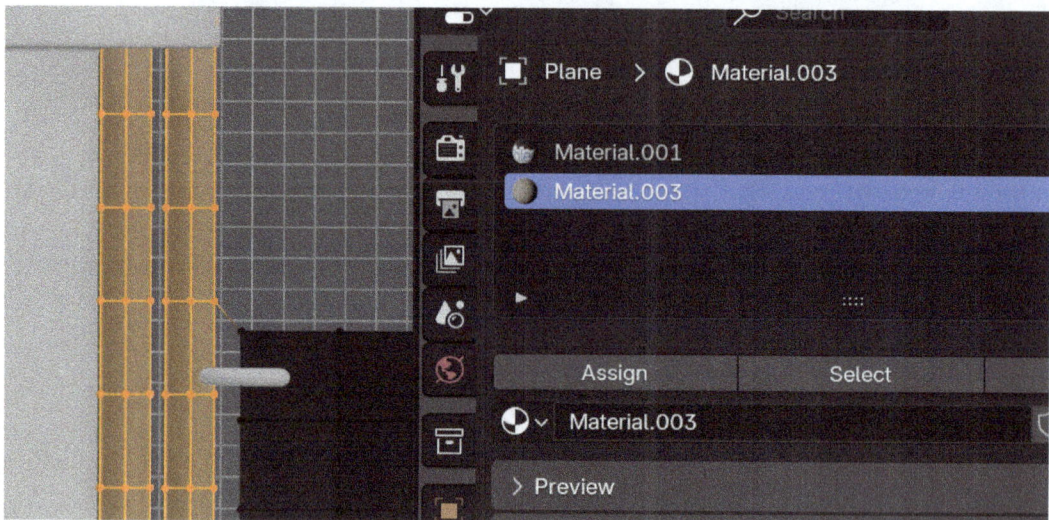

Figure 9.28 – Assigning the material

At the beginning of the chapter, we talked about the hoist of the flag, which is the part that attaches to the rope. To create this, repeat *steps 7–9* but, this time, use a white color for the material! Assign it to the far-left faces of the flag itself. View the following figure:

Figure 9.29 – Creating the hoist

With that done, let's work on the hooks and create a nice gold metallic material!

Creating the hook material

The hooks for flags are usually a silver or gold color, which is pretty simple to do:

1. Select one of the hooks and click **New** to create a new material.
2. Set **Metallic** to 1 and **Roughness** to 0.1. This will give the material a nice glossy look.
3. Then, set **Base Color** to an orange-yellow color, which will give it a gold look.

Figure 9.30 – A gold material

And that material is done! Then, just assign the rest of the hooks to share that material and we can move on!

Creating the flagpole material

The flagpole material is also going to be a nice metallic material except, this time, we are going to give it a silver look:

1. Select the flagpole and create a new material.

2. Set **Metallic** to 1 and **Roughness** to 0.1.

3. As for **Base Color**, let's set this to a light gray color.

And there it is! All the materials are done, and now we can move on to the final touchups before we render the animation!

Rendering the animation

Our scene is coming along great, but for this last section of the chapter, we will be going over some final tweaks and touchups to make our render look good:

1. Let's start by working on the flag. To smooth out the wrinkles and give it an overall better look, let's add a **Subdivision Surface** modifier. Head over to the **Modifier** panel, click **Add Modifier**, and select **Subdivision Surface**. Set both the **Viewport** and **Render** levels to 2.

2. Right now, our flag is completely thin, which isn't very realistic, so let's add a **Solidify** modifier to give it just a little bit of thickness. Set **Thickness** to something much lower, such as 0.002.

3. As for the lighting, I recommend using a **High Dynamic Range (HDR)** image to achieve the most realistic results. You can get very high-quality HDR images for free at polyhaven. com. Once you have found an HDR image that you like, head over to the **World** panel, click the yellow dot next to **Color**, select **Environment Texture**, and open the HDR image in the scene!

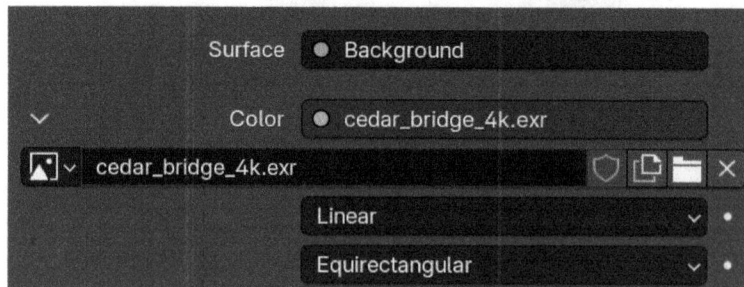

Figure 9.31 – HDR background

4. Next, in the **Render** panel, let's enable **Raytracing** to give us better reflections. Also, make sure to set **Resolution** to `1:1`.

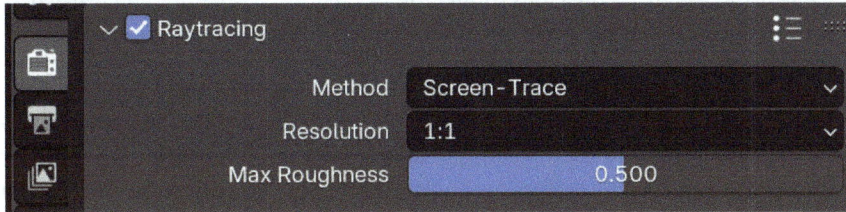

Figure 9.32 – Raytracing

5. In **Color Management**, set **Look** to **High Contrast** to make the colors pop a bit more.

6. After that, you can set up the camera to wherever you like. A good position would be looking up at the flag. This would give a nice perspective and height to the flagpole.

Figure 9.33 – The camera position

7. Finally, the last step is to set the end frame in the Timeline to match the length of your simulation.

At this point, we are ready to render. Make sure to set your output and the file type that you want. From there, head up to **Render** and select **Render Animation**!

Summary

We created a nice realistic flag using the cloth simulation in Blender! Hopefully, you learned a thing or two and created something cool in the process! As always, let's recap what we covered in this chapter.

First, we discussed the different things that make up a flag and the sizes and heights of those. After that, we added and modeled all the objects we needed. We set up the simulation with multiple vertex groups to pin the ropes in place and used **Sewing** to attach the flag to the ropes. We also created the materials and learned how to add the texture to the flag. And finally, we did some final touchups and rendered the animation!

It's always good to practice as well following a tutorial! This way, the steps and things you learned really sink in! I encourage you to create another project using the cloth simulation – maybe a huge medieval banner or a cape flowing in the wind from a character!

Not only is this the end of the chapter but it is also the end of *Part 2* of this book! In the next couple of chapters, we will be diving deep into the rigid body simulation and learning all about what it is and how it works in Blender!

Part 3: Diving into Rigid Bodies

The Rigid Body simulation is all about creating motion with solid objects in Blender. Over the next two chapters, we will learn all about rigid bodies, what they are, and how they work. We will go through all the settings and values and see how to use them effectively in Blender. By the end, we will have created a really cool and interesting rigid body obstacle course animation!

This part has the following chapters:

- *Chapter 10, An Introduction to Rigid Bodies*
- *Chapter 11, Creating a Rigid Body Physics Course*

10

An Introduction to Rigid Bodies

The **rigid body simulation** is another way to add physics to your objects in Blender. Unlike the soft body and cloth simulations, the rigid body simulation won't deform the object. Instead, it will keep the structure of the mesh and make sure everything is rigid. The rigid body system also works very well with the animation system in Blender. This means you can have some objects that are animated and some that aren't, and everything will still interact with each other.

The goal of this chapter is to provide an overview of the rigid body simulation and all its settings. We'll start by learning what this simulation is and how it works. From there, we'll jump straight into the settings and discuss each one. This way, you'll know exactly how everything works and you won't have to guess.

In this chapter, we'll be covering the following topics:

- What is a rigid body simulation?
- Understanding the Rigid Body settings
- Rigid Body World
- Rigid Body Object Menu
- Using rigid body constraints

Technical requirements

This chapter requires that you have Blender version 4.2 or above installed. To download Blender, visit www.blender.org.

The supporting files for this chapter are available here: https://github.com/PacktPublishing/Learn-Blender-4-Simulations-the-Right-Way/tree/main/Chapter%2010.

What is a rigid body simulation?

The **rigid body** simulation is used to simulate the motion of solid objects in Blender. It allows mesh objects to fall, collide with each other, and bounce around without them being deformed. This simulation is great for creating things such as a pile of rocks, something mashing through a wall, or any kind of realistic physics without deformations. Rigid bodies are also often used in films and games to create physics-based effects.

To create a rigid body simulation, you need to have a mesh object selected. Then, you can go to the **Physics** panel and select **Rigid Body**, or go to the **Object** menu and then go to **Rigid Body**. After selecting **Rigid Body**, select either **Add Passive** or **Add Active**:

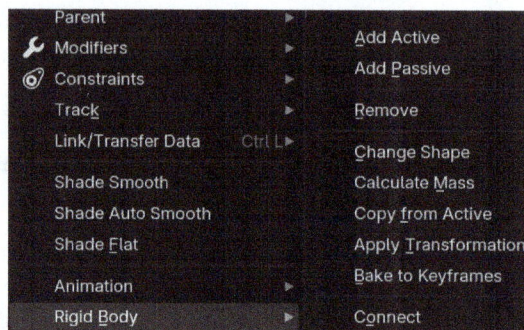

Figure 10.1 – The Rigid Body menu

Active and **Passive** are the two types of rigid bodies you can add in Blender. An active body will react to gravity, collisions, and even force fields, whereas a passive body will stay static and not move but it will still interact with active objects if one collides with it:

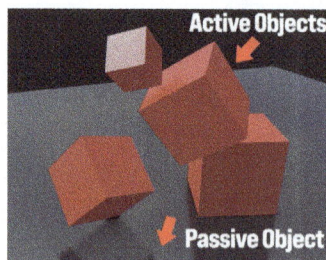

Figure 10.2 – Active and passive objects

Let's say you create a simulation, and the objects move around and collide with each other. Now, you want to apply transformations so that the objects remain in their new location when you restart the timeline. Well, when you create a rigid body simulation, it doesn't create a modifier, unlike the other simulations we've discussed in this book. If you want to apply the transformations, you need to go up to **Object | Rigid Body** and select **Apply Transformation** (*Figure 10.1*). Now, the object will start simulating at that new location.

If you want to remove the simulation, you can click the **X** button next to **Rigid Body** in the **Physics** panel or, once again, go up to **Object | Rigid Body** and choose **Remove** (*Figure 10.1*). I'll be referencing this menu a lot in this chapter, so from now on, let's call it **Rigid Body Object Menu**.

The origin point of the rigid body object will also affect how it's simulated. For example, in the following figure, the origin point is off to the right. Even though nothing is hitting or interacting with the cube, it's being pulled to the right because of the origin point:

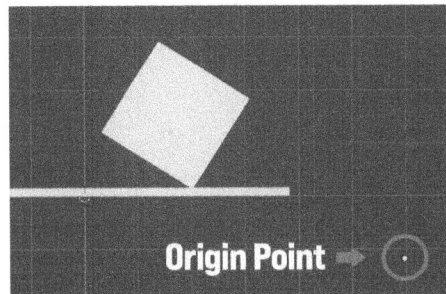

Figure 10.3 – The origin point

So, if an object is flying off in some random direction, double-check where the origin point is. To change where the origin point is, right-click with the object that's been selected, go to **Set Origin**, and select **Origin to Geometry**. This will bring the origin point to the center of the object.

The other aspect of this simulation is rigid body constraints. If you've worked with armatures or animation, you'll be familiar with how these operate. They're used to connect two rigid bodies. You can create a constraint by having two rigid bodies selected, going to **Rigid Body Object Menu**, and clicking **Connect**. An **Empty** object will be created between these two rigid bodies; this is the controller for that constraint:

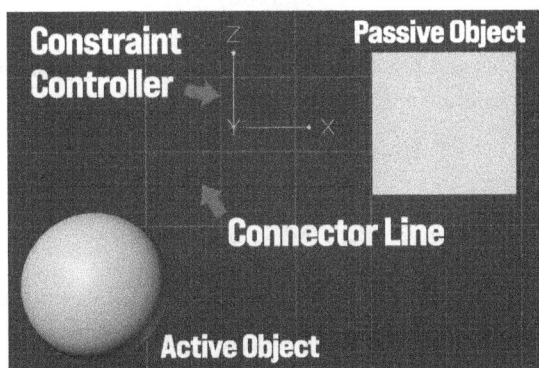

Figure 10.4 – Connected constraints

Using constraints allows you to limit the location and rotation of rigid bodies. This can be very useful for creating things such as a hinge for a door or an elevator that moves up and down. If this sounds complicated, don't worry – we'll be going over rigid body constraints in more detail later in this chapter!

One very important thing that needs to be mentioned is that if you change the scale of any rigid body, you *need* to remember to apply the scale so that all the scale values go back to 1. If you don't do this, Blender won't understand the scale of the objects and you'll get strange collision results. Remember that to apply the scale of an object, make sure the object is selected, press *Ctrl + A* or *Cmd + A*, and select **Scale**.

Now that you understand how the rigid body simulation works in Blender, let's jump into the settings and talk about each one!

Understanding the Rigid Body settings

This section is all about the settings for the rigid body simulation. As always, let's start at the top and work our way down!

When you first select **Rigid Body** in the **Physics** panel, you'll be able to select which **Type** of rigid body you want. As mentioned earlier, there are two types – **Active** and **Passive**:

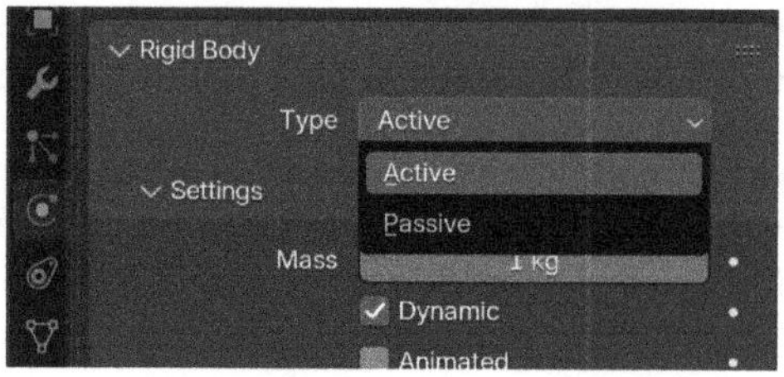

Figure 10.5 – Rigid Body – Type

Active means it will have physics and react to gravity and other forces. **Passive** will make the rigid body stay static, but it will still interact with other rigid bodies.

Settings

The following options can be found underneath the **Settings** tab:

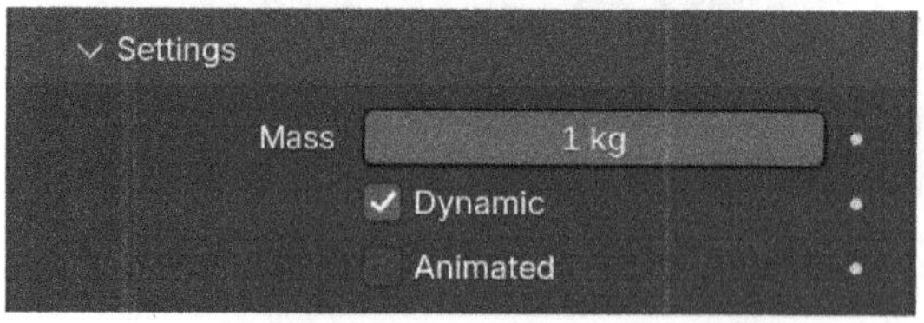

Figure 10.6 – Settings

Let's take a look at these in more detail:

- **Mass**: This is where you set how much the rigid body should weigh in the simulation. As you can probably guess, the weight of the object will affect how it interacts with other rigid bodies and forces. You can type this number in manually or you can let Blender calculate it automatically. In the **Rigid Body Object Menu** area, you can select **Calculate Mass**. This will bring up a large menu containing all the different types of real-world materials:

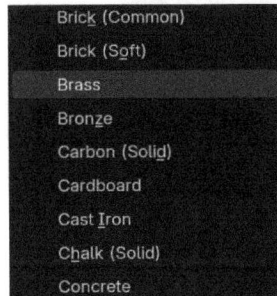

Figure 10.7 – The Calculate Mass menu

Mass is also calculated based on the size of the mesh. For example, if a cube is *2 x 2 meters* and you select **Gold** for the calculation, Blender will treat the cube as a completely solid block of gold and **Mass** is going to be set at 154256 kg or 340076 Ib. This is quite heavy, so make sure you choose the right mass for your simulation.

- **Dynamic**: This allows you to turn the rigid body object off and on. This setting can also be animated, which can be useful if you want the rigid body to stop interacting with the simulation at a certain point in the timeline.

- **Animated**: This setting allows you to move the rigid body object around using animation data and keyframes. And it will still interact with the simulation! This is extremely useful and can be applied to many simulations. The other great thing is that the **Animated** checkbox in *Figure 10.6* can also be toggled off and on using animation keyframes. For example, you can have a cube fly into other cubes using location keyframes:

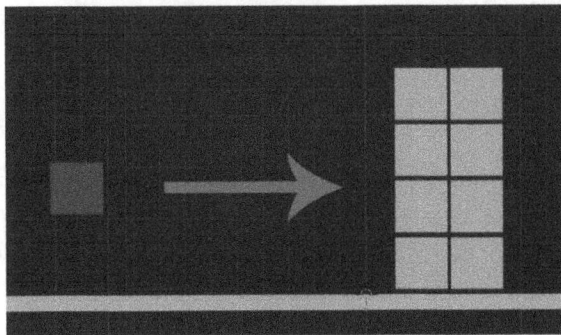

Figure 10.8 – Cube Animated on

Right before the last location keyframe, you can toggle the **Animated** checkbox off. This will allow the cube to keep its velocity and momentum from the previous keyframe and crash into the other cubes, as shown in the following figure:

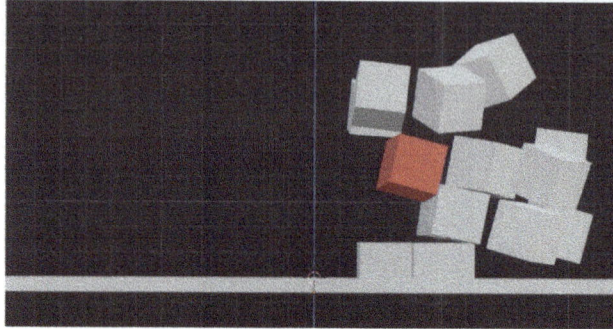

Figure 10.9 – Cube Animated off

If you don't toggle off **Animated**, the cube will follow the keyframes you've set up and stop at its intended location.

While we go through all these settings, I recommend that you test them out for yourself so that you can see how they work. This will help you understand this simulation much better!

Collisions

Next up, we have the **Collisions** tab. Here, we can change the way the rigid bodies collide with other objects and how they respond to surfaces:

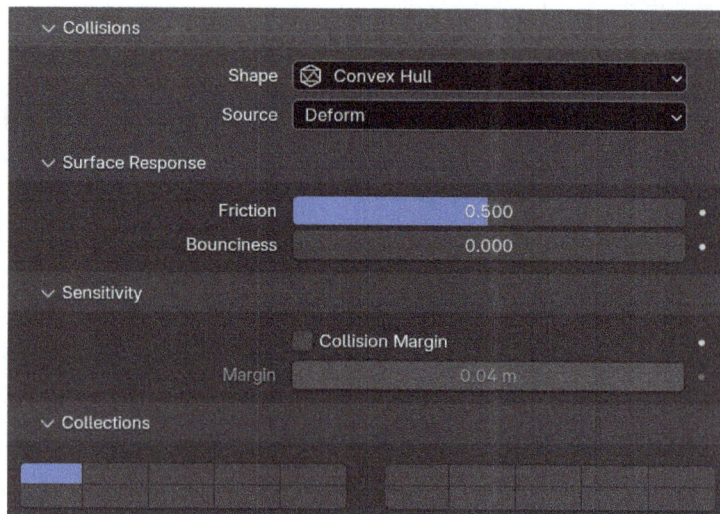

Figure 10.10 – The Collisions tab

Let's look at the options that are available in more detail:

- **Shape**: This controls the collision boundary of the object. With this menu, you can select many primitive shapes to be the collision area: **Box**, **Sphere**, **Capsule**, **Cylinder**, **Cone**, **Convex Hull**, **Mesh**, and **Compound Parent**. If a cube object has a **Shape** value of the **Sphere** option, then the collision will be in the shape of a sphere rather than the cube itself:

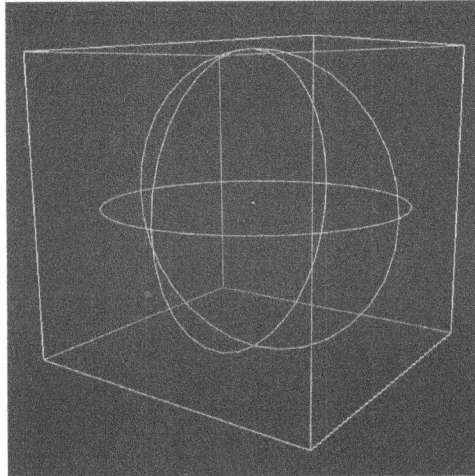

Figure 10.11 – Sphere

The same goes for the other primitive shapes.

Convex Hull works a bit differently. You can think of this collision area as being shrink-wrapped around the object. This method works very well with simple meshes that aren't too complex:

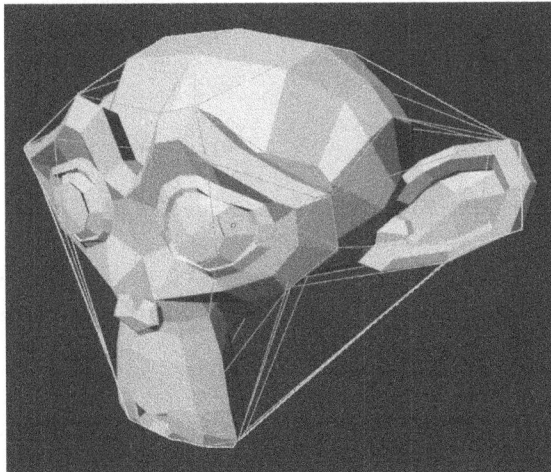

Figure 10.12 – Convex Hull example

The **Mesh** shape is made up of triangles and encompasses the entire object. This is used for more complex collision areas. The **Mesh** method is slower and can sometimes cause errors, so only use it if you need to.

The last shape we need to discuss is **Compound Parent**. This takes any objects that are parented to that mesh and uses them as the collision boundary.

What is parenting?

Parenting means attaching one or more objects to a single parent object. This way, when you move, rotate, or scale that parent object, those translations will also affect the "children" meshes attached to it.

The following figure shows that all the cubes are parented to the icosphere. With the icosphere set to **Compound Parent**, it will use the cubes as the collision boundary, not the sphere itself:

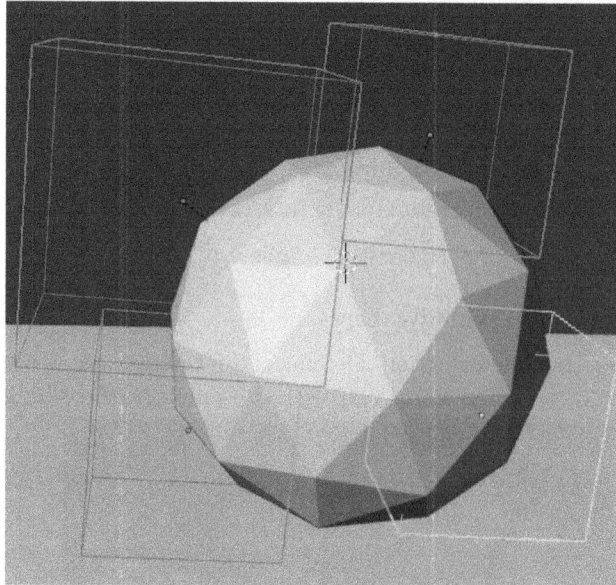

Figure 10.13 – Compound Parent example

- **Source**: This also controls the collision boundary. In this menu, there are three options to choose from:

  - **Base**: This will ignore any modifiers and only use the base mesh for the collision.

  - **Deform**: This will allow any modifiers or shape keys that change the shape of the mesh to be taken into account with the collision

- **Final**: This also includes all the modifiers and deformations that have been applied to the mesh.

With **Shape** set to **Mesh** and **Source** set to **Deform**, a **Deforming** checkbox will appear. This allows the mesh to deform as the simulation plays, which can be useful in some situations. For example, if you have a modifier that changes the geometry on the mesh during the simulation (such as **Displacement** or **Simple Deform**), the collision shape will also change and be more accurate with **Deforming** checked.

Inside the **Collision** tab, there are three submenus, the first of which is the **Surface Response** tab. Here are the available settings:

- **Friction**: This setting controls how sticky the surface will be. Lower values will make the surface like ice and higher values will prevent sliding.

- **Bounciness**: This is exactly what it sounds like – this is the amount of bounciness the surface will have when an object collides with it. Note that this setting won't have an effect until you also change the **Bounciness** setting on *both* objects that are colliding.

In the following figure, the **Bounciness** setting of the cube on the left is set to 0, that of the cube on the right is set to 2, and that of the plane is set to 1. As you can see, the cube on the right is bouncing much higher:

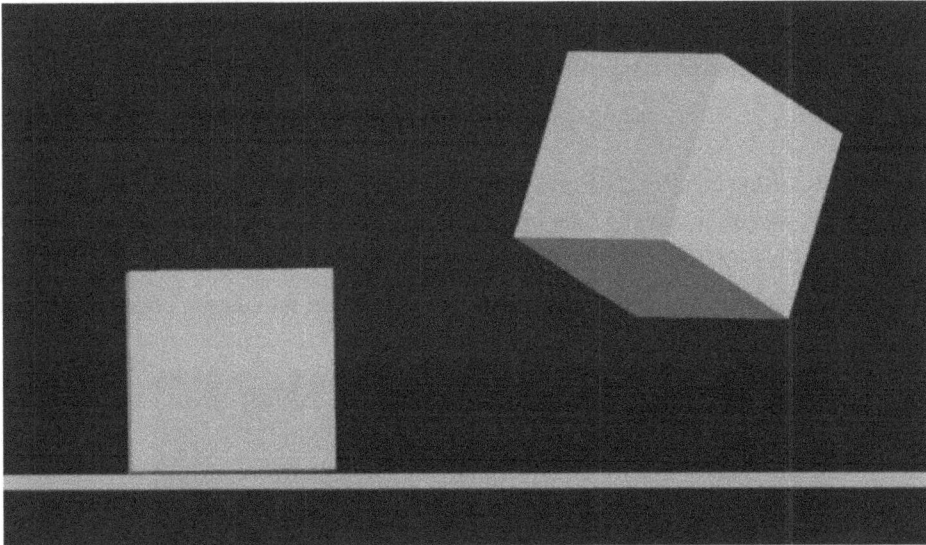

Figure 10.14 – Bounciness example

The next submenu in the **Collision** tab is the **Sensitivity** tab:

- **Collision Margin**: When this checkbox is checked, you'll be able to set the **Margin** value. This value controls the collision distance from other objects. The following figure shows a cube with a **Margin** value of 0.4 m for the plane underneath. As you can see, there's a large distance between the two objects:

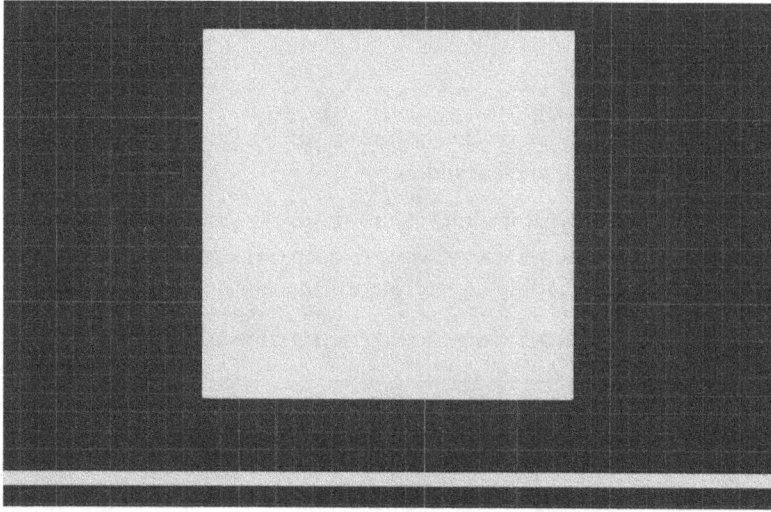

Figure 10.15 – Collision margin

Note that this setting behaves strangely when **Mesh** and **Cone** are selected for **Shape**. If a high distance is set, this will make the rigid bodies bounce and not collide properly. Make sure that you set this value to something low or 0 if those shapes are being used.

The last thing in the **Collisions** tab is **Collections**. Here, you can set custom collision groups for the simulation:

Figure 10.16 – Collections

The main purpose of this tab is to provide **Collections** boxes so that you can set up rigid body collision groups. For example, if one rigid body object has the first box selected and another rigid body has the second box selected, they'll both be simulated but they won't collide or interact with each other because they have different collision groups.

Another thing you can do with this system is have multiple boxes highlighted on one or more objects at the same time. You can achieve this by holding *Shift* and selecting the collision groups you want. This will cause any rigid body objects with those same highlighted boxes to collide with each other.

This can be useful for creating effects where one rigid body will pass through another without colliding but then collide with a different rigid body later on.

Dynamics

The **Dynamics** tab allows you to control the physics of the rigid body a bit more. Note that this only works for **Active** rigid bodies:

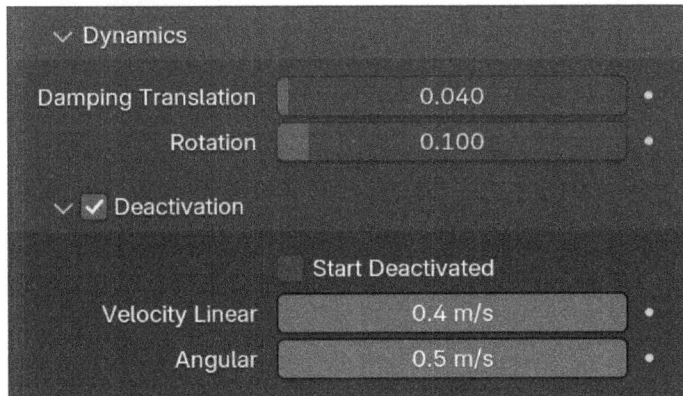

Figure 10.17 – Dynamics

Let's take a look at the settings that are available in more detail:

- **Damping Translation**: This controls how fast a rigid body will lose its velocity and come to a stop. Higher values will dampen the movement and make the object stop very quickly.

- **Rotation**: This works in the same way. If an object is spinning, this value controls how fast that object will lose its angular velocity and come to a stop.

- **Deactivation**: When this is checked, Blender stops simulating the rigid body when the velocity of that object is lower than the **Linear** and **Angular** values. Sometimes, when working with rigid bodies, they jitter around, even when they are stationary. **Deactivation** allows them to stop being simulated and will help prevent jitteriness. This will also help save memory in the scene.

- **Start Deactivated**: This will make the rigid body not move until another rigid body comes into contact with it. This can be useful if you want an object to not move until another object touches it.

And there we go! That is all the settings for **Rigid Body** in the **Physics** panel. We still have a lot to go over in this chapter, so let's talk about **Rigid Body World**!

Rigid Body World

Rigid Body World is located in the **Scene** panel; it's where you can set which collection will be simulated, the speed, and the steps per frame. It's also where you bake in the simulation:

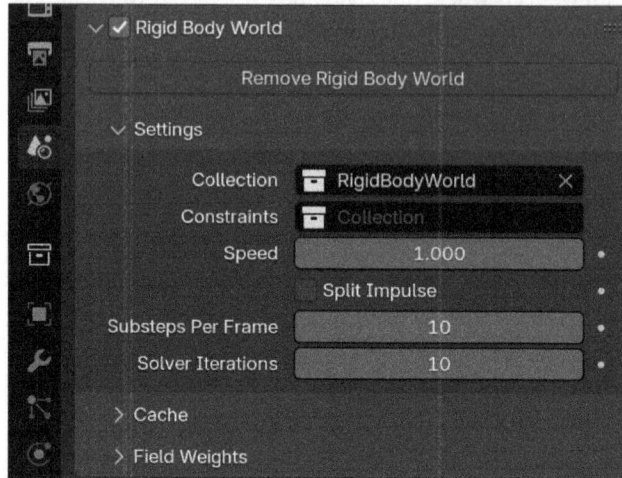

Figure 10.18 – Rigid Body World settings

When you first add a rigid body to the scene, the rigid body world is created. Without this, nothing would be simulated; you always need the rigid body world. You can disable this world by unchecking it or by clicking **Remove Rigid Body World**. Now, let's talk about the settings in this panel:

- With **Collection** called **RigidBodyWorld** selected, *every* rigid body in *every* collection can be simulated. However, if you choose a specific collection, then only the objects in that particular collection will be simulated.

- **Constraints**: In *Figure 10.18*, this collection is currently empty. This is because it's not created until you create a rigid body constraint. Once you do this, a new collection will be created called **RigidBodyConstraints**:

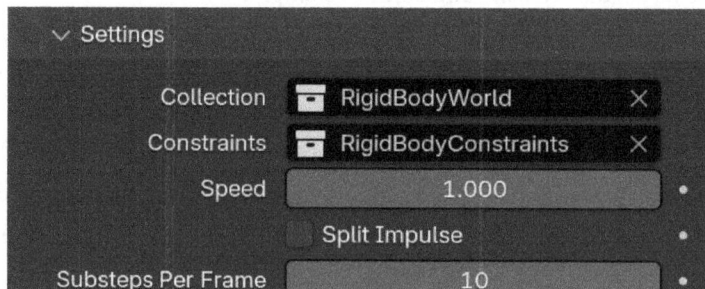

Figure 10.19 – RigidBodyConstraints

You won't see these collections in **Outliner** but if you go to the **Object** panel with one of the rigid bodies selected and go to the **Object Properties** tab, you'll see them inside that **RigidBodyWorld** collection:

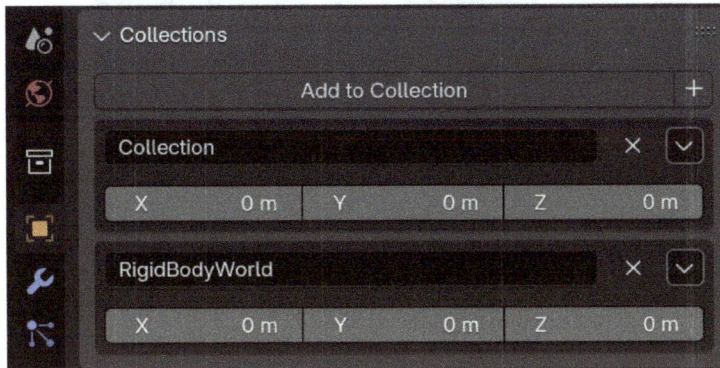

Figure 10.20 – Object collections

- **Speed**: This controls the overall speed of the simulation. Higher values will increase the simulation's speed, while lower values will slow it down.

- **Split Impulse**: This helps reduce any extra velocity that builds up when two objects collide. For example, in the following figure, two cubes are colliding with each other. With **Split Impulse** on, the cubes will collide and come to a stop quickly. With **Split Impulse** off, the cubes will collide, bounce off, and fly in opposite directions:

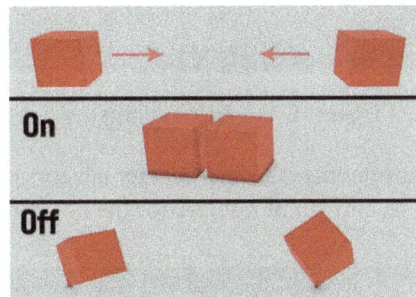

Figure 10.21 – Split Impulse

- **Substeps Per Frame**: This is the number of steps that will happen per second of animation. Increasing this value will give more accurate results but also increase the bake time. If you have fast-moving objects, it's recommended to turn this value up.

- **Solver Iterations**: This works like **Substeps Per Frame** except that it deals with rigid body constraints. Increasing this value will give more accurate results for constraints but also increase the bake time.

- **Cache**: This tab is where you can set the **Simulation Start** and **End** frames and bake the simulation. This should all be familiar since it works the same as the soft body and cloth simulations:

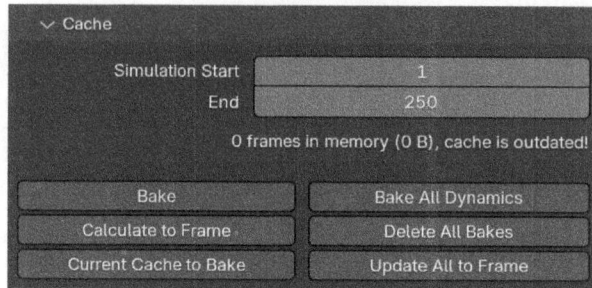

Figure 10.22 – The Cache tab

- **Field Weights**: You can add different force fields to control the movement of rigid bodies. The influence of these force fields can be controlled in the **Field Weights** tab. The **Gravity** setting and strength of every force field can be changed here. You can also select an **Effector Collection** value if you want to limit which forces affect the simulation:

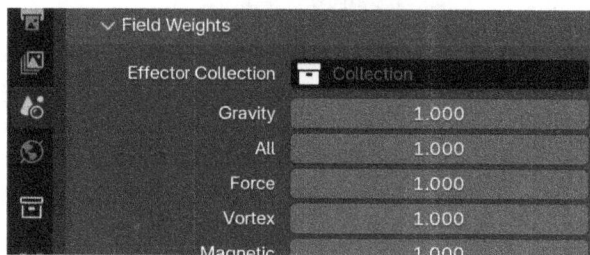

Figure 10.23 – Field Weights

The other place to control the gravity is in the **Gravity** tab above the **Rigid Body World** tab. Here, you can turn it off or set a different number for the downward force. You can even set a different axis for gravity:

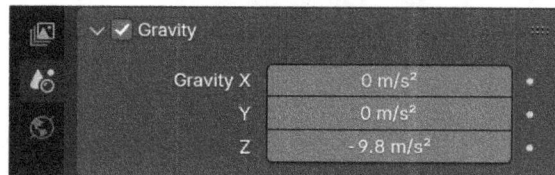

Figure 10.24 – The Gravity tab

Before we move on to the rigid body constraints, let's discuss a couple more options for the rigid body simulation and how to add many rigid body objects at once using the **Rigid Body Object Menu** area.

Rigid Body Object Menu

As mentioned earlier in this chapter, the **Rigid Body Object Menu** area can be found by going to the **Object** menu and then to **Rigid Body**. Here, you'll find a couple of options that we've already discussed, but also a couple of new ones:

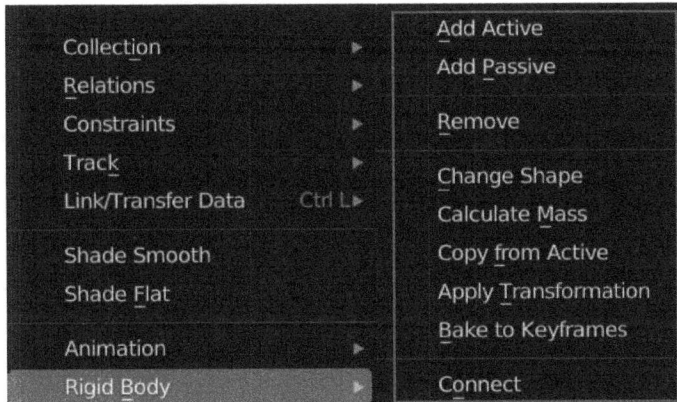

Figure 10.25 – Rigid Body Object Menu

- If you want to create many rigid bodies at once, it's very easy! Make sure all the objects are selected and click **Add Active**. Now, each one you selected will have the **Active** rigid body applied to it.

- The same goes for **Add Passive**.

- You can also remove all the rigid bodies by selecting **Remove**.

- **Change Shape** allows you to change the collision boundary for all the objects you have selected.

- **Calculate Mass** is something we talked about earlier, so let's move on to **Copy From Active**. If you've changed some settings on one object and want to copy those changes to another, this option can do that! Make sure all the objects you want to copy are selected and the one with those settings is the **active object**, then click on **Copy From Active**. Now, each object you've selected will have those exact settings applied. This is very useful for applying the same settings to many objects at once.

- Let's skip **Apply Transform** since we mentioned it earlier, and look at **Bake to Keyframes** instead. This option allows the movement of the rigid body to be converted over to keyframes. This can give you way more flexibility with the object because now, you're dealing with keyframes rather than a simulation. This is very useful when you want to work with other simulations because now, you're dealing with animation data rather than rigid body data, which doesn't translate over to other simulation types.

- Finally, **Connect** allows you to connect two rigid bodies to create a constraint.

Speaking of constraints, let's talk about **rigid body constraints** and how they work with the simulation in Blender!

Using rigid body constraints

Rigid body constraints allow you to connect two rigid bodies and create a *joint* between them. This joint can constrict the movement of the rigid body. For example, one of the constraints you can create is a hinge. This could be very useful for creating things such as a door or a lever.

For this to work, you need to have two rigid bodies selected and then go to the **Rigid Body Object Menu** area and click **Connect**. This will create an **Empty** object between these objects; this is the controller for the constraint. **Empty** is an object with a single coordinate in a 3D space. This object has no geometry or surface, so it won't be rendered. These objects act as handles for many different purposes:

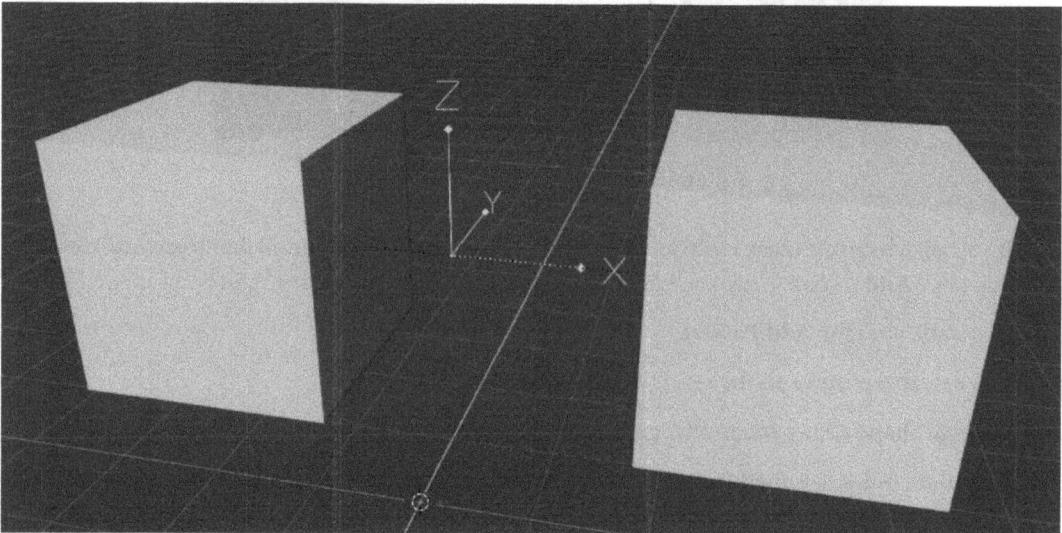

Figure 10.26 – Empty object constraint

You can have one of the rigid body objects be the constraint controller by going to the **Physics** panel and selecting **Rigid Body Constraint**:

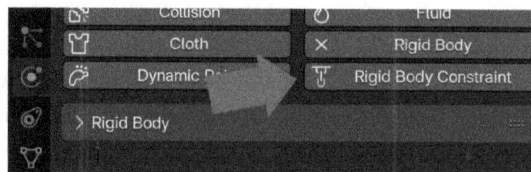

Figure 10.27 – Rigid Body Constraint

Doing this doesn't allow for much customization since the *joint* location will be where the origin point is on the object. Using an **Empty** object as the *joint* is much better and you'll be able to move it anywhere in the scene.

Now that we understand what a rigid body constraint is, let's jump into the settings and learn exactly how they work.

Constraint settings and types

When we first create a constraint using the **Connect** feature, an **Empty** object will be created. When you select this **Empty** object, you'll be able to change the **Type** of constraint and a couple of different settings. First, let's go through the settings; we'll talk about each type of constraint after:

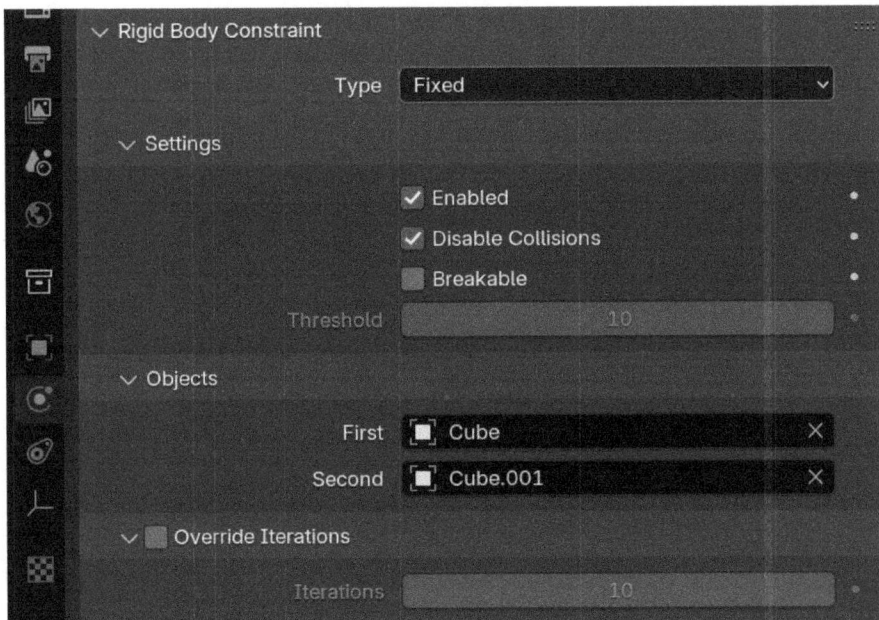

Figure 10.28 – Constraint settings

Let's look at these settings in more detail:

- **Type:** This allows you to change which type of constraint you want. At the time of writing, there are eight different types; we'll go through each one shortly.

- The **Enabled** checkbox: This allows you to toggle between the constraint being enabled or disabled. This setting can also be animated.

- **Disable Collisions:** When checked, the two rigid bodies that are connected won't collide with each other.

- **Breakable**: This allows the connection between the two objects to be broken. **Threshold** determines the amount of force required to break that connection.

- **First** and **Second**: These are the objects that are connected. You can either click the dropdown menu and search for the name or use the **Eye Dropper** tool and click on the object in the **3D Viewport** area.

- **Override Iterations**: This will overwrite the current **Solver Iterations** in the **Rigid Body World** tab for that specific constraint. This can be useful if you have a constraint that requires more iterations than what's been set in the **Rigid Body World** tab.

Some of the settings are different for the different types of constraints, but we'll go through those when we get there! To make the following subsection easier to understand, I've created a `Rigid Body Constraints Examples.blend` file that contains examples of each constraint in different collections. Go to `https://github.com/PacktPublishing/Learn-Blender-4-Simulations-the-Right-Way/tree/main/Chapter%2010` to download that `.blend` file.

When you open this `.blend` file, you'll see eight collections in the **Outliner** area that contain the different types of constraints:

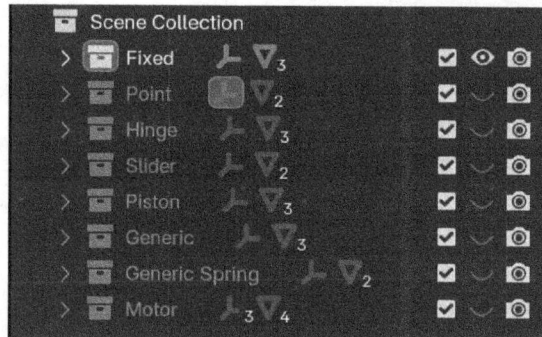

Figure 10.29 – Constraint collections

To switch between the different collections, you can press the number keys on the top of your keyboard or hold *Ctrl/Cmd* and left-click on the eye icon on the right-hand side. This will hide the other collections but keep the one you've selected visible. Then, all you have to do is play the simulation to see what the constraint does!

Now that we've discussed the common settings, let's jump into the specifics and talk about each of the eight types of rigid body constraints in Blender. We'll start with the **Fixed** constraint!

Fixed

The **Fixed** constraint allows two objects to move as one. It connects them and they'll fall and rotate as if they were one solid object:

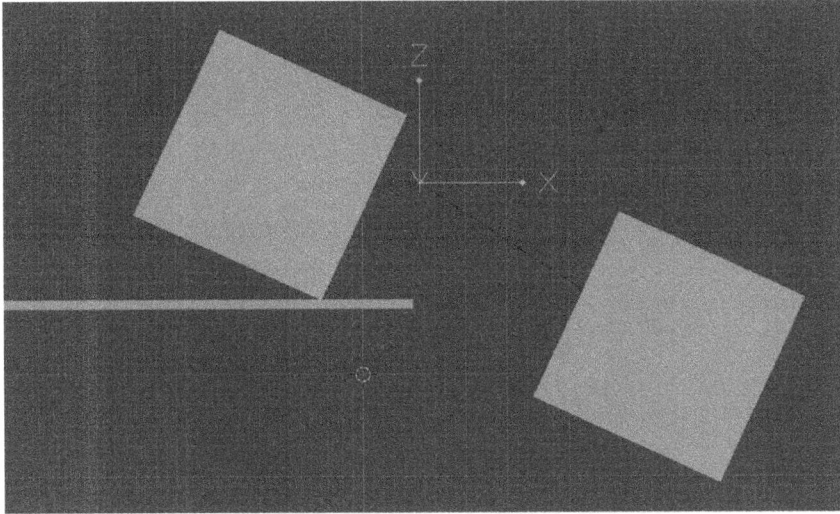

Figure 10.30 – Fixed constraint

Point

The **Point** constraint acts as a rope between the two objects. In this example (see the following figure), the top cube is set to **Passive**, and it connects to an **Active** object. As you can see, the bottom cube will fall and swing as if attached to a rope:

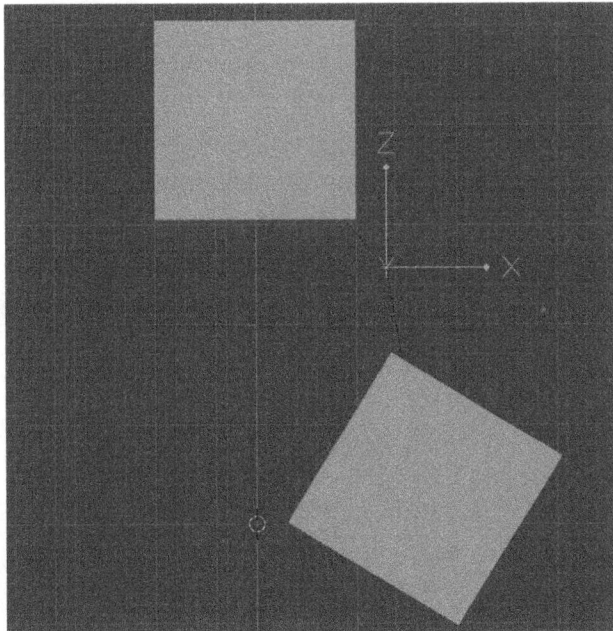

Figure 10.31 – Point constraint

Hinge

The **Hinge** constraint acts as a hinge for a door. It creates a rotation point that's based on the location of the **Empty** object. The rotation is also constricted to the local Z-axis for the **Empty** object. While you can rotate the **Empty** object at a different angle, make sure you have the Z letter pointing in the direction you want the hinge to be:

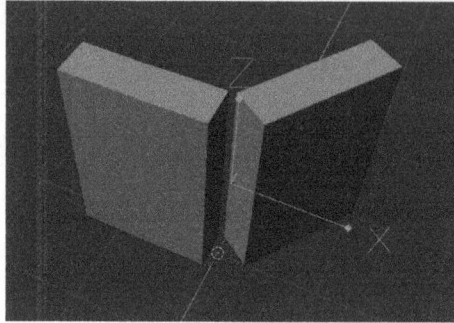

Figure 10.32 – Hinge constraint

In the settings for the **Hinge** constraint, there's a new option: **Z Angle**. Turning this option on allows you to limit the rotation of the hinge using the **Upper** and **Lower** values. Without any limits, the hinge will be able to spin all the way around without stopping.

Slider

The **Slider** constraint allows the object to slide along the local X-axis of the **Empty** object. The movement is restricted to the X-axis, so make sure you rotate the **Empty** object in the direction you want the slide to happen.

In the settings for the constraints, there's an **X-Axis** checkbox. With this enabled, you can set how far away the rigid body can slide using the **Upper** and **Lower** values:

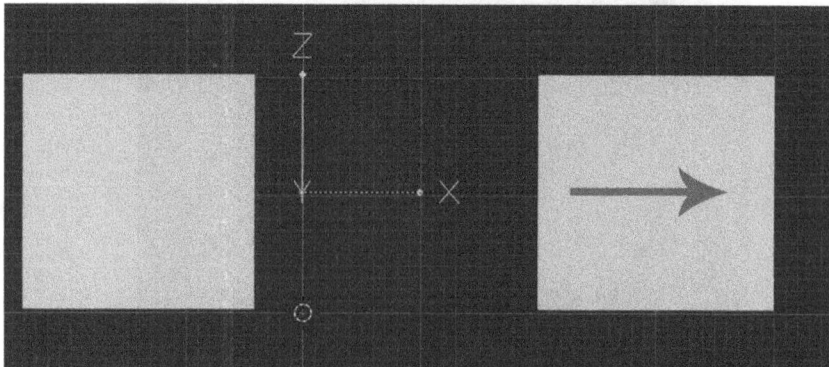

Figure 10.33 – Slider constraint

Piston

The **Piston** constraint combines both the **Hinge** and **Slider** constraints into one. This constraint allows the rigid body to slide and rotate along the **Empty** object's local X-axis. As mentioned previously, in the settings for the constraint, there are the same options for limiting the movement and rotation using the **Upper** and **Lower** values:

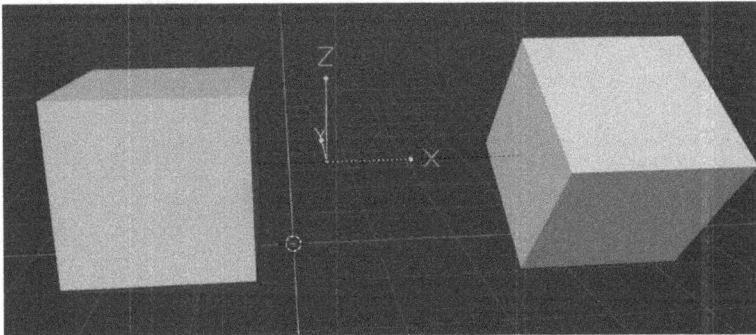

Figure 10.34 – Piston constraint

Generic

The **Generic** constraint covers all the functions we just talked about. Here, you can set limits for the movement and rotation of the X, Y, and Z axes. When you clamp every value to 0, this constraint will act like the **Fixed** constraint. If you set the **Linear** values to 0 but leave the **Angular** values unchecked, it will act like the **Point** constraint.

Every constraint we've learned about thus far can be created using the **Generic** constraint. The name suits it pretty well:

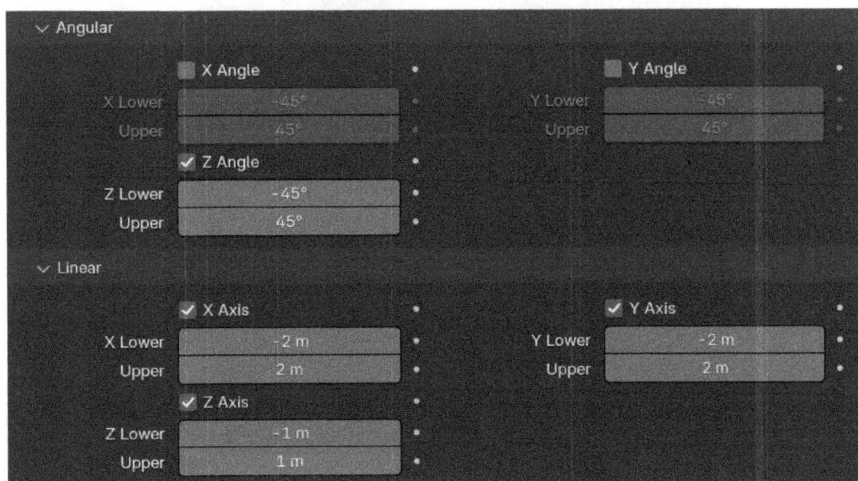

Figure 10.35 – Generic constraint

Generic Spring

The **Generic Spring** constraint is similar to the **Generic** constraint. It has all the same **Angular** and **Linear** limits, plus the addition of **Spring** settings for the *X*, *Y*, and *Z* axes:

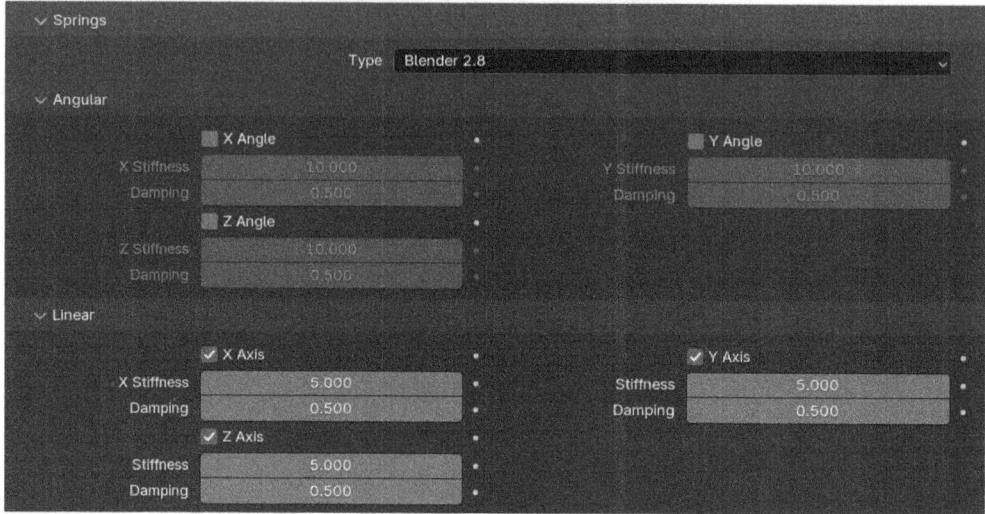

Figure 10.36 – Generic Springs constraint

If only the springs are enabled and not the movement/rotation restrictions, it will act as a springy rope for the constraint. You can see this by playing the animation with the **Generic Spring** collection visible in the `.blend` file:

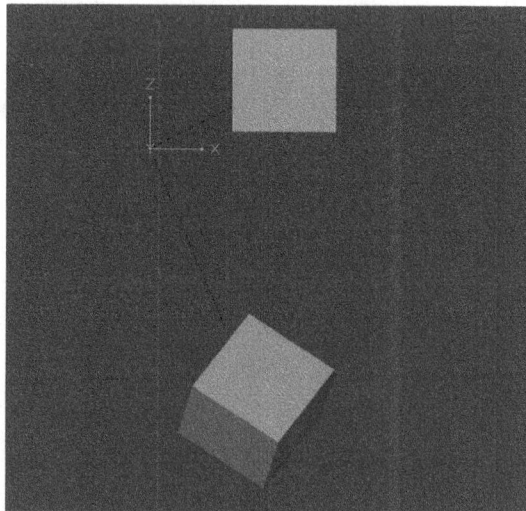

Figure 10.37 – Generic Spring constraint

Stiffness controls how strong the spring will be. Higher values will make the spring very stiff and it won't bend as much.

Damping will dampen the effect of the spring and slow it down. Higher values will make the rigid body fall much slower.

Motor

The last rigid body constraint we have is the **Motor** constraint. This constraint creates a motor-like function where the object will move and/or rotate in a certain direction until the end of the simulation. The **Motor** collection contains an example of a platform rising into the air and a gear rotating:

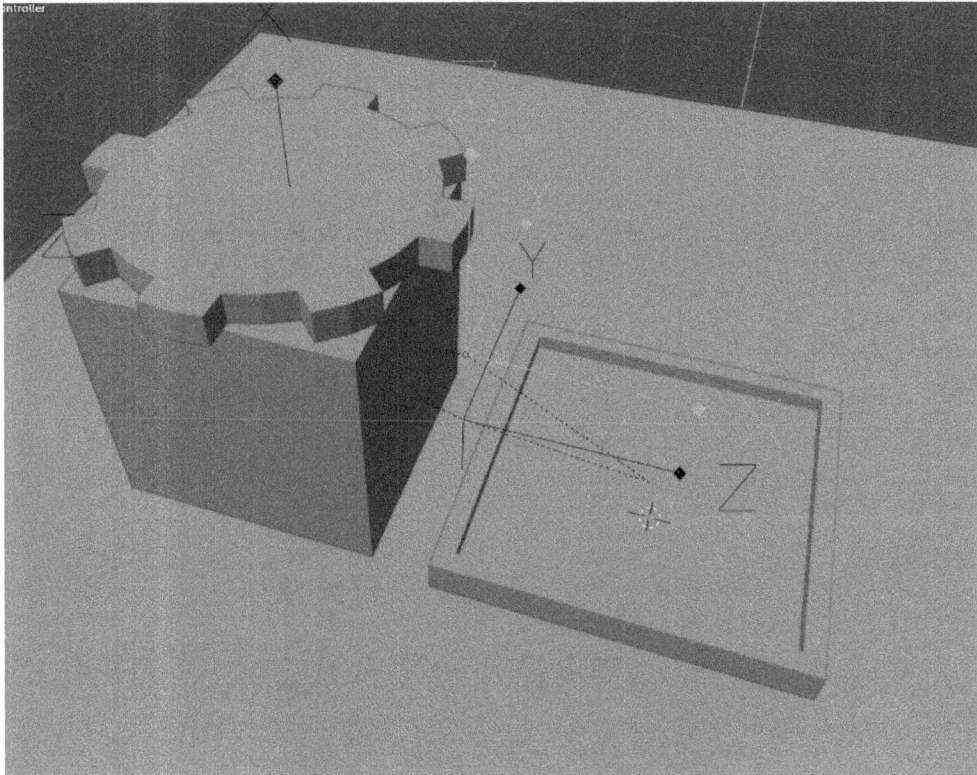

Figure 10.38 – Motor constraint example

There are two motor functions that we can use. **Angular** is for rotating the object and **Linear** is for moving it:

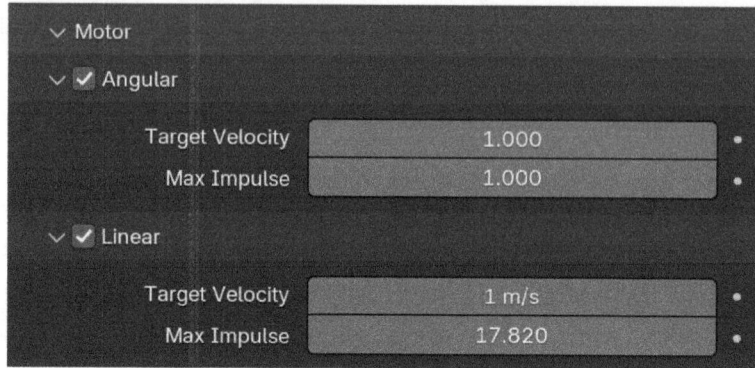

Figure 10.39 – Motor settings

The **Angular** settings are for the rotation. This works by taking the *X*-axis of the **Empty** object and rotating the rigid body along that axis. You can see this by playing the animation and looking at the gear object.

Linear is for the movement. Instead of *X*, **Linear** uses the -*X* direction of the **Empty** option and moves the rigid body along that axis. In this case, you'll notice that the **Motor** constraint has been rotated upside down, so the -*X* direction is pointing straight up. This will cause the platform to rise.

Another issue that might come up is a random rotation, which you don't want for the **Linear** movement. To prevent this, you can lock the rotation in the **Properties** panel. To open this panel, press *N*. If you select the rising platform in the **Motor** collection, you'll notice that all rotation is locked. This ensures there's no unwanted rotation:

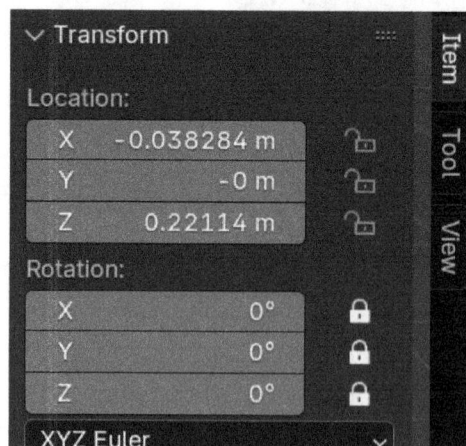

Figure 10.40 – Locked properties

Now, let's look at the two settings that are available in **Angular** and **Linear**:

- **Target Velocity**: This controls the speed of the movement/rotation.

- **Max Impulse**: This controls the strength of the motor. For example, let's say you have a platform rising into the air. If the weight of that object is greater than the **Max Impulse** setting, that platform won't be able to move.

Keep in mind that you can have both the **Angular** and **Linear** motors working at the same time. By doing so, you could create something such as an elevator rotating as it rises into the air!

One last thing to mention is that you can combine multiple constraints into one object. In the **Motor** collection, you'll notice another empty object. This is a **Generic** constraint and what it does is set a limit for how high the platform will go up. In this case, it's 3 meters. So, you don't need to have only one constraint per object – you can have as many as you want and they'll all work together!

Feel free to play around with all the settings and different constraints! Test them out so that you understand how they work!

Summary

And there it is! In this chapter, we learned everything there is to know about the rigid body simulation in Blender! Hopefully, at this point, you have a grasp of all the cool and unique things that can be created using this system! Once again, let's recap so that we remember everything we've covered!

First, we discussed what the rigid body simulation is and what you need to know to get started. After that, we jumped into the settings and learned about active and passive objects, collision shapes, and much more! Next up was the **Rigid Body World** tab, and how you can use that panel to set the length and the speed, as well as bake the simulation! Another thing we learned about is the **Rigid Body Object** menu and how you can copy settings from one rigid body to another! We ended this chapter by understanding every type of constraint there is in the simulation.

The rigid body simulation is probably one of the most useful simulations there is. It can be applied to so many different scenes and animations. Speaking of which, in the next chapter, we'll be taking what we learned here and putting it to the test by creating a nice, satisfying animation!

Join our community on Discord

Join our community's Discord space for discussions with the author and other readers:
`https://packt.link/learn-blender-simulations-discord-invite`

11

Creating a Rigid Body
Physics Course

Now that we have a good understanding of how the rigid body simulation works in Blender, let's take everything we learned in the last chapter and apply it to a real project! In this chapter, we will be learning how to use the rigid body simulation to create a full physics-based animation.

In this animation, we will first simulate a swinging wrecking ball that crashes into a domino. That will cause a chain reaction of falling dominos, which will trigger a button that moves up an elevator. Inside that elevator is a sphere. As the sphere moves up, it will eventually pass through a couple of hinge constraints and end up crashing into a large tower of cubes, finishing off the animation. If that sounds like a lot, don't worry! We will go through it step by step and cover each aspect of this animation in detail.

The goal of this chapter is to understand how to use a rigid body simulation in a practical way to create a nice, interesting animation! By the end, you will have a good understanding of the rigid body system and how to use it in your future projects.

In this chapter, we'll be covering the following topics:

- Creating the simulation
- Adding the camera animation
- Setting up the render

Technical requirements

This chapter requires you to have Blender version 4.2 or above installed.

To download Blender, visit www.blender.org.

Also, make sure to download the setup file for this tutorial here: `https://github.com/ PacktPublishing/Learn-Blender-4-Simulations-the-Right-Way/tree/ main/Chapter%2011`

Creating the simulation

Before we get started, make sure to download the `Rigid Body Course Setup.blend` file. This will include a basic scene, with all the components for our animation, such as the swinging wrecking ball, the dominos, the elevator, the tower, and more. Each object already has a material in place, but feel free to change these to your liking. You can also look in the **Outliner** at the top right to see each object's name, so it's easy to navigate.

Once you are familiar with the scene, we can go ahead and start creating the simulation. If you would like to download the finished scene, `Rigid Body Project File.blend`, for reference, you can do that as well!

When working with complex rigid body simulations, Blender tends to crash and be unresponsive. Remember to constantly save your Blender file throughout this tutorial so that you don't lose progress if and when the program crashes.

Simulating the wrecking ball

Let's get started by simulating a swinging wrecking ball crashing into one of several blue cubes! To do this, we'll use the rigid body **Object** menu to add physics to the chains and wrecking ball at once:

1. Select the **Chain Top** object, all 12 chains, and the **Wrecking Ball** object and head up to **Object | Rigid Body | Add Active**.

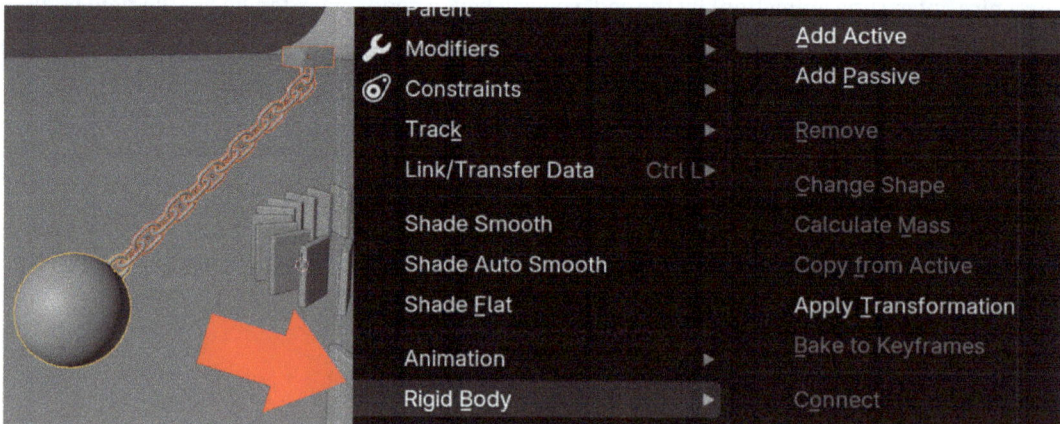

Figure 11.1 – Wrecking ball physics

2. There are a couple of settings we need to change for these chains:

    I.   With all of them still selected, head over to the **Physics** panel: set **Mass** to 4 kg. This will prevent the chains from breaking from the weight.

    II.   Next, let's change the shape of the collision. Because these chains are interlocking, **Convex Hull** will not work. Remember the **Convex Hull** collision boundary is basically shrinkwrapped around the object. That means, in this case, there will be a collision inside the empty part of the chain. To fix this, we instead need to use **Mesh**; this way, the collision works properly, and the chains don't break.

    III. Finally, let's set **Margin** in **Sensitivity** to 0 m. This will make sure the chains touch each other and don't jitter around!

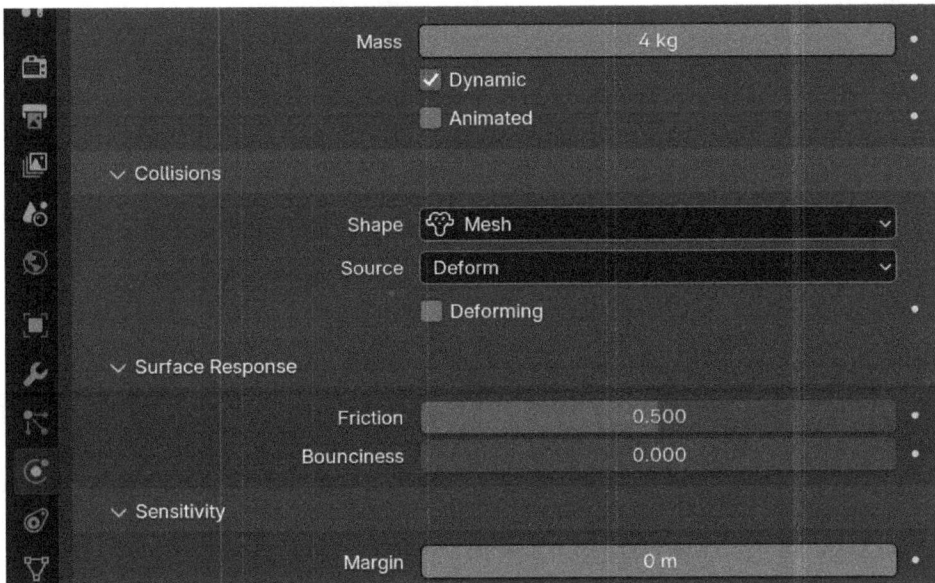

Figure 11.2 – Wrecking ball settings

3. Now, let's copy those changes to the rest of the chains. You can do this by making sure that they are all still selected and the one with those changes is the *active object*, and then head to **Object | Rigid Body | Copy From Active**.

4. Select the wrecking ball object. In real life, this would weigh a lot more, so let's set **Mass** to 20 kg in the **Settings** tab. Also, change **Damping Translation** and **Rotation** to 0.400 in the **Dynamics** tab. This will make the wrecking ball stop swinging as the animation plays.

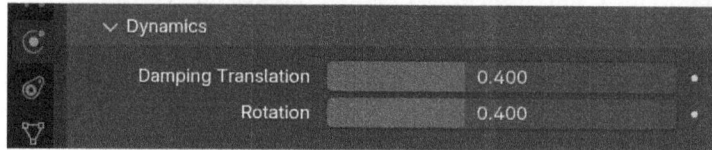

Figure 11.3 – Damping values

5. Then, select the **Chain Top** object and turn off **Dynamic**. This will make sure it stays floating and doesn't fall.

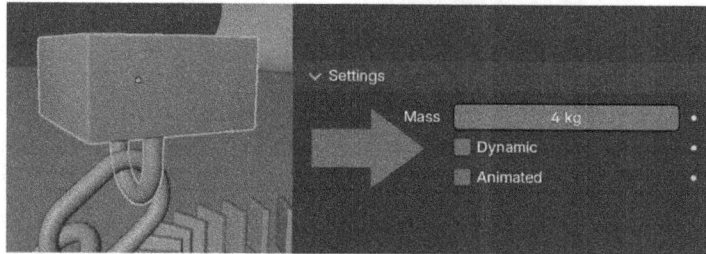

Figure 11.4 – Chain Top settings

Normally, the **Passive** type is used for platforms or bigger surface areas; however, **Active** with **Dynamic** turned off is better for more complicated meshes.

From here, you will be able to play the animation and the wrecking ball should swing! Next up, let's create the domino effect!

Creating the domino effect

Now that we have the wrecking ball swinging, let's have it crash into one of the **Domino** objects, causing a chain reaction, just like dominos would in real life. We want the dominos to fall in a sequence and eventually end up hitting the **Button Cube** object. This is what triggers the elevator to move upward!

1. For starters, let's select all the **Domino** objects in the scene. From there, go up to **Object | Rigid Body** and click on **Add Active**.

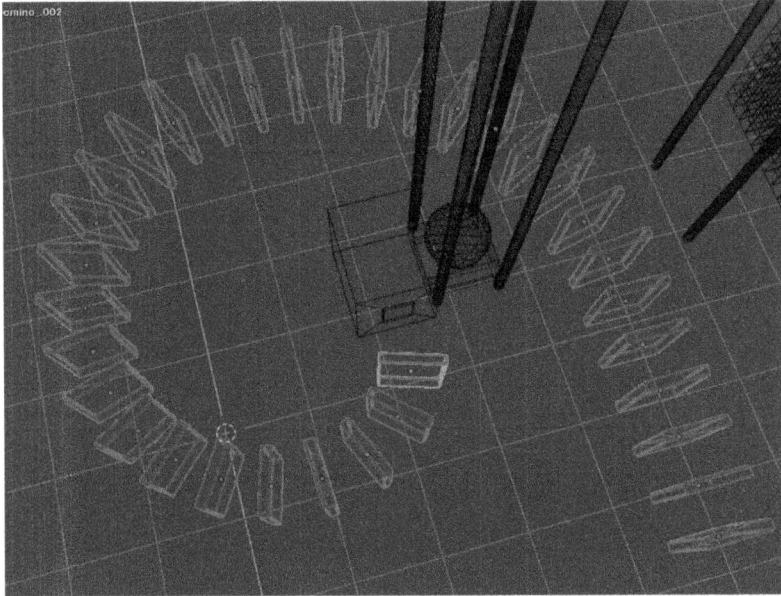

Figure 11.5 – Selected cubes

2. We don't need to change any settings in the **Physics** panel; the default values will work perfectly fine for these objects. Also, another important step is to select the **Floor** object and select **Add Passive** in the rigid body **Object** menu. This way, the cubes stay where they are and don't fall through the floor!

Feel free to change the shape of the domino line to how you like. You could have it go all the way around the scene or split off in two directions! Just make sure that it eventually comes around and hits the **Button Cube** object because this is what triggers the elevator to go up, which we will talk about now!

Before moving on, this is a good time to save the Blender file. You can do this by pressing *Ctrl + S* or by going up to **File | Save**.

Simulating the elevator

Next up is the elevator that carries the sphere to the top of the course. To create this, we will be using a motor constraint! Let's first start by animating the button on the **Button Cube** object to turn green when the last domino hits it:

1. Select the **Button Cube** object and set it to a **Passive** rigid body. This way, it will interact with the scene.

2. Now, to make it turn green, find the frame when the cube hits the button. You can find the frame by playing the animation from the beginning of the timeline (unfortunately, simply scrubbing through the timeline will not work). For my scene, it was at **Frame 122**, but yours may be slightly different.

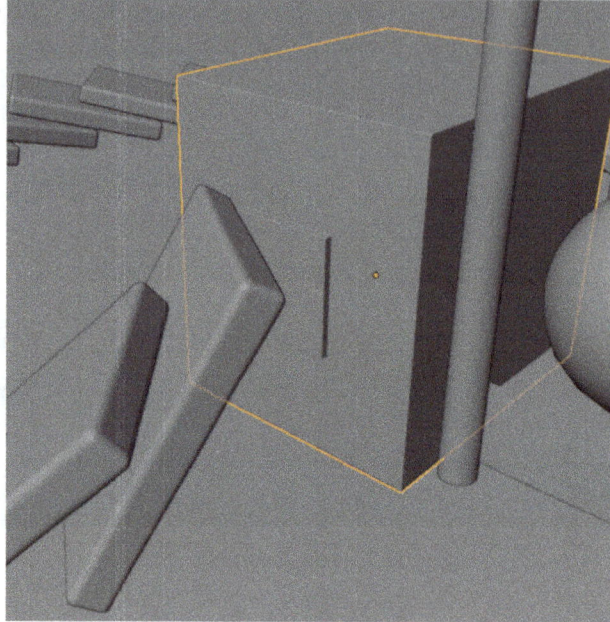

Figure 11.6 – Frame 122

3. Let's head over to the **Material** panel and select the **Button Light** material.

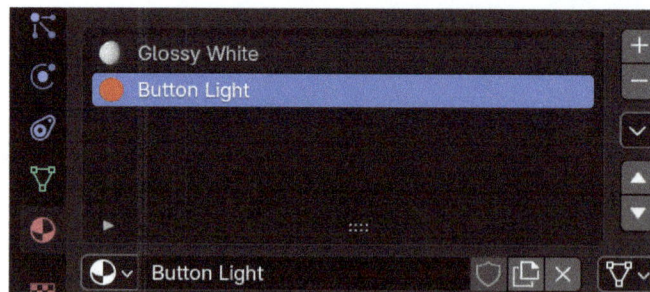

Figure 11.7 – The Material panel

4. Let's go to the previous frame (**121**) and add a keyframe to the **Color** value in the **Emission** shader. You can do this by hovering your mouse over the color and pressing *I*, or by clicking the little dot next to the color.

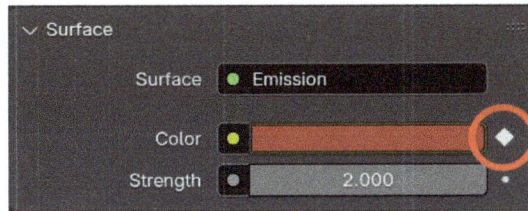

Figure 11.8 – The Emission Color keyframe

5. Jump to the next frame (**122**), change the color to a nice green, and add another keyframe. Now, when the cube hits the button, it will turn green!

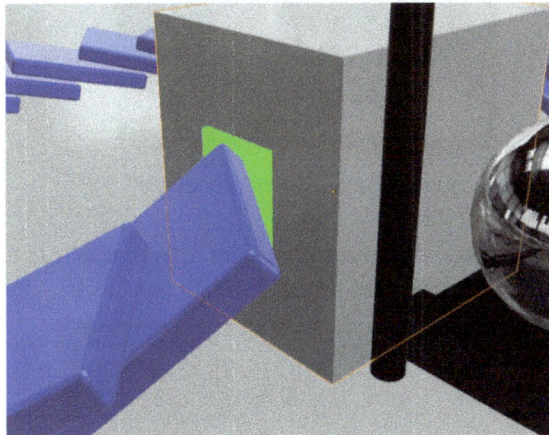

Figure 11.9 – The button turning green

6. To create the motor constraint, let's set the **Elevator Platform** object to be an **Active** rigid body, set the collision shape to **Mesh**, and the **Sensitivity** margin to 0 m.

Figure 11.10 – Elevator settings

7. With the **Elevator Platform** object still selected, press *N* to open the **Properties** panel. Let's lock all the **Rotation** and **Location** axes *except* for the **Z** location; this way, when we add the motor constraint, it will only move up along the **Z** axis.

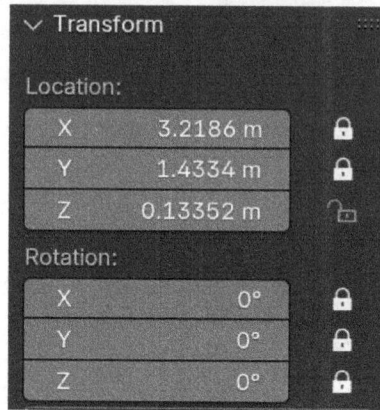

Figure 11.11 – Locked properties

8. Select both the **Button Cube** and **Elevator Platform** objects and head to **Object | Rigid Body | Connect**. This will create a constraint between these two objects.

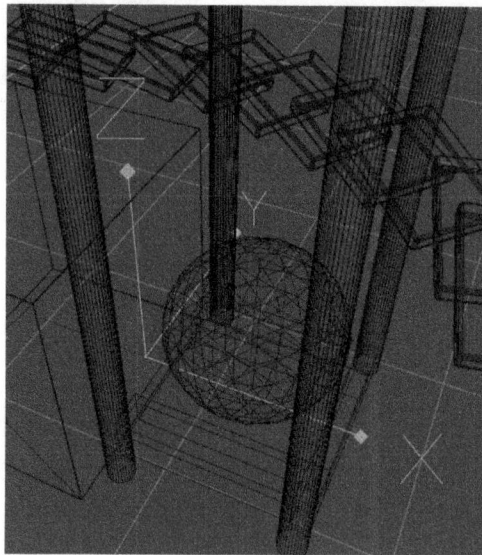

Figure 11.12 – An empty constraint

This constraint will have **X**, **Y**, and **Z** handles. Keep the rotation of these handles in mind because they determine the direction and rotation of a lot of the constraint types.

9. Select the **Constraint** object that has been added and change a couple of settings in the **Physics** panel:

    I.   Change **Type** to **Motor**.

    II.   Enable **Linear** and set **Target Velocity** (which controls the speed) to 2 m/s.

    III. Set **Max Impulse** (which controls the strength of the motor) to 250, a strong enough value to carry the sphere up.

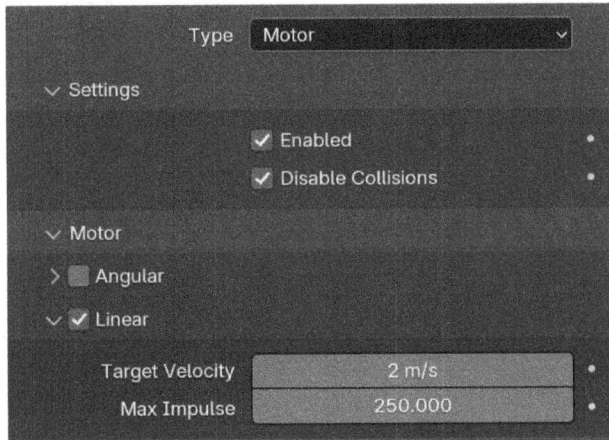

Figure 11.13 – The Motor settings

10. When working with motor constraints, the -*X* direction is the way the motor will go. With this in mind, let's rotate the motor constraint so that the **X** direction is pointed downward. This will cause the elevator to move up!

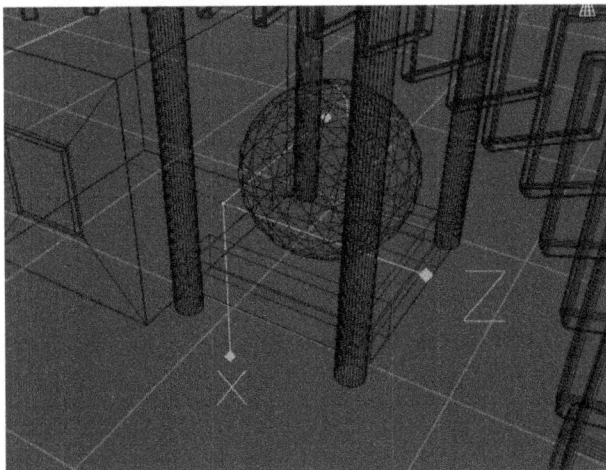

Figure 11.14 – Motor constraint rotation

11. Make sure to play the animation to see whether everything is working properly, and the platform is rising.

12. We don't want the elevator platform to move until the button turns green, so let's jump to the frame right before the button turns green (**121**), uncheck **Enabled** in the **Constraints** settings, and add a keyframe.

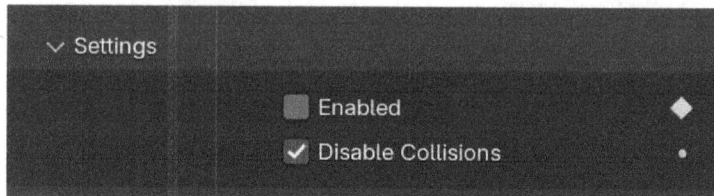

Figure 11.15 – Animating Enabled

13. On the next frame (**122**), turn on **Enabled** and add another keyframe. And there we go – the motor constraint won't turn on until **Frame 122** when the last domino hits the button!

14. The other thing we want is for the elevator to stop at a certain point, which we can do by adding a **Generic** constraint:

I.   Select **Elevator Platform** and **Button Cube** and connect them again by going to **Object | Rigid Body | Connect**.

II.   Select the new constraint object that has been added and change **Type** to **Generic**.

III. In the **Linear** tab, turn on **Z Axis** and set **Upper** to 6 m. This will cause the elevator to stop when it reaches 6 meters in the air, and this is the exact height we need to reach the platforms at the top!

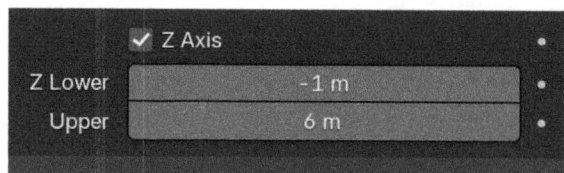

Figure 11.16 – Generic constraint settings

15. Finally, select **Sphere**, and set it to be an **Active** rigid body with a mass of 4 kg.

Before you play the animation, make sure to save your Blender file again. After that, play the animation, and make sure that everything works properly and the elevator rises into the air!

If the elevator stops too early, you may want to change **Z Lower** to a value of -6 m in the generic constraint settings. This is because the **Upper** and **Lower** values are determined by which object was *active* when the **Button Cube** and **Elevator Platform** objects were connected.

Figure 11.17 – The elevator rising

Next up, we will animate a cube smacking into the sphere and shooting it along the platform!

Animating the rigid bodies

When the sphere reaches the top of the elevator, we are going to have a cube slide out and hit it, sending it around the half circle! To do this, follow these instructions:

1. Firstly, we need to extend the rigid body simulation because currently it only lasts for 250 frames. So, open the **Scene Properties** panel and, in the **Rigid Body World** tab, underneath **Cache**, set **End** to 500.

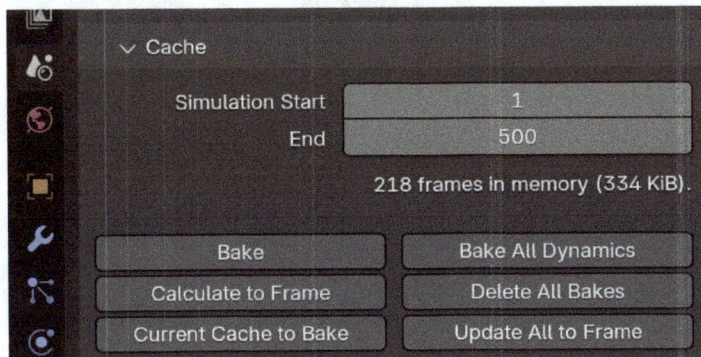

Figure 11.18 – The Cache panel

Now, the simulation will last for 500 frames rather than only 250.

2. Now, let's add physics to the **Cube Hit** object. Select it and give it an **Active** rigid body, with the **Animated** checkbox checked.

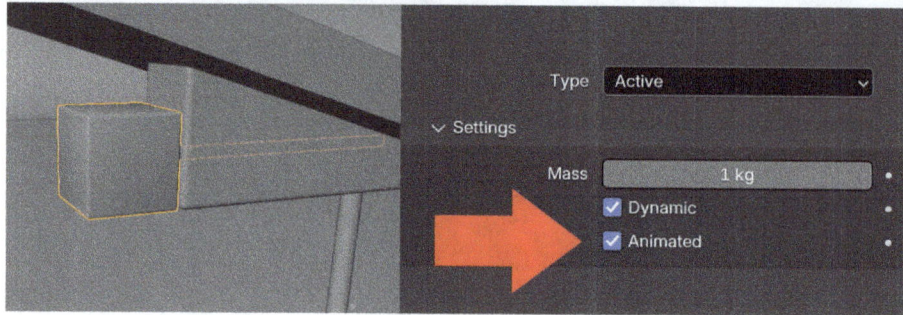

Figure 11.19 – Cube Hit physics

3. Play the animation until the elevator reaches the top and stops bouncing. For my scene, it was at **Frame 220**. If your scene is taking a long time to calculate, you can set **Start** for the simulation to the frame right before the motor constraint activates (around **122**). This way, you don't have to wait; just remember to set it back to 1 when you do a final bake!

4. With the **Cube Hit** object selected, let's press *K* and add a **Location** keyframe on **Frame 230**.

5. Five frames later, let's move the **Cube Hit** object inside the **Sphere** object and add another **Location** keyframe.

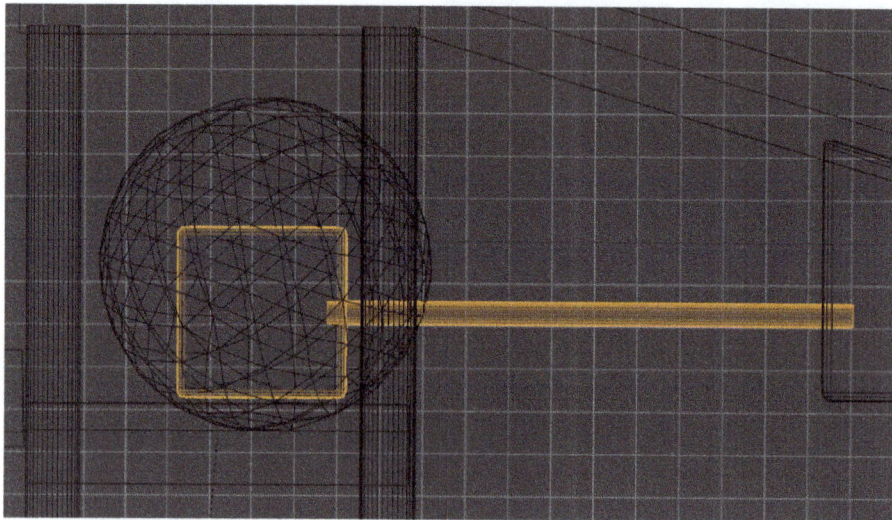

Figure 11.20 – Hitting the sphere

Over the course of five frames, the cube will extend outward and smack the sphere, sending it around the half circle.

6. Now, let's add physics to the rest of the objects! Select **Platform 1** and **Platform 2**. Give them both a **Passive** rigid body type, with **Shape** set to **Mesh** and **Margin** to 0 m.

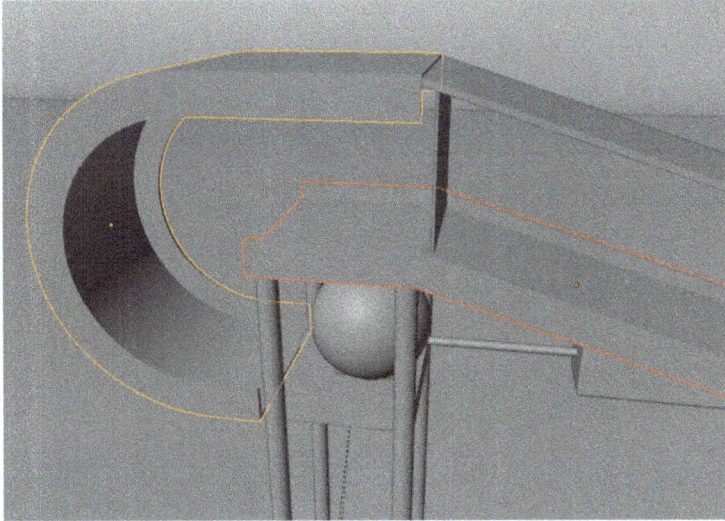

Figure 11.21 – The platform settings

7. If the **Sphere** object does not make it all the way around the circle, you can set **Friction** in the surface responses of **Platform 1** to around 0.1. This will make the sphere slide a bit more.

With that done, let's move on to creating the **Hinge** constraints!

Creating the hinges

The last obstacle for the sphere to go through, before it crashes into the tower of cubes, is a series of walls that rotate using the **Hinge** constraint. To add this, do the following:

1. Select the **Wall 1** object and give it an **Active** rigid body.

2. We want the **Sphere** to easily push the wall up, so let's set **Mass** of **Wall 1** to 0.001 kg.

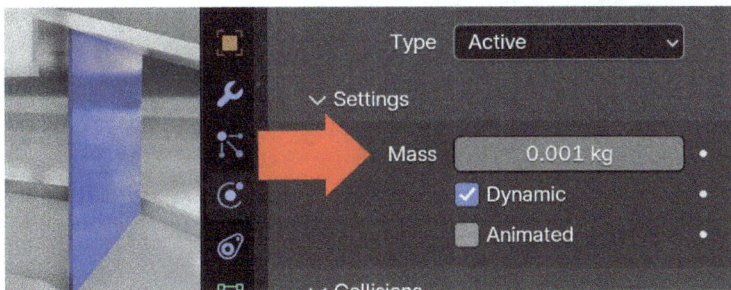

Figure 11.22 – The wall settings

3. To create the constraint, select both **Wall 1** and **Platform 2**. Just as before, let's head up to the rigid body **Object** menu and select **Connect**. This will create an empty object that is used for the rotation point of the hinge! Then, change the constraint type to **Hinge**.

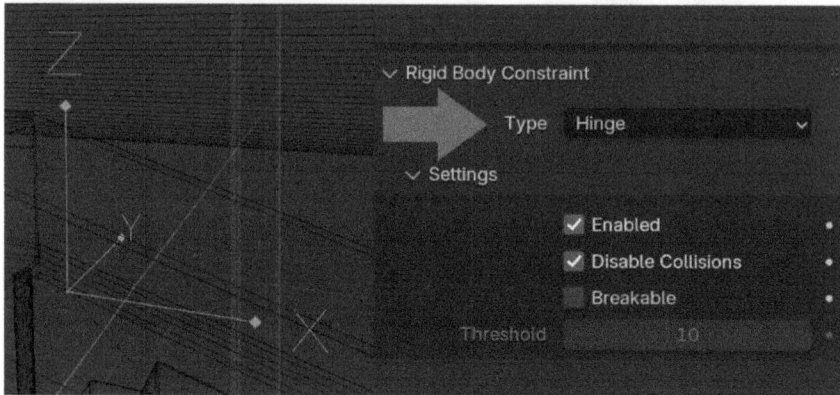

Figure 11.23 – The Hinge constraint

4. The **Hinge** rotation is based on the **Z** angle of the constraint. So, if you want it to behave like a door, have **Z** (as shown in *Figure 11.23*) pointed up, and place it on the side of the wall. If you want the hinge point to be at the top, rotate the constraint so that the **Z** angle is pointed sideways, and then place it on the top of the wall (like in *Figure 11.24*).

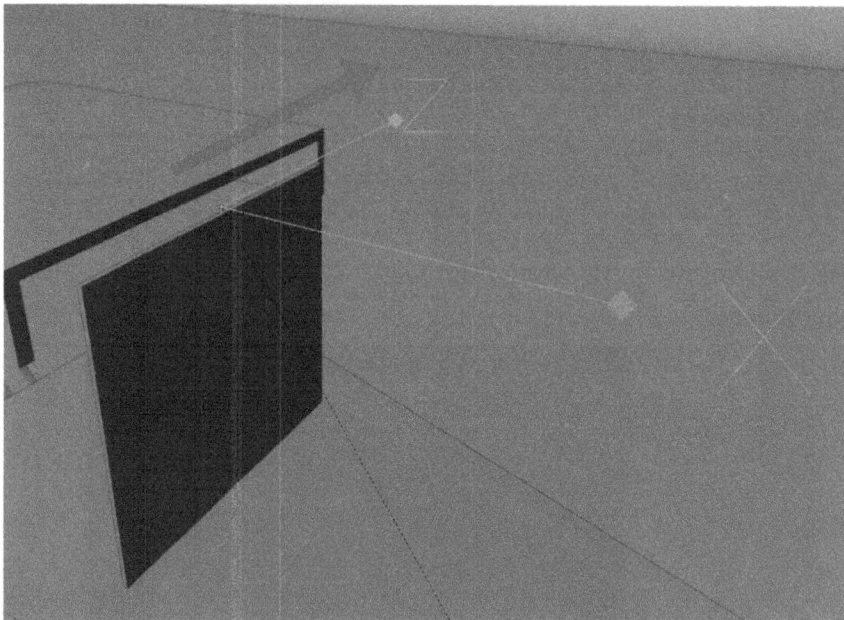

Figure 11.24 – Z angled down

5. At this point, you can duplicate both the wall and the **Hinge** constraint by pressing *Shift + D* and moving along the platform. This way, the sphere will go through multiple walls before falling out! Make sure that the walls aren't hitting the lower platform, as this will cause issues in the simulation.

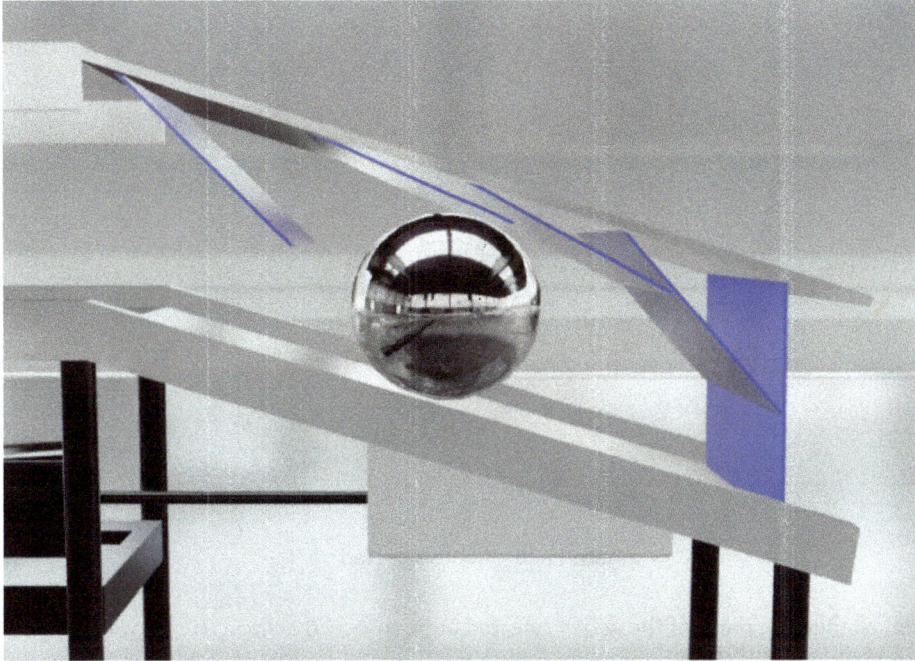

Figure 11.25 – Adding walls

And now, we get to the fun part of this project – collapsing the tower of cubes!

Collapsing the cubes

Adding physics to the 2,880 cubes that are piled up on the right side is very simple to do, so let's go ahead and get started:

1. First, select one of the cubes to make it the active object.
2. Next, go to the **Wireframe** view by pressing *Z* and selecting **Wireframe**. Then drag a box around all the cubes to select them.

3. Go to the rigid body **Object** menu and select **Add Active**. This will give each cube an **Active** rigid body.

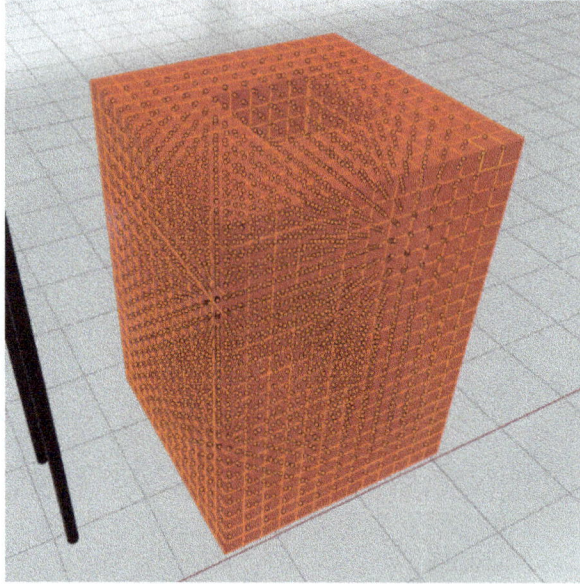

Figure 11.26 – Cubes selected

4. Then, change the mass of the active selected cube to `0.001 kg`. This way, the sphere can crash through all of them very easily.

The other important step is to turn on **Deactivation** in the **Dynamics** tab and check **Start Deactivated**. The **Deactivation** checkbox allows the rigid body objects to stop simulating if the movement or rotation of the object is slower than what's set for **Velocity Linear** and **Angular**.

Start Deactivated allows the rigid body object to *not* simulate until another object comes in contact with it. Since there is a slight gap between each of the cubes in the tower, when we play the animation, they will fall down just slightly. This may cause some of the cubes to move around or fall off the tower, which we don't want. Turning **Start Deactivated** on will ensure that they don't simulate until the sphere crashes into them.

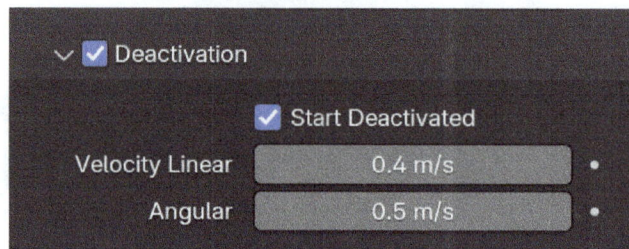

Figure 11.27 – Deactivation

5. Now, we need to apply those changes to the rest of the objects. Head back up to the rigid body **Object** menu and select **Copy From Active**. This will copy all those changes we just made to the rest of the cubes instantly!

6. Next, select each of the **Column** objects holding up the platforms and add a **Passive** rigid body to each! Now, the cubes will collide with them as well.

7. Now, we can bake in the simulation! Remember to save your file again, then head back to the **Scene Properties** panel, and go down to the **Rigid Body World** tab. Inside the **Cache** tab, make sure that the start frame is at 1 and the end frame is set at 500, and click **Bake**!

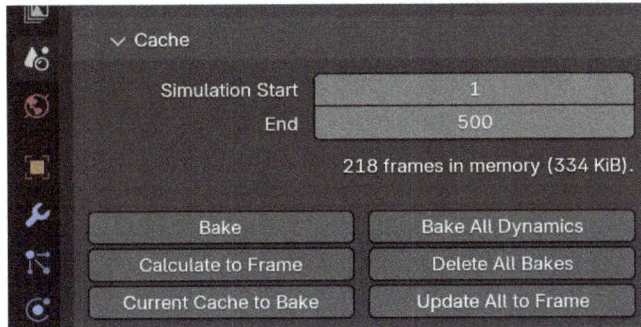

Figure 11.28 – The Cache panel

Once the bake is finished, you will be able to play the animation and see your simulation in real time! Play through it and make any changes you like. Maybe add some of your own obstacles to the scene!

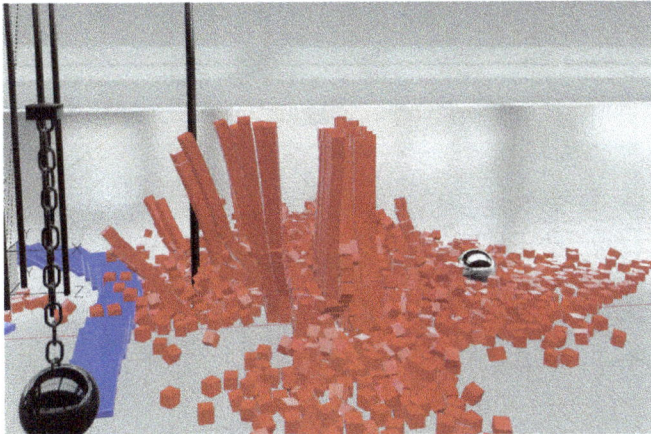

Figure 11.29 – Frame 384

You could have the sphere hit another button, releasing multiple spheres that crash into the cubes, or maybe add in some force fields to totally mess with the rigid bodies. Use your imagination and have fun with it! Once you are happy with the simulation, we can move on to the camera animation!

Adding the camera animation

The next step in our project is to set up the camera to follow the progress of the simulation, starting out with the wrecking ball, moving up the elevator, following the sphere around the half circle, and finally zooming out to see all the cubes collapse.

There are two main ways to move the camera around:

- You can select **Camera** and press *G* to move the camera manually.
- You can open the **Properties** panel by pressing *N*, and in the **View** tab, check **Camera to View**. This will allow you to move the camera around just as you would move around the viewport.

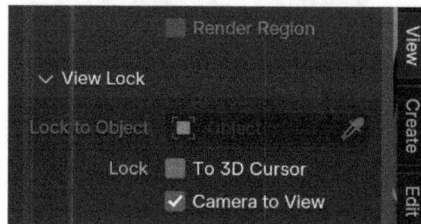

Figure 11.30 – Camera to View

You can use whichever method you prefer!

Now, let's start animating the camera:

1. Let's start by going into the camera view by pressing *0* on the numpad or by going to **View** | **Cameras** | **Active Camera**.

2. Next, select the camera and head over to the **Object Data** panel. Here, we can set **Focal Length** and what object to focus on. Check **Depth of Field**, and in **Focus on Object**, select **Sphere**.

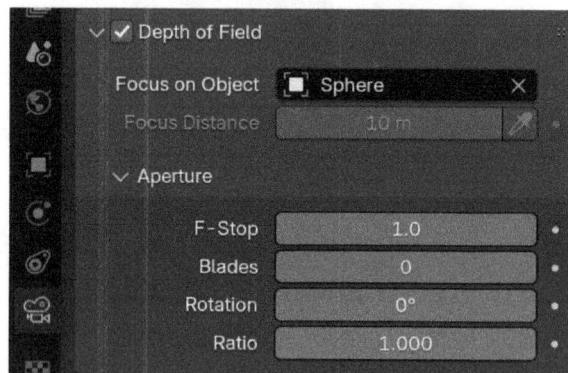

Figure 11.31 – Depth of Field

3. **F-Stop** controls how strong the depth of field will be. Lower values will make the background blurrier. Let's set this to `1.0`.

4. From here, skip to **Frame 1**, position the camera looking at the scene, press *I*, and select **Location & Rotation** to add a new keyframe.

5. The next step is to play the animation for about 100–200 frames and position the camera where you like to add a new keyframe. Repeat this step until you complete the animation. Remember that you can always fine-tune the location of keyframes in the timeline if you don't like how the animation looks.

If this part is a little tricky for you, you can download `Rigid Body Course Project File.blend` for reference from here: `https://github.com/PacktPublishing/Learn-Blender-4-Simulations-the-Right-Way/tree/main/Chapter%2011`

Now that the camera animation is done, let's finish this scene by changing a couple of render settings in EEVEE!

Setting up the render

In the last part of this tutorial, we will set up some render settings in EEVEE to help the scene have nice reflections and colors when we render the animation:

1. Head over to the **Render** panel and turn on **Raytracing**. This will add shadows, reflections, and everything else that makes your renders in EEVEE look good! While we are here, let's set **Resolution** to **1.1**.

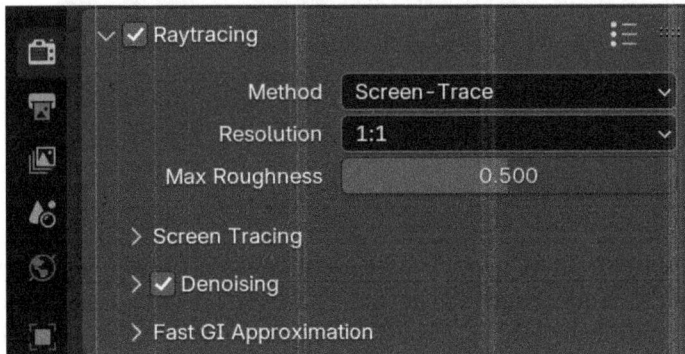

Figure 11.32 – Raytracing

2. Check **Motion Blur** as well. The **Shutter** value sets the strength of the blur. A default value of 0.5 will work well here. Let's also set **Steps** to 16 to give us a better quality blur.

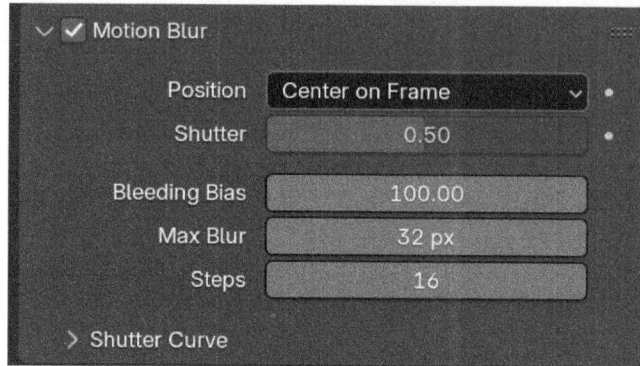

Figure 11.33 – The Motion Blur settings

3. Finally, open the **Color Management** tab and set **Look** to **High Contrast**. This will make everything pop a bit more.

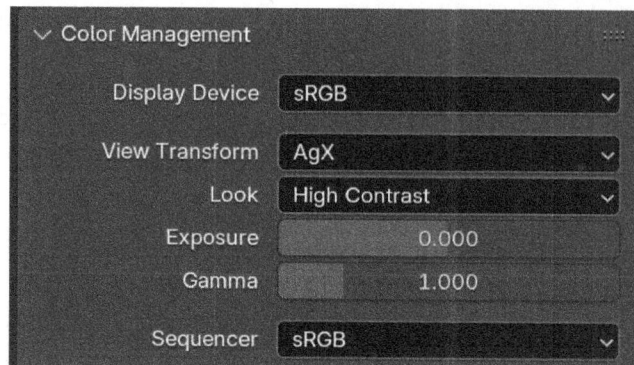

Figure 11.34 – Color Management

And that is it! From here, we can render the animation! Head over to the **Output** panel and set a directory for where you want your animation to render. I recommend rendering this animation as an image sequence just in case of any crashes. If you don't remember how this is done, refer to *Chapter 4*.

But there it is! We have now created an entire rigid body obstacle course! This doesn't have to end here. You can add more obstacles or other things to the simulation. For example, you could add a **Wind** force field at the end to push all the red cubes offscreen or have the sphere object trigger something that causes multiple spheres to crash into the tower!

Another cool idea would be to animate the speed of the simulation when the sphere crashes into the tower. This could have a cool slow-motion effect! It's all up to you and your imagination!

Summary

Hopefully, at this point, you have a good understanding of the rigid body simulation in Blender and feel confident about creating your own scenes and animations! You can always come back to this chapter or the previous one if you need a refresher.

Let's do a quick recap to establish everything we learned today. First, we discussed how to simulate a swinging wrecking ball that crashes into a domino object, causing a chain reaction of other dominos falling over. We also learned about animating the color of materials in Blender. From there, we learned about motor and hinge constraints and how to use them practically in a simulation. We also saw how to animate rigid bodies and how to simulate thousands of cubes all at once. Finally, we set up the camera animation and render settings and exported the animation.

The rigid body simulation in Blender is very powerful and can be used to create many different scenes and animations. So, go play around with it and create your own simulations! This is also the end of *Part 3* of this book. In *Part 3*, we will discuss a topic that not a lot of people know about – Dynamic Paint!

Get This Book's PDF Version and Exclusive Extras

UNLOCK NOW

Scan the QR code (or go to packtpub.com/unlock). Search for this book by name, confirm the edition, and then follow the steps on the page.

Note: Keep your invoice handy. Purchases made directly from Packt don't require an invoice.

Part 4: Understanding Dynamic Paint in Blender

In the final couple of chapters of this book, we will learn all about one of the most powerful simulations in Blender: Dynamic Paint. Step by step, we will cover all the settings, values, and what it takes to create a simulation using this amazing tool. After that, we'll cover how to create a paintbrush animation and a rainfall simulation. Finally, taking everything we learned throughout this book, we will combine multiple simulations to create a burning-up effect!

This part has the following chapters:

12

An Introduction to Dynamic Paint

Dynamic paint is a topic that isn't covered very often. It may seem complicated and hard to understand at first, but once you learn and start playing around with it, you will find that it is a very powerful tool in Blender. Dynamic paint allows you to turn your objects into brushes and canvases. Using this tool, you can create mesh displacement, image sequences, color maps, dynamic weight paint, and much more. Effects such as footprints in the snow, painting on walls, ripples in water, raindrops, and fire trails can easily be achieved using dynamic paint!

In this chapter, we will be covering what dynamic paint is and how to use it efficiently in Blender, starting with the basics and progressing from there. Just as with the previous simulations we have discussed in this book, we will learn what each setting does and how to use it the right way!

In this chapter, we'll be covering the following topics:

- Getting started with dynamic paint
- Creating a paint simulation
- Understanding the canvas
- Using brushes

Technical requirements

This chapter requires you to have Blender version 4.2 or above installed.

To download Blender, visit www.blender.org.

Basic knowledge of Blender will also help in this chapter.

The supporting files for this chapter can be found here: https://github.com/PacktPublishing/Learn-Blender-4-Simulations-the-Right-Way/tree/main/Chapter%2012.

Getting started with dynamic paint

There are two things you will always need when working with dynamic paint: a **Canvas** object and a **Brush** object. **Canvas**, of course, is the object that will be painted on with the **Brush** object. To create a dynamic paint simulation, make sure you have a mesh object selected, then head over to the **Physics** panel and select **Dynamic Paint**:

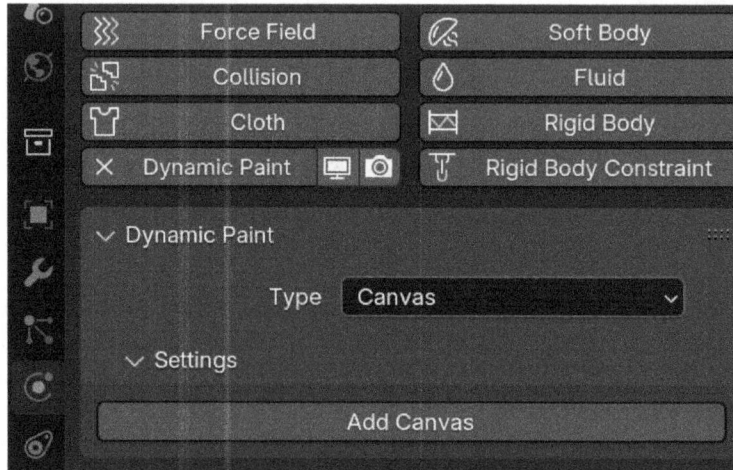

Figure 12.1 – Adding Dynamic Paint

From here, you can choose to either add a **Canvas** or a **Brush** object by selecting from the **Type** menu. When you select **Add Canvas**, you can decide to paint directly on the vertices using the **Vertex** format, or you can export the paint as images using the **Image Sequence** format:

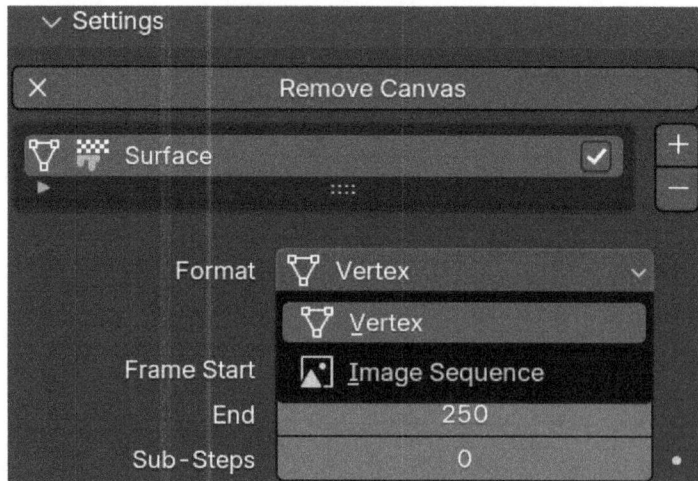

Figure 12.2 – The Format type

Both **Format** types have their advantages and disadvantages, which we will talk about once we get into the settings!

After you decide which **Format** type to use, you can then select which **Surface Type** option you want!

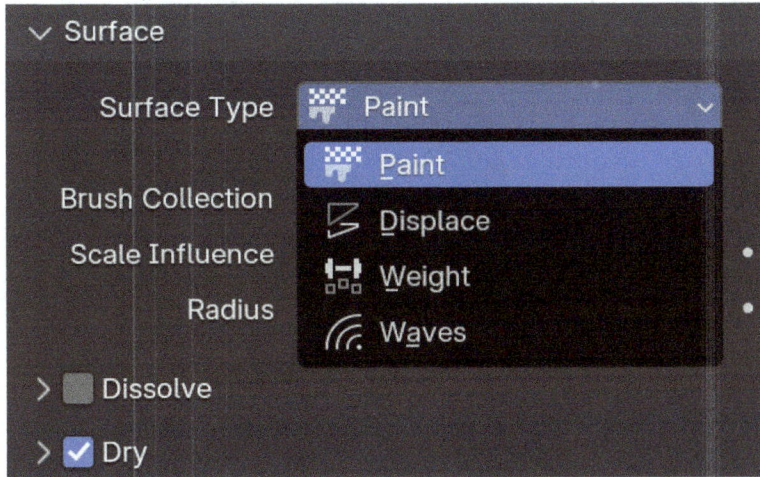

Figure 12.3 – Surface Type settings

With the **Vertex** format selected, there are four **Surface Type** options (**Weight** is not available with the **Image Sequence** format):

- The **Paint** type is exactly what you would expect. It outputs color information that is displayed on the canvas. This can be used to create paintbrush effects, cool and interesting materials, and a huge variety of other things!

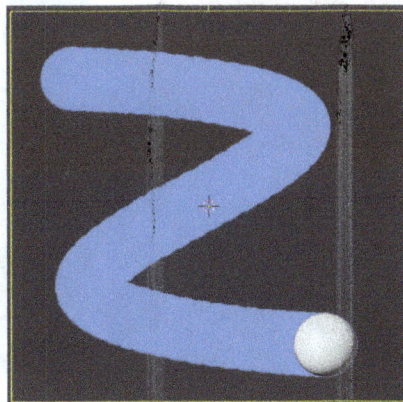

Figure 12.4 – An example of the Paint type in action

- The **Displace** type displaces your mesh based on the size of the **Brush** object. This can be useful for creating tire tracks, footprints, and much more!

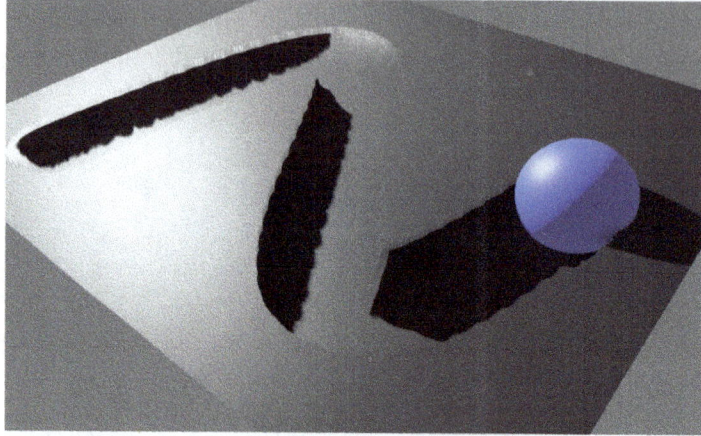

Figure 12.5 – An example of the Displace type in action

- **Weight** allows you to create a dynamic weight paint map. Blender uses weight paint for almost everything – simulations, particle systems, modifiers, materials, and more. For example, in *Chapter 15*, we will be using **Weight** to control where the fire simulation is on our mesh. Using this **Weight** type can be extremely powerful and can allow you to create some very interesting simulations!

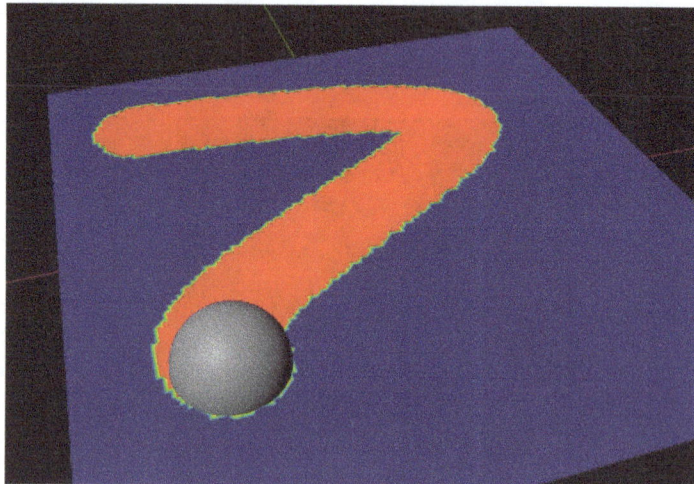

Figure 12.6 – An example of the Weight type in action

- And finally, **Waves** allows you to create waves as if your brush was moving through water. This can be very useful for creating ripples in an image of water, raindrops, or skipping stones on a lake.

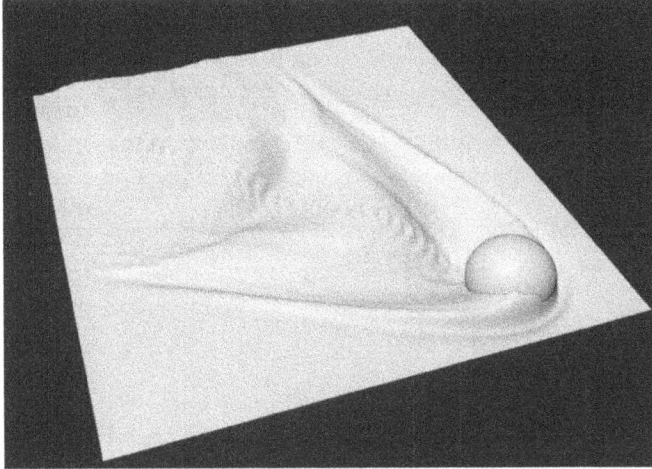

Figure 12.7 – An example of the Waves type in action

There are a lot more ways to customize the canvas to your liking, which we will discuss in this chapter! Before we dive into all the settings and values, let's quickly cover the **Brush** object!

To add a dynamic paint brush, select a mesh object, then head over to the **Physics** panel and select **Dynamic Paint**. Change **Type** to **Brush** and click **Add Brush**:

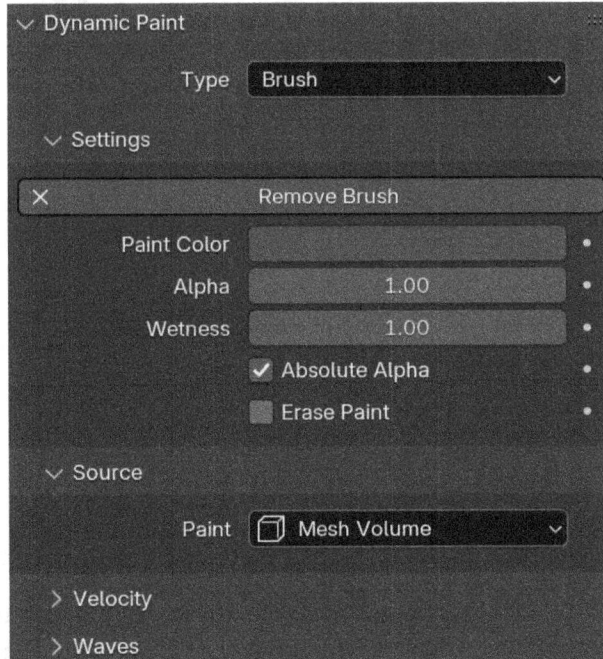

Figure 12.8 – The Brush settings

In the settings, you can change **Paint Color**, the **Proximity** around the brush that will affect the canvas, the **Depth** of the displacement, and the strength **Factor** of the waves. You can even use a particle system as a **Brush**! This could be very useful for creating raindrops and particle paint effects.

Are you starting to see the power of dynamic paint and all its potential in Blender? There are so many ways to use this physics system to create interesting and dynamic (pun intended) animations!

Now that you have an understanding of what dynamic paint is all about, let's create a simple paint simulation together!

Creating a paint simulation

Creating a basic dynamic paint simulation is a little tricky to set up, so let's create one together and go over the process! To make things easier to understand, I recommend downloading the `Paint Startup.blend` file from here: `https://github.com/PacktPublishing/Learn-Blender-4-Simulations-the-Right-Way/tree/main/Chapter%2012`.

This file includes a basic animation of a sphere following a curve on a plane:

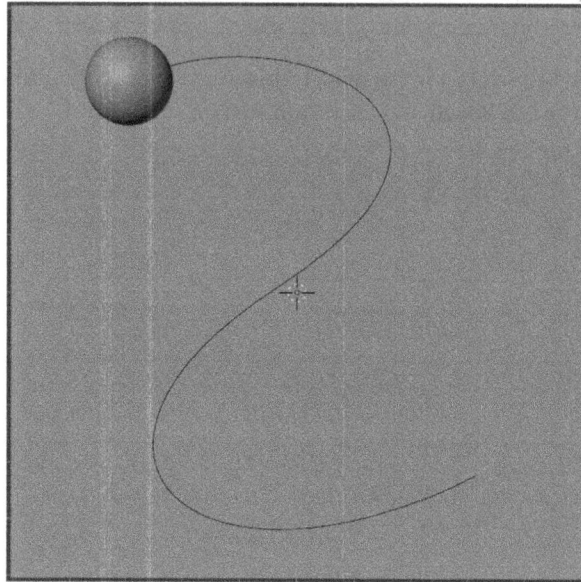

Figure 12.9 – The Paint Startup.blend example

Let's start out by adding a dynamic paint simulation to the plane and the sphere object:

1.   Select the **Plane** object and head over to the **Physics** panel. Select **Dynamic Paint**, make sure **Type** is set to **Canvas**, and then click on **Add Canvas**:

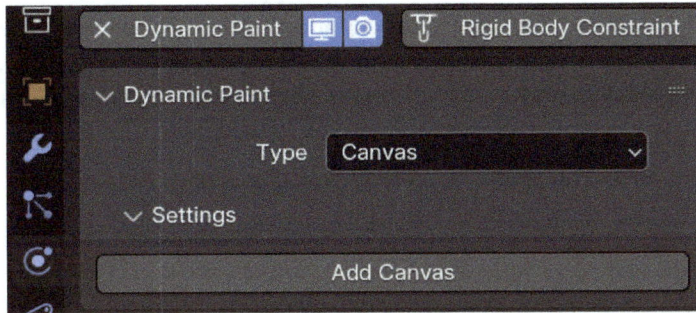

Figure 12.10 – Adding the canvas object

2.   Let's do the same thing for the **Sphere** object, except let's set **Type** to **Brush** and click **Add Brush**!

3.   Even though we have a brush and a canvas in the scene, we can't see anything when we play the animation. This is because we need to set up the **Output** details for the color information first! When using the **Vertex** format, these values are output to the **Color Attribute** field of the object.

Select the **Canvas** object and head down to the **Output** tab at the bottom:

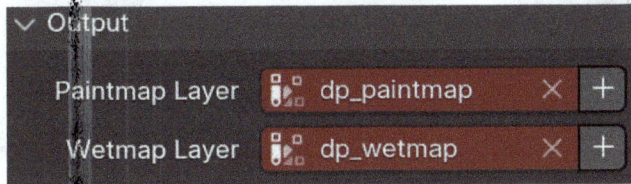

Figure 12.11 – The Output tab

4.   Click on the + icon for both **Paintmap Layer** and **Wetmap Layer**. **Paintmap Layer** is just the basic color information from the brush and **Wetmap Layer** gives us values that determine how "wet" or how "dry" the paint is. We will cover both of these layers in more detail later, in the *Surfaces* section of this chapter!

5.   With that done, we are now outputting the paint and wetness information to the vertex colors! You can also see this by looking at the **Object Data Properties** panel in the **Color Attributes** tab:

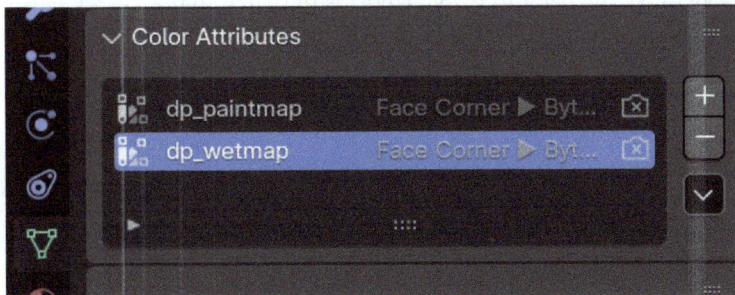

Figure 12.12 – The Color Attributes tab

When using the **Vertex** format, we are directly affecting the color of each vertex of the mesh. These colors are then output as **Color Attributes**, as you can see in *Figure 12.12*. Keep in mind that the color is only affecting the vertices, not the edges or faces. If you have a large gap between the vertices, there will be a gradient of color to the connecting vertices.

6. If you would like to see this paint color affect the canvas, you could do so in a couple of ways:

    - You can open the material node setup, add a **Color Attribute** node (see *Figure 12.13*), and select **dp_paintmap** from the dropdown menu. You can also select **dp_wetmap** in the **Color Attribute** node as well, if you would like to preview what the wetmaps look like.

    Now the paint color will appear when you render.

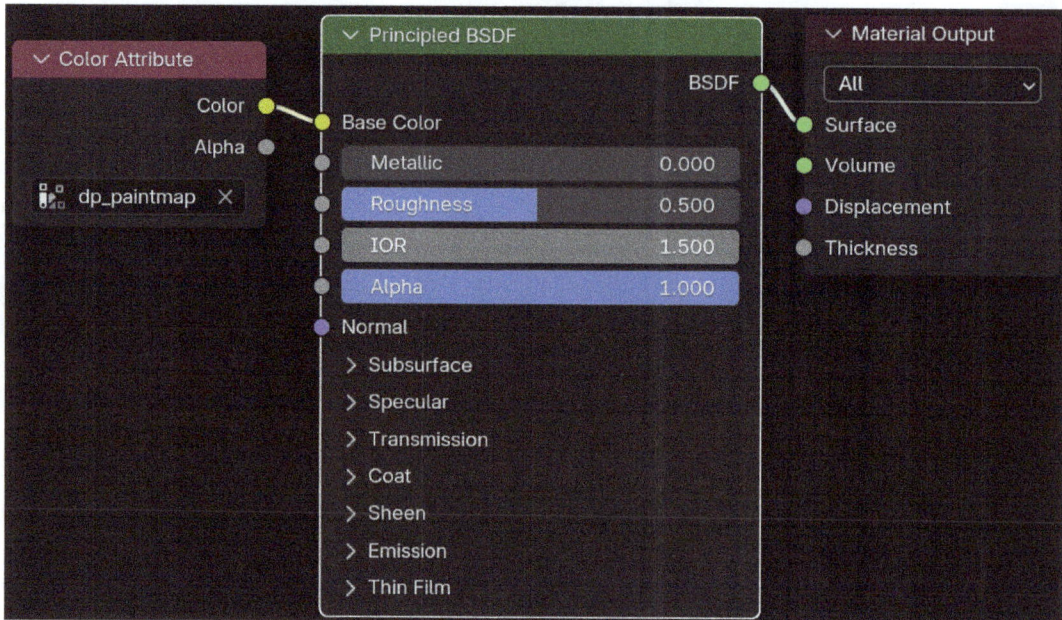

Figure 12.13 – The Color Attribute node

    - Another way to see the paint in the viewport is to switch to the **Vertex Paint** mode in the top left corner. You can toggle between the **dp_wetmap** or **dp_paintmap** by selecting from the dropdown menu.

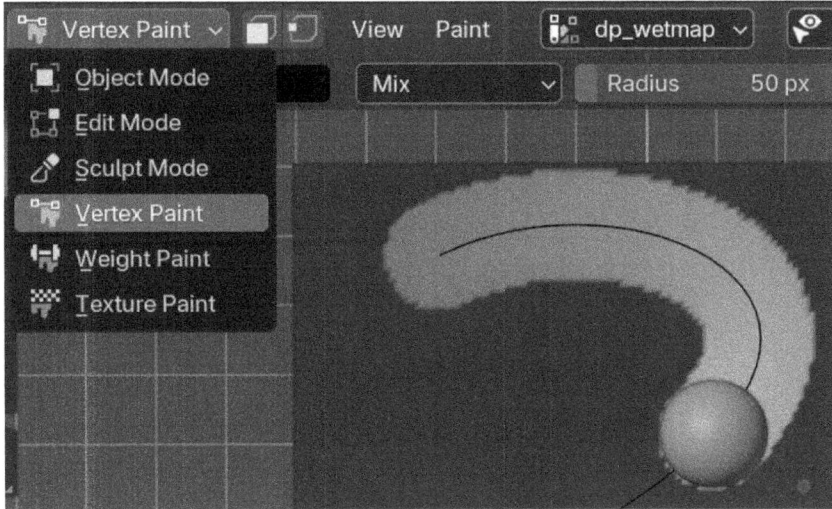

Figure 12.14 – Vertex Mode

- And, lastly, if you don't want to be stuck in **Vertex Paint** mode, you can head to the **Viewport Shading** menu and select the **Attribute** mode:

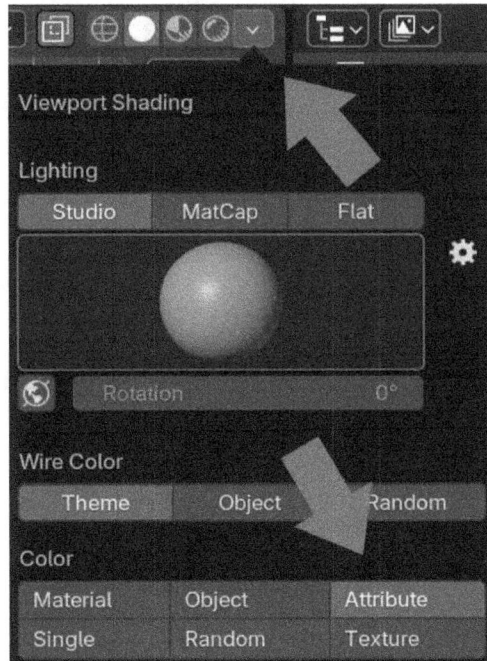

Figure 12.15 – The Attribute mode in the Viewport Shading menu

Now, you should be able to see the brush painting on the canvas in **Object** mode!

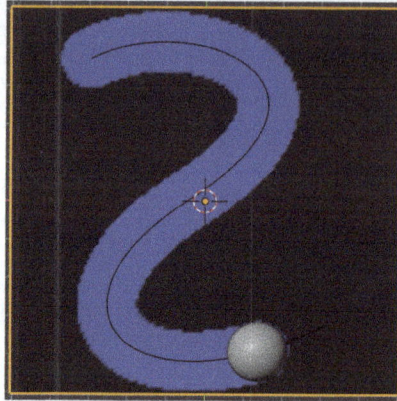

Figure 12.16 – A Brush object painting on the canvas

If you would like to see how the wetmap layer looks, you can do that by selecting **dp_wetmap** in the **Color Attribute** tab. Take a look at *Figure 12.12* to see that menu. Here's a preview of what a wetmap would look like:

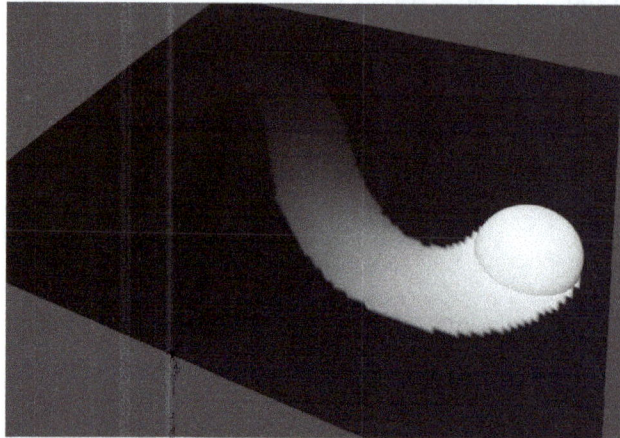

Figure 12.17 – A wetmap preview

Now that we understand how to set up a dynamic paint simulation, let's go over the settings, starting with the canvas!

Understanding the canvas

We have covered how to create a dynamic paint simulation, but let's now get a bit more technical and discuss all the settings for the **Canvas** object:

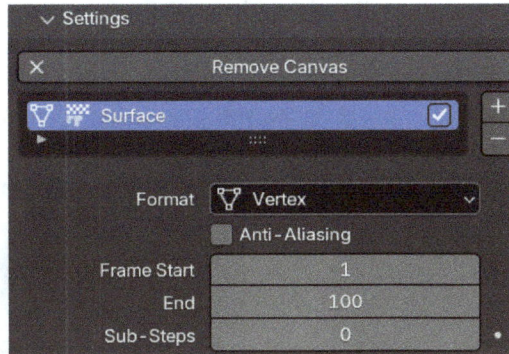

Figure 12.18 – The canvas settings

Settings

Starting at the very top, let's cover the **Settings** tab:

- **Remove Canvas**: This obviously allows you to remove the canvas from the object you have selected.

- **Surface layers**: Below **Remove Canvas**, you have your surface layers. In *Figure 12.18*, the name of the layer is **Surface**; you can rename it by double-clicking on it. You can add or remove layers by clicking the + and – buttons on the side and you can also toggle the visibility by checking the checkbox.

  These layers all work independently from each other, meaning you can have multiple layers with different surface types, and you can change the settings for each individually. For example, in the following figure, there are three surface layers. One is set to **Paint**, another set to **Displace**, and the last is set to **Waves**:

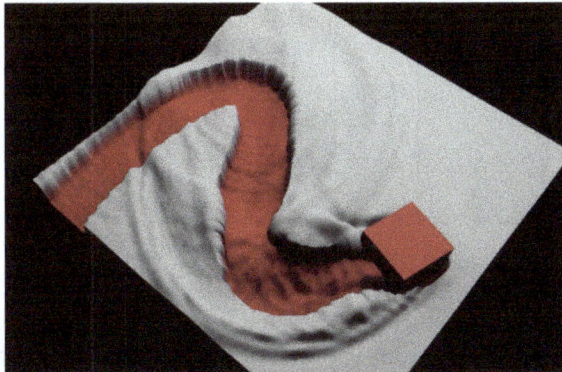

Figure 12.19 – Three surface types

Using multiple layers at the same time can create some very interesting animations!

- **Format**: We mentioned **Format** briefly earlier in this chapter. There are two options to choose from, **Vertex** and **Image Sequence**:

  - **Vertex**: This allows you to paint directly on the vertices of the canvas. This is useful because you can see your result in real time and this makes it very easy to test out settings to find exactly what you want! The downside of using this method is that it requires a lot of geometry for it to look good. In the following figure, you can see the differences between a low poly mesh and a high poly mesh:

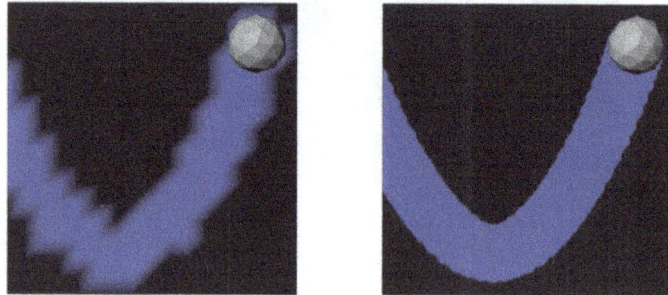

Figure 12.20 – A low poly mesh (left) and high poly mesh (right)

  - **Image Sequence**: This allows you to export the paint information as a set of images. You can set the directory for where these images will be generated in the **Output** tab. We will cover exporting in more detail in the *Cache and Output* section.

Once the images are generated, import them into the material, textures, displacement, or whatever you want! This method does not require any geometry for it to work, meaning you can have a very high-quality paint map with very little geometry on your canvas.

When the **Image Sequence** format is selected, a **Resolution** setting will appear, and this is where you set the size of the images being exported. Keep in mind that the higher the resolution, the longer it will take to bake or export:

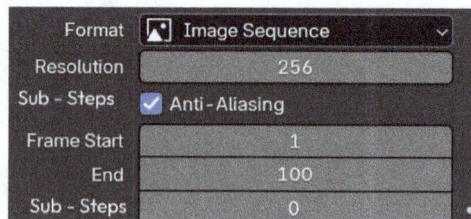

Figure 12.21 – The Resolution settings

The downside of this method is that it's much slower to work with because you need to rebake and export all your images every time you want to make a change.

- **Anti-Aliasing**: This smooths out the edges of the paint. This effect is pretty subtle, but it does help if the edges of the paint are too sharp. The following figure is an exaggerated effect of anti-aliasing:

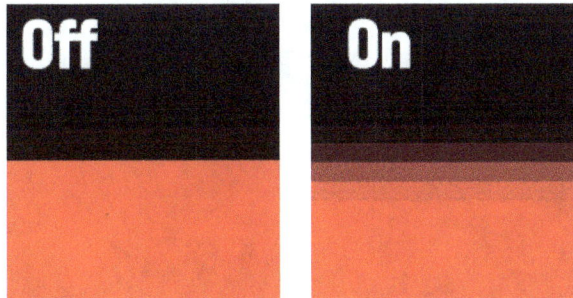

Figure 12.22 – An example of the Anti-Aliasing setting in action

- **Frame Start** and **End**: These, of course, determine when the simulation will start and end!
- **Sub-Steps**: This option adds extra steps per frame. Sometimes, when you have a very fast-moving brush, the paint will skip over some areas. Turning up **Sub-Steps** will help the simulation be much more accurate.

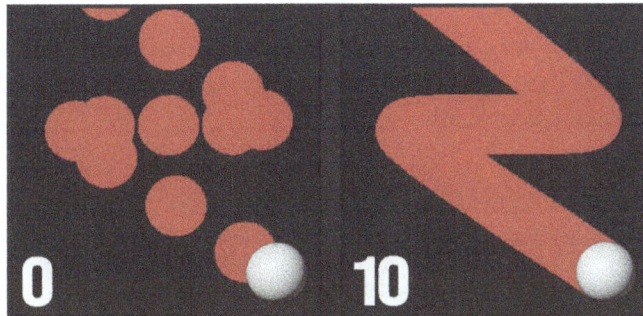

Figure 12.23 – An example of the Sub-Steps option in action

Now that we have covered the values in the **Settings** tab, let's jump into the **Surface** tab and learn all about the different **Surface Type** options!

Surfaces

There are four **Surface Type** options to choose from when working with dynamic paint simulations: **Paint**, **Displace**, **Weight**, and **Waves**. Each of these is unique and can do a lot of cool things!

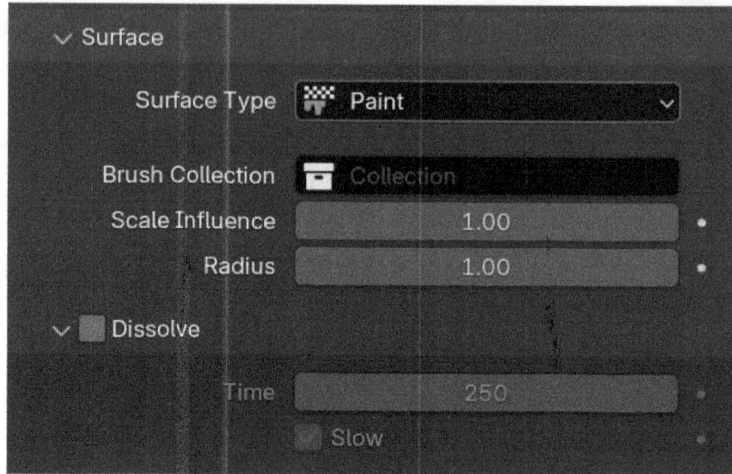

Figure 12.24 – The common Surface settings

Let's start by looking at the common settings and then we will go over each type:

- **Surface Type**: This, of course, allows you to choose which type of dynamic paint you want for your brush!

- **Brush Collection**: This allows you to limit the brushes used on the canvas to that specific collection. This can be useful if you have multiple dynamic paint simulations and you don't want them interacting with each other.

- **Scale Influence**: This sets the percentage of influence the brush has on the simulation. This can be visualized easily with the **Displace** surface type:

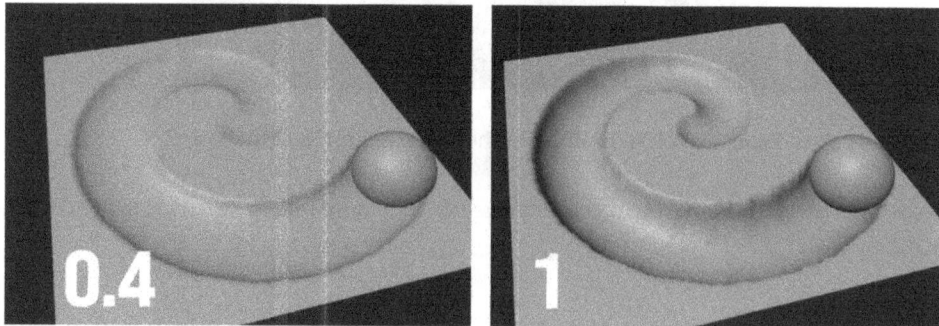

Figure 12.25 – An example of the Scale Influence option in action

- **Radius**: This controls how big or small the area around every brush that affects the canvas is (keep in mind this setting only works when **Source** is set to **Proximity** for a brush – we will cover this in more detail when we talk about brushes).

Figure 12.26 – An example of the Radius settings in action

- **Dissolve**: This is another common setting for the **Paint**, **Displace**, and **Weight** types (**Dissolve** is not available when using the **Waves** surface type.) When enabled, it will dissolve the effect of the brush over time. How fast it dissolves is set by the **Time** value. When it is set to `100`, it will take approximately 100 frames until the effect completely dissolves. When **Slow** is checked, the way it dissolves will be much smoother and slower:

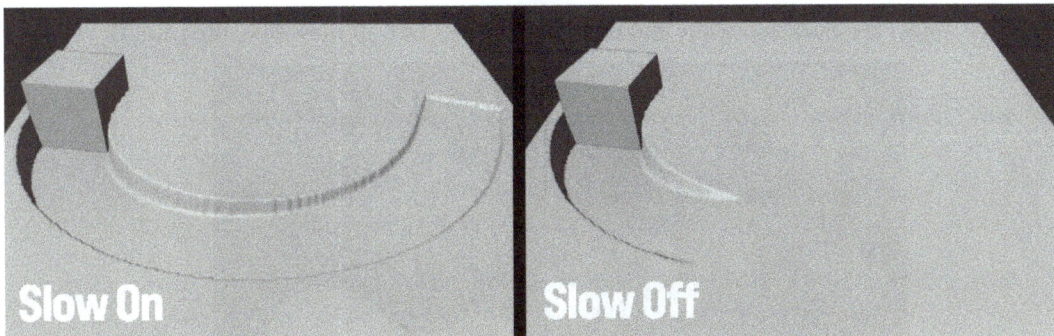

Figure 12.27 – An example of the Dissolve settings in action

If you are using the **Dissolve** option with **Paint Surface Type**, you need to remember to uncheck **Dry** in the **Surface** tab, or it will not work. It's not recommended to use this method to dissolve the paint because it seems to be a bit buggy and does not work as intended. A lot of the time, you will get a hard edge when dissolving and not a smooth transition. A better option would be to use a wetmap to dissolve the paint. This way, you have more control and it will be much smoother.

Now that we have covered the common settings for **Surface**, let's go through the individual settings for each type, starting with **Paint**!

Paint

Paint is the basic surface type that outputs color information and wetness values. The color of the paint is based on the color set by the brush. This can be changed in the **Brush** settings:

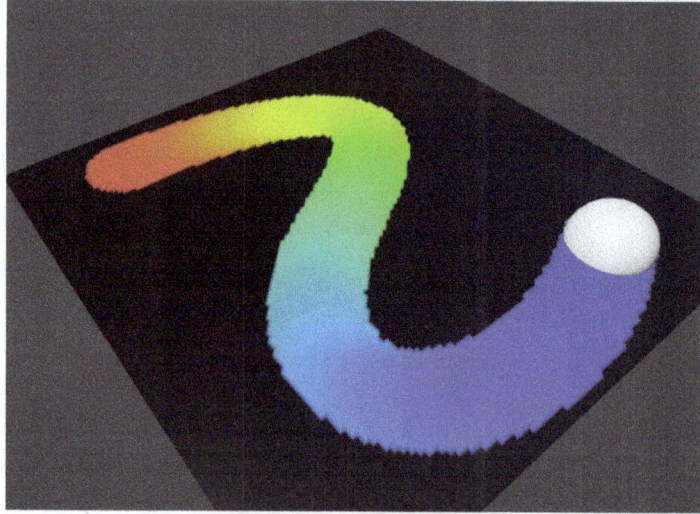

Figure 12.28 – The Brush color

The wetness values are black and white and these define how "wet" or how "dry" the paint is:

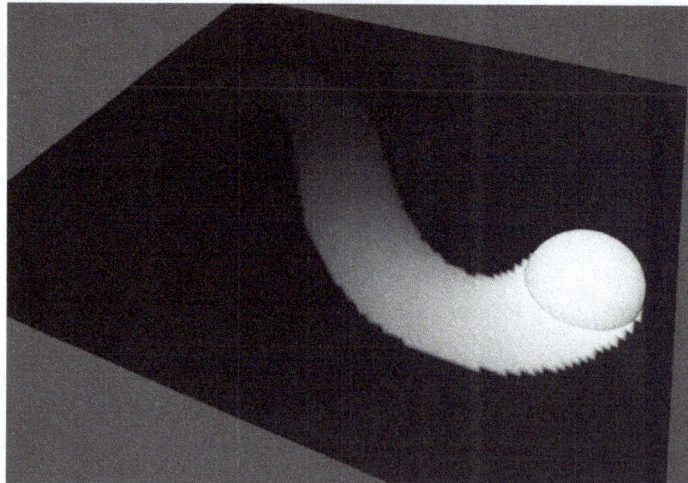

Figure 12.29 – An example of a wetmap layer

A wetmap can be very useful as a mask for the material and defining which parts are supposed to be glossy or wet. If you want to create an animation of paint drying, you can do that using dynamic paint.

How fast or slow the drying happens can be changed in the **Dry** tab:

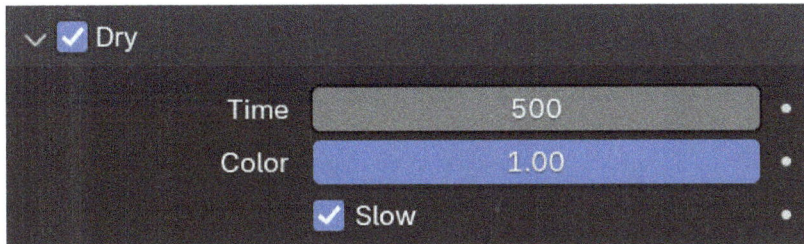

Figure 12.30 – The Dry settings

Dry tab

Let's look into the options on the **Dry** tab:

- **Time**: Controls how fast the drying will happen in terms of frames.

- **Color**: Defines when the wetness level of the paint starts to shift to the background. An easier way to understand this would be that it helps to blend the spreading paint as it dries:

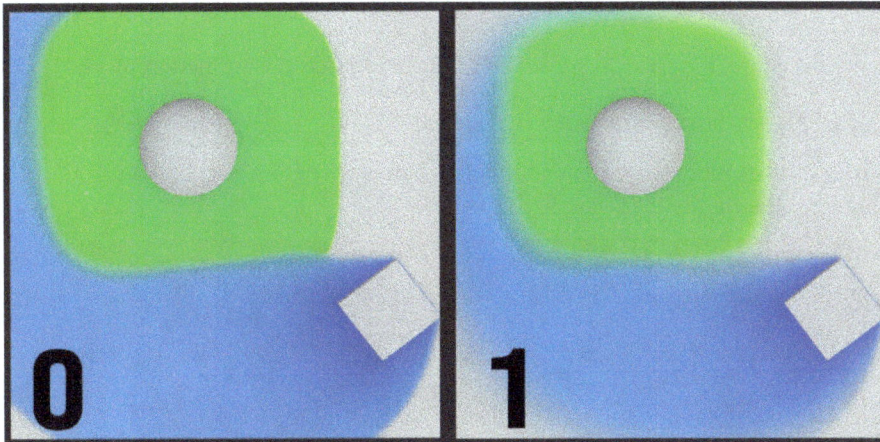

Figure 12.31 – An example of how the Dry Color setting works

- **Slow**: This allows the paint to dry more slowly and smoothly.

Next up, let's explore the **Effects** tab.

Effects tab

In *Figure 12.31*, you may have noticed that the paint is spreading from the brushes. This is one of three **Effects** features you can add to the canvas:

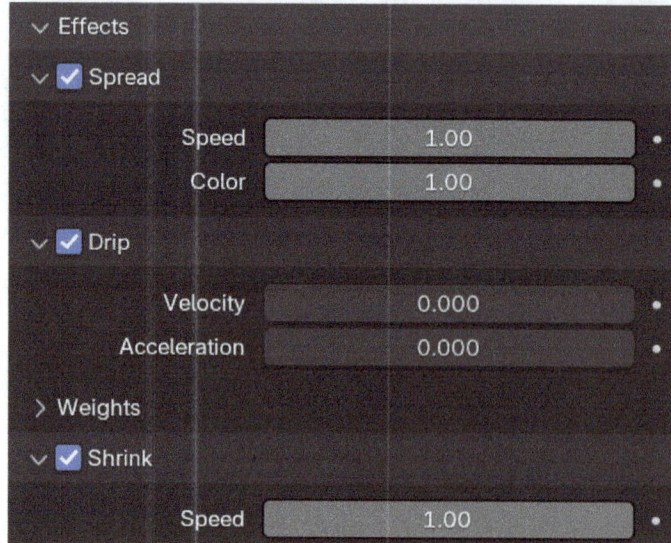

Figure 12.32 – The Effects settings

- **Spread**: This allows the paint to spread from the brushes as the animation plays:

  - **Speed**: This sets how fast the paint will spread.

  - **Color**: This helps blend two colors of paint as they spread into each other. You can see the different values in the following figure:

Figure 12.33 – An example of Color Spread in action

- **Drip**: This allows the paint to react to gravity. For example, in the following figure, there are some brushes on a vertical canvas and, as you can see, gravity is affecting the paint and making it drip down:

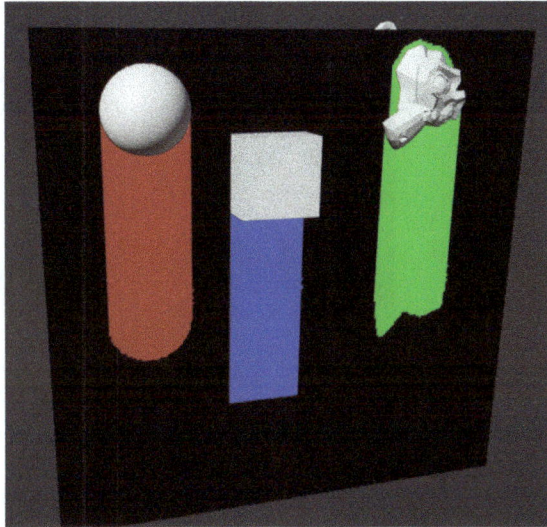

Figure 12.34 – An example of the Drip setting in action

- **Velocity**: This takes the velocity of the canvas and affects the paint accordingly. The higher you set this, the more the movement of the canvas will affect the paint. For example, when the canvas moves quickly to the right, the source of the paint moves as well. Then, it will start to drip in that new location. This is visualized in the following figure:

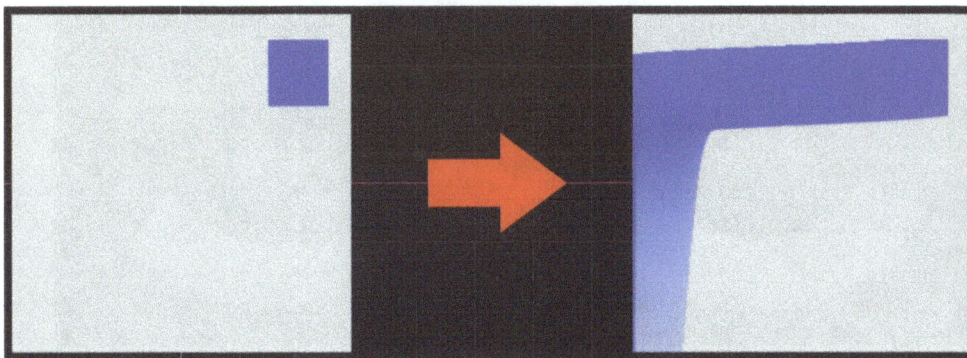

Figure 12.35 – An example of the Velocity option in action

- **Acceleration**: This works similarly to **Velocity**; the difference is that the paint will still react to the movement of the canvas, but the source of the paint will not move. Once the canvas has stopped moving, the paint will drip down in the same location as where it started:

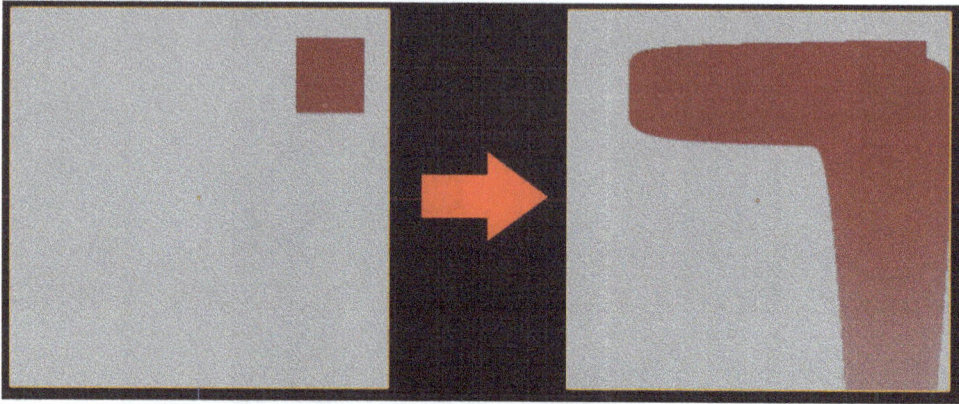

Figure 12.36 – An example of the Acceleration option in action

The **Drip** effect also reacts to force fields! If you want to add some wind movement to the paint, you can do that! You can control the strength and influence that the force fields have in the **Weights** tab.

- **Shrink**: This effect only changes the wetmap layer. Instead of drying normally, the wetmap layer will shrink at each end:

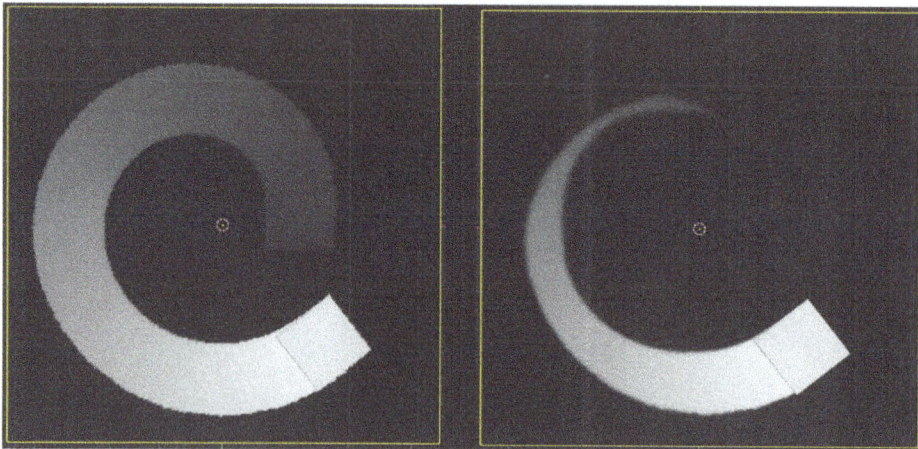

Figure 12.37 – An example of the Shrink option in action

You can also control the amount of shrinking and how fast it is with the **Speed** value.

Now, let's take a look at the **Initial Color**!

Initial Color

Below the **Effects** tab, we have the option to select an **Initial Color** setting for the canvas. This will allow the canvas to have a starting color instead of just automatically being black.

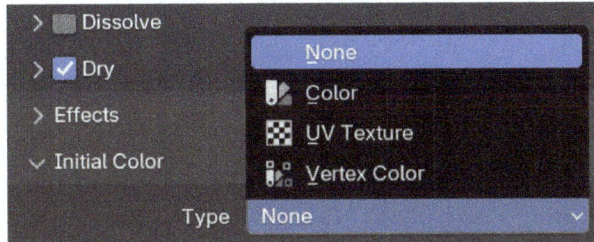

Figure 12.38 – The Initial Color settings

If you select **Color**, you will be able to choose a specific color for the background of the canvas. You can also select **UV Texture** or **Vertex Color**:

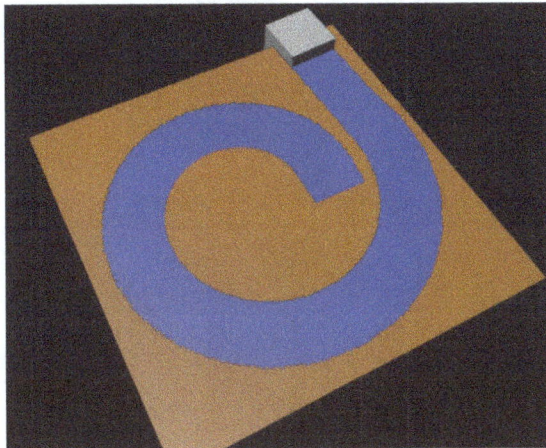

Figure 12.39 – An example of the Initial Color option in action

And finally, when using the **Vertex** format, remember to always output the paint color information on the **Output** tab.

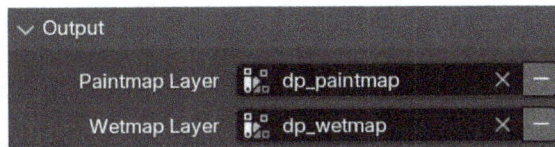

Figure 12.40 – The Output tab

And that is all the settings for the **Paint** surface type! Next up, let's talk about the **Displace** type!

Displace

The **Displace** type allows you to indent the mesh based on the size and scale of the **Brush** object! This can be very useful for creating footprints, tire tracks, objects landing in dirt or snow, and a lot more:

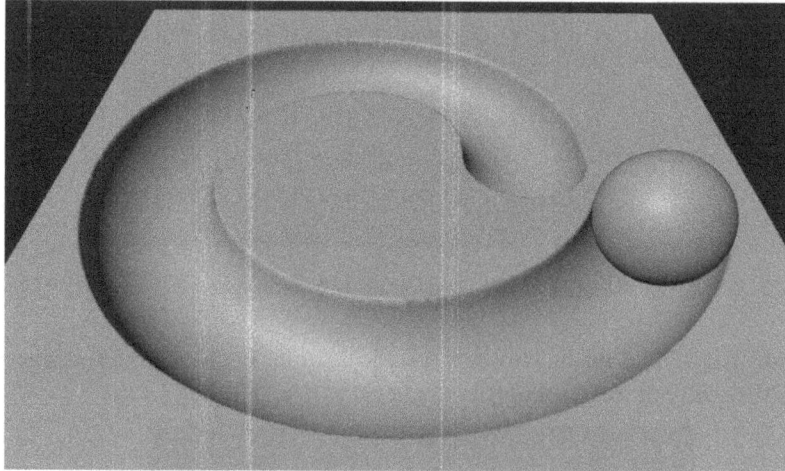

Figure 12.41 – The Displace surface type

There are only three settings that we need to go over for the **Displace** surface type:

Figure 12.42 – The Displace settings

- **Max Displace**: Sets the maximum amount of displacement that the brush can have on the canvas. This setting is in meters, so if the value is set to 1, then the brush can only displace 1 meter on the canvas. A value of 0 means the displacement can be indefinite.

- **Displace Factor**: Multiplies the displacement depth. For example, if the displacement depth is 1 meter and you set the **Displace Factor** to 3, the depth will now be 3 meters. This value can also be set to a negative number and that will cause the displacement to go up rather than down:

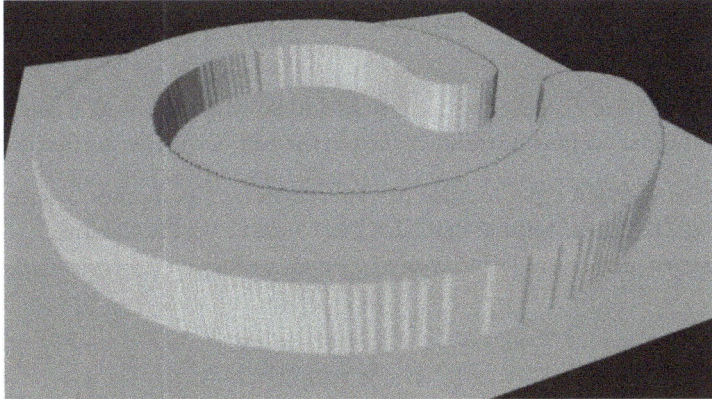

Figure 12.43 – A negative Displace Factor setting in action

- **Incremental**: allows new displacement to be added on top of existing displacement. This could be useful for creating a digging animation.

And that is all the settings for the **Displace** surface type! Next up, let's look at **Weight**!

Weight

The **Weight** surface type allows you to paint a vertex group on the canvas. This can be extremely useful because almost everything in Blender can be influenced by a vertex group. For example, using the **Weight** type, you can easily paint a trail of fire. Another example would be painting hair particles. In the following figure, a cube is painted on a plane using the **Weight** surface type. This **Weight** surface type then controls the density and size of the particle system:

Figure 12.44 – The Weight surface type in action

Most of Blender's modifiers can also be influenced by vertex groups! The things you can create are almost limitless!

Throughout this book, we have discussed vertex groups and how they are used in certain simulations. If you would like a refresher on how it works, check out the *Soft Body Goal* section in *Chapter 6*.

When you first select the **Weight** type, you also need to remember to output to a vertex group. Scroll down to the bottom of the canvas settings and click the + next to **Vertex Group**:

Figure 12.45 – The Vertex Group option under Output settings

Also, if you want to see how the simulation looks, make sure to switch to the **Weight Paint** mode:

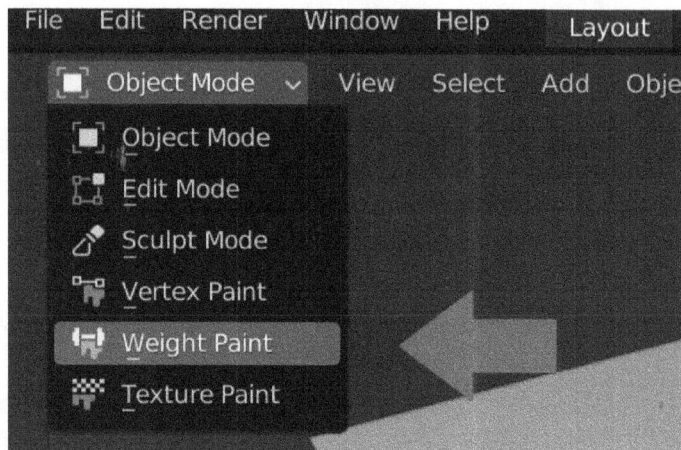

Figure 12.46 – The Weight Paint mode

There are two settings we need to discuss when using the **Weight Surface Type**:

- **Scale Influence**: Adjusting this in the canvas settings will affect the weight being painted. A value of 0.5 will paint 50% weight.

- **Dissolve**: Another cool trick would be to enable **Dissolve**. This will make the weight disappear as the animation plays! You can see an example of this in the following figure:

Figure 12.47 – Scale Influence and Dissolve

The **Weight** surface type is very powerful and can be used in so many ways! Definitely check it out and experiment with different modifiers and simulations!

Waves

The last **Surface Type** to talk about is **Waves** and this is one of the coolest ways to use dynamic paint! It basically allows you to turn your canvas into water and have the brush create waves and ripples as it moves around:

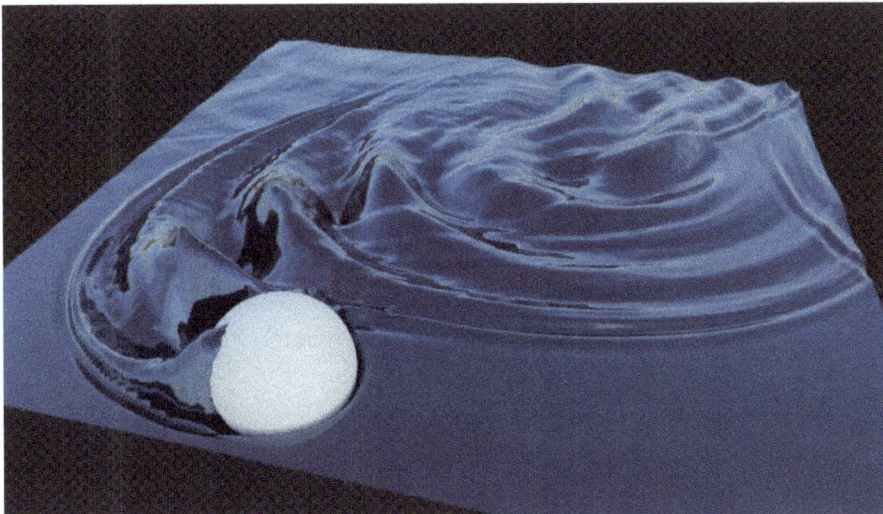

Figure 12.48 – An example of the Waves type in action

In the canvas settings, there are a lot of ways to customize how these waves behave. Let's go through them one by one:

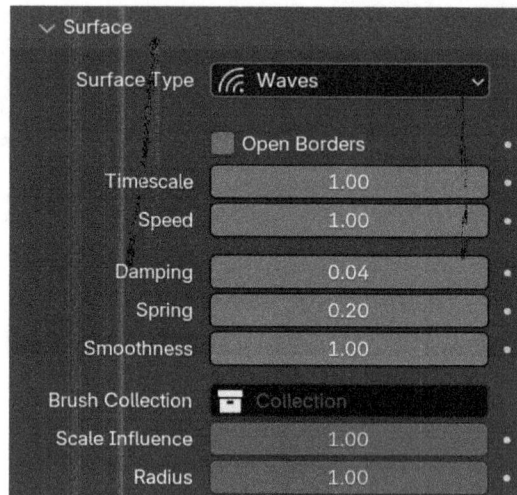

Figure 12.49 – Waves settings

- **Open Borders**: This allows the waves to pass through the edges of the canvas instead of reflecting from them. Normally, when this is unchecked, the waves will hit the edge of the canvas and bounce back.

- There are two speed settings here: **Timescale** and **Speed**. The difference between these two settings is that **Timescale** will speed up the simulation without affecting the overall outcome. **Speed** will speed up the movement of the waves, thus changing the outcome of the simulation.

  So, if you want to slow down or speed up the simulation without affecting how it looks, use the **Timescale** setting.

- **Damping**: This controls how fast the waves disappear. When set to 0, the waves will continue moving and never stop bouncing around, whereas when it's set to a higher value (max of 1), the waves will lose their strength and eventually disappear.

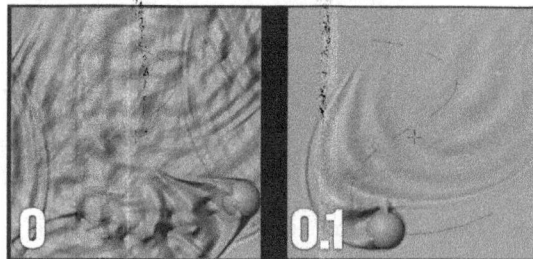

Figure 12.50 – An example of the Damping option in action

- The **Spring** value goes from 0 to 1, and it determines the strength/force with which the waves will be pulled back down to the flat ground. Higher values tend to make the waves a bit bouncier and springier:

Figure 12.51 – An example of the Spring setting in action

- **Smoothness**: This smooths out the waves and gets rid of any bumps or sharp areas. The values range from 0 to 10:

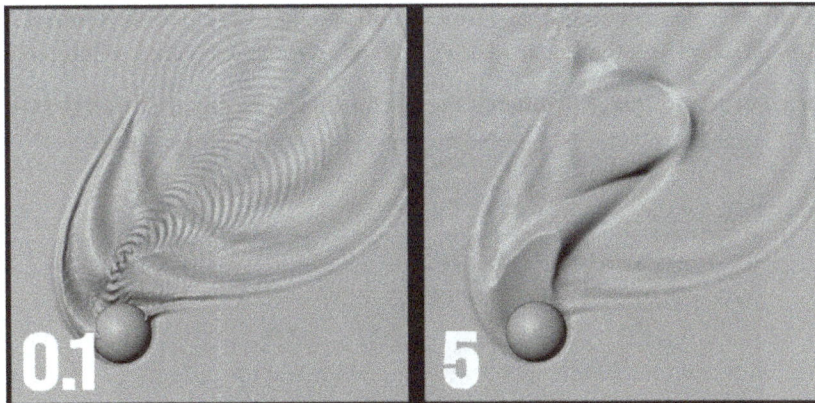

Figure 12.52 – An example of the Smoothness setting in action

Now that we have covered every surface type and all the settings associated with each one, next, let's take a look at the **Cache** tab and talk about baking and exporting!

Cache and Output

The **Cache** and **Output** tabs are where you bake the simulation and generate **Vertex Groups** and **Paintmap Layers** (mesh data layers) and export the **Image Sequences**, respectively. With the **Vertex** format selected, you will see a familiar list of settings:

Figure 12.53 – The Cache tab

If you haven't saved your blend file, all these settings will be grayed out. Make sure you save your project – only then will you be able to bake the simulation!

When you bake the simulation, the cache will be locked in and if you want to make changes, you will need to free the bake. It's generally recommended to bake the simulation before rendering. This will ensure that there are no issues and that the rendering process goes smoothly.

Since we have gone over these settings many times in this book, let's skip to the **Output** tab. If you would like a refresher, check out the *Understanding soft body settings and values* section in *Chapter 6*.

When you change **Format** to **Image Sequence**, the **Cache** tab will be replaced with the **Output** tab:

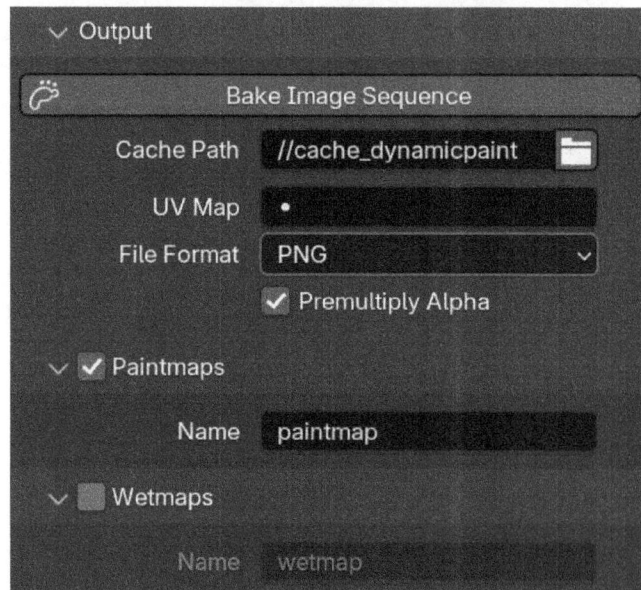

Figure 12.54 – The Output tab

- **Bake Image Sequence**: When this is clicked, Blender will export all the images from the simulation and place them in the directory set by the **Cache Path** field. You can choose which folder the images will export to by clicking the **Cache Path Folder** icon.

- **UV Map**: For most basic canvas objects, such as planes, spheres, or cubes, there should already be a UV map you can select. Selecting **UV Map** tells Blender how to properly export the images so they can be mapped to the canvas. If, however, you modeled or changed the canvas, you may need to UV unwrap your object. UV unwrapping is a topic that we don't have time to cover in this chapter. If you would like to learn more about this topic, here is a great resource: `https://youtu.be/7JUN1j6mR0U?si=-pZsq8Nw1nd5RChY`

- **File Format**: There are two types of file formats when exporting images: **PNG** and **OpenEXR**. **OpenEXR** is a better and higher-quality image file than **PNG**, but the file size is much bigger. Normally, **PNG** will work perfectly fine for most simulations.

- **Premultiply Alpha**: This allows you to export transparent images so that only the paint will show up and not the canvas. And at the bottom, you can decide to either export the **Paintmaps**, **Wetmaps**, or both.

And there we go! We have now talked about everything there is to know about the **Canvas** object in the dynamic paint simulation. The last thing we will learn about in this chapter is the **Brush** object and all its settings.

Using brushes

Now that we have covered the canvas, let's discuss the brush and all the ways to customize how it behaves in the simulation!

Settings

Let's start by looking at the **Settings** tab:

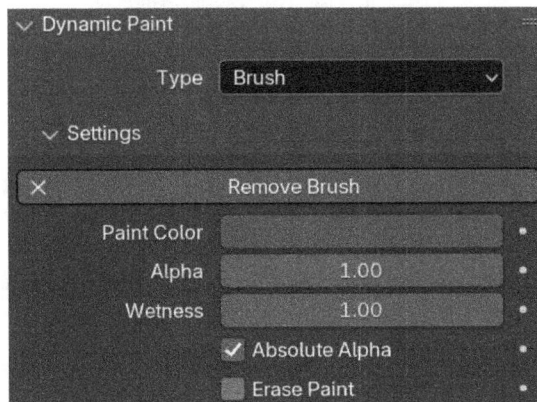

Figure 12.55 – The Brush settings

- **Paint Color**: This obviously allows you to change what color is being painted on the canvas. This color can also be animated to create a cool effect, as you saw in *Figure 12.28*.

- **Alpha**: This, which ranges from 0 to 1, controls the transparency of the paint. The lower this value, the more transparent the paint will be:

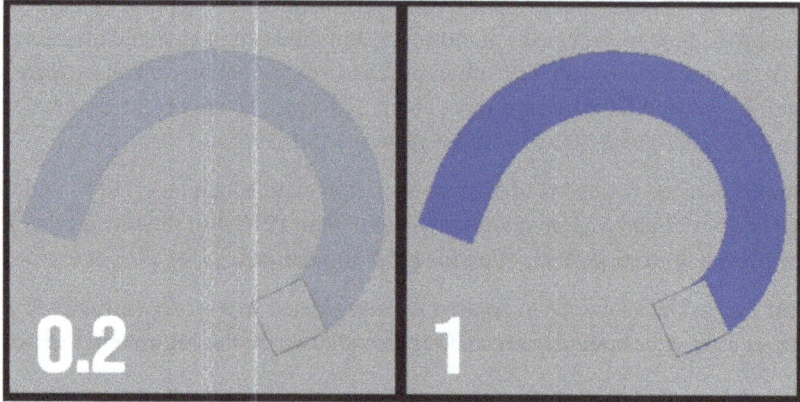

Figure 12.56 – An example of the Alpha option in action

When using the **Weight** surface type in the canvas settings, this value now controls the strength of the weight the brush will paint.

- **Wetness**: This sets how wet the brush will be. You can see the values in the following figure:

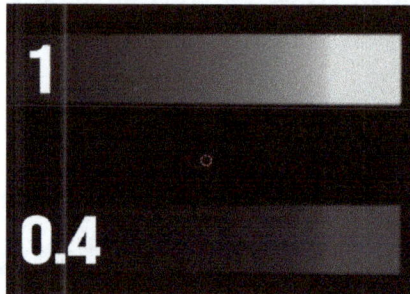

Figure 12.57 – An example of the Wetness setting in action

- **Absolute Alpha**: This deals with transparent brushes. If unchecked, the brush will constantly add paint to every single frame, thus increasing the alpha value. If it is checked, then the alpha value of the brush will stay the same throughout the simulation. Normally, it's better to leave this setting checked.

- **Erase Paint**: If this is checked, your brush will now turn into an eraser and delete paint instead of adding it.

Next up, let's take a look at **Source**!

Source

The **Source** menu is where you set how the brush will paint on the canvas:

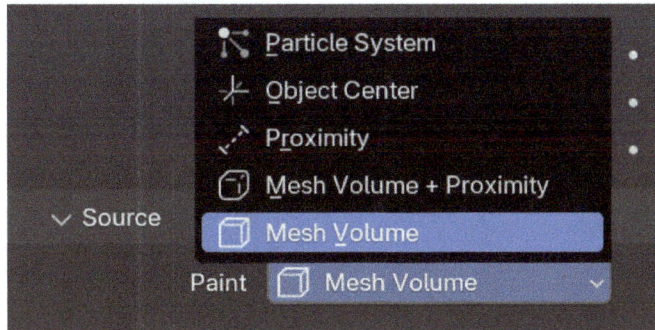

Figure 12.58 – The Source menu

Let's discuss each of the five **Paint** methods individually, starting with the **Mesh Volume**:

- **Mesh Volume**: When **Mesh Volume** is selected, the size of the brush object determines where the paint will be. Only the parts of the canvas intersecting with the geometry of the brush will be painted:

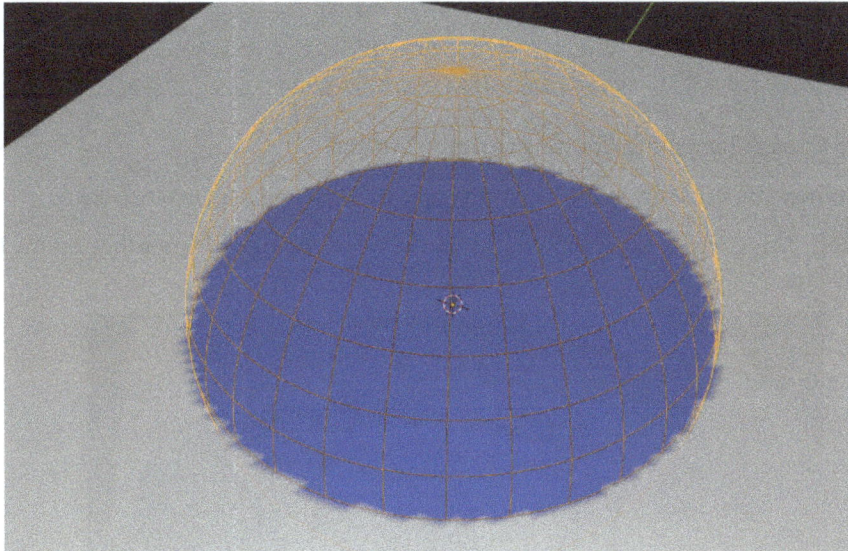

Figure 12.59 – The Mesh Volume option

- **Proximity**: This allows you to paint in proximity around the brush. Keep in mind that the inside of the mesh may not be painted if it's far away from the surface of the mesh, as you can see in the following figure:

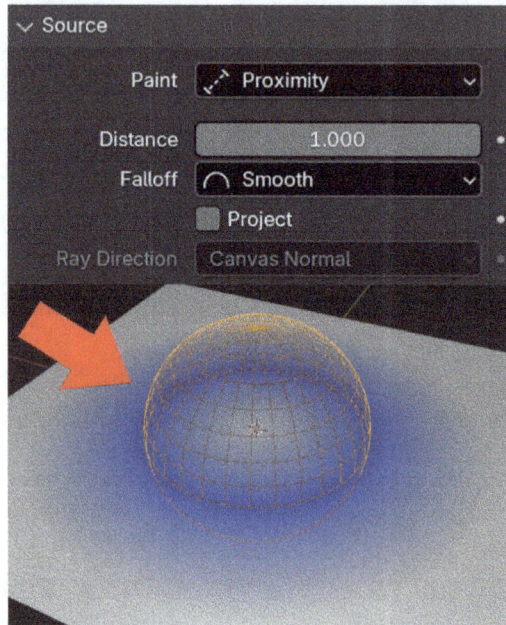

Figure 12.60 – The Proximity settings

Let's go through the settings for the **Proximity** brushes:

- **Distance**: You can control the **Proximity** area by changing the **Distance** value.

- **Falloff**: This controls how smooth it is. In the following figure, **Smooth** is on the left and **Constant** is on the right:

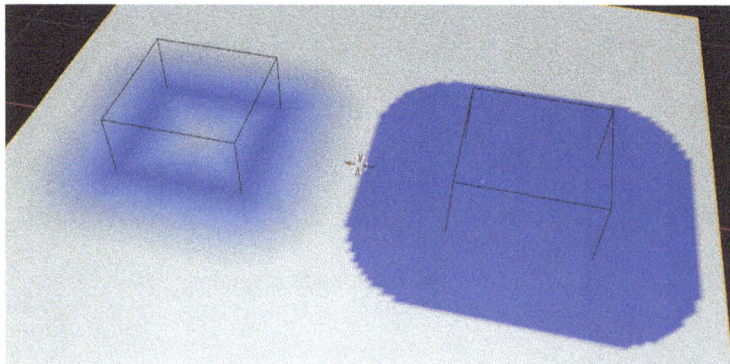

Figure 12.61 – An example of the Falloff option in action

- **Project**: This allows you to project the brush onto the canvas. In the following example, there is a floating cube set to **Project** paint type. You can see it's basically acting like a projector casting down onto the canvas.

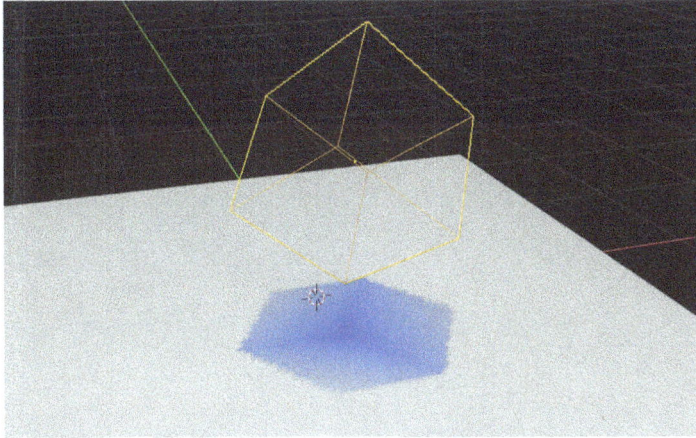

Figure 12.62 – An example of the Project option in action

- **Mesh Volume + Proximity**: With this method, you can also combine the two sources we just talked about. In this example, there is a smooth falloff with the **Proximity** but nothing inside the **Mesh Volume** is now solid.

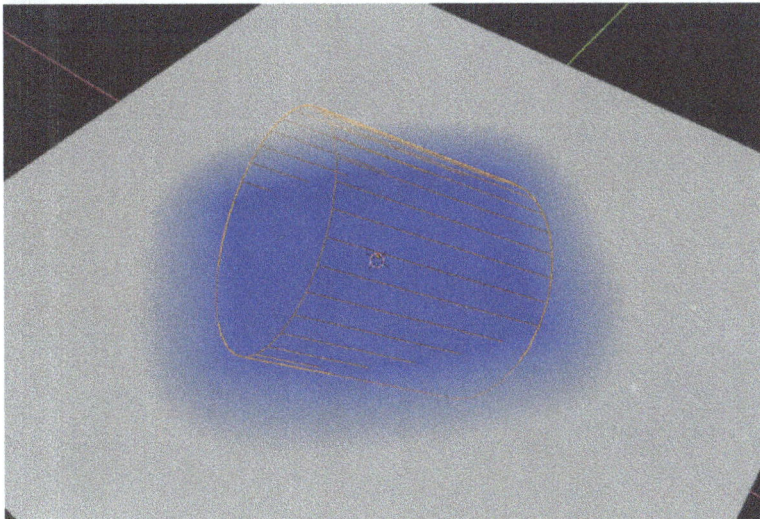

Figure 12.63 – Mesh Volume + Proximity example

- **Object Center**: This disregards the mesh, takes the position of the origin, and paints an area around it:

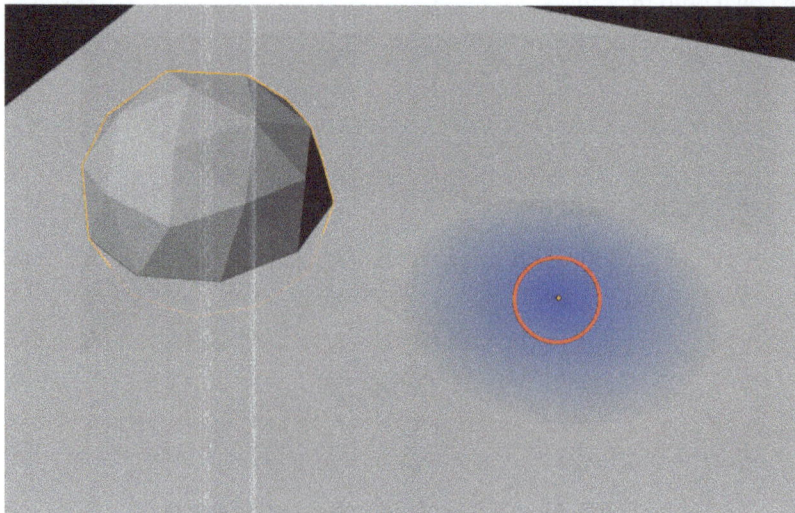

Figure 12.64 – Using the Object Center setting

- **Particle System**: This allows you to select a particle system to be the brush:

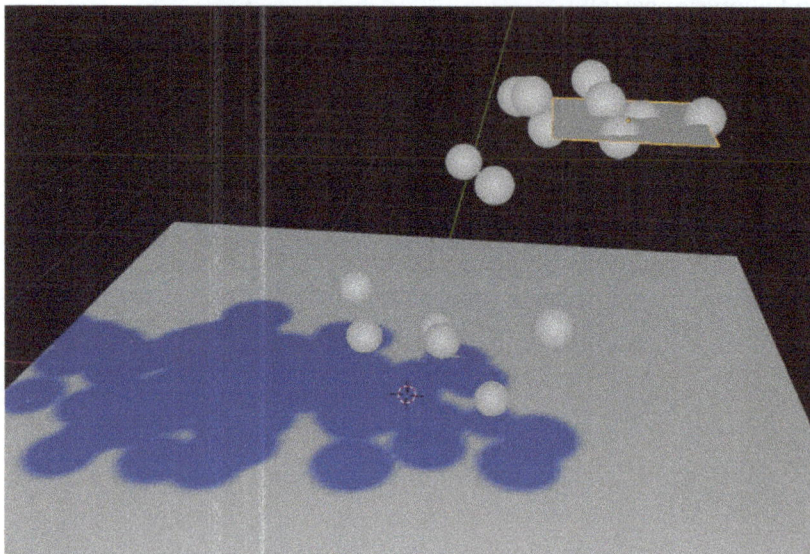

Figure 12.65 – An example of a Particle System brush

When you select a particle system to be the brush, there are a couple of settings you can change:

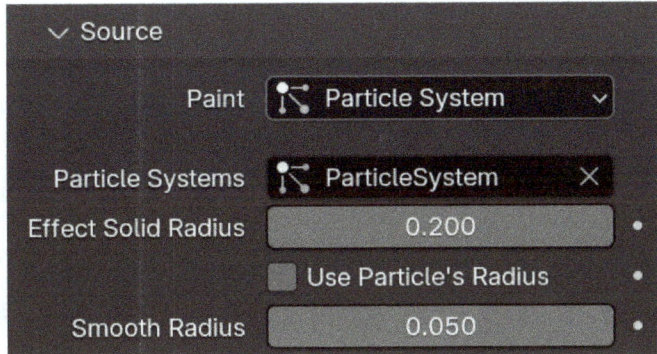

Figure 12.66 – Particle System settings

- **Effect Solid Radius**: This sets the radius around each particle that will affect the canvas.

- **Use Particle's Radius**: This allows the size of the particle to determine the radius. This can also be controlled in the **Particle Systems** settings.

- **Smooth Radius**: This controls the smoothness around each particle when painting. Lower values will make the edges of the paint sharper, while higher values will smooth it out.

Using a particle system as a brush in the simulation can be very useful for creating interesting particle paint effects. Not only do the particles work with the **Paint Surface Type** but also **Waves**, **Displace**, and **Weight**. In the following figure, we've set up a particle system to act as raindrops!

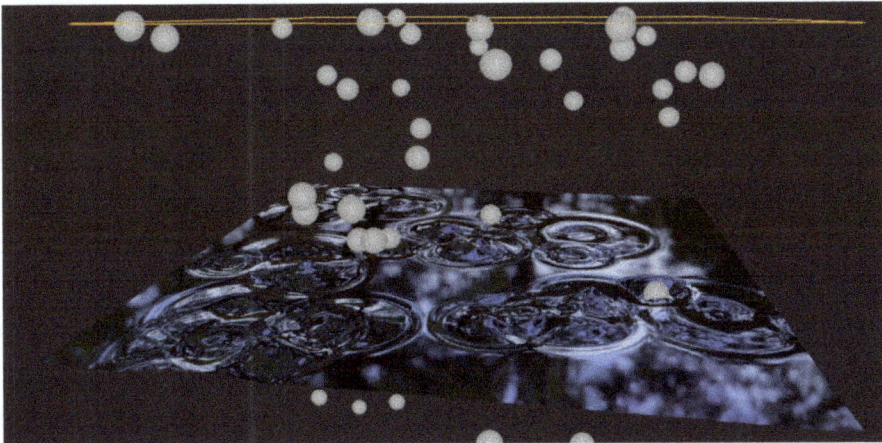

Figure 12.67 – Particle rain effects

Now that we have learned about the **Source** settings for the brush, let's talk about the **Velocity** tab!

Velocity

The **Velocity** tab allows you to influence the way the brush behaves based on speed! Let's go through the settings:

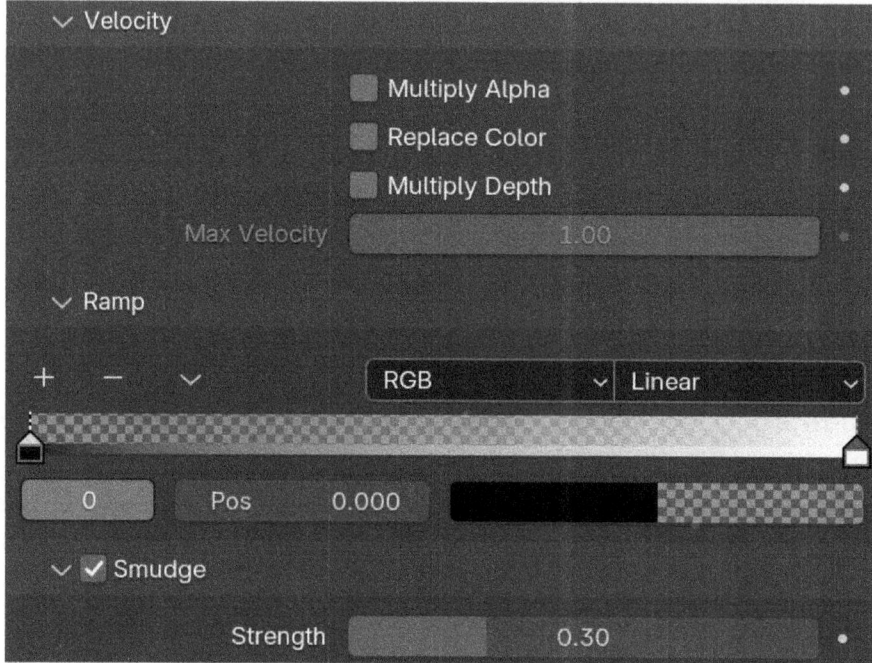

Figure 12.68 – The Velocity tab

- **Multiply Alpha**: When this is checked, the transparency of the brush will change depending on how fast it moves across the canvas. Faster velocities will increase the alpha and lower velocities will decrease the alpha. If you want to invert this so that faster movement will decrease the alpha, you can do that by flipping the values in **Ramp**.

- **Replace Color**: This does the exact same thing but rather, for the color of paint. This color can be controlled in the **Ramp** settings.

- **Multiply Depth**: This allows you to change the depth of the displacement based on the speed of the brush.

- **Max Velocity**: This gives you control over how fast the brush needs to move to influence the canvas. In the following figure, the color and displacement on the canvas change based on how fast the cube moves. The cube starts moving slowly and gains speed over time. That's why you see an increase in the displacement and change of color.

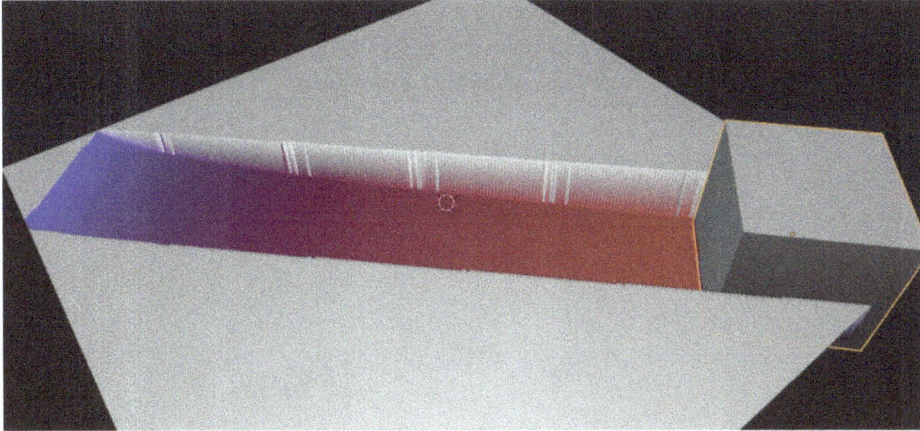

Figure 12.69 – The Multiply Depth and Replace Color settings in action

- **Smudge**: This enables the brush to smudge any paint that is already on the canvas. This can be used to create a messy paint look! In the following figure, the brush is completely transparent with **Smudge Strength** set to 0.4:

Figure 12.70 – An example of the Smudge option in action

With that done, let's take a look at the last tab for the brush settings!

Waves

The last couple of settings we need to discuss for the brush are on the **Waves** tab. This is where you can set how your brush is going to affect the waves in the simulation. So, let's dive in:

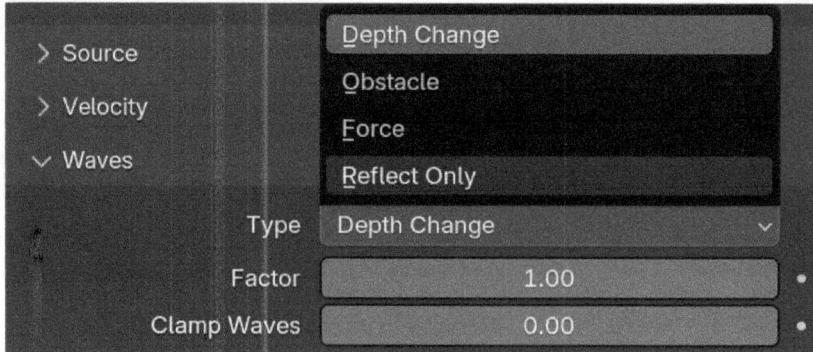

Figure 12.71 – The Waves settings for the brush

- **Type**: From this menu, you can choose what effect the brush will have on the waves:

    - : This will not create any waves – rather, it will reflect and bounce back waves that hit the object.

    - **Obstacle**: This constantly affects the surface of the canvas, creating and reflecting waves even when it's not moving. This may sound good in theory, but when testing this type, you may find that it leaves strange displacement on the canvas and can cause weird issues.

    - **Force**: This directly affects the velocity and movement of the waves. For example, if a wave passes through where the **Force** brush has been applied, the wave will dissipate.

Figure 12.72 – An example of the Force settings in action

- **Depth Change**: This is the default type; it will only create waves on the canvas when the brush is moving. If the brush is still, there will be no waves created. This type usually creates the best and cleanest results.

- **Factor**: This controls the strength of the brush on the waves. Higher values tend to create bigger and taller waves. Negative values will invert the wave pattern, making it look like the waves were created from underneath the canvas rather than on top:

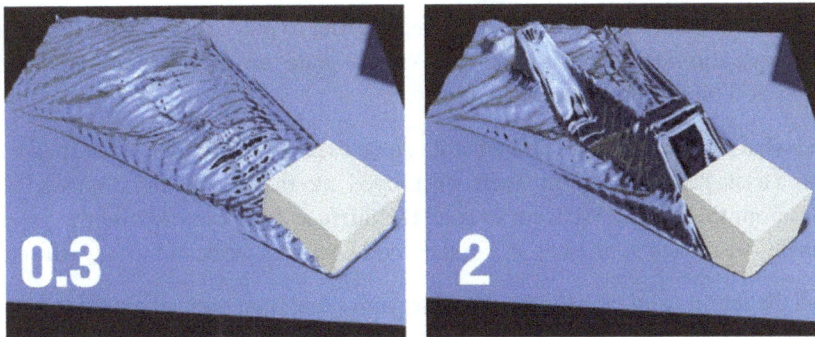

Figure 12.73 – An example of the Factor setting

- **Clamp Waves**: This setting allows you to clamp down on the height or depth of the waves. If your waves are too tall, try setting this to a low value, such as 0.2 or so. When set to 0, there will be no clamping.

That is all the settings for the brush in the dynamic paint simulation! This simulation is very powerful and can allow you to create so many awesome animations! One of the most interesting things you could do is to combine different simulations. By using the **Weight** surface type, you could paint a trail of fire!

Figure 12.74 – A trail of fire

Another use would be to create a fluid simulation splattering on a wall. Then, using the fluid as a brush, you can easily create a paint splash effect! You can also combine multiple dynamic paint simulations. With the **Displace** and **Paint** surface types, you could create a wood carving animation! The possibilities are endless!

Summary

The Dynamic Paint simulation in Blender is an incredible tool to play around with. It can be used to create so many unique and interesting animations. We have gone through a lot of information in this chapter, and it can be a lot to take in, so let's recap!

First, we learned what dynamic paint is and what it can be used for in Blender. After that, we worked together to create a basic paint simulation. Then, we jumped into the settings and discussed everything there is to know about the canvas. We went over all the **Surface Type** options and the practical uses for each one. Finally, we looked at brushes and understood how they work and what each setting does.

Reading about all the settings and uses for the dynamic paint simulation is great, but for the information to really sink in, the best thing would be to create something yourself. I encourage you to open Blender and play around with this powerful tool.

In the next couple of chapters, we are going to be taking what we learned and applying it to real projects to create some awesome, satisfying animations using dynamic paint.

Join our community on Discord

Join our community's Discord space for discussions with the author and other readers: `https://packt.link/learn-blender-simulations-discord-invite`

13

Creating a Paintbrush Effect

At this point, you should have a good understanding of dynamic paint and how it works in Blender. Now, let's put those skills to the test by creating a paintbrush effect using this simulation! We will learn how to animate a paintbrush along a curve, create hair particles for the bristles, and have the particles paint on a plane object. From there, we will import the color information into the material so that it can be easily customized. After that, we will set up the camera and render the animation. The goal of this chapter is to give you a practical understanding of how to use dynamic paint while also creating something cool in the process!

In this chapter, we'll be covering the following topics:

- Animating the brush
- Creating hair particles
- Simulating dynamic paint
- Adding the materials
- Rendering the animation

Technical requirements

This chapter requires you to have Blender version 4.2 or above installed.

To download Blender, visit www.blender.org.

We will also be using a brush model, which you can download here: https://github.com/PacktPublishing/Learn-Blender-4-Simulations-the-Right-Way/tree/main/Chapter%2013

Animating the brush

To get started with this tutorial, make sure to download the `Paint Brush Startup.blend` file. You can find a link to this in the *Technical requirements* section. This file includes a basic model of a paintbrush, a plane, and HDR for lighting.

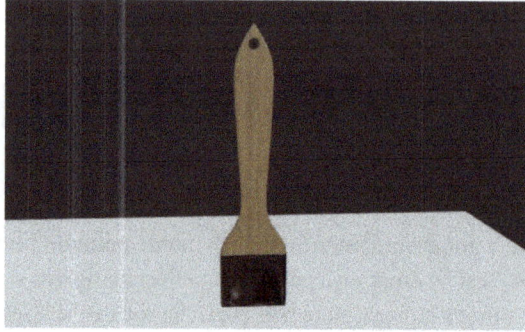

Figure 13.1 – Paintbrush model

The first step is to add a curve object. This is going to be the path for the brush to follow while it paints on the canvas!

Let's go ahead and get started:

1. Press *Shift + A*, go to **Curve**, and select **Bezier Curve**.

2. Go to the **Edit** mode with the curve selected. From here, you will be able to select the points on either end of the curve and rotate, scale, and move them however you like. You can also press *E* to extrude, and this will add more points to the curve. Customize this path however you like, but make sure that the curve stays flat or it might cause issues with the simulation.

    To make sure that the curve is flat, in **Edit** mode, select everything by pressing *A*. Then hit *S* to scale, press *Z* to lock the scale operation to the *Z* axis, type *0*, and press *Enter*.

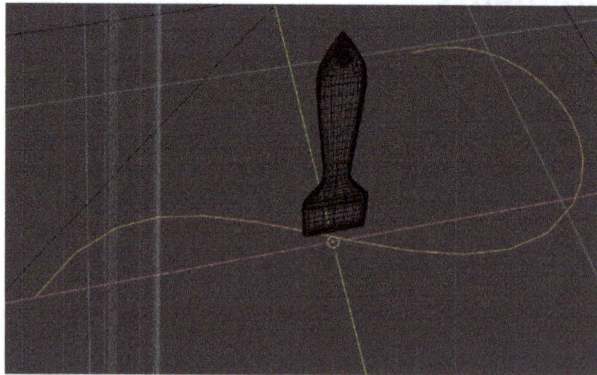

Figure 13.2 – Curve shape

3. Right now, our curve looks a bit low poly. To smooth it out, let's change the **Resolution Preview U** value in the curve **Object Data** panel to a value of 32. This will increase the number of points on the curve and, in turn, make the curve appear more smooth.

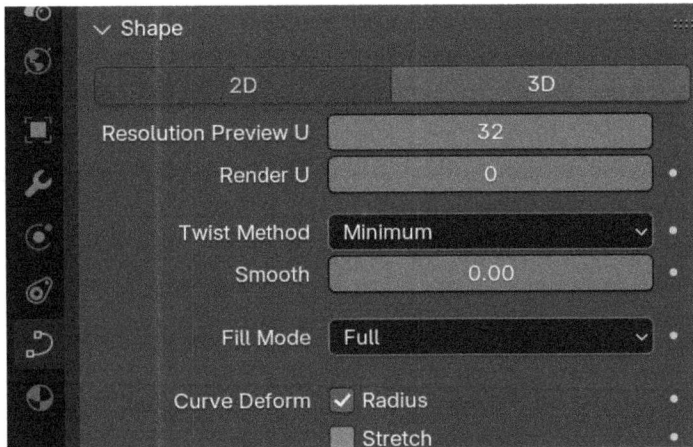

Figure 13.3 – Curve resolution

4. Now we can animate the brush following the curve! Select your **Brush** object and head over to the **Constraints** panel.

5. Click **Add Constraint** and select **Follow Path**. **Target** is going to be the **BezierCurve** we just added. Also, make sure to enable both the **Fixed Position** and the **Follow Curve** checkboxes. **Fixed Position** allows us to control where the brush is located along the curve using **Offset Factor**, and **Follow Curve** lets the brush rotate and follow the banking of the curve.

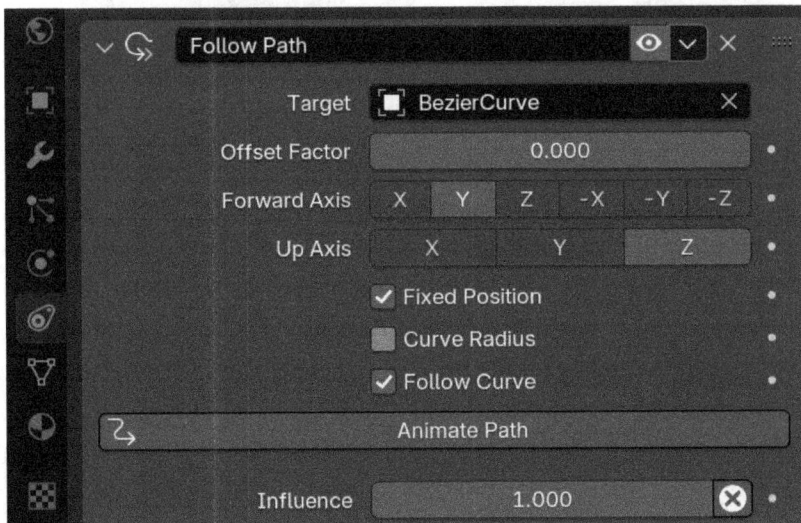

Figure 13.4 – Follow Path constraint

The **Brush** object should have moved to the beginning of the curve. Now the next step is to animate the brush moving down and then following the curve.

6.   In real life, you don't paint with a brush completely vertically. You usually hold the brush at around a 35–45-degree angle as you do the paint strokes. We're going to replicate that with our **Brush** object. With the direction in which the brush will follow the curve, we need to rotate the **Brush** object in the negative direction. Press *R*, then *X*, and then *X* again to lock the rotation to the local *X* axis. Type -35 and press *Enter*.

7.   On **Frame 1**, let's add a **Location & Rotation** keyframe to the brush. You can do this by pressing *K* and selecting **Location & Rotation**.

8.   Jump to **Frame 20**, move the brush back down about *0.1 meters* above the plane, and add another **Location & Rotation** keyframe. View the following figure to see the steps side by side.

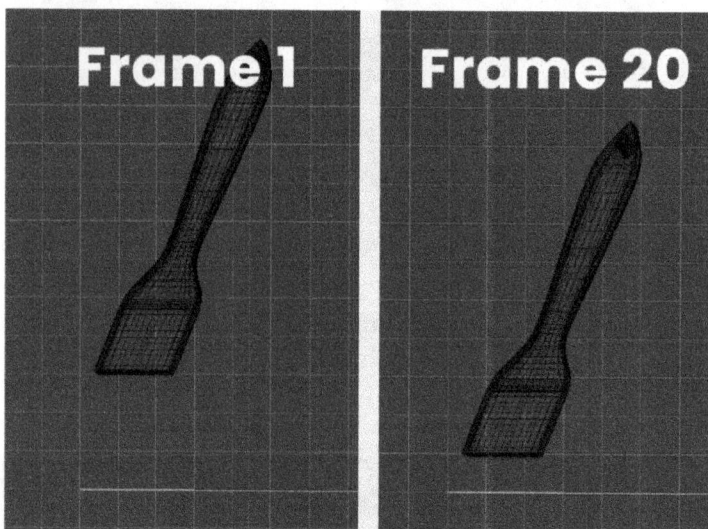

Figure 13.5 – Animated brush progression

9.   In the **Follow Path** constraint, add a keyframe to **Offset Factor** with a value of 0 on **Frame 20**. You can do this by clicking on the small dot next to **Offset Factor**. View *Figure 13.4*. **Offset Factor** controls where the brush is on the curve. With a value of 0, the brush will be positioned at the start and as we increase **Offset Factor**, it will move the brush along the curve.

10. Then, skip all the way to **Frame 230**, set **Offset Factor** to 1, and add another keyframe.

     If you have a longer curve, we recommend extending **End Frame** in **Timeline** and adjusting **Offset Factor** accordingly as it will cause issues if the brush moves too quickly along the curve. If the brush moves around 2 to 3 meters every 100 frames, you should get a nice smooth paint line!

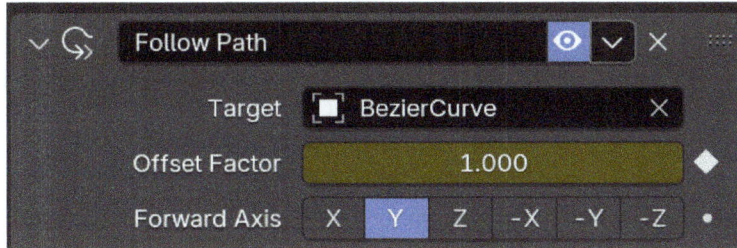

Figure 13.6 – Offset Factor 1

Now, when you restart and play the animation, the brush will move to the position and start following the curve! This is what it should look like on **Frame 120**:

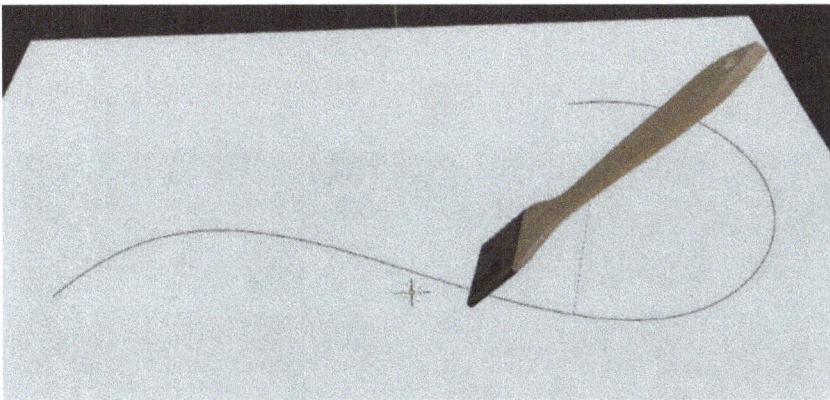

Figure 13.7 – Brush following the curve

Awesome! We now have the brush following the curve all the way around! Again, feel free to customize the curve shape and the position of the keyframes to your liking. But also make sure not to make the brush move too quickly, as this will cause issues with dynamic paint, which we will talk about in the *Simulating Dynamic Paint* section. Once you are happy with it, we can move on to creating hair particles, which we will use to paint on the plane object.

Creating hair particles

Creating the bristles on a paintbrush may seem complex and hard to do, but when we use a hair particle system, we can easily add thousands of bristles to create that look. We can also add physics to the hairs so that they bend and deform as they collide with the plane, giving the look of a real paintbrush. Let's jump straight into it:

1. First, select **Particle Object**, located at the bottom of the brush. This is the object that we will use to emit the hair particles.

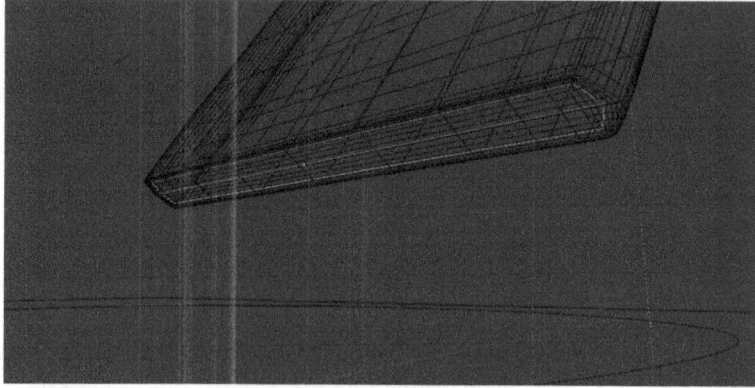

Figure 13.8 – Particle Object

2. Head over to the **Particle System** panel, create a new one by hitting the + button, and then switch the type to **Hair**.

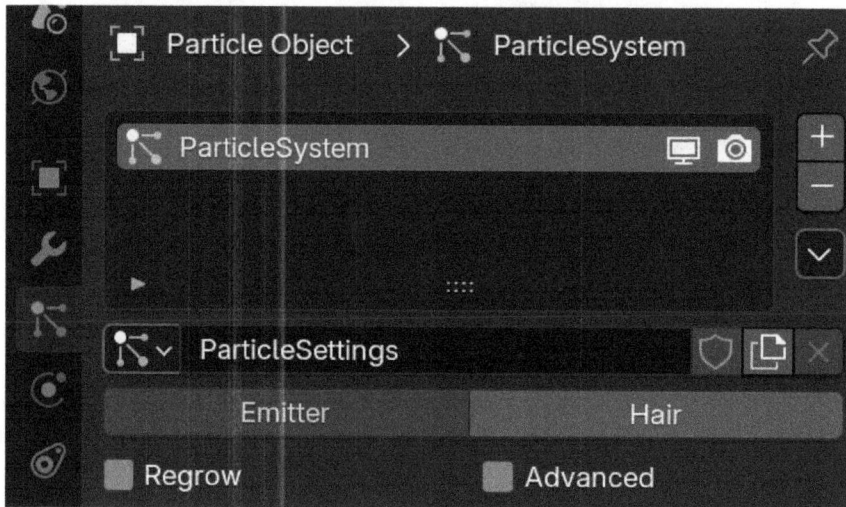

Figure 13.9 – Hair particle system

3. Let's tweak a couple of these settings to get a better result. First, set the number of hair particles to 2000. This will give us double the number of particles. Then, to make the hair shorter, set **Hair Length** to 0.2.

4. Now comes the fun part! Check **Hair Dynamics** in the **Particle System** panel. This will enable the particles to react to gravity so that they bend and deform.

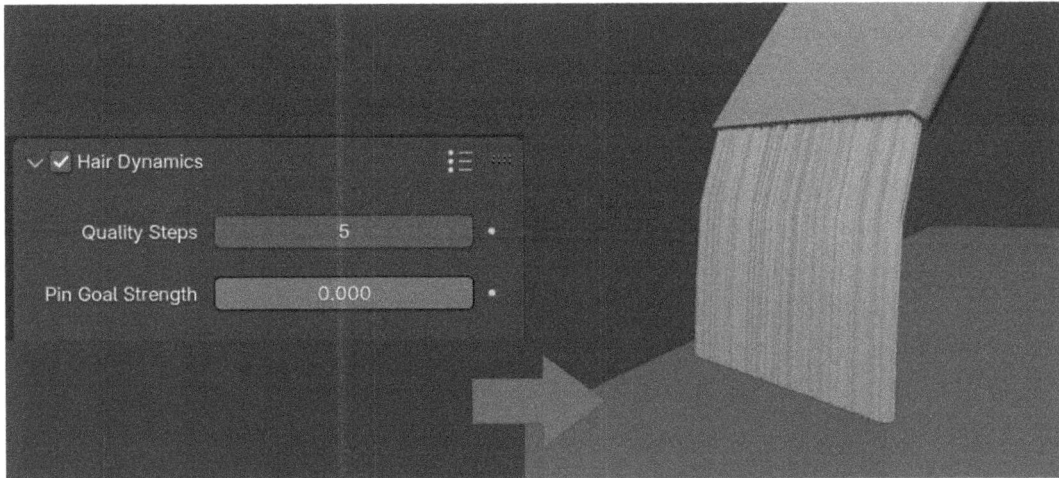

Figure 13.10 – Hair Dynamics

5. In order for the hair to collide with the plane, we need to give the plane object a **Collision** modifier. Select the plane object, head over to the **Physics** panel, and select **Collision**. Also, make sure to set **Thickness Outer** to 0.001 so there is not a big gap between the hair and the plane.

Figure 13.11 – Collision modifier

6. Next up, let's change a couple of settings in **Hair Dynamics** to get a nice paintbrush look:

    I.   Change **Quality Steps** to 10. This will give us a better overall result.

    II.   In the **Collisions** tab, let's set **Quality** to 4 and **Distance** to 0.001.

III.   The hair is also too flimsy, so in the **Structure** tab, let's increase **Stiffness** to 5 and **Random** to 0.5 to give us some random variation.

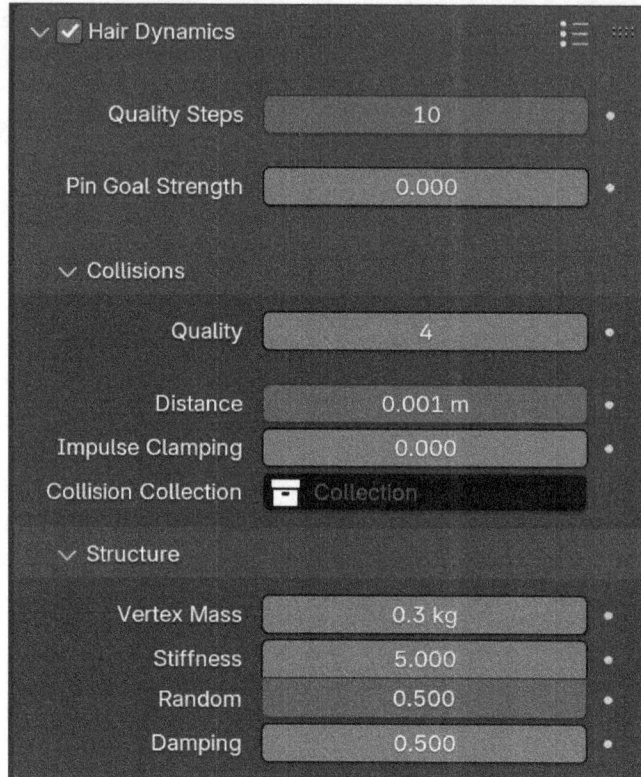

Figure 13.12 – Hair Dynamics settings

7.   Before we bake in the hair dynamics, let's scroll down to the **Viewport Display** tab and set **Strand Steps** to 6.

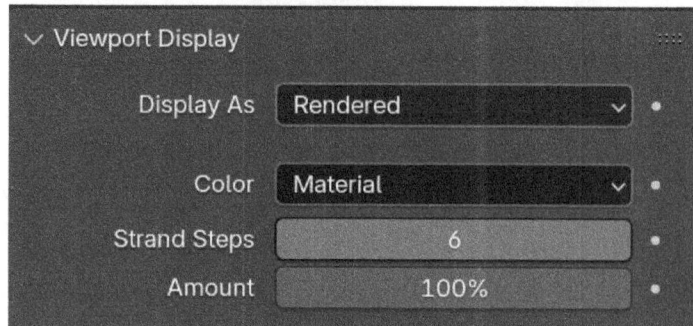

Figure 13.13 – Viewport Display

This will add more points to the hair, smooth it out, and give us a much better look. You can see the differences in the following figure:

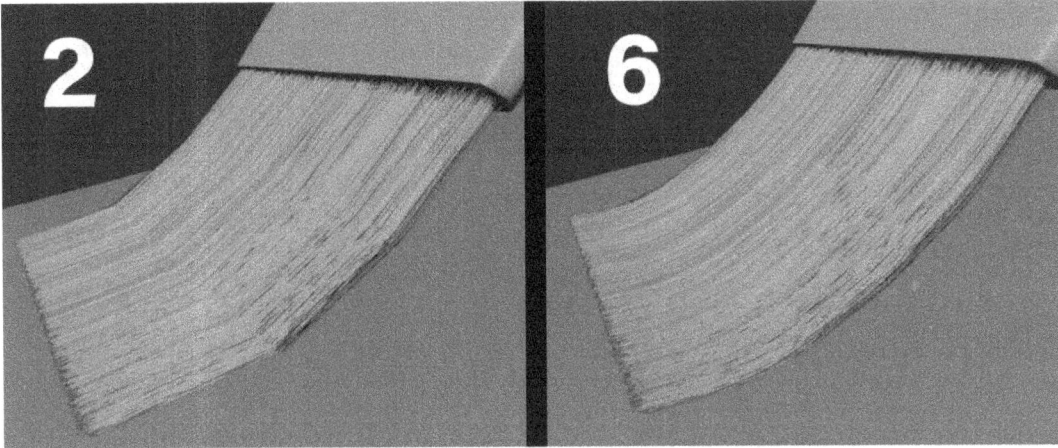

Figure 13.14 – Strand steps example

8. We are now ready to bake this particle system! Head back up to the **Cache** tab, make sure **End Frame** is correct for how long you want the animation to be, and hit **Bake**.

One of the limitations with dynamic paint is you can't use hair particles to paint on a canvas. Only mesh objects will work. So, in order for our simulation to work properly, we need to attach a mesh object to each hair particle. And that is what we will be discussing in the next section!

Simulating Dynamic Paint

As mentioned previously, since hair particles aren't technically a mesh, we can't use them as a brush in the dynamic paint simulation. You may remember from the previous chapter that brushes have an option to use **Particle System** as the source.

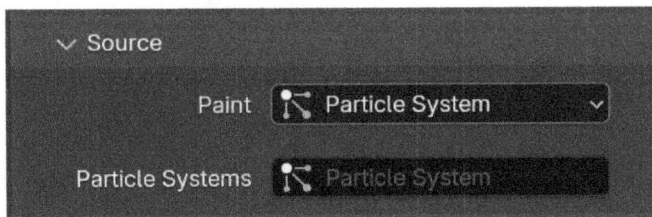

Figure 13.15 – Particle System source

This, however, does not work. This method only works for **Emitter** particle systems and not hair particle systems. To navigate around this, we have to get a little creative. What we are going to do is add a cube object and instance that cube on every single hair particle. That cube is going to be **Brush** in the dynamic paint simulation.

> **What are instances?**
>
> Instancing an object involves duplicating its geometry without replicating the underlying data. This optimization helps render engines, such as Cycles, efficiently manage the same geometry across multiple locations in the scene. In contrast, duplicating an object instead of instancing it increases the scene's data and memory usage. To learn more about instancing, refer to this resource: `https://youtu.be/FGcJ255ZMdY?si=H_Lm-1BcL3HxkcLwA`.

With that said, let's go ahead and instance a cube for the hair particles!

Instancing the cube

Before we add the cube, make sure the cursor is at the center of the grid. This is important because if you add a cube anywhere but the center, it will not line up with the hair when we instance it. You can snap the cursor back to the center by pressing *Shift + C*. Then, follow these steps:

1. Now we can add the cube! Hit *Shift + A*, go to **Mesh**, and select **Cube**. Press *N* to open the **Properties** panel, and let's change **Dimensions** of this cube to fit the hair particles. Set **X** and **Z** to 0.005 and **Y** to 0.2 to match the length of the hair.

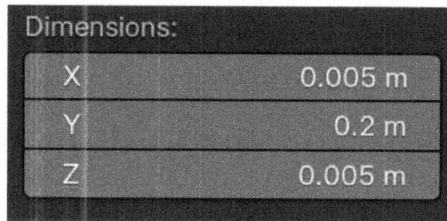

Figure 13.16 – Cube dimensions

2. The next step is to add more geometry to the cube so it bends with the hair. Let's go into **Edit Mode** and press *Ctrl/Cmd + R* to add a loop cut. Position your mouse so the loop cut goes horizontally, type 50, then hit *Enter*. This will add 50 loop cuts down the length of the cube.

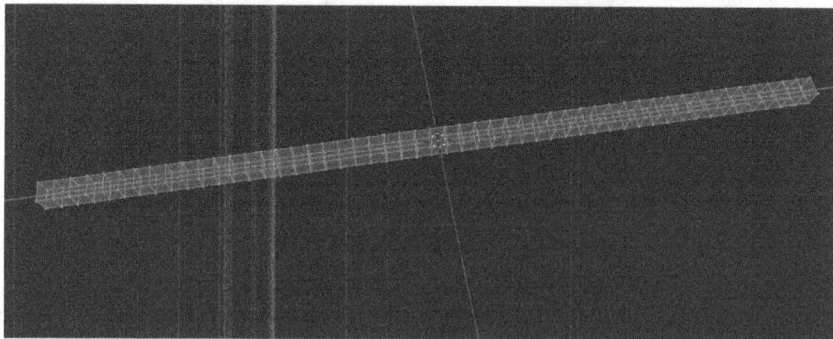

Figure 13.17 – Adding loop cuts

3. Another important step is to apply the scale to our cube. If we don't do this, the cube will not align with the hair particles and the simulation won't work. So, press *Ctrl/Cmd + A* and select **Scale**. Now the scale numbers should be back to 1 and it will work properly!

4. Now let's instance this cube on each hair particle! Select the cube, head over to the **Modifier** panel, select **Add Modifier | Physics**, and select **ParticleInstance**.

5. For **Object**, select **Particle Object** and it should automatically select the particle system as well. After that, check **Create Along Paths** and now the cube should be instanced on each hair particle.

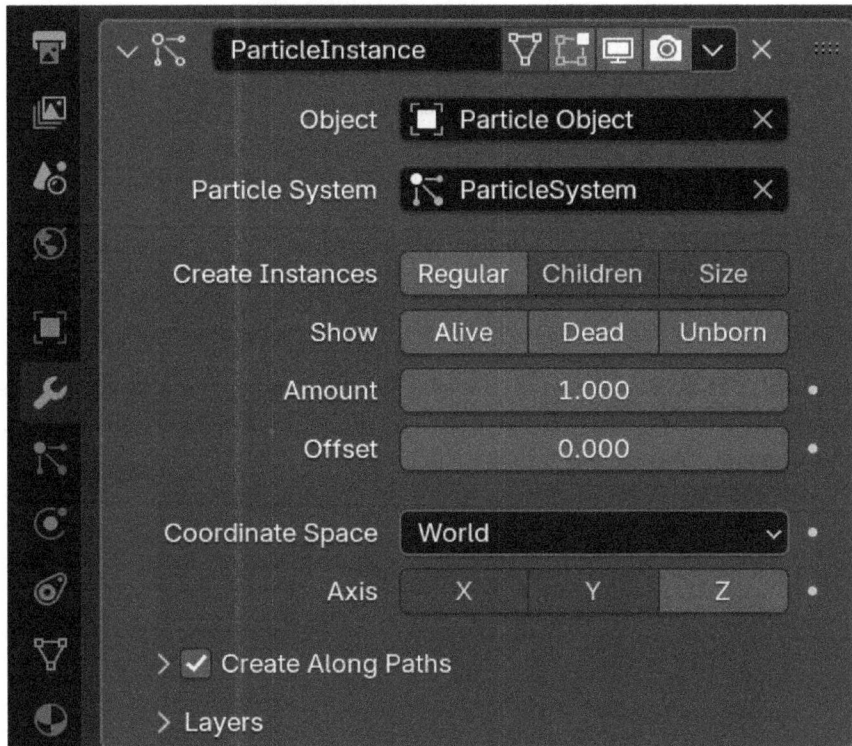

Figure 13.18 – ParticleInstance modifier

Troubleshooting

If the cube did not instance properly, you can try two things. First, make sure you applied the scale for both the cube and **Particle Object**. You can do this by selecting the objects, pressing *Ctrl + A* or *Cmd + A*, and selecting **Scale**. Second, double-check that the cube is at the very center of the grid. If the cube has moved, this will cause issues with the instancing. You can move it to the center easily by hitting *Alt + G* or *Option + G*.

Here is what the instanced cube should look like!

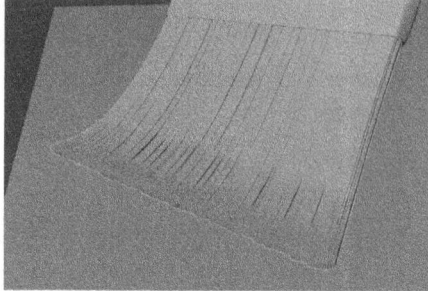

Figure 13.19 – Instanced cube

With that done, we can now move on to creating the dynamic paint simulation.

Creating the simulation

With all the objects in place, we are ready to start creating the dynamic paint simulation! Let's start by adding **Brush**, and then we can move on to **Canvas**:

1. Select the cube that has been instanced on the hair particles and head over to the **Physics** panel. Select **Dynamic Paint**, set **Type** to **Brush**, and click **Add Brush**. Don't worry about **Paint Color**; we will be changing that later in the material.

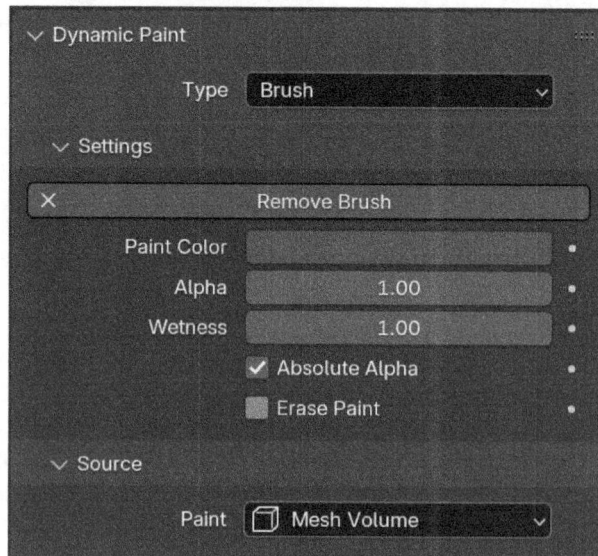

Figure 13.20 – Brush settings

We can leave the rest of the settings at the defaults; we don't need to change anything else.

2. Next, select the plane object. In the **Physics** panel, select **Dynamic Paint**, leave **Type** set to **Canvas**, and hit **Add Canvas**.

3. For this simulation, we will be using **Image Sequence** for **Format**, and for **Resolution**, let's go with 2048. The higher **Resolution** is, the longer it will take to bake. If you have a slow computer, I recommend setting this to 1024. This will still give you a nice image, but it won't look as sharp.

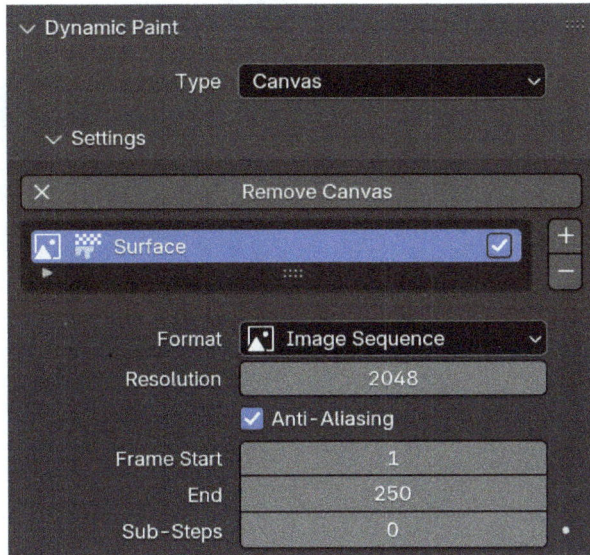

Figure 13.21 – Adding the canvas

4. One thing that needs to be mentioned is **Sub-Steps** in the canvas settings. Normally, with fast-moving brushes, you would turn this setting up to get a nice smooth paint line. The problem is, since the location of the dynamic paint brush (the instanced cube) is being driven by the particle system and not the cube itself, the **Sub-Steps** value is not going to affect the simulation. This means that if the paintbrush object is moving quickly along the curve, you may get a spotty paint line rather than a smooth continuous line even if you increase the **Sub-Steps** value.

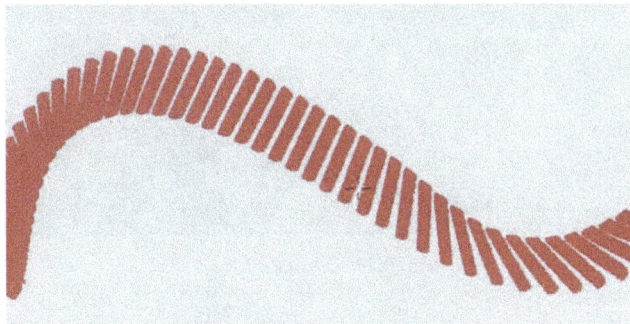

Figure 13.22 – Fast paint line

To help fix this issue, there are a couple of things you can do. Increasing the framerate of the animation will allow the brush to have more frames every second, thus creating a smoother line. Another thing that might help is to increase the number of frames in the animation and have the brush move more slowly along the curve. Since we set up the animation to last from **Frame 20** to **Frame 230**, that should be slow enough to get a nice paint line. With that being said, let's continue and change a couple more settings.

5. Next, let's head down to the **Dry** tab and set **Time** to 200 so the paint dries a bit faster.

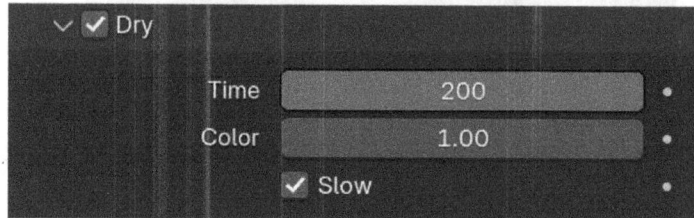

Figure 13.23 – Dry tab

6. In the **Output** tab, we need to set up a folder where the images are going to be exported. Click on the folder icon in **Cache Path** to set a new directory. We recommend creating a new folder in the same folder as your Blender file.

7. Select **UVMap** in the drop-down menu and make sure to export both **Paintmaps** and **Wetmaps** by checking both boxes.

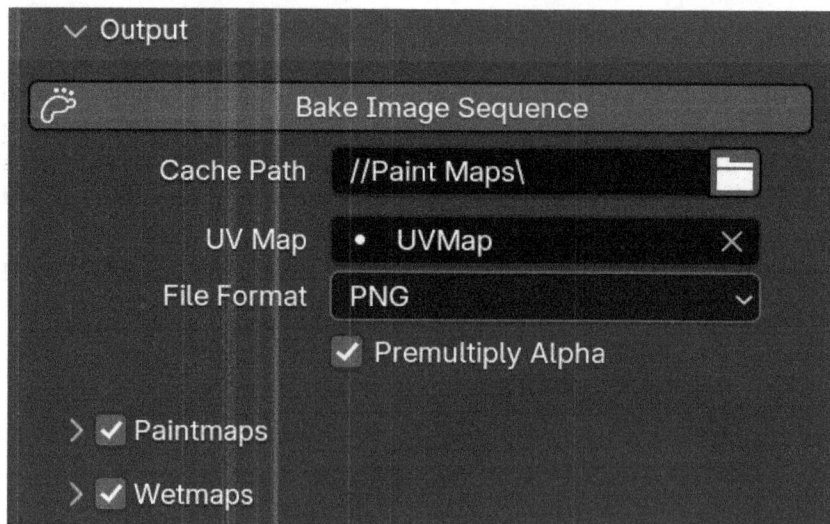

Figure 13.24 – Output tab

8. Before you bake the image sequence, move the plane object up slightly so brush and the canvas intersect. This will make sure all the cubes paint on the canvas.

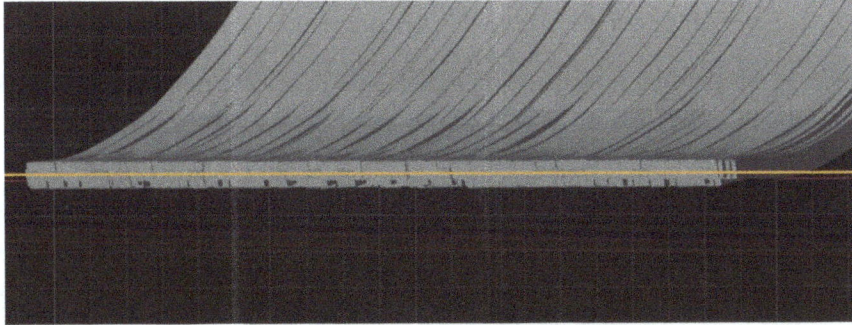

Figure 13.25 – Canvas and brush positions

Great! Now the simulation is ready to be baked! In the **Output** tab, click on **Bake Image Sequence** and all the images will be exported to the folder you set for **Cache Path**.

Once this has finished baking, we will create the materials for both **Canvas** and the hair particles.

Adding the materials

Now that we have exported all the dynamic paint images, let's import them into the material for our canvas! After that, we will learn how to create a material for the hair particles. Let's get started!

Creating the canvas material

The first thing we need to do before we start working on adding nodes to the material is to separate the paintmaps and the wetmaps. When we baked the image sequence, both the paintmaps and wetmaps were put into the same folder.

So, let's select all the wetmap.png files and move them into a new folder, as you can see in the following figure:

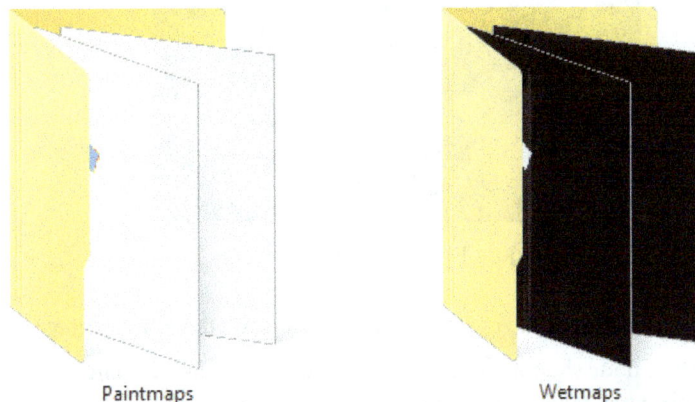

Paintmaps   Wetmaps

Figure 13.26 – Image folders

With that done, we are ready to jump back into Blender and start creating the materials:

1. Head over to the **Shading** workspace, then click **New** to create a new material for the plane object. It's always a good habit to name your materials as well so that they are easy to find later.

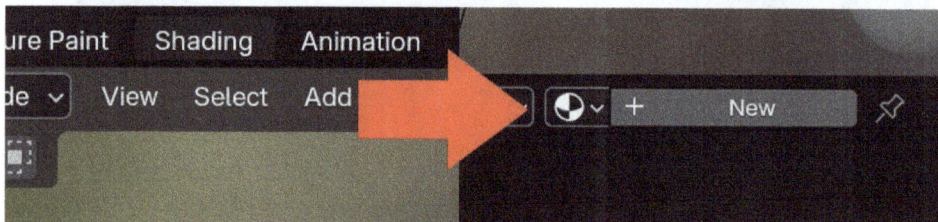

Figure 13.27 – Creating a new material

2. Let's first add the paintmaps to the material. Press *Shift + A*, go to **Texture**, and select the **Image Texture** node.

3. Click **Open** and navigate to where the images are located on your hard drive. Once you have found the folder, double-check that you are sorting by **Name** and not **Modified Date**. **Name** will sort the images alphabetically by their file name. **Modified Date** will sort them by the date/time the image was created. Since the **Frame 1** image was created first, this will make the image sequence play backward.

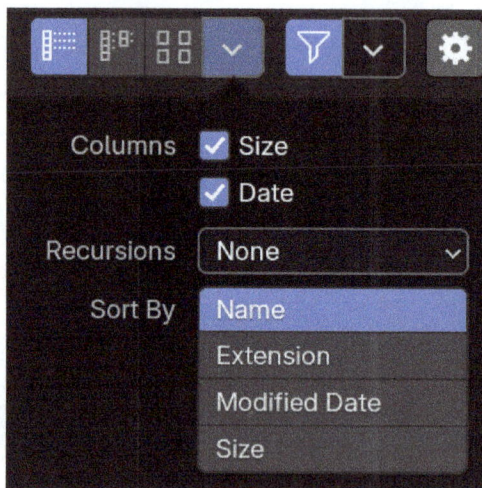

Figure 13.28 – Sort By menu

4. Then, all you have to do is press *A* to select everything and click **Open Image**.

5. Your **Image Texture** node should now have turned into an **Image Sequence** node. To make sure this is working properly, take the **Color** output and plug it into **Base Color** of the **Principled BSDF** shader. Also, check **Auto Refresh** so the image sequence will update every frame.

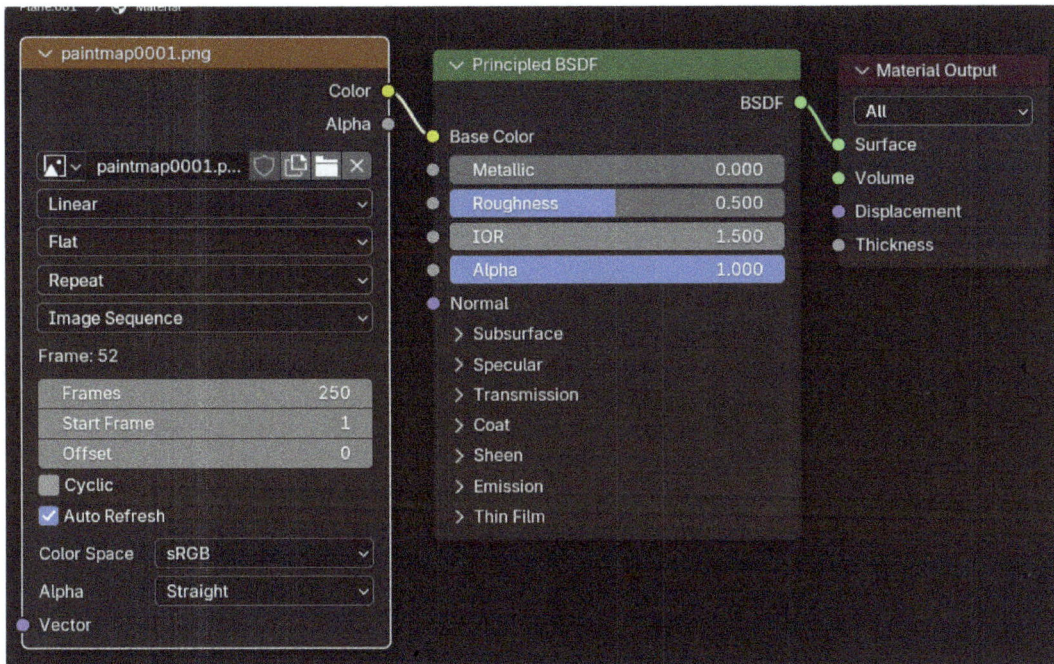

Figure 13.29 – Testing the material

When you play your animation now, you should see the paint spreading across the canvas as the paintbrush object moves along the curve!

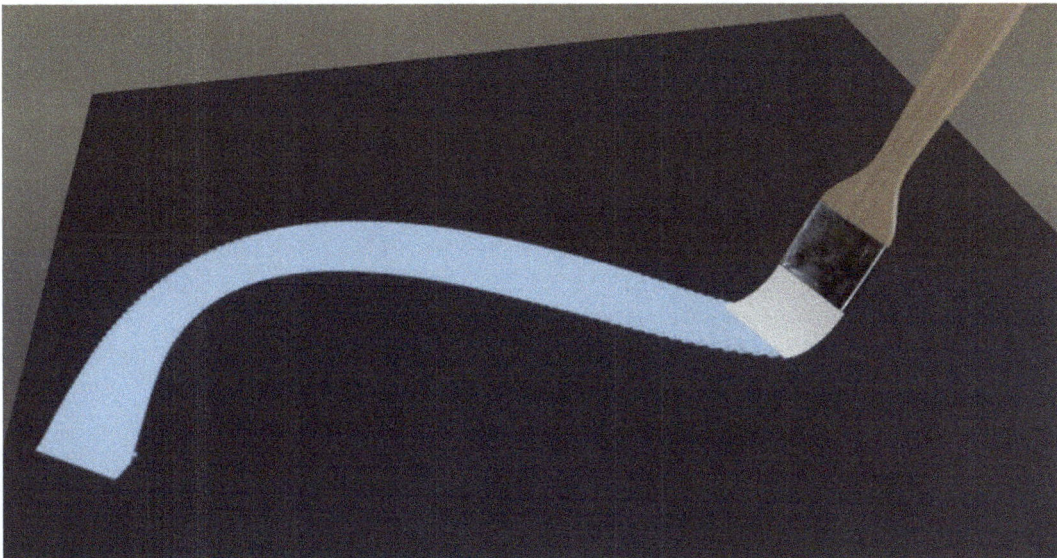

Figure 13.30 – Painting on the canvas

Using Vertex Format

If you decide to use **Vertex Format** for dynamic paint in future simulations, you can take that color information and plug it directly into the material using the **Color Attribute** node! View the following figure to see the setup!

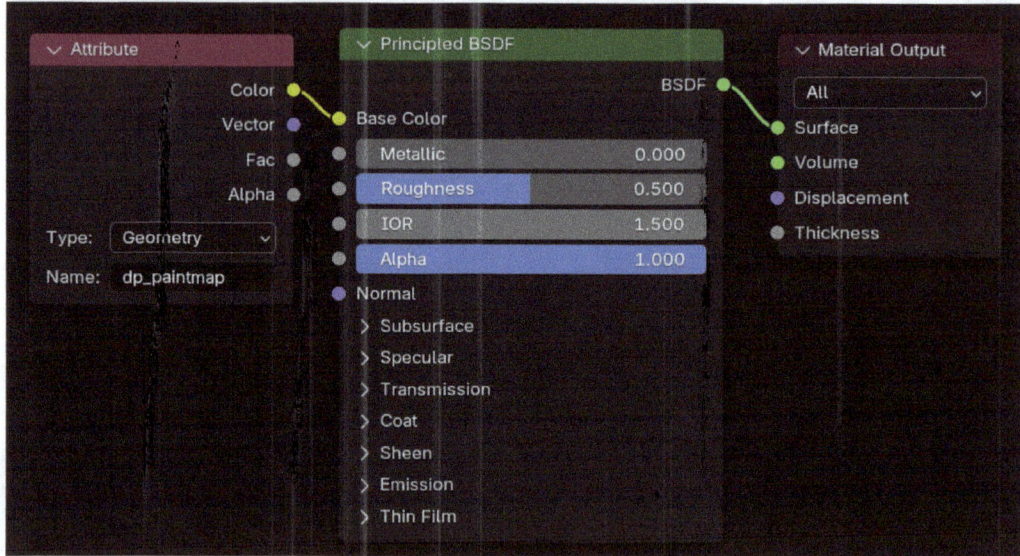

Figure 13.31 – Color Attribute node

6. Great! Now that we know it's working, we can tweak the colors and then add the wetmaps. Let's press *Shift + A*, go to **Color**, and add a **Mix Color** node. This node will allow us to change the color of the canvas and the paint super easily.

    The **Alpha** output from the **Image Sequence** node sets the canvas to black and the paint to white. We can use this to create a mask so we can easily change the colors to our liking.

7. Take **Alpha** from **Image Sequence** and plug it directly into **Fac** of the **Mix Color** node. Then take the **Mix Color** output and plug that directly into **Base Color**. The **A** color of the **Mix Color** node now controls the canvas, and the **B** color controls the paint. Choose whatever colors you like! For this scene, we went with a white canvas and a red paint color.

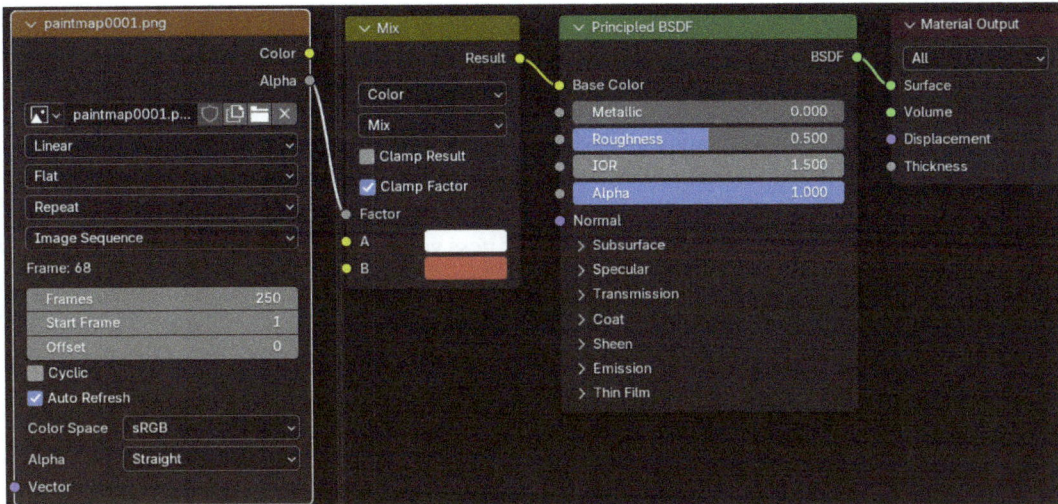

Figure 13.32 – Adding the Mix Color node

8. You may have noticed the paint looks a bit spotty. To prevent the spotty look, you can add a **Color Ramp** node. Press *Shift + A,* go to **Converter**, and select **Color Ramp**. Place it between the **Image Sequence** and the **Mix Color** nodes. Dragging the white handle closer to the black handle will help clamp down on that spotty look.

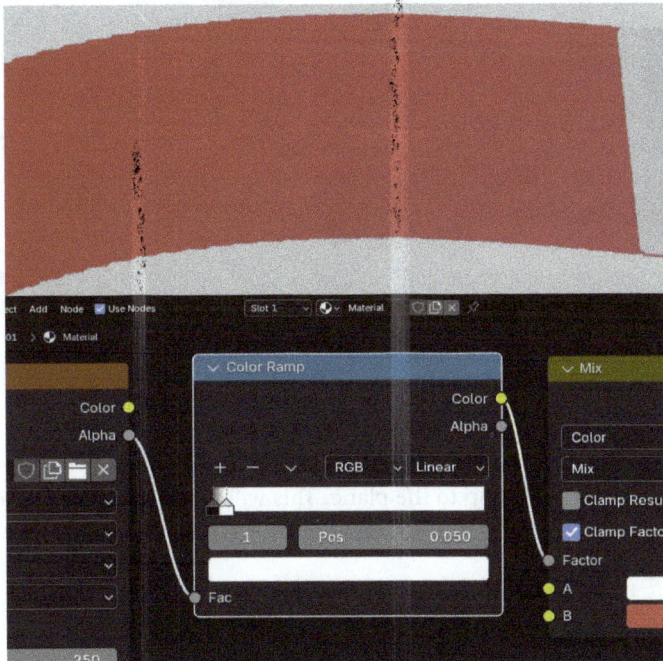

Figure 13.33 – Color Ramp fix

9. Now we can add the wetmaps. Select the **Image Sequence** node and press *Shift + D* to duplicate it. Place it below, click on the folder icon, and navigate to the wetmaps folder. Press *A* to select everything and click **Open Image**.

10. If you don't remember, wetmaps are black-and-white values on the canvas that visualize the paint drying over time. We can use these values to control the **Roughness** value of the material. This will give the look of wet paint that slowly dries over the course of the animation. Let's take the **Color** output and plug it into the **Roughness** value of the **Principled BSDF** shader.

11. The effect is currently the opposite of what we want. We need to invert the wetmaps to make the paint appear glossy while keeping the canvas diffuse. To do this, press *Shift + A* and add another **Color Ramp** node.

12. Flip the colors of **Color Ramp** so that the black handle is on the right side and the white handle is on the left. Then move the black handle until it's about halfway and set **Interpolation** to **Ease**.

Here is what the full material setup should look like:

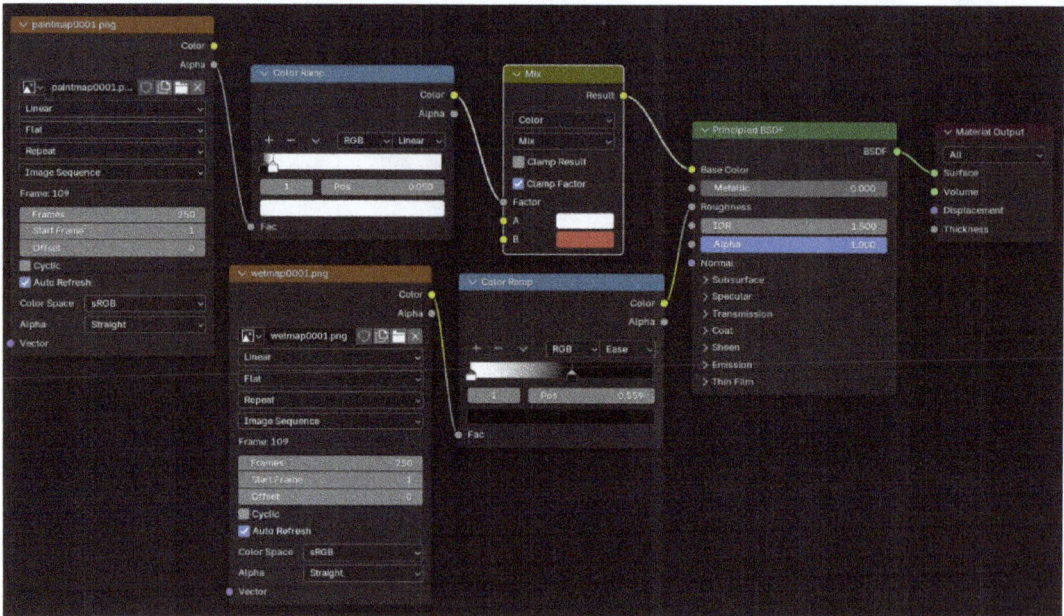

Figure 13.34 – Full canvas material

13. The last step is to add some bump to the plane. This will give the plane more detail and make the final result more interesting. Here are the steps!

    I.   Press *Shift + A*, go to **Texture**, and add a **Noise Texture** node.

    II. Next, add a **Bump** node! Press *Shift + A* and then go to **Vector | Bump**.

III.   Take **Fac** from **Noise Texture** and plug it into the **Height** on the **Bump** node. Then take the **Normal** output and plug that into the **Normal** input of the **Principled BSDF** shader.

IV.   Now for the values. Set **Scale** to 500, **Roughness** to 0.9, and **Strength** of **Bump** to 0.3. Here is the full setup.

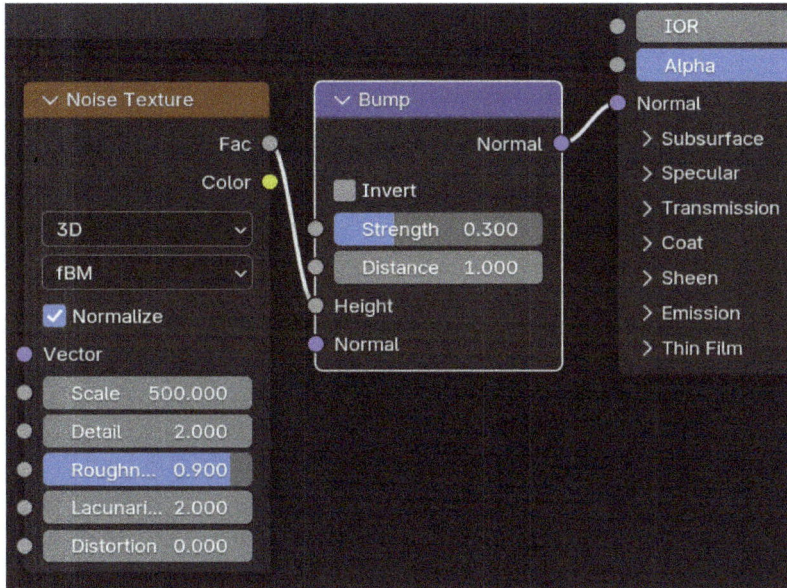

Figure 13.35 – Adding Bump

If you would like to make the animation a bit more interesting, you could have the **Image Sequence** node plug into the **Emission** input of the **Principled BSDF** shader. This will give the look of the brush painting glowing paint on the canvas!

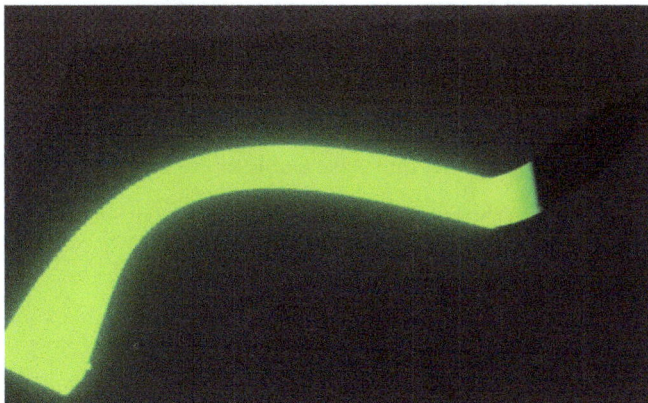

Figure 13.36 – Glowing paint material

Another idea would be to plug an **Image Texture** node into the **B** color input of the **MixRGB** node. So, instead of painting a solid red color, the brush will paint an image texture instead! Feel free to get creative and experiment with different images to create some interesting effects!

Once you are happy with how the canvas looks, we can move on to creating the hair material!

Creating the hair material

This next material we will create is pretty easy to set up! What we will be doing is creating a gradient effect where the top of the hair is one color, and it blends into another color near the bottom:

1. To get started, let's first hide the instanced cubes so we can see the hair particles. Up in **Outliner**, click on the **Eye** and **Camera** icon to hide this object. This will hide it from the view and from the render as well.

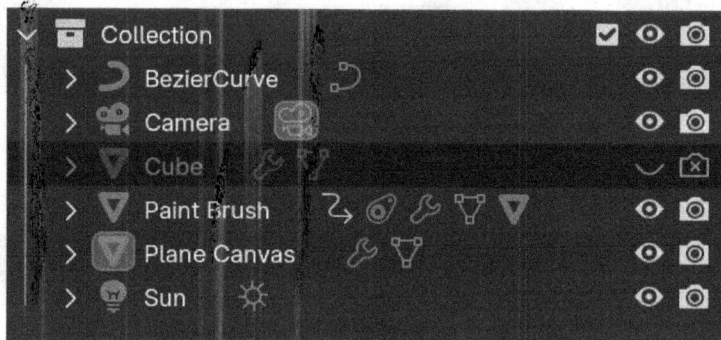

Figure 13.37 – Hiding the instanced cubes

2. Next, select the hair particles and click **New** to create a new material.

3. To create that gradient effect, there are two nodes we need to add. The first one is a **Curves Info** node. Press *Shift + A*, go to **Input**, and select **Curves Info**.

4. The other node we need is **Color Ramp**. Add it between **Curves Info** and the **Principled BSDF** shader.

5. In the **Curves Info** node, the **Intercept** output is what we need. Let's plug it into **Color Ramp**, then take **Color Ramp** and plug that into **Base Color** of the **Principled BSDF** shader.

    The hair particles should now have turned into a black-and-white gradient.

Figure 13.38 – Hair particle gradient

6. We can control the colors of the gradient with the **Color Ramp** handles. For the handle on the right, choose the same color as you did for the paint. As for the left handle, let's go with a light gray color. Here is the full node setup:

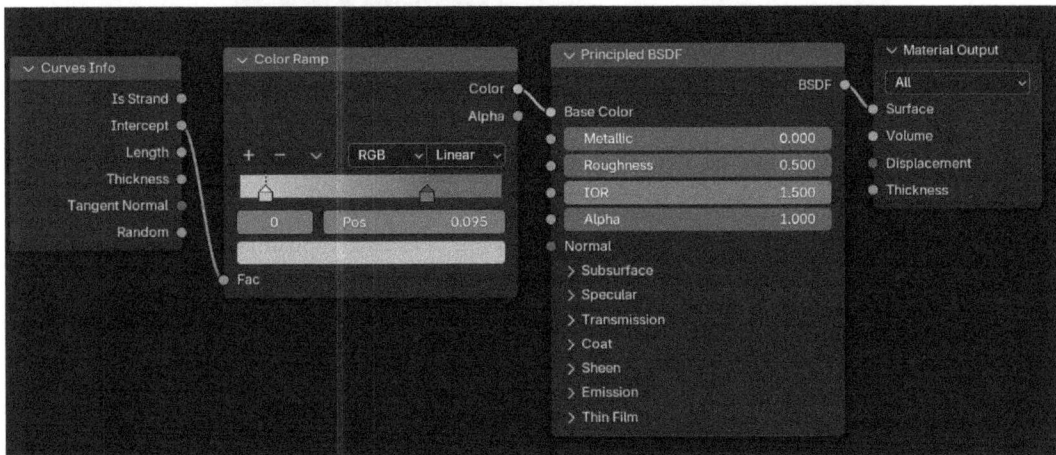

Figure 13.39 – Hair material node setup

That is basically all we really need to do for this material! If you want to add more to this material, you could take the **Intercept** output from the **Curve Info** node and have that control the **Roughness** value in the **Principled BSDF** shader. This can give the look of wet paint on the particles, but I will leave that up to you. For now, let's move on to the final render settings, and then we can render this animation!

Setting up the render

This tutorial is almost done! The final steps we need to do are setting up the render, animating the camera to follow the paintbrush, and rendering the animation. Let's start by taking a look at the EEVEE settings and changing them to make the whole scene look much better:

1. In the **Render** panel, let's turn on **Raytracing** to get nice reflections in the materials. Set **Resolution** to **1:1**.

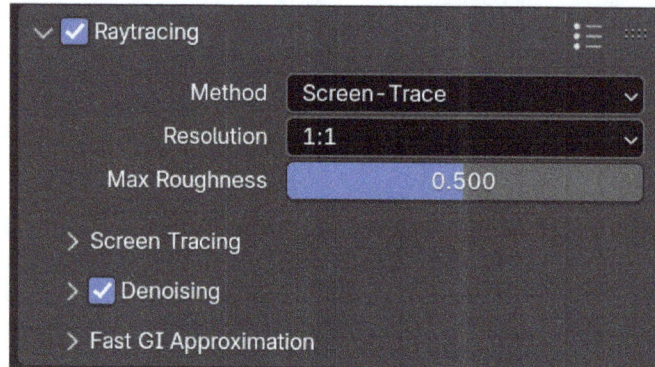

Figure 13.40 – EEVEE render settings

2. In the **Color Management** tab, let's set **Look** to **High Contrast**. This will really make the colors in our scene pop!

3. For the **Camera** animation, we recommend jumping to **Frame 1**, positioning **Camera** to the view you want, and then adding a keyframe. You can do this by selecting **Camera**, hitting *I*, and selecting **Location & Rotation**.

4. Around **Frame 100**, rotate and move **Camera** so that it's facing the paintbrush, then add another keyframe. Repeat this step at around **Frame 160** and then **250**. Remember, you can always move the keyframes by selecting them in **Timeline** and pressing *G*.

5. If you want to delete a keyframe, select it and press *X*, and choose **Delete Keyframes**.

Figure 13.41 – Deleting keyframes

6. If you would like to add a nice look to the camera, enable **Depth of Field** in the **Camera Data Properties** panel. For **Focus on Object**, select **Paint Brush**.

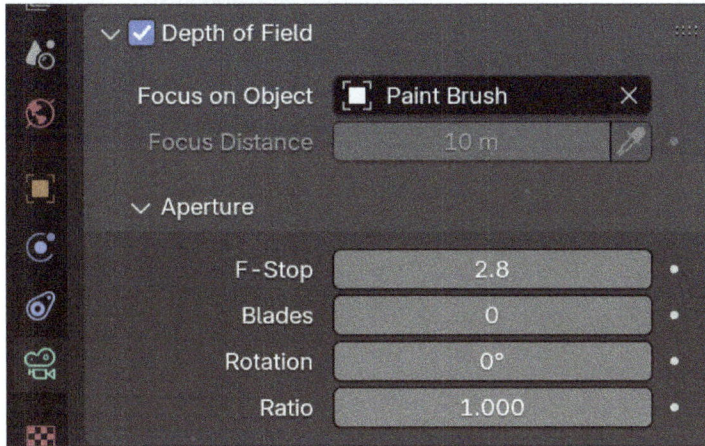

Figure 13.42 – Depth of Field

Once you have your camera set up, you are ready to render the animation. If you need a refresher on how to render animations in Blender, check out *Chapter 4.*

Figure 13.43 – Final result

If you would like to see the final result, or if you want to download this chapter's project file, you can do that by visiting the following link: `https://github.com/PacktPublishing/Learn-Blender-4-Simulations-the-Right-Way/tree/main/Chapter%2013`

Feel free to add to or change up the animation however you like! Maybe add two or three paintbrushes and have the colors mix together. You could even spell out a word using the brushes! Just remember that **Sub-Steps** does not work using this method, so you will have to slow down the brush so the paint line is not spotty.

Summary

We have now finished this tutorial and created a paintbrush animation using dynamic paint in Blender. Hopefully, now you have an even greater understanding of this powerful simulation and all the fun and unique things that can be achieved. Just like always, let's recap so everything sinks in.

First, we learned how to have an object follow a curve using the **Follow Path** constraint. After that, we created hair particles and gave them physics, so they bend and deform. Then we instanced a long cube on each hair particle and used that as the brush in the dynamic paint simulation. We created the canvas, set up all the settings, and made an image sequence. With all the images exported from dynamic paint, we imported images into the material for the canvas and then learned how to customize the colors easily. We also discussed the hair particle material and created a nice gradient. Finally, we set up the camera and rendered the animation!

I hope you are ready because, in the next chapter, we will be moving away from **Paint Surface Type** and instead be taking a look at **Waves** and learning how to create a really nice raindrop effect!

14

Creating a Raindrop Effect

For the next project in this book, we will be using dynamic paint and particles to create a realistic raindrop effect on a lake! With the knowledge gained in this chapter, you will be able to add raindrop effects to puddles on a road or create a boat traveling across an ocean, leaving a trail of waves! There are many different ways to use this effect, and it can definitely add another level of detail to your renders and animations!

We will first start by adding all the objects we will need for the scene. From there, we will learn how to use the particle system to create rainfall! After that, we will jump into the dynamic paint simulation and learn how to use the **Waves** surface type to create realistic raindrops. Finally, we will create a nice water material and render the animation using EEVEE!

In this chapter, we'll be covering the following topics:

- Setting up the scene
- Creating the rain particles
- Simulating the waves
- Creating the water material
- Setting up the render

Technical requirements

This chapter requires you to have Blender version 4.2 or above installed.

To download Blender, visit www.blender.org.

Make sure to also download the startup file found here: https://github.com/PacktPublishing/Learn-Blender-4-Simulations-the-Right-Way/tree/main/Chapter%2014.

Setting up the scene

To get started, make sure to download the `Raindrop Effect Startup.blend` file. You can find the link in the *Technical requirements* section. This `.blend` file includes a couple of rocks with nice textures, an HDR for lighting, and a bit of camera animation. What we'll be doing first is adding a plane object to be the canvas for our simulation. After that, we'll add a bigger plane for the background, animate displacement, and rearrange the rocks for a nice aesthetic. Open the Blender file and let's get started:

1. Press *Shift + A* to add a plane object. This is going to be the canvas in our simulation.

2. We need to scale this plane up so that it fits the scene a bit better. Select the plane and open the **Properties** panel and set **Dimensions** for **X** and **Y** to `13` meters. Doing this causes the **Scale** numbers to change, so let's press *Ctrl + A* or *Cmd + A* and click **Scale**. This will bring those numbers back down to `1.000`.

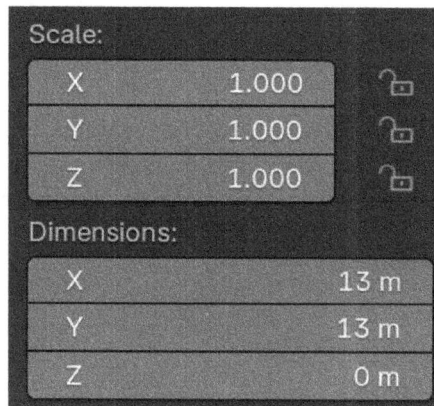

Figure 14.1 – The plane dimensions

When working with dynamic paint, it's always important to apply scale to your objects, especially if you are working with the **Displace** or **Waves** surface type. When the scale numbers are not set to `1.000`, you may see inaccurate simulations. While testing for this chapter, we noticed some of the rain particles were not creating waves. The reason for this was that the scale was not applied on the canvas. Always remember to apply scale!

3. Next, we need to add more geometry to the plane for it to create waves. To do this, go into **Edit Mode,** and with the entire mesh selected, right-click and select **Subdivide**. Open the **Subdivide** menu at the bottom left and set **Number of Cuts** to `100`.

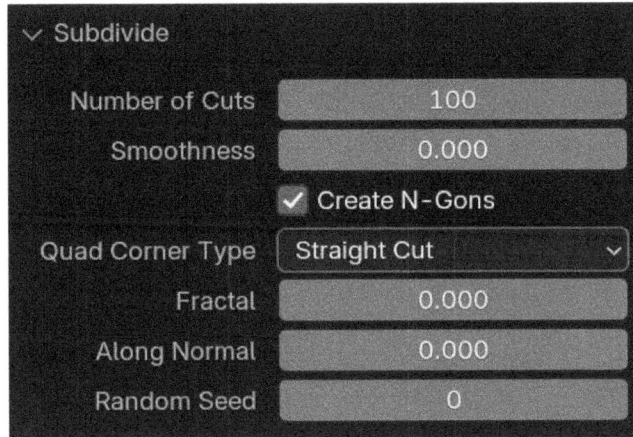

Figure 14.2 – Subdividing the plane

4. Unfortunately, we still need more geometry, and we can't set **Number of Cuts** higher than 100. So, instead, let's right-click again and select **Subdivide**. This will add double the amount of geometry to the plane.

5. Let's repeat *step 4* one more time and that should give us enough geometry on the plane for the waves to look nice. With everything selected, right-click again and choose **Subdivide**.

6. If we go into the camera view by pressing *0* on the numpad or by going up to **View | Cameras | Active Camera**, we can see the edge of the plane.

Figure 14.3 – The edge of the plane

7. This doesn't give the illusion of a big lake, so to fix that, let's add another plane object and scale it up. Press *Shift + A*, go to **Mesh**, and select **Plane**.

8. In **Dimensions**, let's set **X** and **Y** to 65 meters, and then, of course, press *Ctrl + A* or *Cmd + A* and apply the **Scale**.

9. We don't need the big plane object extending behind the camera, so let's move it forward until the edges of both plane objects line up. Then, move it slightly down so that they are not intersecting.

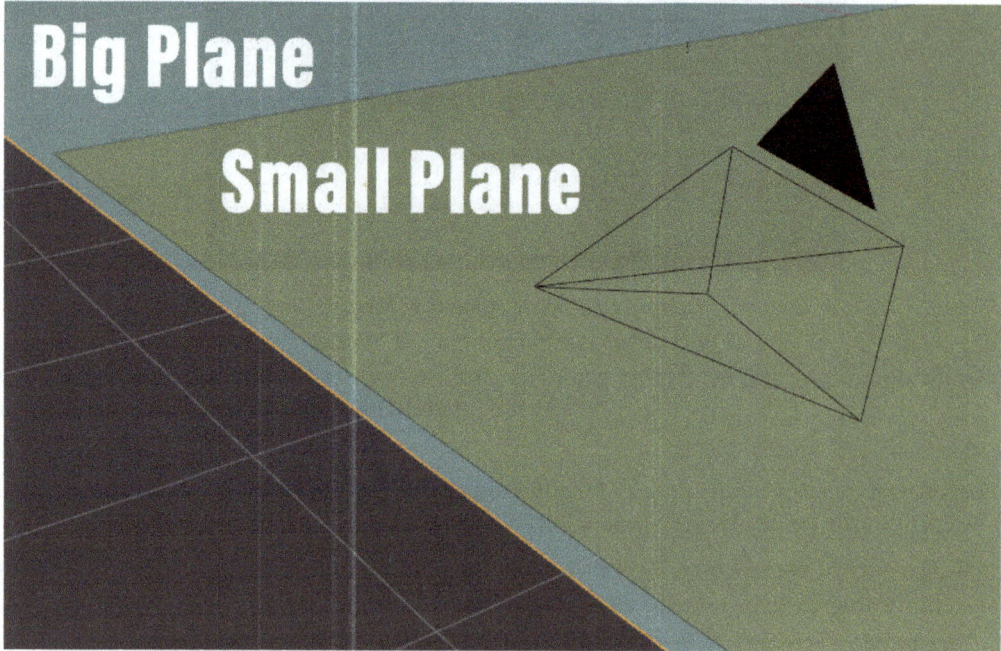

Figure 14.4 – Moving the big plane

Why are we using two plane objects?

The reason we are using two plane objects is that we want a lot of geometry close to the camera to create nice smooth waves, but we don't need that level of detail in the distance. That would just be a waste of memory on your computer, and it would increase render times.

---

10. The next step is to fake the raindrop effect on this bigger plane using a **Displace** modifier! Since the bigger plane will be viewed from a distance, it will still give the effect of "waves" without all the extra geometry you would need for a dynamic paint simulation.

Select the bigger plane object and head over to the **Modifier** panel. Select **Add Modifier | Generate | Subdivision Surface** and set **Mode** to **Simple**. **Simple** will subdivide the mesh without effecting the shape, where as **Catmull-Clark** will add more subdivions while also rounding the edges of the mesh. And set the **Viewport** and **Render** levels to 8. This will give us a lot more geometry on our mesh so the **Displace** modifier works properly.

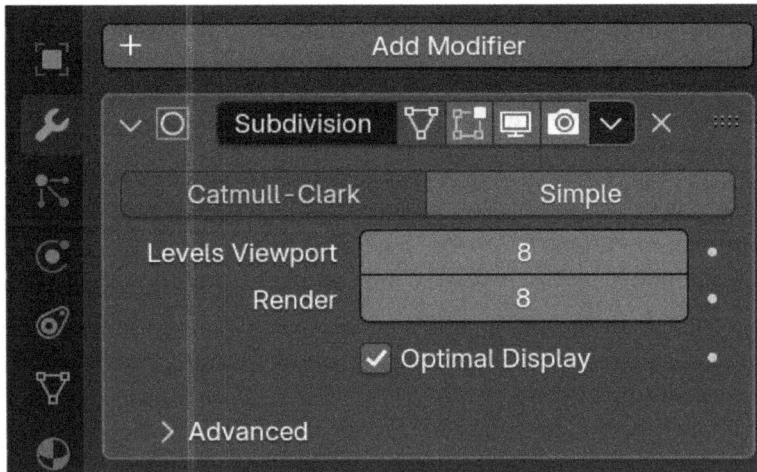

Figure 14.5 – The Subdivision Surface modifier

11. After that, let's select **Add Modifier** | **Deform** | **Displace**.

12. Click **New** to create a new displacement texture, and then head over to the **Texture** panel.

13. Change the type of texture to **Clouds**, and in the **Clouds** tab, set the **Size** value to 0.10.

Figure 14.6 – A displacement texture

14. Currently, the displacement is way too strong. Let's jump back over to the **Modifier** panel and lower the strength of the **Displace** modifier to 0.070.

15. The last thing we need to do is animate the location of this displacement texture. This will give the illusion of raindrops in the distance. Here is how we do that:

    I.   Press *Shift + A* and go to **Empty | Plane** to add a new empty object.

    II.   On **Frame 1**, press *K* and add a **Location** keyframe to the empty object.

    III.   Next, skip all the way to the end of the animation (**Frame 200**) and move the empty object 0.5 meters along the **X** axis. You can do this by pressing *G*, then *X*, typing 0.5, and then hitting *Enter*. Then, press *K* and add another **Location** keyframe.

    IV.   We need to change the interpolation of these keyframes to **Linear** so that the empty object moves at a constant rate throughout the entire animation, rather than speeding up and slowing down. Select both keyframes in the **Timeline** by dragging a box, then press *T*, and choose **Linear**.

16. With that done, we can jump back over to the **Displace** modifier. Switch **Coordinates** to **Object**, and in the **Object** menu, select **Empty**.

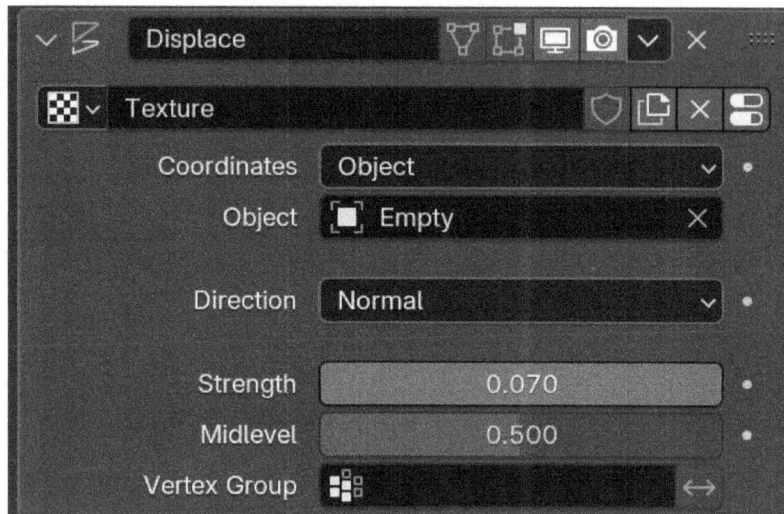

Figure 14.7 – The Displace modifier

If correctly done, the displacement on the bigger plane should be moving as the empty object moves! This will give the illusion of raindrops in the distance!

17. With the bigger plane object still selected, you can right-click and select **Shade Smooth** to smooth out all the displaced geometry.

18. The last step is to position the rocks around the scene. I recommend going into the camera view and placing the rocks. This way, you know what they will look like when you do the rendering. Scale, rotate, and move them around until you fill out the scene. If you want to add more rocks, you can press *Shift + D* to duplicate. Here is what the scene looks like so far:

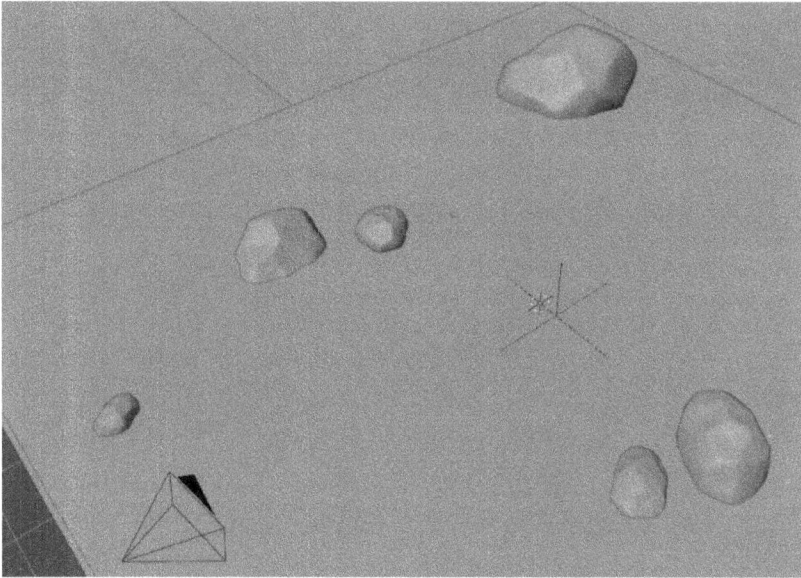

Figure 14.8 – Rock positions

Great! Now that we have the scene filled out, let's create the rain using a particle system!

Creating the rain particles

To create this particle system, let's first add an emitter object to emit the particles into the scene:

1. Press *Shift + A* and add another plane object. Let's scale it to be the same size as the smaller plane and then move it up about four meters above the water.

2. To create the particle system, head over to the **Particle System** panel and click + to create a new one.

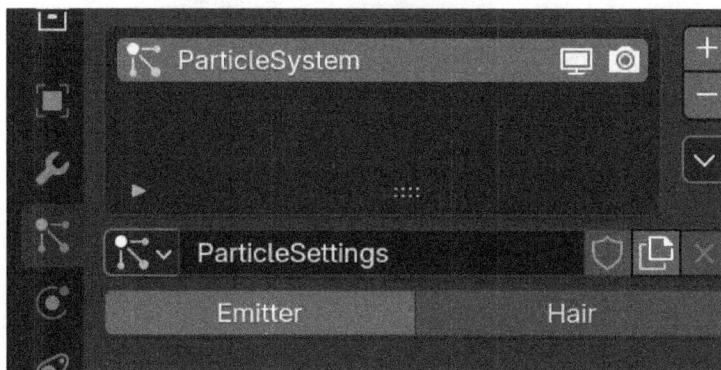

Figure 14.9 – New particle system

3. Now, let's decide how much rain we want there to be. Do you want it to be pouring down or just a light sprinkle? Let's go with something in the middle and create light rain. To do this, set the number of particles to 3000.

4. For **Frame Start**, set it to -50 so that it looks like it's already raining when we play the animation. For **Lifetime**, set it to 35 so that the particles disappear after they go beneath the water.

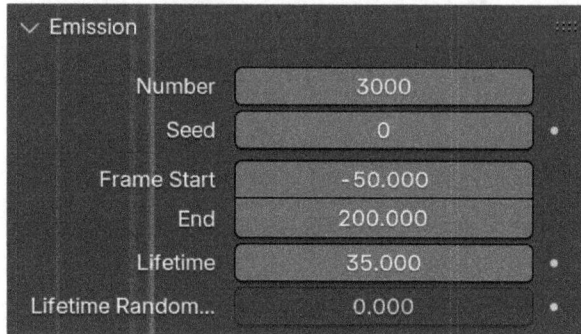

Figure 14.10 – Emission settings

5. In the **Velocity** tab, set **Normal** to 0 and **Object Aligned Z** to -1. This will cause the particles to have a starting velocity along the -**Z** axis.

6. The particles are moving a bit too fast right now. To fix that, head down to the **Physics** tab and set **Damp** to 0.050. This will slow down the particles just a little bit.

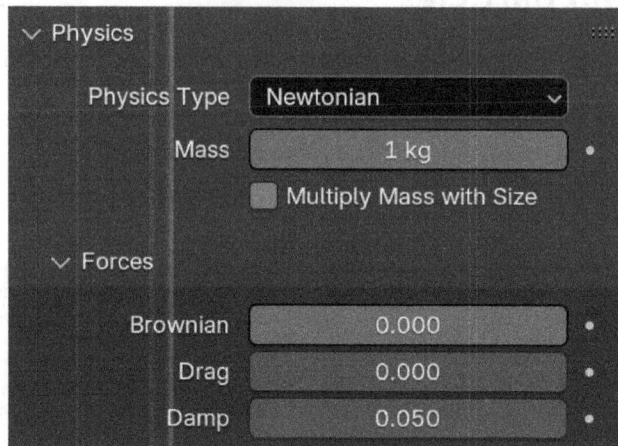

Figure 14.11 – The Physics tab

7. Now, we need an object to represent each particle. Since a raindrop is spherical, let's use an icosphere! Press *Shift + A* and add an icosphere object. Move it out of the way so that you can't see it from the camera, and then scale it down by 0.2. Then, of course, always remember to apply the scale! Press *Ctrl + A* or *Cmd + A* and select **Scale**.

8. You can also right-click and select **Shade Smooth** to smooth out the edges of the icosphere.

9. Select the plane with the particle system again, and in the **Render** tab, switch **Render As** to **Object**, and then for **Instance Object**, select the icosphere you just added. Also, make sure to turn off **Show Emitter** so that the plane does not show up in the render!

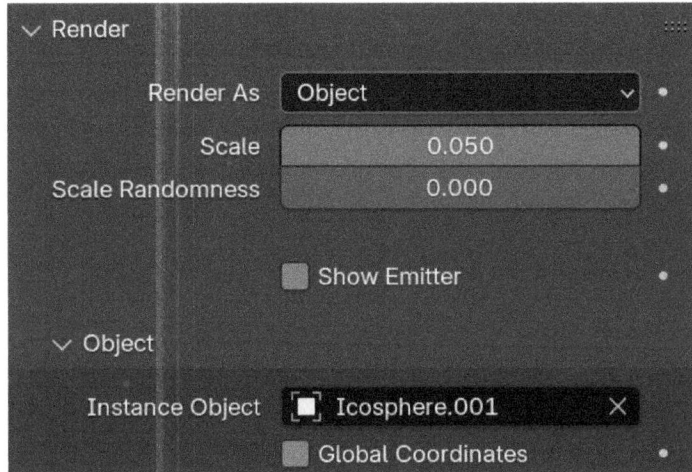

Figure 14.12 – The Render tab

10. Now, we are ready to bake in the particle system! Head up to the **Cache** tab and click on **Bake**!

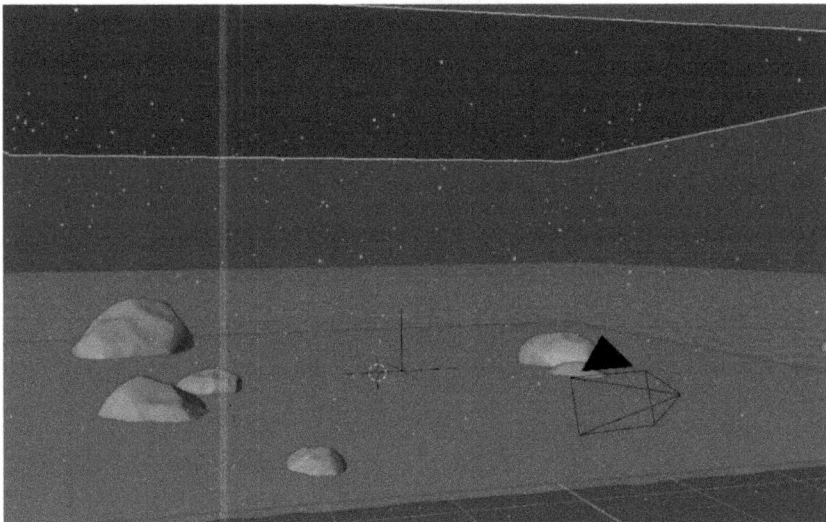

Figure 14.13 – Rain particles

With all that done, we are ready to move on to creating the dynamic paint simulation!

Simulating the waves

Now, the part you have been waiting for – let's create the dynamic paint simulation and simulate the raindrop effect! Let's start by creating the canvas, and then we can move on to the brush objects:

1. Select the smaller plane object and head over to the **Physics** panel. Select **Dynamic Paint**, make sure that **Type** is set to **Canvas**, and click **Add Canvas**.

2. The **Frame Start** and **End** settings should already be the correct values we need. Let's also make sure to change **Sub-Steps** to 5 to help make the simulation more accurate.

Figure 14.14 – The dynamic paint settings

3. Head down to the **Surface** tab and set **Surface Type** to **Waves**. We are going to be changing some settings in **Waves**, so let's go through them one by one:

    I.   First, let's turn on **Open Borders** so that the waves don't bounce off the edge of the mesh.

    II.   Next, change **Timescale** to 0.30 to slow down the simulation.

    III. **Speed** controls how fast the waves move; let's also slow this down by changing it to 0.40.

    IV.   To help the waves to dissipate a bit faster, set **Damping** to 0.20.

    V.   Finally, to make the waves bounce a bit more, you can change **Spring** to 0.50.

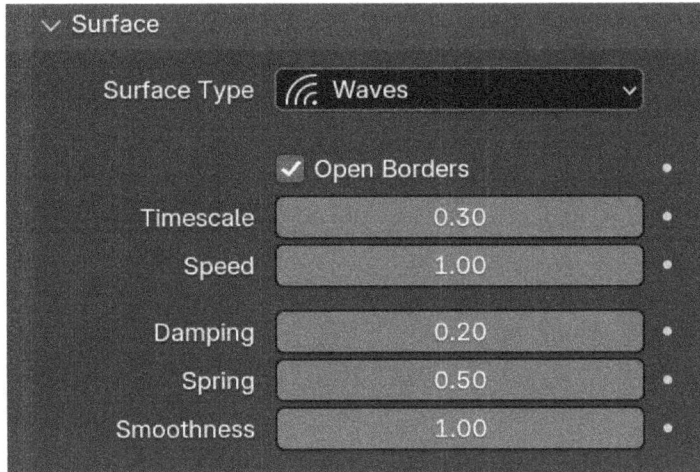

Figure 14.15 – Wave canvas settings

That is all the settings we need for the canvas! Next, let's select the plane object with the particle system and add it to the simulation:

1. Select your particle system object and head over to the **Physics** panel. Select **Dynamic Paint**, switch **Type** to **Brush**, and click **Add Brush**.

2. In the **Source** tab, switch **Paint** to **Particle System**, and select **ParticleSystem** from the **Particle Systems** dropdown menu.

3. Next, check **Use Particle's Radius**. This will allow the radius affecting the canvas to be the exact size of the particle.

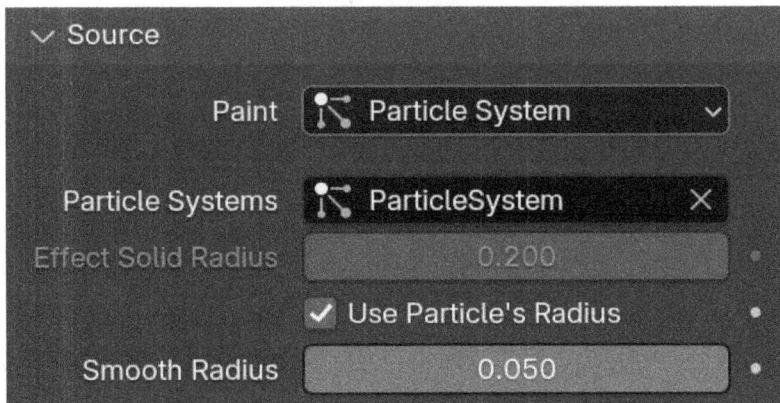

Figure 14.16 – The brush source settings

Now, when you restart the **Timeline,** you should see the particles creating waves on the canvas!

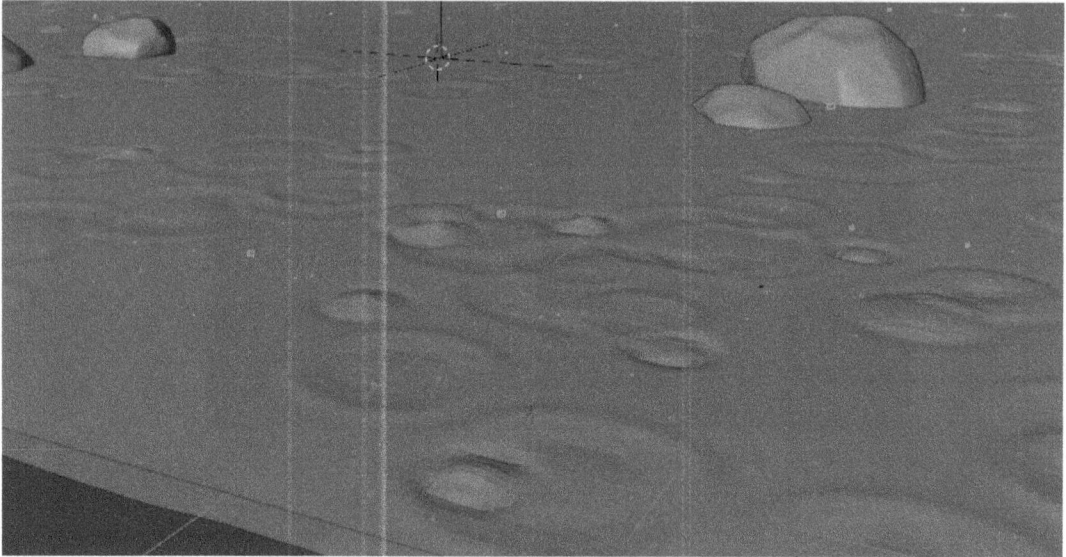

Figure 14.17 – Simulating waves

If you want to create bigger splashes, you can set **Factor** in the **Brush Waves** tab to a higher value. You can see the different values in the following figure:

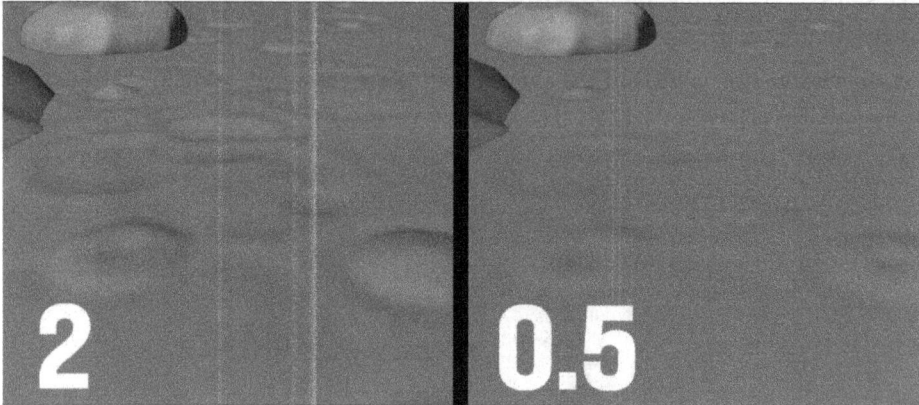

Figure 14.18 – The waves factor

4.   Also, make sure to select your canvas object, and right-click and select **Shade Smooth** to make sure faces are nice and smooth.

5.   Finally, let's allow the rocks to interact with the simulation as well! Select one of the rocks in the scene, and in the **Physics** panel, choose **Dynamic Paint**, switch **Type** to **Brush**, and click **Add Brush**.

6. In the **Waves** tab, switch **Type** to **Reflect Only**. This will allow the rocks to reflect any waves that hit them!

Figure 14.19 – Reflect Only

7. We need to repeat this process for every rock in the scene. However, that is a little tedious. To speed it up, select every rock object, and then select the rock object with the **Brush** settings last. This will make the brush object the **active object**. Then, press *Ctrl* + *L* and select **Copy Modifiers**. Now, all the rocks should have the same brush settings applied to them.

8. Once you are happy with how everything looks, we can bake in the simulation! Select your canvas once again, and in the **Cache** tab, click on **Bake**!

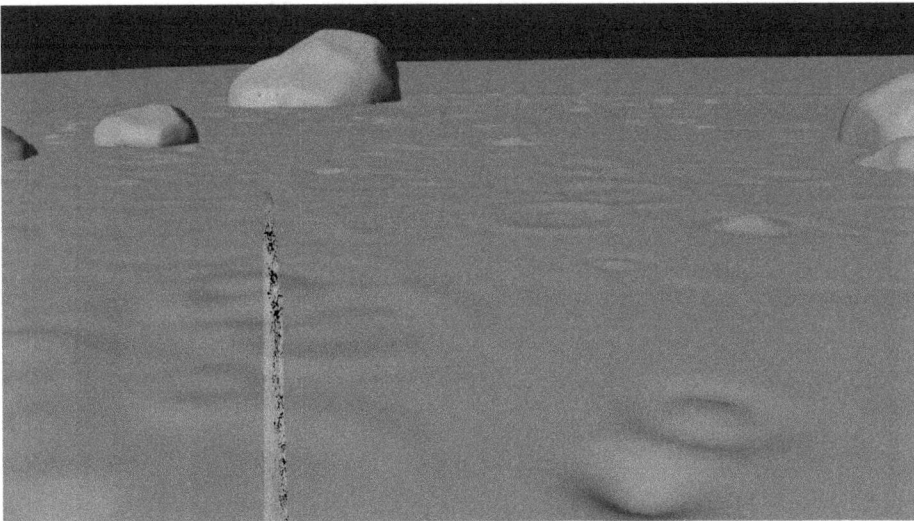

Figure 14.20 – A baked simulation

There we go! The simulation is done and ready to go! Next, let's create some nice water materials!

Creating the water material

There are two materials that we need to create: water and raindrops. Let's create the water material first:

1. Select the canvas object, and head over to the **Shading** workspace at the top. Create a new material by clicking the **New** button.

2. Name this material `Water` so that it's easy to find later.

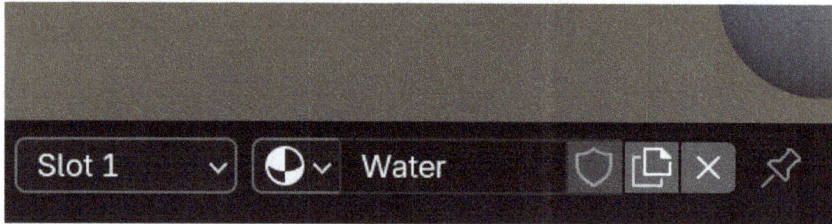

Figure 14.21 – The material name

3. Set **Base Color** in the **Principled BSDF** shader node to a nice dark blue. If you want to use the same color we're using, the hex code is `#274C7A`.

4. To make the lake glossy and reflective, set **Roughness** to `0`.

5. Finally, set **Transmission Weight** to `1` to give the look of glass and **IOR** to `1.333`. IOR stands for *index of refraction*. This is basically how light passes through objects. In this case, the IOR of water is `1.333`. There is also a long list of other IOR values for different real-life materials, which you can reference here: `https://pixelandpoly.com/ior.html`.

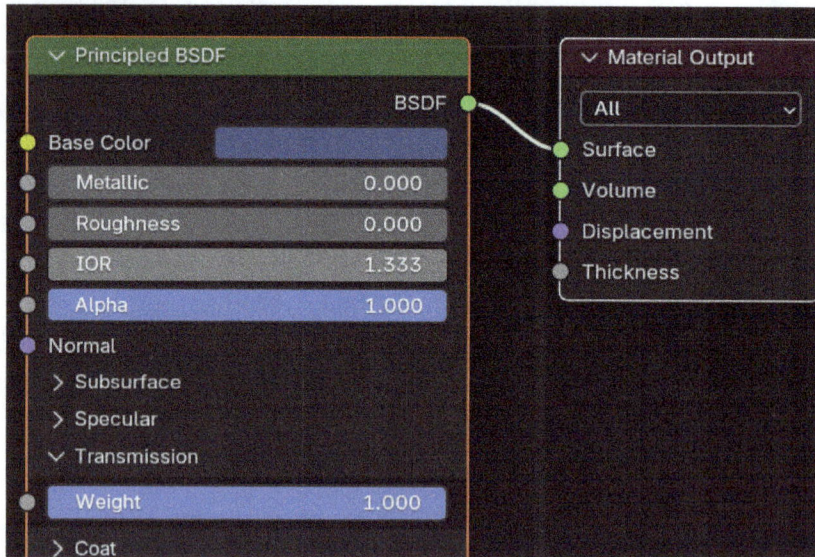

Figure 14.22 – The Principled shader

6. Right now, the water looks a bit flat, so let's give it a bump! This will increase the detail and make the water look like it's moving around in the wind! Press *Shift + A*, go to **Texture**, and add a **Noise Texture** node.

7. Next, let's add a **Bump** node. Press *Shift + A*, go to **Vector**, and add a **Bump** node.

8. Now, we need to plug all the nodes together! Take **Fac** from **Noise Texture** and plug that into **Height** of the **Bump** node. Then, take **Normal** from the **Bump** node and plug that into **Normal** of the **Principled BSDF** shader. It should look like this:

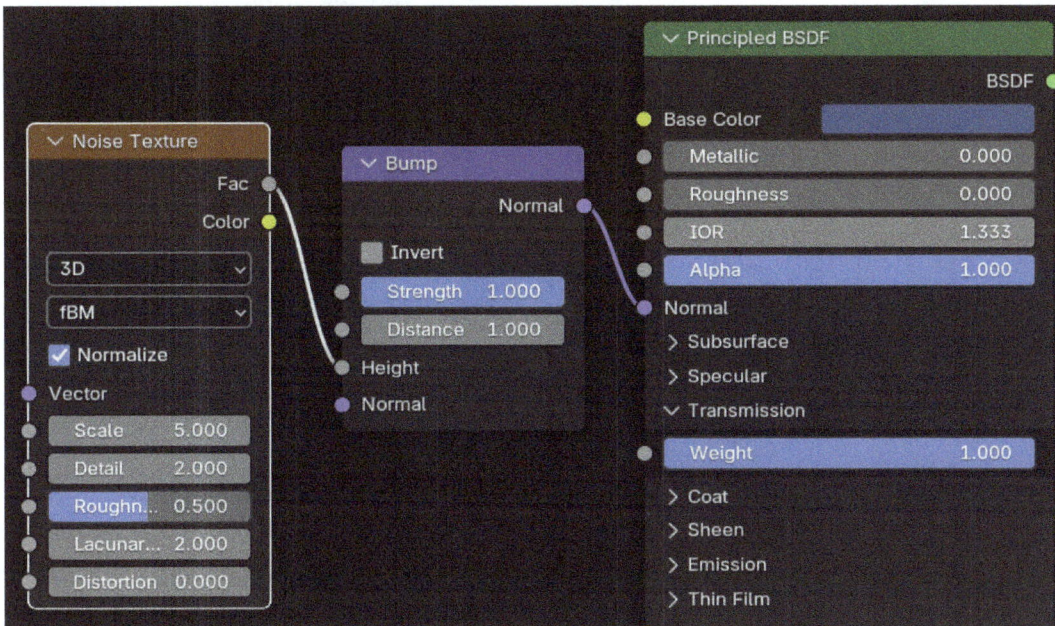

Figure 14.23 – The Noise and Bump nodes

9. Right now, the water looks a bit too bumpy, so let's change some values in these nodes to make it look better:

   I. Starting with **Noise Texture**, let's switch the mode from **3D** to **4D**.

   II. A **W** value should have appeared. Increasing this value will allow the water to look like it's moving. Let's add a driver to this value so that the **W** value automatically increases over the course of the animation. To do this, type in the **W** field `#frame/1500`. Set **Scale** to 75 to make the bumps smaller and **Detail** to 2.

What are drivers?

Drivers allow you to control different property values using functions or mathematical expressions. In this case, with the #frame function, the value will match whichever frame you are on (frame 5 = value of 5). Then, if we divide it with the #frame/10 function, on frame 5, the value will be 0.5. This is just a simple example, but there are many more complex drivers that you can add.

III.   The bumps on the water are way too strong now, so let's bring **Strength** in the **Bump** node down to 0.050 and **Distance** down to 0.100. Here is what it should look like now:

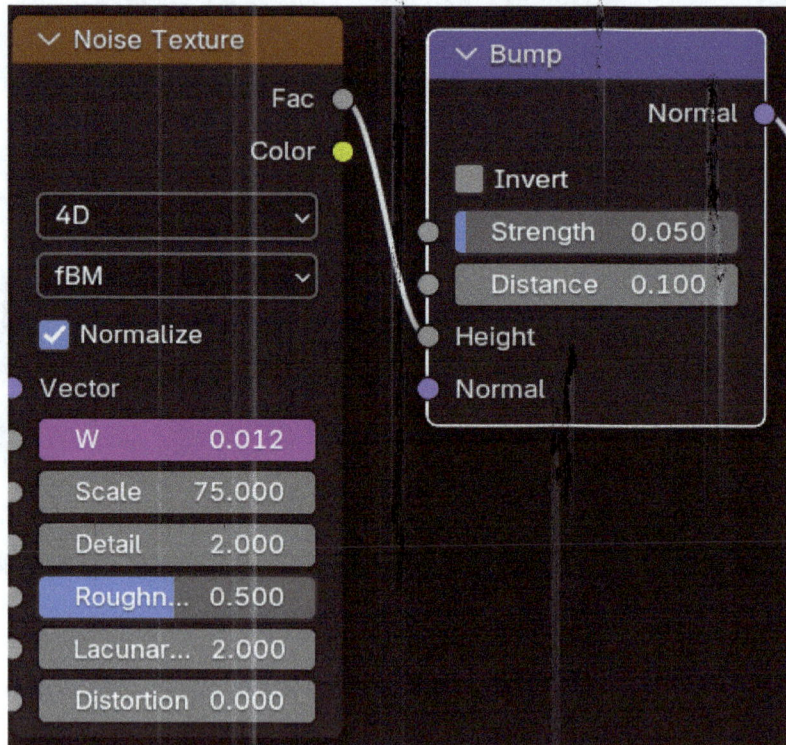

Figure 14.24 – The Noise Texture and Bump values

If we now take a look at the water, it should have a lot more detail and not be as flat!

Figure 14.25 – Water with bumps

1. Let's give the bigger plane that same material by selecting the object, and in the **Shader Editor** workspace, click on the **Browse Material** button and choose the **Water** material.

Figure 14.26 – The Browse Material button

If you press *Z* and go into **Rendered View**, you will be able to see what the scene looks like so far!

Figure 14.27 – A water material preview

2.   Now, let's create the particle material! Select the icosphere object, click the **Browse Material** button, and choose the **Water** material.

3.   We are going to be changing the color of this material. Right now, the **Water** material is shared across three other objects (the particle, the plane, and the bigger plane). That is why you see **3** next to the material. We want to duplicate this material so any changes we make won't affect the other objects. To do this, hit the **3** button next to the name.

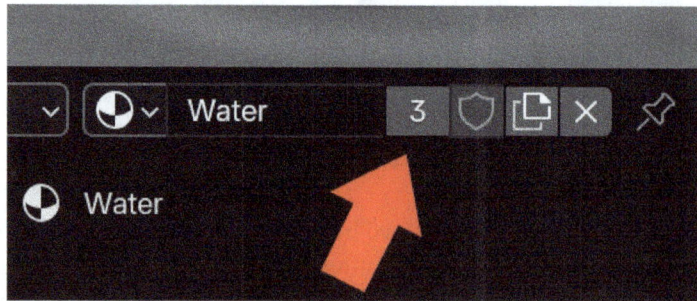

Figure 14.28 – Duplicating the material

Now, we can change this material without affecting other objects!

4.   All we really need to do is set **Base Color** to a very light blue color. If you want to use the exact color we used, the hex code is `#B1D4E5`. We can also delete the **Noise Texture** and **Bump** nodes, as we won't need them for the raindrops.

Figure 14.29 – The particle material

Awesome! All the materials are now done, and our scene is really starting to look nice! Before this project ends, let's set up the render and really make this raindrop effect look great!

Setting up the render

Now that everything is set up, we are basically ready to render the animation. Before we do that, let's quickly go over some EEVEE settings to really make our animation pop:

1. Head over to the **Render** panel, turn on **Raytracing**, and set the **Resolution** setting to 1.1. This will give the water accurate reflections and overall give the scene a much more realistic look.

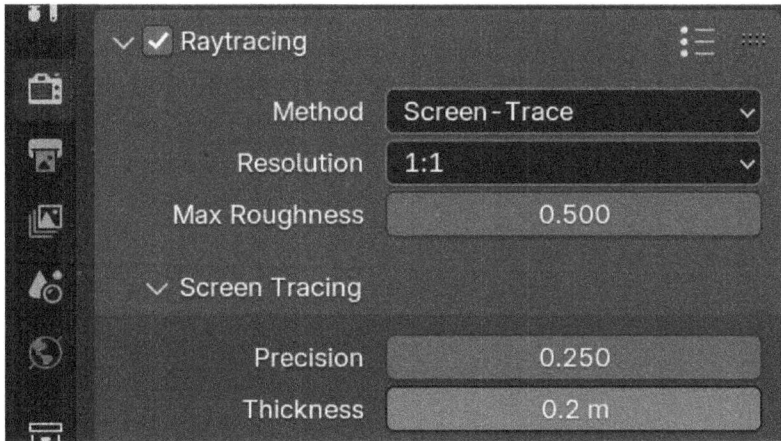

Figure 14.30 – Setting up raytracing

2. To give the rain the look of motion, let's enable **Motion Blur**! The **Shutter** value sets how strong the motion blur will be. Let's bring this down to 0.25. The **Steps** value is also important. The higher you set this, the better the motion blur will look, but it will take longer to render. A value of 8 will work well for this scene.

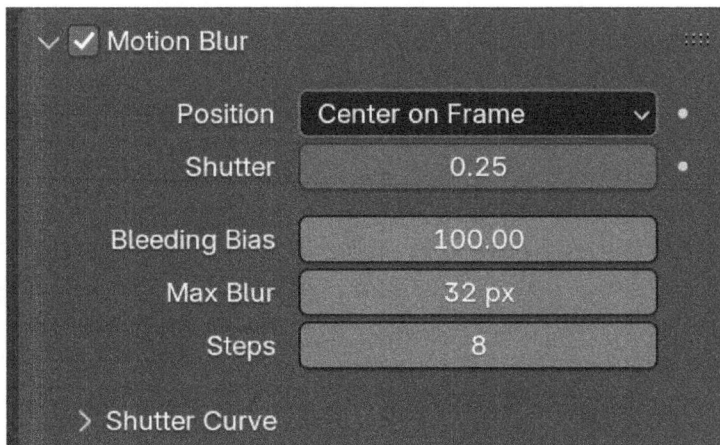

Figure 14.31 – The Motion Blur settings

3. To give the overall scene a better look, open the **Color Management** tab and set **Look** to **High Contrast**.

4. Finally, the last thing we can set up is some depth of field! Select the camera and head over to the **Object Data Properties** panel.

5. Enable **Depth of Field**, and for **Focus on Object**, you can either add a new empty object or use the same one we used for the **Displace** modifier.

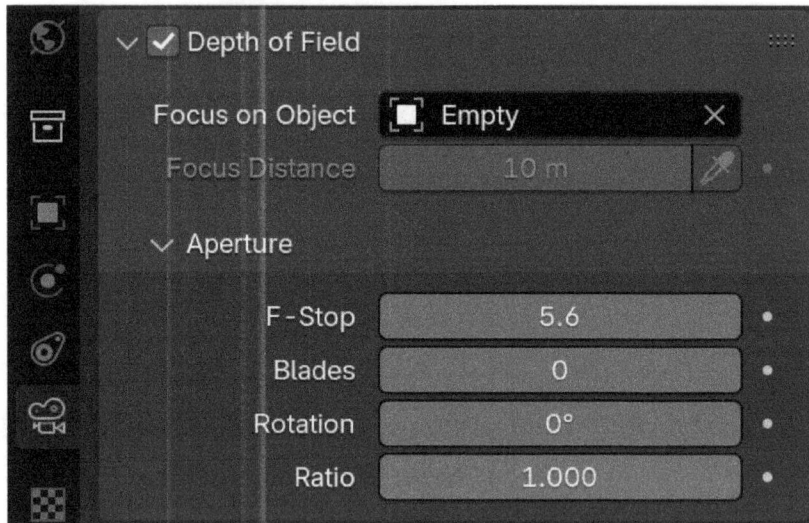

Figure 14.32 – Depth of Field

6. The **F-Stop** value controls how shallow the depth of field will be. Lower values will make the render more shallow, and higher values will make the render crisp and sharp. This value is a personal preference so set it to what you think looks good, or if you would like to copy us, we set it to 5.6.

With that done, we are ready to render the animation! Feel free to add some more elements to the render as well! Maybe add a couple of trees along the shoreline or hanging above the camera. You could also have a boat going along the water in the distance, creating even more waves! Have fun with it and experiment with different ideas! Once you are ready, just set an **Output** directory and then render the animation! Remember, if you need a refresher on how to render animations, check out *Chapter 4*.

Figure 14.33 – The final result – frame 83

Also, if you would like to download and play around with this project's finished `.blend` file, you can do that by following this link: `https://github.com/PacktPublishing/Learn-Blender-4-Simulations-the-Right-Way/tree/main/Chapter%2014`.

Summary

The dynamic paint simulation is a great tool, and it has so many practical uses! Creating a paintbrush and a raindrop effect is just a small portion of what you can do using this simulation. I encourage you to jump into Blender and experiment with cool and interesting ideas. The limit is your imagination!

Let's go through and recap what we learned in this chapter. First, we added all the objects that we needed for this scene! After that, we learned about particle systems and creating rainfall. Next up was the dynamic paint simulation. We learned how to use the particle system to create waves, and we tweaked settings to get the most realistic results. After that, we added the water materials and set up the render.

I hope you enjoyed learning about dynamic paint over these last three chapters and that it has helped you with your own projects and animations. Every simulation discussed in this book has its own uses and can help drastically with a lot of different scenes and projects. For the final chapter in this book, we will be combining fire, cloth, and dynamic paint to create a burning-up effect!

Join our community on Discord

Join our community's Discord space for discussions with the author and other readers:
https://packt.link/learn-blender-simulations-discord-invite

15

Creating a Burning-Up Effect

Over the course of this book, we've discussed and learned about every physics simulation that Blender has to offer. One thing we haven't discussed is combining these effects together. This is what this chapter is all about!

We will be combining the following simulations to create a burning-up effect in Blender: **Dynamic Paint**, **Cloth**, and **Fire**. The goal of this chapter is to demonstrate the process of managing multiple simulation types on one object while keeping in mind the order of the modifier stack. Remember that the order of the simulation modifiers greatly influences the outcome of the simulation.

We'll start out by creating an animated vertex group using dynamic paint on a plane object. Next, we'll add the cloth simulation and use the **Mask** modifier to slowly remove parts of the mesh. After that, we will use the vertex group we created to determine where we want the fire to appear on the object. Finally, we'll create a fire and burnt material, then render out an animation!

In this chapter, we'll be covering the following topics:

- Dynamic weight painting
- Creating the Cloth simulation
- Using the Mask modifier
- Simulating the fire
- Adding burnt and fire materials

Technical requirements

This chapter requires you to have Blender version 4.2 or above installed.

To download Blender, visit www.blender.org.

Make sure to also download the setup file, which includes a couple of mesh objects and lights: https://github.com/PacktPublishing/Learn-Blender-4-Simulations-the-Right-Way/tree/main/Chapter%2015

Dynamic weight painting

Let's begin by opening the `Burning Effect Setup.blend` file, whose link you can find in the *Technical requirements* section. This file includes a plane, a couple of area lights, and some render settings already in place. This plane object is going to be our canvas, cloth, and inflow object for this simulation.

We'll start out by creating a new brush object to paint weight on the canvas. Then, from there, we'll use a new vertex group to mask out the canvas and determine where the fire should be. That will create the look of the **Plane** object burning up!

Let's go ahead and get started by creating the first simulation for this project, dynamic paint!

1. We already have the canvas for our dynamic paint simulation so now we need to add a brush object. Press *Shift + A* and then click on **Mesh | Icosphere**.

2. Before you do anything else, make sure to open the menu at the bottom left and set **Subdivisions** to 6, which will increase the amount of geometry on the icosphere, and set **Radius** to 1.5.

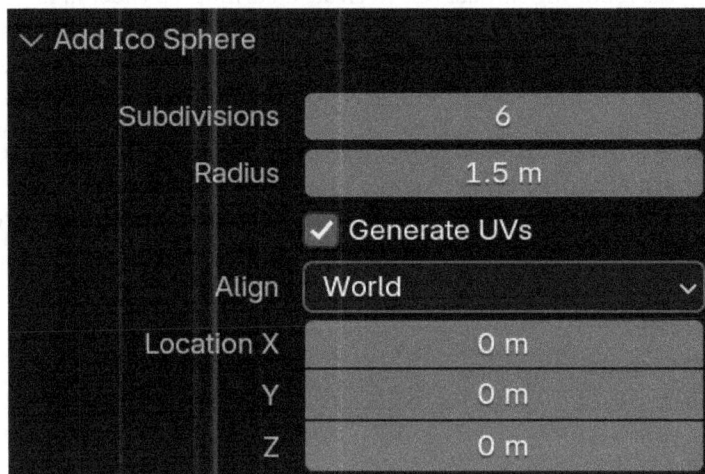

Figure 15.1 – Add Ico Sphere menu

The next step is to have this icosphere paint weight on the canvas, which we will use later to determine where the fire appears on the plane. To do this, we need to animate the icosphere moving up the plane. Here are the steps!

I.   Position the icosphere beneath the plane object.

II.   On **Frame 1** press *K* and, add a **Location** keyframe to the brush.

III.   Jump all the way to **Frame 250**, move the icosphere up until it envelops the plane object completely, and add another **Location** keyframe.

IV.   In the Timeline, select both keyframes by drawing a box around them. Then, with your mouse hovering over the **Timeline,** press *T* and select **Linear**. This will make the brush move at a constant speed throughout the animation.

> **Keyframe interpolation**
>
> The normal interpolation between keyframes is a **Bezier** curve, which means the animation will start out slowly, speed up in the middle, and slow down at the end. Changing the interpolation to **Linear** will make the brush object move at a constant rate rather than speeding up and slowing down.

V.   One last step on our brush object before we start simulating is to add a **Displace** modifier. This will give the simulation a much more natural look, so the weight painting isn't a perfect icosphere shape. To do this, head over to the **Modifier** panel and select **Add Modifier | Deform | Displace**.

VI.   Set **Coordinates** to **Global** and **Strength** to 0 . 3. Setting **Coordinates** to **Global** will make the displacement change over time as the object moves upwards.

Figure 15.2 – Displace modifier

VII. Finally, jump to the **Texture** panel and change **Type** to **Clouds**. Now the icosphere's surface should look like the **Cloud** texture with bumps and ripples all throughout.

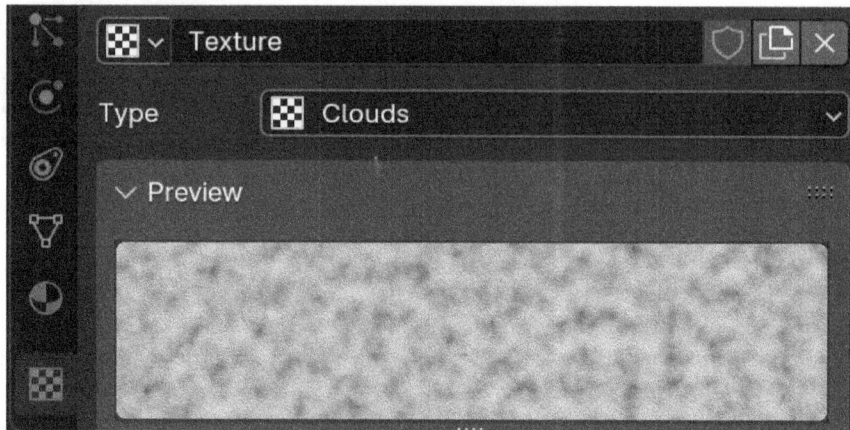

Figure 15.3 – Texture type

Now, when we play the animation, the icosphere will move upward and the **Cloud** texture displacement will also move along the surface of the mesh, giving the icosphere a much more random and varied look. With that done, let's create the dynamic paint simulation!

3. Select the **Plane** object and head over to the **Physics** panel. Choose **Dynamic Paint** and, for **Surface Type**, we can leave it on **Canvas**.

4. Scroll down to the **Surface** tab and change **Surface Type** to **Weight**.

5. Next, in the **Output** tab, make sure to hit + to add a new **vertex group**.

Figure 15.4 – Canvas settings

That's all we need to do for our canvas object! Now let's move on to the brush settings!

6. Select **Icosphere**, in the **Physics** panel, choose **Dynamic Paint**, and, for **Type**, change it to **Brush** and click **Add Brush**.

7. In the **Source** tab, change **Paint** to **Mesh Volume + Proximity**. For **Distance**, let's go with a value of 0.250. This will create a smoother transition for the weight being painted.

And that is it! If you want to see what your vertex group will look like, you can select the **Plane** object and go into **Weight Paint** mode. Make sure you restart the animation and play it from the start, or you won't be able to see it. Here is what it currently looks like on **Frame 120**.

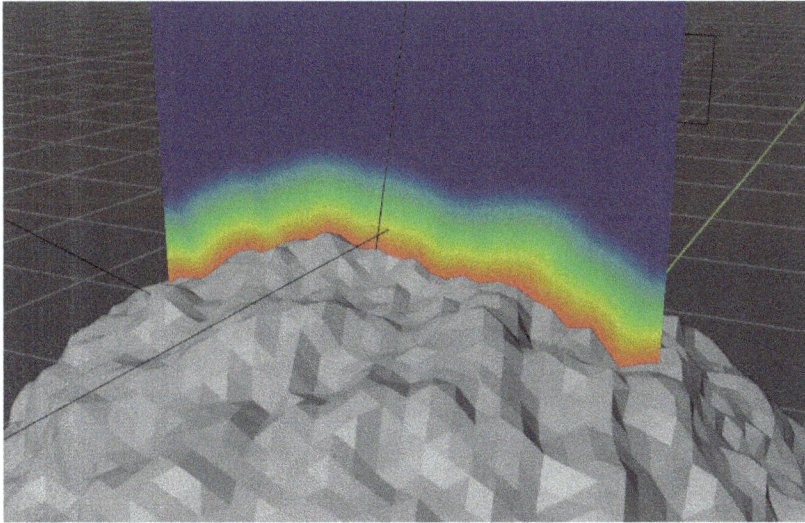

Figure 15.5 – Weight painting

If you are happy with how it looks, go ahead and bake the dynamic paint simulation in by selecting the **Plane** object. In the canvas settings, scroll down to the **Cache** tab and click on **Bake**! For the next step in our burning-up effect animation, we will be using the **Cloth** simulation!

Creating the Cloth simulation

The dynamic painting section of this project is done! Now let's use the **Cloth** simulation on our plane object to have it flow and move around in the wind as it's burning up!

1. Firstly, we need to add a **Wind** force field to add some movement to the plane. Press *Shift + A* and then click on **Force Field | Wind**. Make sure to rotate and position the **Wind** force field on the left side of the plane.

2. In the **Physics** panel, set **Strength** of this force field to 2500. That should give the cloth some nice flow and movement.

3. If we add the **Cloth** simulation to our plane object right now, it will just fall due to gravity. To prevent this, let's create a new pin group and lock the top row of vertices from moving.

4. With the plane selected, head over to the **Data** panel and create a new vertex group by hitting the + button.

5. In **Edit** mode, select the top row of vertices on the plane. You can easily do this by holding the *Alt* or *Option* key and left-clicking anywhere along the top row of vertices. Then click **Assign** in the **Data** panel.

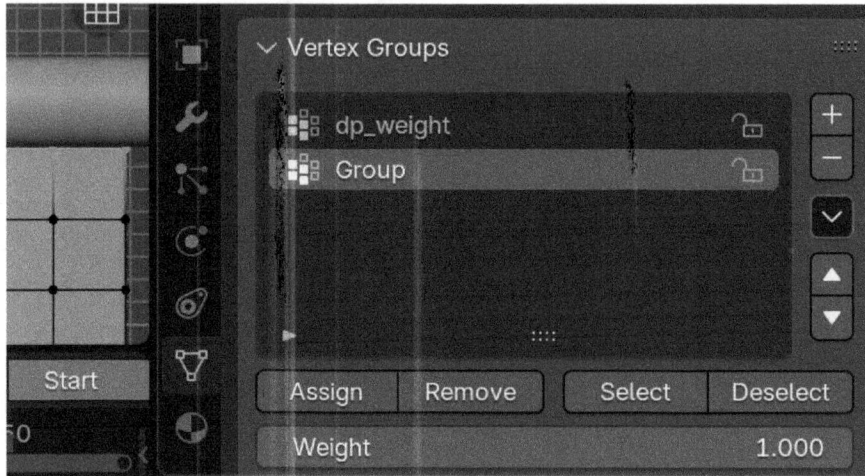

Figure 15.6 – Vertex group assigning

6. Now we are ready to work on the **Cloth** simulation! Head over to the **Physics** panel once again and choose **Cloth**!

7. In the **Physical Properties** tab, set **Vertex Mass** to 0.2 kg. This will make each vertex on our plane weigh just a little less.

8. In the **Shape** tab, let's select the vertex group that we just created for the pin group. Make sure to select **Group** and not **dp_weight** as this group is for the fire and masking, and not for the cloth simulation.

9. Finally, check **Self Collision** and set **Distance** to as low as it can go, which is 0.001.

That is all we need to do for the cloth simulation settings! Feel free to play around with the position and rotation of the **Wind** force field as this can affect how the cloth will move and flow. Once you are happy with the results, open the **Cache** tab and select **Bake**!

Using the Mask modifier

So far, we have set up two simulations, dynamic paint and cloth. The next step in this project is to use the **Mask** modifier to remove parts of the mesh. This modifier works by using a vertex group to mask out parts of the object. In this case, we want to use the vertex group we created with dynamic paint!

1. Select the **Plane** object if it's not already selected and head over to the **Modifier** panel. Click **Add Modifier | Generate | Mask**.

2. In the **Vertex Group** drop-down menu, select **dp_weight**, which is the vertex group we created with the dynamic paint!

3. Right now, the **Mask** modifier is removing parts of the mesh that are *not* assigned to the **dp_weight** group. This is the opposite of what we want. To invert the masking selection, click on the double-sided arrow next to the **Vertex Group** drop-down menu.

4. Finally, check the **Smooth** checkbox to help give the mask a smoother transition and bring up **Threshold** to 0.850. This means that only a weight value greater than 0.850 will be removed.

Figure 15.7 – Mask modifier settings

Remember, vertex group values range from 0 to 1, with red being a value of 1 and blue being a value of 0 (see *Figure 15.5*). Since we set the **Threshold** value to 0.850, the **Mask** modifier will only remove parts of the mesh that are almost that red color. To see an example of this, view the following figure:

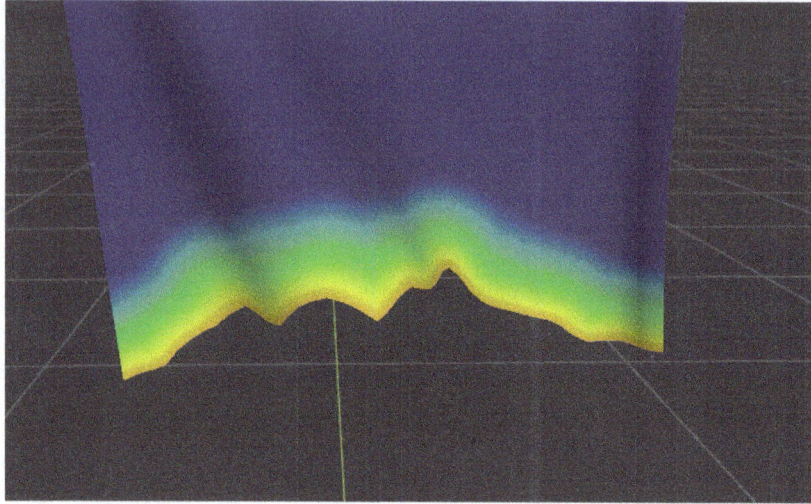

Figure 15.8 – Mask weight example

5.   We also don't need the icosphere object in the scene anymore, so let's toggle both the viewport and render visibility by clicking the eye icon and camera icon in the Outliner.

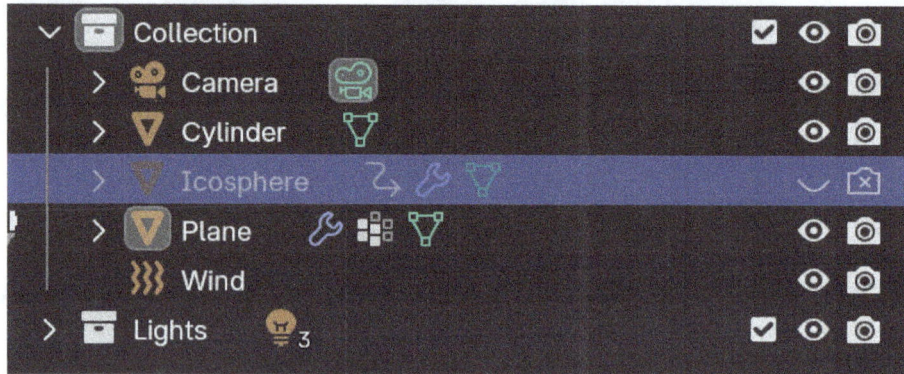

Figure 15.9 – Icosphere visibility

Now, when we play the animation, the plane should be flowing in the wind from the force field and slowly be masked away! If everything looks good, we can move on to adding fire!

Simulating the fire

The final simulation that we'll be adding is fire! We'll be taking the plane and using it as an inflow object to emit fire into the scene. The simulation is going to work by taking the **dp_weight** group and assigning it to the vertex group for the inflow. This will restrict the fire to only appear at the bottom of the plane as it's being masked away.

Adding the domain

To get started with creating the simulation, we need a domain object in the scene.

1. Let's press *Shift + A* and then go to **Mesh** and add a new **Cube** object.

2. Next, scale the domain object to the size that you need. If you would like to use the same dimensions we used, view the following figure:

Figure 15.10 – Domain dimensions

3. Move the domain up so it encapsulates the **Plane** object, and since we changed the scale, we need to press *Ctrl + A* or *Cmd + A* and apply **Scale**.

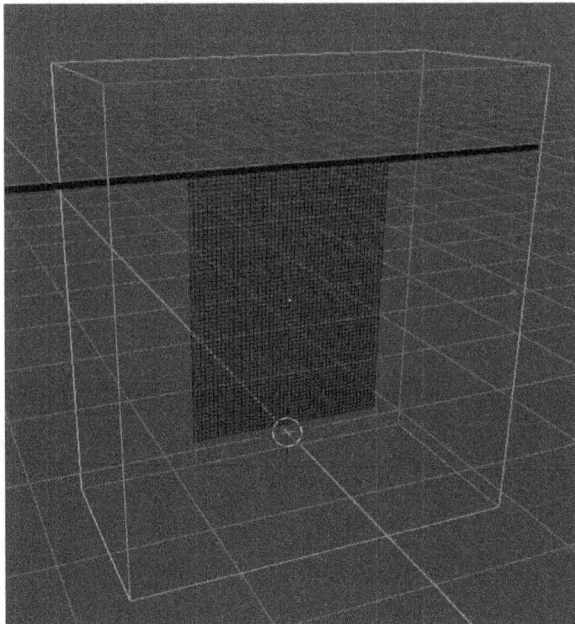

Figure 15.11 – Domain size

4. Now let's add the fire! With the domain selected, head over to the **Physics** panel, select **Fluid**, and for the type choose **Domain**.

5. For **Resolution**, let's go with a high value of 256. If you have a slower computer, **Resolution** of 128 will work well too.

6. We've also noticed that the fire moves a bit too fast in the simulation. To help fix this issue, set **Timescale** to 0.7. This will slow down the movement of the fire by 30%.

7. Let's also change **CFL Number** to 4. This will help improve the bake time a little bit.

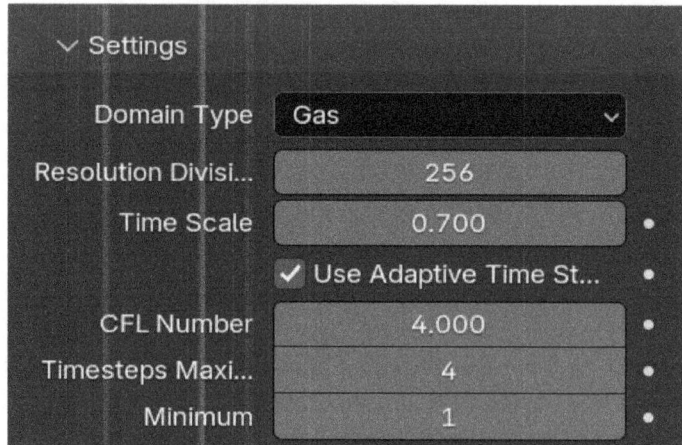

Figure 15.12 – Domain settings

8. Next, scroll down a little bit and enable **Adaptive Domain** by clicking the checkbox. This will adaptively change the size of the domain based on where the fire is located inside. With **Adaptive Domain** enabled, the bake time will drastically improve!

9. In the **Fire** tab, bring **Reaction Speed** up to 0.8. This setting controls the height of the flames. The higher the value, the shorter the flame will be.

10. Let's also set **Vorticity** to 0.6. This will give the flames just a little bit more randomness and variation.

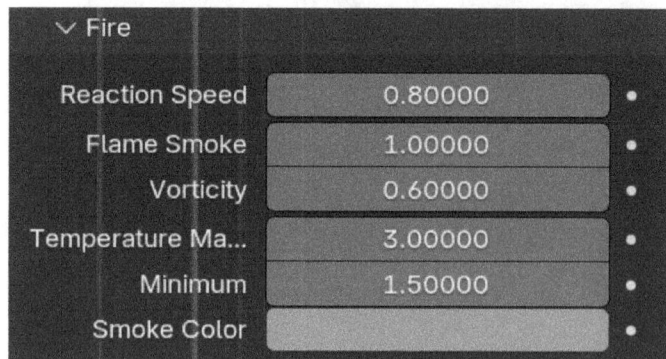

Figure 15.13 – Fire settings

11. Now open the **Cache** tab. If you would like to save your simulation data, set a new directory by clicking the folder icon. If you don't do this, the data will automatically be deleted after you close the project, which means that the next time you open this blend file, you will have to rebake the simulation. This can be a good thing though, to save on hard drive space.

12. Let's change **Type** to **Modular**, so we can bake in the simulation later. Make sure **Frame Start** and **End** match your desired length of the simulation.

13. Let's also check **Is Resumable**, just in case we need to pause the bake.

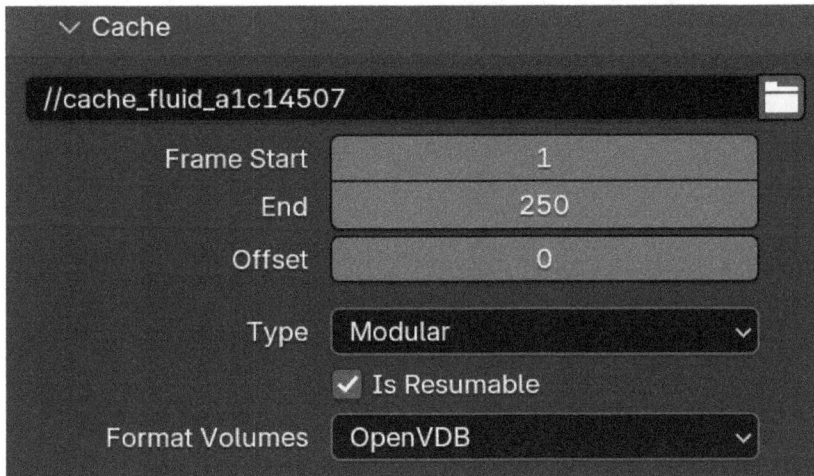

Figure 15.14 – Cache settings

14. Finally, open the **Field Weights** tab. Right now, we have a **Wind** force field with **Strength** of 2500, which we used for the cloth simulation. With **Strength** that high, the fire will go crazy if we keep it enabled. Instead of deleting the force field, let's just set the **Wind** value in **Field Weights** to 0. This will prevent the **Wind** force field from affecting the flames.

With that done, let's set up the inflow object and bake in the simulation!

Setting up Inflow

Now that the domain is done, it's time to create the inflow object!

1. Select the **Plane** object, and in the **Physics** panel, choose **Fluid** and change **Type** to **Flow**.

2. For **Flow Type** choose **Fire**, and for **Flow Behavior**, we need to go with **Inflow**, so it constantly adds fire to the scene.

3. For the most important part, in the **Vertex Group** menu, select **dp_weight**. Now the fire will only appear at the very bottom of the plane object as it's being masked away.

4.   Lastly, open the **Flow Source** tab and set **Surface Emission** to a value of 1. This will bring the fire closer to the surface of the mesh.

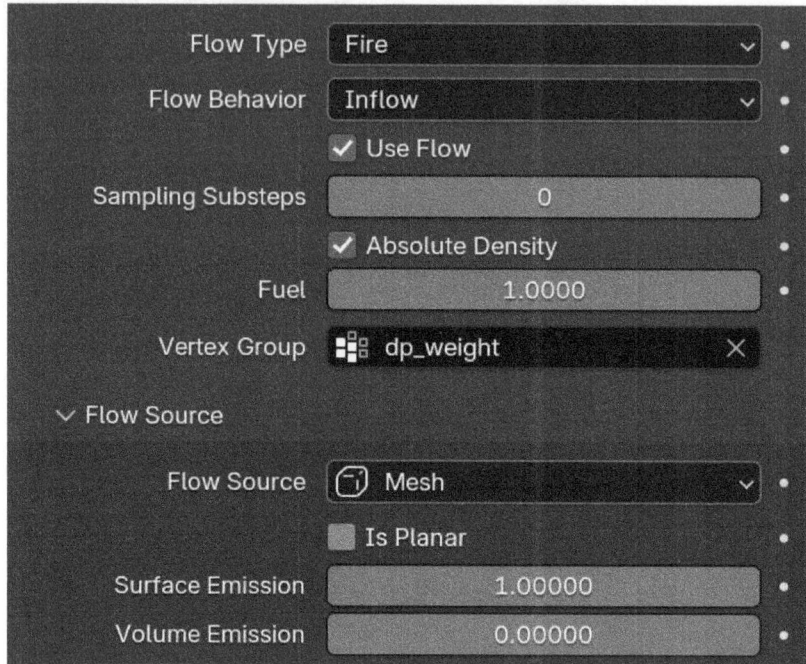

Figure 15.15 – Inflow settings

That is all we need to do for the inflow object! Let's now select the domain. In the **Settings** tab, click on **Bake Data**! Once the bake has finished, we move on to creating the fire material and adding a burning look to the plane!

Adding burnt and fire materials

All three simulations are done and working properly on our plane object. Next, we'll create the materials for our fire and **Plane** object!

Domain material

We'll start out with the domain fire material and then focus on the plane next!

1.   Head over to the **Shading** workspace at the top of your screen.

Figure 15.16 – Shading workspace

2. Make sure your domain object is selected then click **New** to create a new material.

3. We don't need the **Principled BSDF** shader, so go ahead and delete it. Then, add a **Principled Volume** shader. Press *Shift + A* and then go to **Shader | Principled Volume**.

4. Take the **Volume** output and plug it into the **Volume** input of the **Material Output** node.

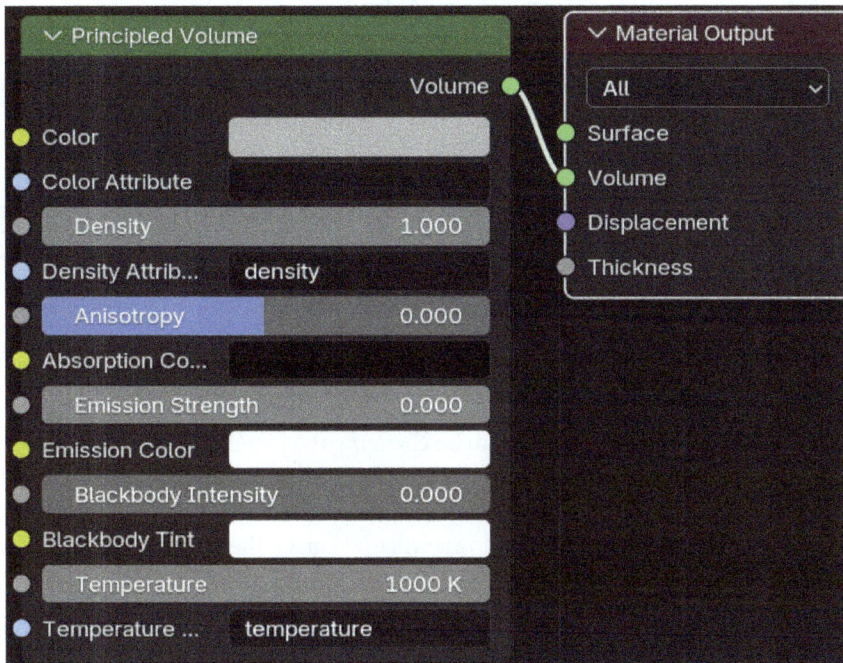

Figure 15.17 – Principled Volume Shader

5. We are going to be creating a material similar to that in *Chapter 3*. We will be adding the **Heat** attribute to control **Emission Strength** and **Emission Color**. To do this, add the **Attribute** node by pressing *Shift + A* and then going to **Input | Attribute** and placing it on the left side of the **Principled Volume** node.

    As mentioned in *Chapter 3*, the **Heat** attribute only works in Cycles, so if you aren't already in the Cycles render, change to it now.

6. In the **Name** field, type the word heat (all lowercase).

7. Next, let's add a **Color Ramp** node to control how the **Heat** attribute looks! Press *Shift + A*, then go to **Converter | Color Ramp**.

8. Take the **Fac** output of the **Attribute** node and plug it into the **Fac** input of the **Color Ramp** node.

9. Then, to change the brightness of the flames, let's add a **Math** node. Press *Shift + A* and then go to **Converter | Math**. Place the node between the **Color Ramp** and **Principled Volume** nodes and change **Mode** to **Multiply**.

10. Take the **Color** output from the **Color Ramp** node and plug it into the top input of the **Math** node, then take the **Value** output from the **Math** node and plug that into **Emission Strength** of the **Principled Volume** node. The bottom value of the **Math** node now controls how bright the flames will be. Let's go with a value of 100!

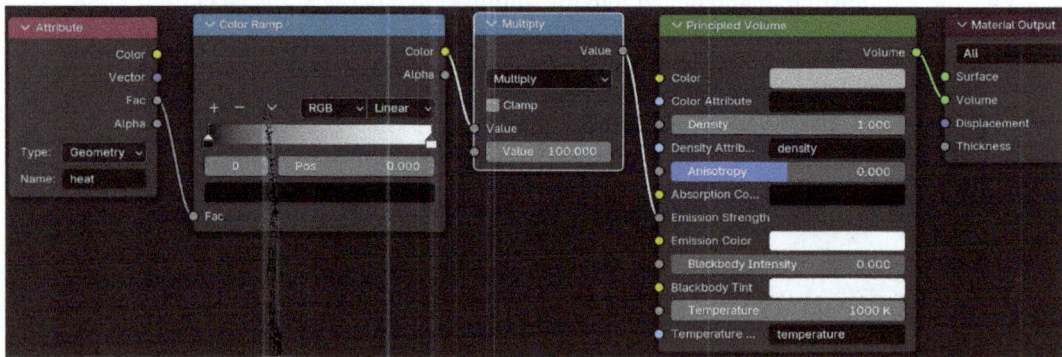

Figure 15.18 – Emission Strength node setup

11. With the **Color Ramp** node, we're going to be changing the positions of the handles just a little bit. First, move the white handle towards the middle, then add a new handle by clicking the + button. Move this new handle almost all the way to the right, but leave just a little bit of room, and then change the color to black. What this will do is make the very bottom of the fire more transparent. This will make it easier to see the burnt material when we add that in.

12. The last node we need to add is for **Emission Color**. What we can do is select the **Color Ramp** node and press *Ctrl + Shift + D*. This will duplicate the **Color Ramp** node while keeping the connection to the **Attribute** node. Place this new **Color Ramp** node beneath the first one.

13. Take the **Color** output and plug it into **Emission Color** of the **Principled Volume** node.

14. As for the handles on this new **Color Ramp**, take the black handle and move it to the 0.7 position on the right. Next, change the color of the white handle to a more yellow/orange color.

15. And finally, add one more handle by clicking the + button. Position this new handle in the middle between the black and yellow handles. Change the color to a darker orange. View the following figure to see the full node setup:

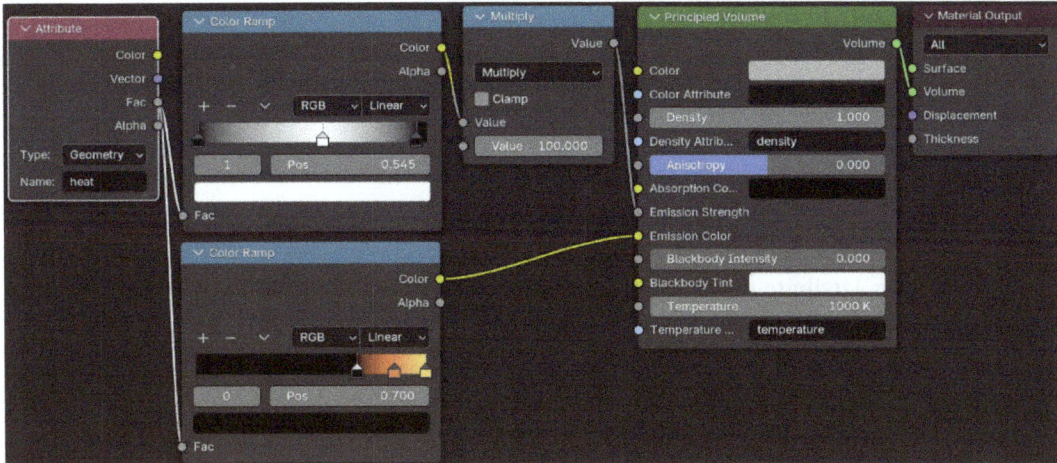

Figure 15.19 – Domain node setup

If we go into the rendered view now, here is what the fire should look like:

Figure 15.20 – Fire render preview

Next up on the list is the **Plane** burnt material!

Burning material

If you light a piece of paper on fire in real life, the fire will change the color of the paper as it's burning. That is what we will be replicating here with the **Plane** object:

1. To get started, select the **Plane** object. You will see a basic material already in place with an image texture and a **Bump** node to add some depth.

2. To create this color change as the plane burns up, we'll be adding three different nodes. The first one is an **Attribute** node. Press *Shift + A*, then go to **Input** and add an **Attribute** node, and place it above the **Image Texture** node.

3. In the **Name** field, we'll be using the vertex group we created at the beginning of this chapter: **dp_weight**. One thing to note about using vertex groups in material node setups is that it only works in Cycles. EEVEE does not support vertex groups influencing materials. Since we are already in Cycles, this should not matter, but it's good to know for future projects.

4. To get **dp_weight** to influence the material, we need to mix the **Image Texture** and **Attribute** nodes together. Press *Shift + A* and then go to **Color** and add a **Mix Color** node.

5. Take **Fac** from the **Attribute** node and plug it into **Factor** of the **Mix** node. Then take **Color** from **Hue/Saturation/Value** and plug it into the **A** input.

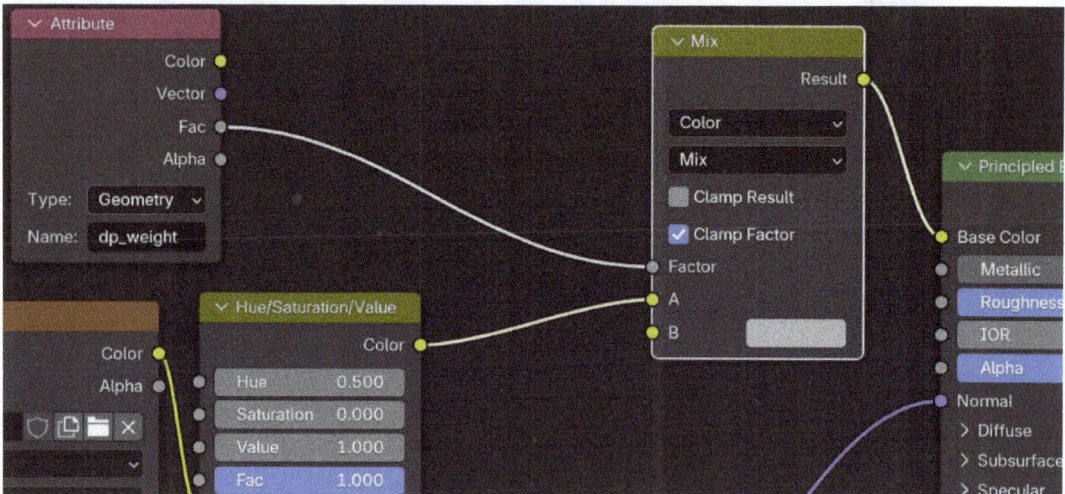

Figure 15.21 – Adding the Mix node

6. The **B** input color now controls what the burnt area will look like. Let's change this color to black.

7. The last node we will be adding is another **Math** node. Press *Shift + A*, go to **Converter**, and select **Math**. Place it in between the **Attribute** and **Mix** nodes.

8. With **Mode** set to **Multiply**, the bottom value controls how dark the burnt areas will be. A value of 2 will work well here. Here is the full node setup.

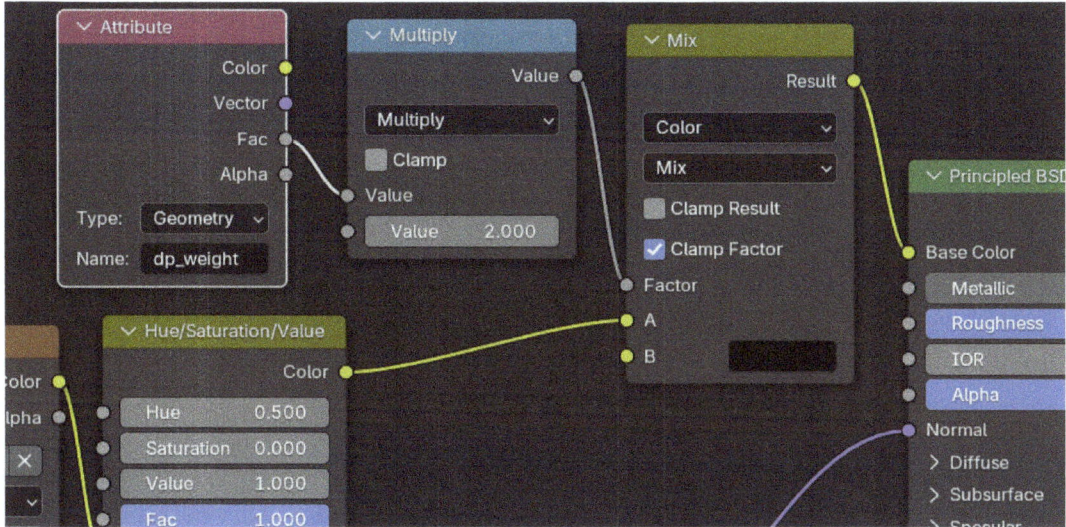

Figure 15.22 – Burnt material setup

When we play the animation, the areas on the **Plane** object with fire should now display a very dark color, indicating that they are burning. Here is an example of the simulation before and after the color change:

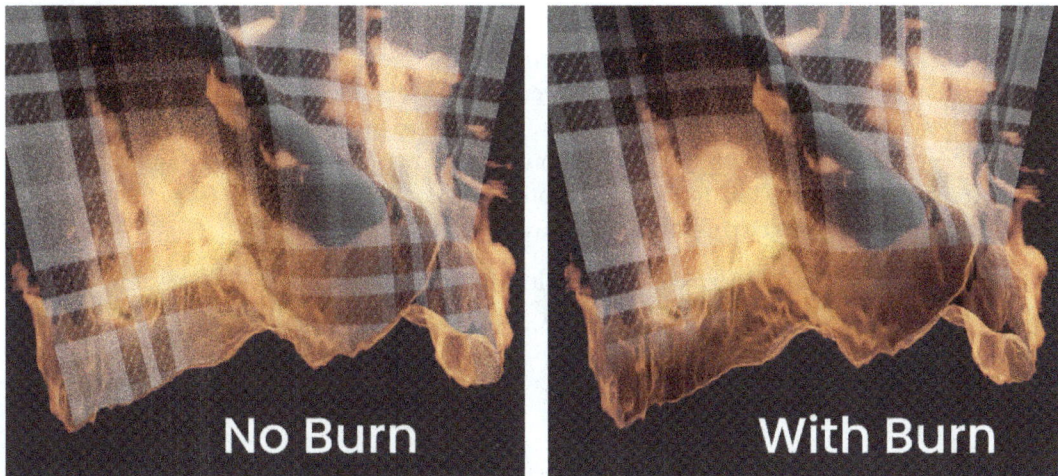

Figure 15.23 – Simulation before and after the application of the burn effect

And there we go – that is it for this project! At this point, we are ready to render out the final animation. If you need a refresher on how to render animations in Blender, there is a full breakdown in *Chapter 4*. The following figure is a rendered image of **Frame 80**.

Figure 15.24 – Frame 80 rendered

If you would like to download this project's Blender file, you can do that here as well: `https://github.com/PacktPublishing/Learn-Blender-4-Simulations-the-Right-Way/tree/main/Chapter%2015`

One last thing that needs to be mentioned is the order of the simulations we created and why it's important. If any of the three simulations we used weren't created in the order that was shown in this chapter, this project would not have worked properly. If we created the cloth simulation first, it would be much harder to create a smooth transition with the brush because the plane would be flowing and moving in the wind. Likewise, the fire simulation would not work either because we needed the dynamic paint simulation to determine where the fire would be on the plane.

So, for future projects when you decide to use multiple simulations at once, be mindful of which simulation needs to be created first in order for everything to work properly!

Summary

Physics simulations are everywhere nowadays: movies, TV shows, commercials, and even health and education. Everything we talked about in this book is just a small portion of what you can do using these simulations. I encourage you to jump into Blender and experiment with cool and interesting ideas. The limit is your imagination!

Let's do a quick recap of everything we learned about in this chapter! First, we added an icosphere and went through the process of displacing the mesh as it moves upwards. From there, we created the dynamic paint simulation using **Weight Surface Type**. After that, we used the cloth simulation and a force field to have the plane flow and move in the wind. The last simulation we created was fire. We discussed how to use the vertex group we created earlier to determine where we want the fire to appear. Finally, we created the fire material using the heat attribute and **Color Ramp**. We also added a burn effect to the **Plane** object wherever there was fire.

I hope you enjoyed learning about all the simulations that Blender has to offer and that it helps you with your own projects and animations. Every simulation discussed in this book has its own uses and can help drastically with a lot of different scenes and projects. Remember to keep learning and if you ever need a refresher on a certain simulation in Blender, you can always open this book again!

Index

‹packt›

packtpub.com

Subscribe to our online digital library for full access to over 7,000 books and videos, as well as industry leading tools to help you plan your personal development and advance your career. For more information, please visit our website.

Why subscribe?

- Spend less time learning and more time coding with practical eBooks and Videos from over 4,000 industry professionals

- Improve your learning with Skill Plans built especially for you

- Get a free eBook or video every month

- Fully searchable for easy access to vital information

- Copy and paste, print, and bookmark content

At www.packtpub.com, you can also read a collection of free technical articles, sign up for a range of free newsletters, and receive exclusive discounts and offers on Packt books and eBooks.

Other Books You May Enjoy

If you enjoyed this book, you may be interested in these other books by Packt:

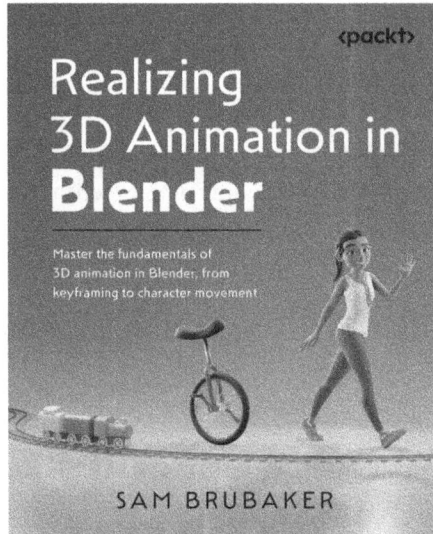

Realizing 3D Animation in Blender

Sam Brubaker

ISBN: 978-1-80107-721-7

- Become well-versed with the simple rules of keyframing and interpolation
- Understand the function and behavior of Blender's animation curves
- Bring a character to life with Blender 3D character animation
- Utilize multiple cameras and the video sequence editor for advanced shot composition
- Get to grips with Blender's mysterious non-linear animation tool
- Explore advanced features such as physics simulation and camera techniques

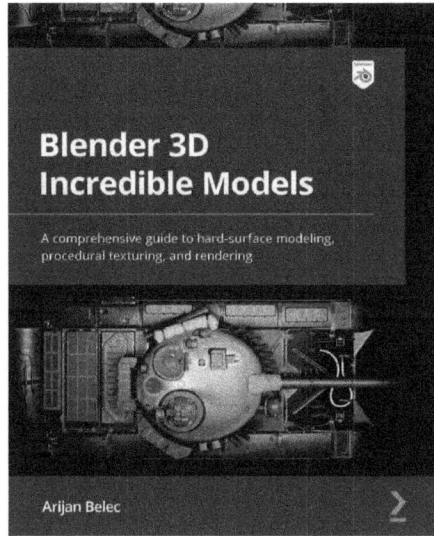

Blender 3D Incredible Models

Arijan Belec

ISBN: 978-1-80181-781-3

- Dive into the fundamental theory behind hard-surface modeling
- Explore Blender's extensive modeling tools and features
- Use references to produce sophisticated and accurate models
- Create models with realistic textures and materials
- Set up lighting and render your scenes with style
- Master the use of polygons to make game-optimized models
- Develop impressive animations by exploring the world of rigging
- Employ texture painting and modifiers to render the tiniest details

Packt is searching for authors like you

If you're interested in becoming an author for Packt, please visit `authors.packtpub.com` and apply today. We have worked with thousands of developers and tech professionals, just like you, to help them share their insight with the global tech community. You can make a general application, apply for a specific hot topic that we are recruiting an author for, or submit your own idea.

Share Your Thoughts

Now you've finished *Learn Blender Simulations the Right Way, Second Edition* we'd love to hear your thoughts! Scan the QR code below to go straight to the Amazon review page for this book and share your feedback or leave a review on the site that you purchased it from.

`https://packt.link/r/1-836-20005-6`

Your review is important to us and the tech community and will help us make sure we're delivering excellent quality content.

www.ingramcontent.com/pod-product-compliance
Lightning Source LLC
Chambersburg PA
CBHW081040220326
41598CB00038B/6938